Collecting Sports Legends

by Joe Orlando

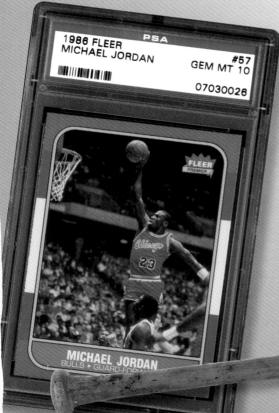

Acknowledgements

Author: Joe Orlando
Layout and Design: Type F Graphic Arts
Contributing Writers: Brian Bigelow, Steve Grad and Rob Rosen
Copy Editor: Jonathan Garner, Claire Grad and Rebecca Tran
Cover Design and Image Preparation: Don Hallack
Image Coordinator: Annabelle Caberte

A special thank you goes out to all of the industry experts who kindly shared their thoughts about the hobby and contributed to the content of this book. That list includes, but is not limited to, Greg Bussineau, Al Glaser, Harvey Goldfarb, Steve Hart, Andy Madec, Brian Seigel, Kevin Struss and John Taube.

In addition, many of the collectibles pictured in this guide were provided by various hobbyists and auction houses. That list includes Tony Arnold, John Blattner, Levi Bleam, Robert Block, John Branca, D'Orsay Bryant, Glen Chaytor, Bruce Ciemny, Robert Clark, The Dreier Collection, Darin Deschaine, Bill Dodge, Steve Eberhardt, Paul Fleetwood, Marshall Fogel, Frank Foremny, Craig Froelich, Al Glaser, Ross Greene, William Hilsenrath, Scott Ireland, Jon Isaacson, Michael King, David Kohler, Eric Kramer, Carl Lamendola, Peter Leonard, Don Louchios, Mastro Auctions, Andy Madec, Thomas Malito, Dan Markel, Jeff Mazzeo, Memory Lane, Inc., Charles Merkel, Mile High Card Company, Matt Mueller, Julius Narancik, Anthony Nex, Stephen Park, Jason Peeples, John Pink, Dan Potter, Jay Radke, Jim Ragsdale, Michael Rakosi, Chris Raney, Doug Rivard, Larry Robbins, Kevin Roberson, Robert Edward Auctions, Rob Rosen, Randy Ruble, SCP Auctions, Paul Sacco, Brian Seigel, Pete Shelters, Wendell Smith, Stephen Soloway, Ronald Sparschu, Don Spence, Joe Squires, Kevin Struss, Harold Sturner, Stephen Sutherland, Dominic Terranova, Joe Tocco, Robert Utley, Joe Verno, John Vineyard, Michael Wachs, Mark Winter, Jeffrey Wolf, Henry Yee and Colin Yu.

Published by:
Zyrus Press Inc.
P.O. Box 17810, Irvine, CA 92623
Tel: (888) 622-7823 / Fax: (800) 215-9694
www.zyruspress.com
ISBN# 1-933990-21-X
978-1-93390-21-7

PSA Address: P.O. Box 6180
Newport Beach, CA 92658
PSA Phone Number: (800) 325-1121
PSA website: www.psacard.com
PSA/DNA website: www.psadna.com

ZYRUS PRESS

Contents

77	1949 Bowman #84 Roy Campanella
77	1949 Bowman #224 Satchel Paige
78	1949 Bowman #226 Duke Snider
78	1950 Bowman #98 Ted Williams
79	1950-51 Toleteros Josh Gibson
79	1951 Bowman #1 Whitey Ford
80	1951 Topps Major League All-Stars Robin Roberts SP
80	1952 Bowman #1 Yogi Berra
81	1952 Bowman #101 Mickey Mantle
81	1952 Bowman #196 Stan Musial
82	1952 Bowman #218 Willie Mays
83	1952 Red Man Tobacco #15N Willie Mays
83	1952 Topps #1 Andy Pafko
84	1952 Topps #191 Yogi Berra
84	1952 Topps #261 Willie Mays
85	1952 Topps #312 Jackie Robinson
85	1952 Topps #314 Roy Campanella
85	1952 Topps #407 Eddie Mathews
86	1953 Bowman #33 Pee Wee Reese
86	1953 Bowman #93 Billy Martin/Phil Rizzuto
87	1953 Bowman Black and White #39 Casey Stengel
87	1953 Stahl-Meyer Franks Mickey Mantle
88	1953 Topps #1 Jackie Robinson
88	1953 Topps #82 Mickey Mantle
88	1953 Topps #244 Willie Mays
89	1954 Bowman #66 Ted Williams
90	1954 Dan Dee Mickey Mantle
90	1954 Red Heart Stan Musial SP
91	1954 Topps Ted Williams (2)
92	1954 Topps #94 Ernie Banks
93	1954 Topps #201 Al Kaline
94	1955 Topps #123 Sandy Koufax
94	1955 Topps #124 Harmon Killebrew
95	1955 Topps #210 Duke Snider
96	1955 Topps Double Headers #69 Ted Williams
96	1956 Topps #135 Mickey Mantle
97	1957 Topps #1 Ted Williams
97	1957 Topps #18 Don Drysdale
98	1957 Topps #35 Frank Robinson
99	1957 Topps #302 Sandy Koufax
99	1957 Topps #328 Brooks Robinson
99	1957 Topps #407 Yankee Power Hitters
100	1958 Bell Brand Sandy Koufax
101	1958 Hires Root Beer #44 Hank Aaron
102	1958 Topps #47 Roger Maris
102	1958 Topps #418 World Series Batting Foes
103	1959 Bazooka Mickey Mantle
103	1959 Fleer #68 Ted Signs for 1959
104	1959 Topps #514 Bob Gibson
104	1960 Topps #148 Carl Yastrzemski
105	1962 Topps #1 Roger Maris
106	1962 Topps #387 Lou Brock
106	1963 Topps #537 Pete Rose
107	1964 Topps Stand-Up #77 Carl Yastrzemski SP
108	1965 Topps #16 Joe Morgan
108	1965 Topps #477 Steve Carlton
109	1966 Topps #126 Jim Palmer
109	1967 Topps #569 Rod Carew
109	1967 Topps #581 Tom Seaver
110	1968 Topps #177 Nolan Ryan
111	1968 Topps #247 Johnny Bench
112	1968 Topps 3-D Roberto Clemente
112	1969 Topps #500 Mickey Mantle White Letter
113	1969 Topps Supers #28 Reggie Jackson
114	1971 Topps Greatest Moments #1 Thurman Munson
114	1973 Topps #615 Mike Schmidt
115	1975 Topps #228 George Brett
116	1979 Topps #116 Ozzie Smith
116	1980 Topps #482 Rickey Henderson
116	1982 Topps Traded #98TCal Ripken, Jr.
117	1983 Topps #482 Tony Gwynn
118	1984 Fleer Update #U-27 Roger Clemens
119	1987 Donruss #36 Greg Maddux
119	1987 Fleer #604 Barry Bonds
119	1989 Upper Deck #1 Ken Griffey, Jr.
121	1993 SP #279 Derek Jeter
121	1994 SP #15 Alex Rodriguez

BASKETBALL

122	1933 Goudey Sport Kings #3 Nat Holman
122	1957 Topps #17 Bob Cousy
123	1957 Topps #77 Bill Russell SP
123	1961 Fleer #3 Elgin Baylor
124	1961 Fleer #8 Wilt Chamberlain
125	1961 Fleer #36 Oscar Robertson
125	1961 Fleer #43 Jerry West
126	1968 Topps Test #5 John Havlicek
126	1969 Topps #25 Lew Alcindor
127	1970 Topps #123 Pete Maravich
127	1972 Topps #195 Julius Erving
128	1980 Topps Larry Bird/Magic Johnson
129	1992 UD #1 Shaquille O'Neal
129	1996 Topps Chrome #138 Kobe Bryant

FOOTBALL

130	1933 Goudey Sport Kings #4 Red Grange
131	1933 Goudey Sport Kings #6 Jim Thorpe
131	1935 National Chicle #9 Knute Rockne
132	1948 Leaf #1 Sid Luckman
132	1948 Leaf #6 Bobby Layne
133	1948 Leaf #34 Sammy Baugh
133	1950 Bowman #1 Doak Walker
134	1950 Bowman #5 Y.A. Tittle
134	1950 Bowman #45 Otto Graham
135	1950 Topps Felt Backs Joe Paterno
135	1951 Bowman #4 Norm Van Brocklin
135	1951 Bowman #20 Tom Landry
136	1952 Bowman Large and Small #1 Norm Van Brocklin
136	1952 Bowman Large and Small #16 Frank Gifford
137	1952 Bowman Large and Small #144 Jim Lansford SP
137	1954 Bowman George Blanda #23
138	1955 Topps All-American #37 Jim Thorpe
139	1955 Topps All-American #68 Four Horsemen
139	1955 Topps All-American #97 Don Hutson
139	1957 Topps #119 Bart Starr
140	1957 Topps #136 Johnny Unitas
141	1957 Topps #151 Paul Hornung
141	1958 Topps #62 Jim Brown
142	1962 Topps #1 Johnny Unitas
142	1962 Topps #17 Mike Ditka
143	1962 Topps #28 Jim Brown
143	1962 Topps #90 Fran Tarkenton
144	1965 Topps #122 Joe Namath
145	1966 Philadelphia #31 Dick Butkus
145	1966 Philadelphia #38 Gale Sayers
145	1970 Topps #90 O.J. Simpson
146	1971 Topps #156 Terry Bradshaw
146	1972 Topps #200 Roger Staubach
146	1976 Topps #148 Walter Payton
147	1981 Topps #216 Joe Montana

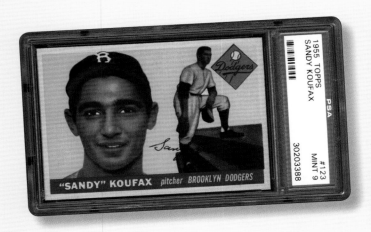

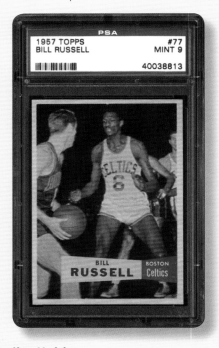

170 Building a Dream
A Look at Collecting the Top 30 Complete Sets in the Hobby
by Brian Bigelow

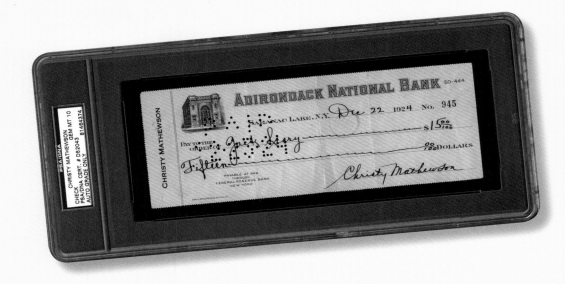

A Look Inside

Collecting Sports Legends was constructed with the singular purpose of providing a definitive guide to the most important collectibles from the world of sports in each of the categories covered. The diversity of the items discussed should appeal to collectors of varying interests, and this guide includes chapters on collecting **individual trading cards, complete sets, autographs, game-used bats, tickets and unopened packs.**

Within each chapter, there are collectibles that originate from the 1800s to those that extend all the way to the post-2000 era, spanning well over 100 years of sports history. Several leading industry experts and knowledgeable hobbyists were asked for their input. While there will always be room for friendly debate, we feel these lists provide the most accurate reflection of what truly is the best of the best.

Before finalizing each list of elite collectibles, we considered things such as the popularity, scarcity and historical importance of each item. It would be easy to comprise a list based on pure market value or strict scarcity, but that would require little creativity, insight or thought. Even though there are many items within this book that most of us can only dream of owning based on their value or scarcity, the goal of this book was not to simply fill it with collectibles that no one could afford or find. We wanted to provide a nice blend of items while still maintaining the integrity of the list.

For example, there are numerous individual trading cards that were excluded, including many cards from the 19th Century. Cards of that nature are infinitely tougher to find and more valuable than a Cal Ripken, Jr. or Joe Montana rookie, but it would be nearly impossible to keep those modern-era cards off the list considering each athlete's impact on the game and the popularity of each card within the hobby. When it came to evaluating tough commons versus star cards, the struggle continued. Our staff made sure that we included some of the more important commons on the individual card list, mainly condition rarities within landmark sets, but they represent the cream of the crop.

The dilemma regarding scarcity and popularity presented itself within each category, not just individual trading cards. There are plenty of sports autographs that are worth not just more, but considerably more, than many of the names that made the cut but demand was a critical factor in making our final determination. We could have included several obscure, virtually impossible autographs from baseball's beginnings, but the reality is that more people are interested in owning a Johnny Bench or Nolan Ryan autograph, despite their relative availability, because of their place in history.

After sifting through this book, it will become abundantly clear that of all the sports covered, baseball simply dominates the lists. While it is true that sports like basketball and football have gained immensely in popularity, in the world of collectibles, baseball remains top dog. The rich history of the game provides hobbyists with storied franchises, colorful characters and a link between players of many different generations. In no other sport are more athletes compared, nor are there more stories told about the legends of the past than in baseball. I may sound biased, but there is something magical about the sport and that magic draws more collectors to it than any other.

We have to admit, this book was a lot of fun to put together. The goal we had in building this guide was to give the new collector an accurate representation of what active collectors desire and why. We just hope the readers enjoy the trip through sports history and time, as seen through these amazing collectibles, as much as we did.

Introduction

As a longtime hobbyist, I'm excited to present a book specifically designed to interest new collectors in the sports memorabilia industry. Our intention is to show you why collecting is an immensely enjoyable hobby.

It has been frustrating to see just how few books have been written about our great hobby. Sports collecting guides have been released through the years, but their scarcity makes the 1909-11 T206 Honus Wagner card seem common. Yes, there are annual price guides hitting bookstores each year, but they do not offer much in terms of insight and do little to generate interest in the collectibles hobbyists all find so fascinating.

The goal of this book is to appeal to the new collector, to show them why these things hobbyists all pursue so intensely are appealing, using a simple and visual format. It is in all of our best interests to help this hobby grow, whether you are a collector, dealer or authentication service. One way to do that is through increased awareness and information. We need to share our knowledge, our motivation and our appreciation for sports collectibles with each other. A collector can inspire a non-collector. What makes us tick, as collectors, is as important to others as the collectibles themselves.

It would amaze most hobbyists to know just how little the average person knows about our industry. Non-hobbyists often find collectibles fascinating but have no idea how to acquire them, what to buy or how to build a collection. I cannot tell you how many times non-hobbyists tell me how interesting they find the material that we sometimes take for granted, simply because we see or handle the material all the time. Their eyes light up when they catch a glimpse of what our hobby has to offer, like a 100-year old Ty Cobb card or a Babe Ruth game-used bat, but it is up to us to encourage a newcomer to act upon that feeling.

There are so many positive aspects about collecting but, like any business, it is important to make you aware of, or remind you of, the darker side. There are large numbers of forgeries and on-line scams that hurt the reputation of our hobby, but this business has come a long way since the 1980s. Third-party authentication and grading has brought peace of mind to those who spend hard earned money on the collectibles they love. The Internet gives hobbyists simple and increased access to those same items, more than ever before. The high-end auction, a huge part of the hobby today, has done much to improve the way our industry is presented and perceived. These aspects have changed this hobby for the better.

The negative side of this hobby is the one typically presented by the naysayer and the uninformed. The side that these people ignore is the side that is safe. It's the side that is filled with millions of authentic collectibles. It's the side that is made up of fathers sharing this hobby with their sons and daughters, the side where long term friendships are made. It's the side that we know exists and the side we all know is wonderful.

That is what I want this book to be about, our hobby in its simplest form.

While we tried to include a diverse selection of items throughout, this book does not cover all the fantastic collectibles that are available to the collector such as original photographs, game-used gloves, game-used jerseys and display pieces. There are items, like the ones mentioned above, that are extremely important and scarce. In fact, many of these items are so scarce that we decided to not cover collectibles of this nature in this particular guide even though some of the finest collections in the world contain them.

In addition, this book is not going to teach the truly advanced collector, a collector of any of the items covered in each section, something they didn't know before. If the reader wants to learn about the history of paper production as it relates to trading cards, this book is not for you. If the reader wants an in-depth analysis performed on the variations found in a particular set that few people care about, picturing players that no one has ever heard of, this book is not for you. If the reader wants to know how Babe Ruth could go out on the town all night long, drink like a fish and then go five for five at the plate the next day, I do too!

All kidding aside, I have enjoyed this hobby my entire life. Unfortunately, it has been a point of frustration for me and others who share my passion that it has not been portrayed the way it should be. It brings great enjoyment to a large number of people from all walks of life. There are plenty of positive reasons to start collecting. In many cases, people just need a little guidance and inspiration from those who are willing to share their experience.

When I walk into a museum or exhibit claiming to showcase an array of fine sports memorabilia, 9 times out of 10, I walk away terribly disappointed. Why? Many of these displays are comprised of questionable material. It's sad to see but it happens all the time. (Most of the time, the people composing these displays do not possess the expertise to know better but they usually put forth their best effort.) More importantly, the obvious reason these displays are lacking in significant material is because 99% of the best sports memorabilia in the world rests in private hands.

You are probably wondering why I am writing about this. It's very simple. I want to illustrate the importance for all of us to share our endeavor with others. Since such a large percentage of the great sports collectibles in existence are held by collectors and not on display where people can see them or gain inspiration from them, we need to find ways of exposing our collections to the rest of the world. While this problem might exist in the world of fine art or coins, there seems to be enough of those collectibles in mainstream circulation to entice people to start collecting.

The material found in our hobby is what makes it so rewarding. Some people who do not have the collector "gene" cannot understand our fascination. They cannot fathom paying large sums of money for an autograph, a card or a bat. What they fail to realize is what sports really means to this country, and to people all over the world. It impacts most American lives. No, baseball players do not cure cancer and boxers do not solve poverty in Third World countries but no one can overlook the impact of sports. It builds confidence in young boys and girls. It teaches us about discipline, how to fail and how to come back from defeat. It brings people together and gives them something to root for. It provides an activity where people can bond and share in a common interest.

While it's true that people find inspiration from all kinds of sources and from all types of people in various professions, the reality is that more people are inspired by athletes and by the sports they play than virtually anything else in our society. Athletes inspire people more than artists, more than scientists, more than astronauts, more than police officers and more than teachers. The reality is that more young men who grew up in the 1950s and 1960s wanted to be like Mickey Mantle than like any President of the era. I am by no means saying this is the way it should be; it's just the way it is.

Let's face it, young boys dream about hitting home runs, making three-pointers and catching touchdowns to win the game. So do grown men. Our outer shells may change over time, but the feelings we have inside rarely do. This is part of what keeps us young at heart. Collecting can play a major role in helping us feel like kids again. We can relive great memories of going to the stadium as a child or explore the history of the game we love through the collectibles that honor and celebrate the figures who shaped it.

Every collector has a driving force behind their motivation. For me, collecting evolved into something very personal. Playing baseball in college had a lasting impact on my life. The experience completely changed who I was as a person and I will be forever grateful for the opportunity. Since I was a catcher, the focus of my collection is on the greatest catchers who ever played the game. It is a way for me to honor the players who set the standard at that position. The driving force behind my collection is about appreciating history. For others, the motivation comes from a different source.

Collecting, like the sport itself, connects people from generation to generation. It provides an escape for all of us who work hard each day and it brings people together. That is what all of this is about. It's about the connection – the connection to the past, to others and to our inner child. This is the driving force behind the endeavor we have all chosen. If we can channel that feeling, the one that keeps us pressing forward, the future of this hobby looks very bright.

Even during tough economic times, the hobby has always found a way to survive. While investments in stocks and real estate may rise and fall, the one thing that these other markets do not possess is emotional attachment. Even though many hobbyists view collecting as a form of investment, as certain collectibles have outperformed many traditional investment strategies over the years, they rarely collect strictly for investment reasons. Their affections for a particular player, team or the sport itself do not change as a result of poor economic conditions. Even with most other types of collectibles, like coins or stamps, this type of sentimental connection is missing. That is part of what makes collecting sports legends unique and the hobby so resilient.

The bottom line is that the hobby has never been better. I hope this book will both inform the current collector and inspire those who have not yet seen what our hobby has to offer.

Happy Collecting.

Joe Orlando has been an advanced collector of sportscards and memorabilia for over 20 years. Orlando attended Westmont College in Santa Barbara, California where he studied communications and was the starting catcher for the baseball team. After a brief stint in the minor leagues, Orlando obtained a Juris Doctor from Whittier Law School in Southern California in the spring of 1999. During the last nine years, Orlando has authored several collecting guides and dozens of articles for Collectors Universe, Inc. Orlando's first book, *The Top 200 Sportscards in the Hobby*, was released in the summer of 2002. Orlando has appeared on several radio and television programs as a hobby expert including ESPN's award-winning program *Outside the Lines* and HBO's *Real Sports*, as the featured guest. Currently, Orlando is the President of PSA and PSA/DNA, the largest trading card and sports memorabilia authentication services in the hobby. He is also Editor of the company's nationally distributed *Sports Market Report*, which under Orlando's direction has developed into a leading resource in the market.

Ten Tips for Building a Collection

By Joe Orlando

If you are thinking about assembling a collection, big or small, it is always best to lay out a plan of action before you start spending your hard-earned money. While this may appear to be common sense to most readers, you would not believe how many people fail to act accordingly. Planning ahead will help whether you collect autographs or trading cards, game-used bats or tickets, or a combination of many different types of collectibles. If you stick to a plan, it will ultimately result in a more enjoyable collecting experience.

Listed below are 10 suggestions that will help a collector accomplish this goal.

1. Select a Collecting Theme and Stick to it

The first thing a collector should do is select a collecting theme. This takes precedence over everything else on this list. Not only will it help you stay focused on your collecting goals, it also will help you maintain your sanity! I have been guilty of not following this suggestion in past years but, when I decided to stop the insanity and stay focused, it enhanced my experience tremendously.

Remember, even if you have virtually endless financial resources at your disposal, you can't own everything. It is always better to start with reasonable collecting goals and then branch out from there. If you want to build a collection around members of *The 500 Home Run Club*, you might start with single-signed baseballs, game-used bats, rookie cards or tickets. However, I do not suggest trying to collect all four at once. Even if you do, at least a theme was chosen, which many hobbyists fail to do. The key is sticking to the theme.

Collectors are tempted, time and time again, to buy things that simply do not fit into the theme of their existing collection. When you appreciate great items, it's hard to resist the opportunity to buy something when the opportunity presents itself. If you collect autographs of Hall of Fame pitchers, it just doesn't make sense to buy a Magic Johnson rookie card and a Wayne Gretzky-signed puck. If you fall victim to your own impulses, you end up with a collection that has no rhyme or reason to it.

A lack of focus will lead to serious frustration.

2. Buy Authenticated/Graded Collectibles

The hobby has changed tremendously in the last 15-20 years and part of the evolution has been the advent of third-party authentication and grading. This has brought peace of mind to collectors across the hobby and provided a more liquid product to dealers who sell collectibles. Of all the benefits this service provides, perhaps none is greater than the simple fact that it helps remove the potential conflict of interest from a transaction.

Prior to the advent of third-party services, the conflict was unavoidable. The typical scenario looked something like this:

A collector approaches a dealer and asks about a Mickey Mantle baseball card on display. The dealer tells the collector how much it costs, which is expected, but the dealer also tells the potential buyer that the card is authentic and in Mint condition. This is where the problem lies. The same person who benefits directly from the sale of the item is the same person who is telling the collector whether or not it's authentic. The seller is also rendering an opinion about the quality of the item. This is a direct conflict of interest no matter how you look at it.

This was simply how a transaction worked before third-party services emerged. This doesn't mean the dealer was trying to defraud the buyer in any way. It took time but hobbyists started to realize, both collectors and dealers alike, that the system didn't make sense. Then along came third-party services. Buying collectibles that have been authenticated and/or graded by a credible third-party will help protect you now and in the future. Even if you witnessed an item being signed yourself, if you decide to sell the autograph or hand the collectible down to a family member at some point, third-party

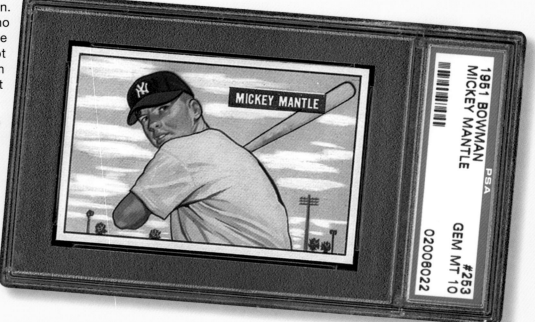

certification will help you achieve the highest possible price for your item or protect the people you give it to.

While the authentication of a collectible is of primary importance, the grading of collectibles is quickly becoming equally as important. After a hobbyist feels comfortable with the authenticity of an item, it is important that they understand the quality, how this item grades against like items in the marketplace. This way, the buyer knows exactly what they are getting at the point of sale. While third-party services do not offer grading for every kind of collectible, I would suggest using the service for collectibles that can currently be graded. Grading is not limited to trading cards anymore. The grading of autographs, game-used bats, packs and tickets are just some of the newer services that have emerged in recent years. These services can help both the buyer and the seller.

Finally, it is crucial that you learn how to distinguish between third-party services. Anyone can generate a letter of authenticity for an autograph or merely place a trading card in a plastic holder. **The key is the name behind the opinion.** This is what ultimately carries weight in the industry and protects you, the consumer. Asking the right questions is a good place to start. How long has the company been in business? How many items have they certified? What is their reputation? What is their market share? How strong is their following? These are just examples, but do as much research as you can.

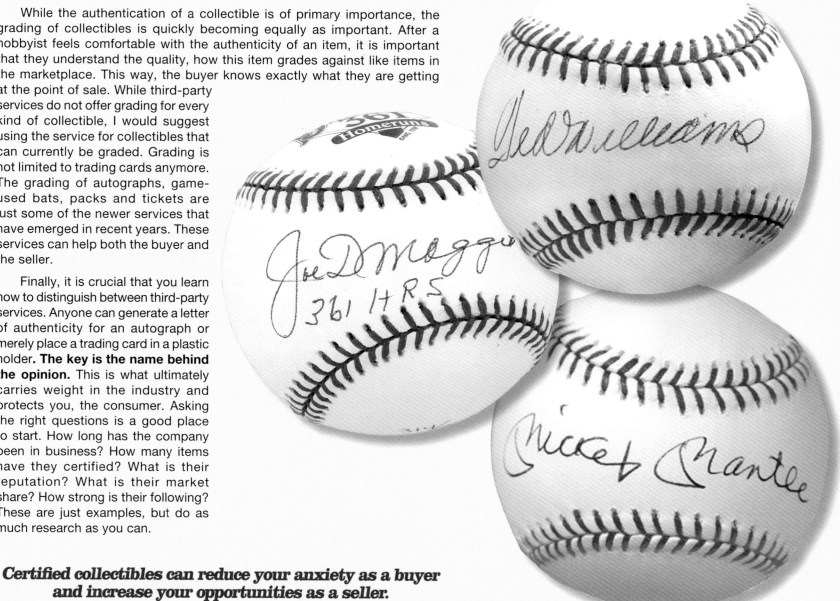

Certified collectibles can reduce your anxiety as a buyer and increase your opportunities as a seller.

3. Ask Questions and Educate Yourself

This picks up where we left things at #2. You can never ask enough questions in this business, whether it's about a third-party service, a dealer, an auction house or a collectible. There is more information available to the collector today, primarily due to the Internet, than ever before. There are websites with ample information about collectibles, their history, their scarcity and their popularity. Take advantage of them!

It surprises me that so many collectors start buying items, sometimes very expensive ones, without learning about them beforehand. If you were buying a car or a watch or a piece of property, you would want to know as much as you can about each item before you buy it. It should be no different here. Talking to experienced collectors and dealers can assist in the process, in addition to reading articles and guides about the hobby. Third-party services can help you remove doubt about the authenticity or grade of an item, which is great, but it's up to you to learn about the historical aspects of the piece.

One purpose of this book is to educate people about the various collectibles covered within, but you can never know enough in this hobby. Even the experts will tell you that they learn more and more each year as new information arises. There's no question that certain collectibles require more extensive research than others. For example, it may take longer to understand what makes a piece of game-used equipment exceptional compared to what makes a baseball card exceptional, but you will be glad you took the time to increase your knowledge no matter where your interests lie.

An informed collector is a happy collector.

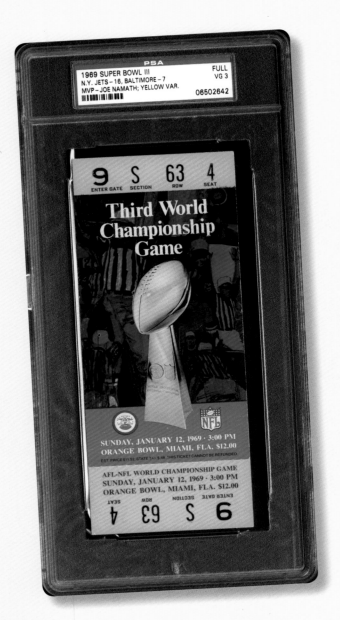

4. Find and Buy from a Reputable Seller

While buying certified collectibles is of primary importance, it is still imperative that you deal with a seller you trust and one who assists you with your collecting goals. This isn't just about being treated fairly as a customer; the seller can be a great resource of information as well. You can learn from his travels and experiences. Since dealers make their living buying and selling collections, they have seen more collectibles than most hobbyists can dream of.

A good dealer is not one who simply sells you items at a good price. A good dealer is one who helps his customers learn more about what they are collecting, imparting knowledge on the people who support them. A good dealer is also someone who may be able to help you sell or trade the item once you decide to let it go. Remember, a good seller can be a good buyer or broker when the time comes for you to part with the item. If a dealer is not willing to support the product or assist you when you need to sell, that is usually a bad sign.

The good news is there are sellers who have the knowledge and are happy to share it with you. There are also dealers who provide a complete service and are willing to build relationships with their clients. You just need to find them. Trust me; it will be worth your while. Research is the key. Talk to fellow collectors and peruse a seller's website so you can fully understand the track record of the person you are considering buying from.

A good dealer can be a great ally.

5. Consider Display or Storage Issues

This is one many of us learn the hard way. We end up buying a bunch of items and then realize, after it's too late, that we have nowhere to put them! This is another issue that seems easy to avoid but I assure you it affects more collectors than you can imagine. It all comes down to your intent as a collector, whether you want to display your collection proudly in your den or tuck most of your items away in a safe deposit box.

For those collectors who choose to display their items, this issue is a significant one. This is especially true for those who enjoy collecting larger items such as game-used jerseys, panoramic photos or vintage advertisement pieces. Even if you have a large home and think you have plenty of wall space, it can run out very quickly. Think of ways to achieve your display goals without mounting everything on the wall. For example, you can save a lot of space by displaying bats on a bat rack versus placing them in a wall frame. It is far more efficient and the racks make for fun displays. In addition, if you choose to display your collection, make sure you get it insured to protect yourself against an unforeseen event.

For those collectors who prefer to keep their holdings behind lock and key, there are different options available, but it is still important that all options are considered before you start building the collection. Some collectors prefer to keep their prized collectibles at the bank or inside a large safe at home. This is understandable considering the value of high-end collectibles, which can reach five, six and even seven figures in price. The problem is that most safety deposit boxes are relatively small and most home safes are incredibly heavy and cumbersome. If you opt to go this route, make sure you have enough space to safely store everything you own.

Thinking about space will help you reach a better place.

6. Avoid Becoming a Bargain Hunter

As a collector, it is always good to be patient and look for a fair price. There is nothing wrong with searching for a good deal. However, when a collector's entire focus revolves around finding a good deal, it can lead that collector right into a trap. That trap is usually filled with items of poor quality and suspect authenticity. We all know collectors who fall into this trap; they become almost obsessed with the idea of finding an item for less than someone else can.

Here is an example of the problem. Most authentic Mickey Mantle signed baseballs sell for at least $600 or more depending on their quality. If you see one available online for $200, your gut instinct should tell you there may be something wrong with the ball. When you become hyper-focused on bargain hunting, it is easy to overlook the obvious and ignore the red flags that could help you steer clear of the item. If all signed Mickey Mantle baseballs sell for $600 or more, odds are that ones offered for less are either in unattractive condition or an outright forgery.

In collecting, there is truth to the old theory, "If it sounds too good to be true, it usually is." This is especially true in today's memorabilia market. With so much information available in the form of sales history websites, price guides and auction results, it has become virtually impossible to find good items at severely discounted rates. Most of the time, if a collectible is offered at a price that appears to be inexplicably low, there's a good reason for the low price which means it's a bad deal for you.

Be price conscious but not price obsessed.

7. Buy the Finest Quality You Can Afford

We have already discussed how becoming a bargain hunter can negatively affect your collecting experience. While we all should try to buy sensibly and stay within our budgets, a focus on buying the best quality you can afford is a good thing. To make this abundantly clear, I am not suggesting that you squander your child's college fund or your retirement savings on high-end sports memorabilia. I simply suggest that quality should take precedence over quantity in this two-step process.

First, you need to establish a fairly firm budget. I say "fairly" firm because you should be slightly flexible when it comes to budgeting, in case something unforeseen occurs. An unforeseen event may minimize your spending ability as a result of a necessary repair to your car or give you the option of increasing your budget as a result of a surprise bonus at work. The key is to establish a sensible budget based on truly disposable income. If you fail to do so, you will inevitably put unnecessary pressure on yourself and your family.

Second, once you establish a sensible budget, you should look at your collecting goals and evaluate how changes in quality may affect them. As quality goes up or down, so does cost. For example, for the price of one 1933 Goudey Babe Ruth #53 in PSA NM-MT 8, you may be able to buy all four Ruth cards from the set in PSA EX-MT 6's and NM 7's. Collectors have different tastes and different budgets. You simply have to ask yourself what level of quality will satisfy you and what your budget will allow.

Over time, there is no question that collectors will pay for quality. It is a simple result of supply and demand. Top quality collectibles always have a way of finding a home, no matter what the economic climate looks like. Even during some of the toughest times in the stock market, fine pieces of sports memorabilia have set records at auction because collectibles offer sentimental value in addition to possible financial gain. While there is never a guarantee that any item will actually increase in value or even retain value, you can never go wrong with quality.

You get what you pay for.

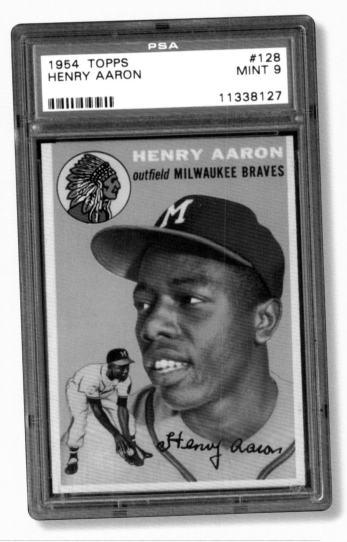

8. Manage Your Emotions but Don't be Afraid to Pull the Trigger

This can be one of the hardest things to deal with on the entire list. Most hobbyists have a real passion for what they do. It's difficult to tell them to shut that passion down, especially when they are looking to add something to their collection, one that may fill a hole. In general, collectors are programmed a certain way. What we call a hobby, some call a sickness! The reality is the vast majority of collectors keep this hobby in perspective so most of us can laugh about the light-hearted criticism.

First, and most importantly, it is crucial for collectors to keep their emotions in check when bidding or buying. This goes back to the concept of sticking to a budget. There will come a point when a collectible reaches a dollar figure that you simply cannot afford. It's alright to let the collectible go if buying it means you have to liquidate your 401(K) in order to pay for it. By planning ahead, this should be avoidable. An emotional buy is never a good one.

Along the same lines, be careful about sharing your desire to acquire something with sellers. It is one thing to give a seller a wish list so they can keep an eye out for items that you need, but it can be dangerous if you express a very high level of interest. For example, don't tell a seller you would be willing to pay any amount of money if he or she could track down something for you. If you show your cards so to speak (no pun intended), there are some sellers who will prey on you like a starving lion that just spotted an injured wildebeest straying from the herd. It's like a boxer who telegraphs his punches. They usually get knocked out cold.

Now that I have scared you to death about controlling your emotions, it's time to flip this approach around. While it is of the utmost importance to manage your emotions for the sake of your own financial well-being, it is also important to take advantage of rare opportunities when they arise. Great items are hard to come by – plain and simple. In fact, many pieces of memorabilia are unique or one of only a handful known to exist. Knowing this, make sure you are not afraid to pull the trigger when the time comes. If you become gun shy, you may regret it because some items only come around once in a great while. As long as that item is within range, take a chance. It might make sense to slightly overpay for an exceptional piece today, especially when you consider the sentimental value it may provide. You will be glad you did.

Collect with your heart but buy with your head.

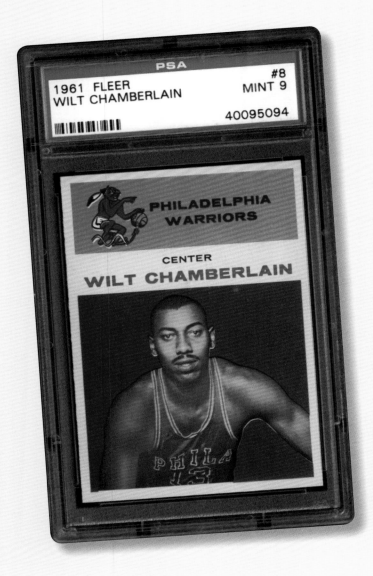

9. Value Expertise Over Origin

Ah, the issue of provenance. Its impact and importance may be the single most misunderstood aspect of collecting. In this hobby, provenance is usually found in some form of documentation used by a seller to support the item that he or she is offering. Some provenance can have a huge impact on the value of a piece while other forms of provenance do not. Let's explore this subject.

The first thing that all collectors must understand is that provenance or origin should never take precedence over expertise. It is also not a replacement for expertise. It is very important that a collectible be able to stand on its own merit before provenance is considered. In other words, if you have a Ted Williams store model bat, a letter from a former player attesting to its use is meaningless because the bat will fail expert review every time. Ted Williams did not use store model bats, no matter what the alleged provenance tells us.

The story changes if a professional model Ted Williams bat, one that exhibits excellent use characteristics and matches factory records, is accompanied by a letter from a former player. Now, the letter or provenance adds to the item. It is like icing on the cake. You now have taken an authentic piece of memorabilia and made it even better because the provenance provides an interesting story about the history of the bat. The provenance doesn't provide the basis for authentication but it adds value to the piece. In some cases, this may result in substantial added value.

In addition, solid provenance is only valuable to the buyer if that provenance travels with the item. In other words, if the item is being sold as originating from a particular collection, estate or person, it is important that the buyer is able to use that provenance someday when it comes time to sell or trade. What good would it do you if I sell you something that allegedly came directly from Willie Mays if you have no way to prove that fact 10 years from now? Look for some tangible support documentation. If you are paying a premium, in part, for the provenance, then you should also be able to reap the benefits from that provenance down the road.

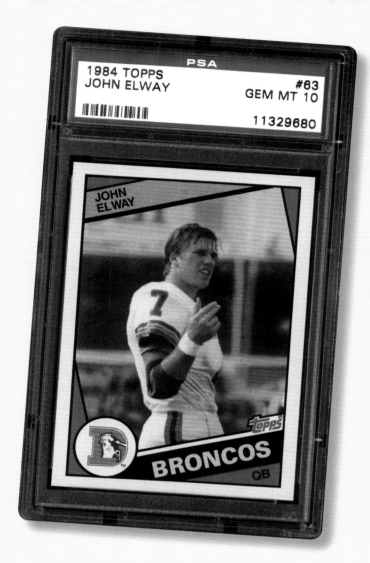

The second thing that all collectors must understand is that provenance, assuming it is legitimate, may or may not affect the value of a collectible at all. If things like prior ownership are important to most collectors, it can add great value. Let's keep going with our Ted Williams bat example. If the Ted Williams game-used bat was used to hit a meaningful home run and was presented to a notable person at one time, then the origin is relevant because it can help tell the entire story, not just the fact that it is a Ted Williams game-used bat. If we are talking about a Ted Williams baseball card, there are very few instances where provenance should impact the value since a card's value, assuming it is authentic, is based solely on condition.

Finally, and most importantly, collectors must understand that some sellers will actually use false provenance to distract potential buyers from the merit of the piece itself. This has become more prevalent in recent times, especially as it relates to some high value items. They will concoct an elaborate story, one that may include newspaper clippings or letters from members of the estate the item allegedly came from, all in hopes of taking your eye off the ball. Don't fall for it! A story is useless if no credible expert will authenticate the item. Most collectors will demand authentication before they buy it. Don't be fooled by fairy tales. Otherwise, you will be left holding the bag (or bat).

Provenance can add great value but there is no substitute for merit.

10. Keep Collecting Fun

Let's face it, there is an investment aspect to buying sports memorabilia, no matter what types of items you collect. If you are going to spend your money on collectibles, you want to make sure you are getting a good value. That is important to all of us, but keeping balance between the collector and investor inside can be tricky. How do we stay true to what we want as collectors, while being intelligent about where we spend our money?

First of all, and I would say this to anyone considering it, do not buy sports memorabilia if you are solely interested in making money. It can be a very risky proposition as very few individuals have the expertise, knowledge and foresight needed to make money. The reality is that none of us have a crystal ball. There is no way to predict the future. We can make educated guesses as to which items may have the best upside but no one knows for sure since collectibles can get hot and cold almost instantly.

In addition, if all of your focus is on making money, the process can leave you with an empty feeling even if you are successful. Most hobbyists are what I would call collectors/investors, people who thoroughly enjoy the material yet, at the same time, are prudent about their purchases. This is the balance we are all looking for and finding that balance will help you achieve peace of mind about your collection. It feels good to buy something you want, and at a fair price. That way, you can justify buying that tough card you need for your 1955 Topps baseball set instead of buying that new lawn furniture. We have all been there whether we were trying to justify our purchase to ourselves or to our significant others!

As collectors, we should appreciate the opportunity we have in this hobby. Think about it for a second. How many things can you buy that may retain most of their value or actually increase in value over time? If you buy a piece of furniture, a television or a car, as soon as you take possession of it, it tends to drop in value rapidly. This is not always the case but your chances of recouping your investment on items such as these are slim to none. That is not to say that these items will not be used and enjoyed, but some of them have expiration dates and others are substantially marked up at the point of sale. They are marked up so much so that their true market value is a mere fraction of what you paid.

Secondly, it is important that collectors buy what they like. It is easy to get caught up in the hype of a hot product or caught up in what others collect but, in the end, you have to be satisfied with your collection. After a hard day at the office, you may want to disappear into your collection to take the edge off or be surrounded by the collectibles you enjoy in your sports den. It's about what makes you happy. Sports collectibles help bring back great memories for many of us and give us something that we can share with family and friends.

Finally, it is important that hobbyists try not to let collector frustration prevent them from enjoying themselves and enjoying the experience that collecting provides. There may be times where you get frustrated because of your inability to locate a needed card or autograph for your collection. There will be other times where you may become frustrated with a fellow hobbyist or dealer due to the way you were treated. This is your hobby and it should be fun. Like any relationship, your collecting experience may endure some rough spots. It is never perfect. You will not always be able to afford what you want or find what you need but take it from those of us who have been collectors for many years, the experience is priceless.

If it's not fun, it's not worth doing.

There you have it. I hope these 10 tips can help you build the collection of your dreams and maximize your hobby experience. It can be an extremely rewarding endeavor if collectors create a plan of action, do their homework and keep it fun. Take it from a fellow collector, these tips work!

Cardboard Classics

A Look Inside
the Top 250 Sportscards in the Hobby

By Joe Orlando

In the following section, I have compiled a list of what many experts consider to be the 250 most important cards in the hobby. While the list is dominated by baseball, it also contains dozens of cards from the worlds of basketball, football, hockey, boxing and golf. From Babe Ruth to Michael Jordan, from Jim Brown to Wayne Gretzky, from Joe Louis to Tiger Woods, legends of the past and present are brought to life through the cardboard classics bearing their image.

The list begins with the top 20 sportscards of all time, ranked in order of importance. At the top is the Holy Grail of sportscard collecting – the 1909-11 T206 Honus Wagner. After the conclusion of the top 20, the journey continues through the remaining 230 cards on the list. The rest are listed in chronological order, unranked, within each category or sport. I chose not to rank all 250 cards for a host of reasons.

First, ranking 20 cards was challenging enough, but ranking 250 of them seemed virtually impossible. In my opinion, there was no question about including each of these great cards on the list, but assigning a numerical ranking to them was another story. As I narrowed the list from 500 to 400 to 300 and eventually to 250 total cards, it became evident that comparing a card like a 1911 T9 Turkey Red Cabinets Jack Johnson to a 1991 Topps Stadium Club Brett Favre card was difficult. It seemed unfair to both cards. The important thing is the vast majority of hobbyists recognize that each card has a place on this list based on a combination of attributes.

Second, while creating this list, I felt it was crucial to maintain its integrity. I did not want to be biased or misleading. For example, the trading card list is heavily weighted towards vintage material. The list wasn't weighted that way simply because I like vintage-era trading cards more or dislike modern-era cards in any way; it was weighted in that manner because I felt it was an accurate reflection of how hobbyists feel about the importance of each card. The reality, due to a plethora of reasons, is that more vintage-era trading cards are considered important by the people who collect.

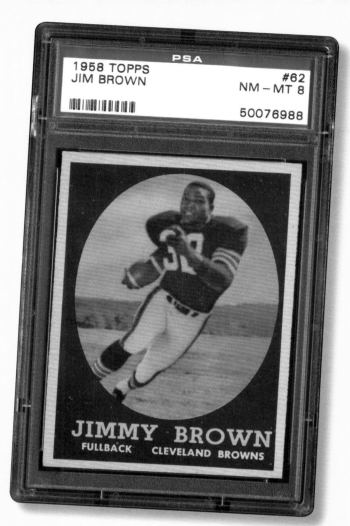

Much of that reasoning lies in the simple fact that, in comparison to vintage material, modern cards can be found in abundance most of the time. This is due, in part, to the volume of cards produced each year. More importantly, it is a result of collectors taking the time to preserve their cards as a result of the evolution of the hobby. During the 1980s, what was once a very miniscule hobby became a phenomenon throughout America. Along with the boom in the industry came awareness about how to better protect trading cards. Things like binders, protective sleeves, nine-count sheets, Lucite holders and specially designed storage boxes were all used to protect the cards that were once handled with great frequency just a decade earlier.

That being said, there is no question that I tried to provide some diversity within the *Top 250* as well. In other words, it would be very easy to fill any top card list with every Sandy Koufax, Mickey Mantle, Willie Mays and Ted Williams card ever manufactured. While there are many cards on this list that feature great players like these legends, I did make a concerted effort to include some examples of cards that originate from fascinating sets. Some of these are mainstream productions while others are regional or test issues. When it made sense to do so, I also incorporated important modern-era cards that capture some of the most significant athletes in sports history.

Finally, please keep in mind that there are so many wonderful cards to collect in this great hobby of ours. This list is a mere sampling of the great cards available to the collector. The hardest part about constructing this section was to limit it to only 250 total cards. I am sure some readers will question why a particular card may or may not have made this exclusive list, but that is part of what makes our hobby fun. So, let the debates begin! Furthermore and most importantly, I hope this section can help bring back memories of opening packs with your friends, watching the games with your dad or rooting for your favorite sports heroes.

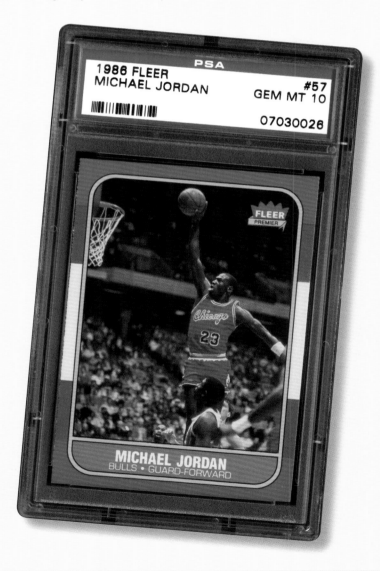

By Joe Orlando

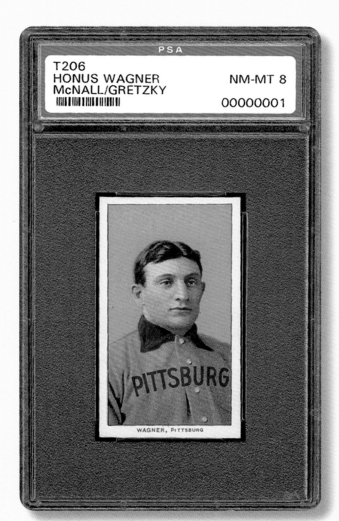

1 1909-11 T206 White Border Honus Wagner

This is the Holy Grail of all trading cards. This card, which resides in one of the most popular sets of all time, features one of baseball's greatest players and it remains the symbol of trading card collecting. This card is also one of the great rarities, though it is not the scarcest in the hobby. That said, this card has taken on a life of its own and no card has ever sold for anywhere close to the sale of the finest example known, the famous PSA NM-MT 8. Once owned by hockey legend Wayne Gretzky and Bruce McNall, that copy sold for an astonishing $2,800,000 in 2007, the only seven-figure price ever paid for a trading card as of this writing. Even low-grade copies have sold for well over $100,000.

The reason behind the rarity has been debated for years. Was it a mere contract dispute? Was it a result of a stand taken by Wagner, not wanting to promote tobacco use to children since the cards were packed with cigarettes? No one knows for sure, but documentation from the era has surfaced supporting the theory that Wagner may have had his younger fans in mind. It is ironic since Wagner was an avid user of tobacco. He is actually pictured on a 1948 Leaf card holding an enormous wad of chew. No matter what theory you believe, the card was pulled from production early, leaving approximately 50 or so known copies in the hobby today. Keep in mind that most of the surviving Wagners have Sweet Caporal backs. Only a few exhibit Piedmont backs, which includes the finest example of them all.

2 1952 Topps #311 Mickey Mantle

This is, perhaps, the most recognizable sportscard in the entire hobby and the anchor of the most important post-war set in existence. Strangely enough, it is not Mickey Mantle's official rookie card, but there is no question that it is the slugger's most important card. Despite a couple of major finds of 1952 Topps cards during the last 25 years, this card has remained difficult to obtain in NM-MT or better condition as many of those "find" examples exhibit poor centering. There are actually two different versions of this double-printed card. The line surrounding the Yankee logo is a solid black on one version, while the other version has a line that is only partially filled. There is also a slight variance in color and focus between the two. Despite the minor difference in appearance, there is no difference in market value. Most of the high-grade examples found today were a product of either the large 1952 Topps find from the New England area during the 1980s or a few smaller finds from Canada over the last two decades. After slugging .530 in 1952, Mantle was well on his way to stardom. This would be the first of 16 All-Star selections for the Yankee Slugger, a man who made the #7 famous.

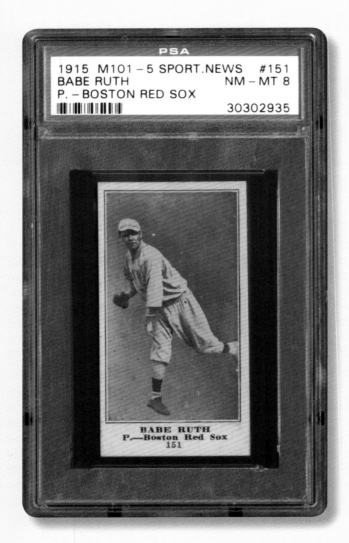

3

1915/1916 (M101-5) Sporting News #151
Babe Ruth

This is the rookie card of the greatest player who ever lived. It is one of his most difficult cards overall, making it one of the most important cards on this list. It pictures a young Ruth, firing the ball as a pitcher for the Boston Red Sox before they traded him to the rival New York Yankees. Ruth was an outstanding pitcher. He compiled a 94-46 record (.671 winning percentage) with 107 complete games, 17 shutouts and a career ERA of 2.28. In the World Series, he was even more impressive. Ruth went 3-0 with an ERA under 1.00! After three full seasons on the mound, the Red Sox began to use Ruth as a part-time outfielder in 1918. The rest is history. After they sent Ruth to New York in 1920, little did they know that it would result in a World Series drought that lasted until 2004. This card, the key to the 200-card M101-5 set, is often found off-center and features a variety of advertising backs, although most existing copies exhibit blank backs.

4

1909-11 T206 White Border Eddie Plank

This is the second most desirable card in the famed T206 set and the only pose of the HOF pitcher. To this day, there is no clear explanation for the rarity of this card, a card that is nearly as tough as the Honus Wagner from the same set. The most prevalent theory is that the card suffered from a poor printing plate, resulting in many of the cards being destroyed since they could not pass quality control. In addition, many of the known examples are found with poor centering from top to bottom. The centering can be so severe that it will cut into the text along the bottom. Eddie Plank, a master of off-speed pitches, was one of the greatest left-handed pitchers in the game. Plank amassed 327 career wins and he remained the all-time leader in wins for a left-hander until Warren Spahn eclipsed the mark about 50 years later in the early 1960's. Plank won 20 or more games on eight separate occasions and he still owns the all-time record for most shutouts by a lefty with 69. What may be most impressive is the fact that Plank entered the league at the age of 26, a late start for someone with such great overall numbers. Plank was elected to the Hall of Fame in 1946.

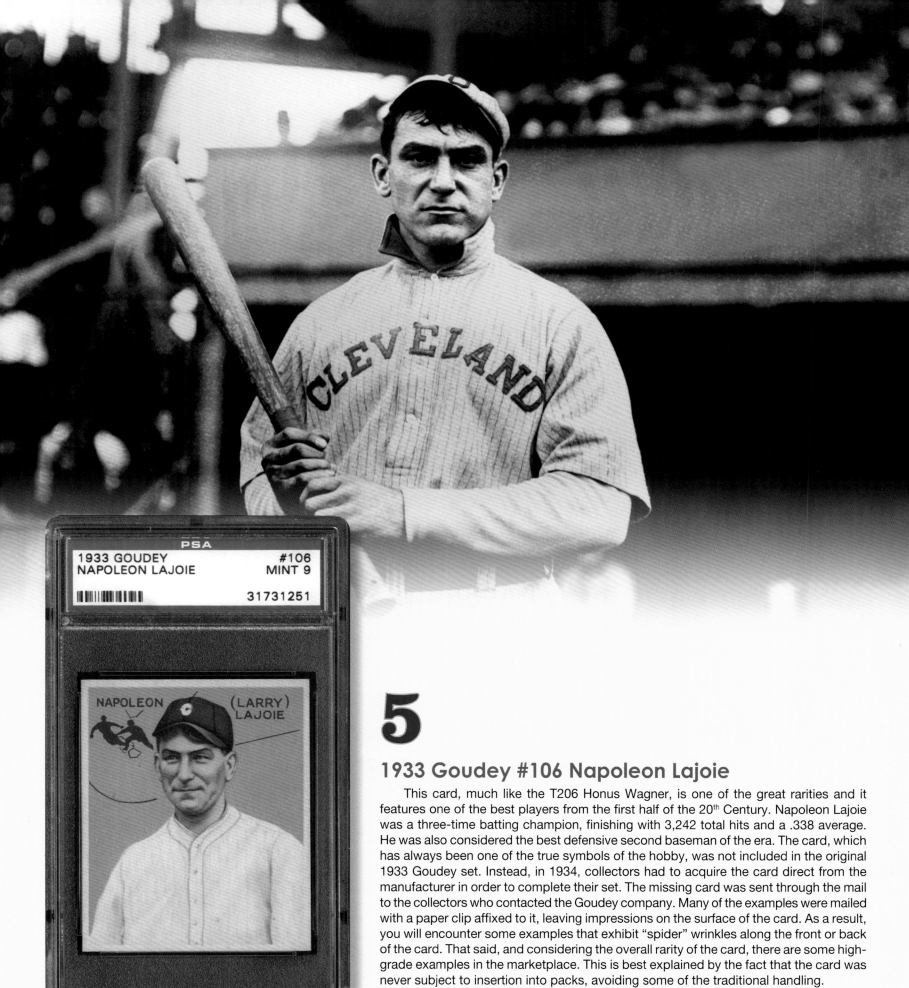

5

1933 Goudey #106 Napoleon Lajoie

This card, much like the T206 Honus Wagner, is one of the great rarities and it features one of the best players from the first half of the 20th Century. Napoleon Lajoie was a three-time batting champion, finishing with 3,242 total hits and a .338 average. He was also considered the best defensive second baseman of the era. The card, which has always been one of the true symbols of the hobby, was not included in the original 1933 Goudey set. Instead, in 1934, collectors had to acquire the card direct from the manufacturer in order to complete their set. The missing card was sent through the mail to the collectors who contacted the Goudey company. Many of the examples were mailed with a paper clip affixed to it, leaving impressions on the surface of the card. As a result, you will encounter some examples that exhibit "spider" wrinkles along the front or back of the card. That said, and considering the overall rarity of the card, there are some high-grade examples in the marketplace. This is best explained by the fact that the card was never subject to insertion into packs, avoiding some of the traditional handling.

6

1911 T3 Turkey Red Cabinets #9 Ty Cobb

This card is, quite simply, the most majestic entry on the entire list. At 5¾" by 8" in size, this amazing card is not only the biggest one on the list, it is also visually stunning. These enormous cards were actually distributed through a redemption program. Collectors could send in coupons in exchange for these cardboard titans. It took 10 Turkey Red Cigarette coupons or 25 Old Mill or Fez Cigarette coupons to claim one card. The set included many great ballplayers from the era such as Walter Johnson, Christy Mathewson and Cy Young, but no card in the set is as desirable as the one featuring the most intense player in the game – Ty Cobb. The image, which is strikingly similar to the T206 *Bat on Shoulder* Cobb, is extremely vibrant. Cobb is shown glaring at the camera with bat in hand, a look that put fear into many pitchers during the early part of the 20th Century. The backs of these giants come two different ways, one with a tobacco advertisement and one with a checklist. Currently, there appears to be no difference in value between the two back variations.

7

1933 Goudey Babe Ruth (4)

This legendary quartet represents the most important component to the ultra-popular 1933 Goudey set and it features the most destructive hitter who ever played the game. *The Sultan of Swat* is pictured on four different cards – #s 53, 144, 149 and 181. The #53 (or Yellow Ruth) is considered to be the toughest, closely followed by the #149 (or Red Ruth) that portrays the slugger in an identical pose. While the #144 (or Full Body Ruth) was double-printed and is more plentiful overall, it is actually harder to find in high-grade than the #181 (or Green Ruth). In fact, there is a subtle difference between the two versions of the double-printed #144 card, with one version exhibiting much better focus and clarity than the other. With the exception of the Napoleon Lajoie rarity, a card that wasn't part of the original set, these four cards represent the core of this elite Goudey production. While this issue is not Babe Ruth's most valuable or scarce, it is arguably his most important and it captures the mighty slugger near the tail end of his career.

8

1951 Bowman #253
Mickey Mantle

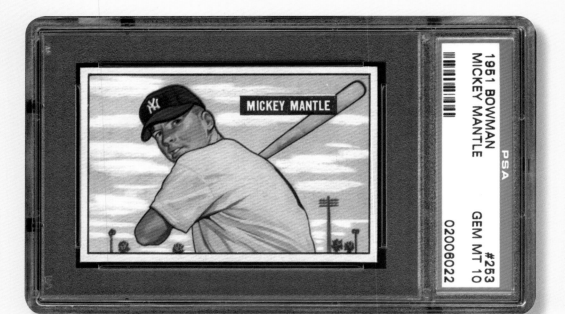

This is the only recognized rookie card of *The Mick*. Mickey Mantle is, quite simply, the most widely collected figure in the hobby. He was the hero of choice during the 1950s and 1960s, inheriting centerfield from another Yankee legend – Joe DiMaggio. This humble country boy moved to the big city where he became the most celebrated player of his generation. In 1951, Mantle made his debut for the Yankees as a part-time player. He managed just 13 homers but many of those were of the tape measure variety, something Mantle was known for throughout his career. This 16-time All-Star was robbed of his blazing speed after suffering a few terrible injuries along the way, but he would go on to become the most powerful slugger in the game. While his 1952 Topps card receives a tremendous amount of fanfare, some collectors forget that this is his only true rookie. This incredibly important card is subject to numerous condition obstacles. As with most high-numbered cards in the set, this card often suffers from print lines, wax stains along the reverse and poor centering.

9

1914/15 Cracker Jack #103 Shoeless Joe Jackson

In most cases, inclusion in the HOF is a key when discussing the best of the best in card collecting. Here is one of the few exceptions. *Shoeless Joe* was banned from the game after the 1919 Black Sox scandal. It was alleged that Joe Jackson helped "throw" the World Series and accepted $5,000 to do so. He hit .375 in the series, driving in six runs and played flawless defense but, in the end, it didn't matter. The ban stuck. Nevertheless, this man is treated as a Hall of Famer and the controversy has done nothing but help bring more attention to his collectibles. This particular card is, arguably, his most popular and attractive issue. Most high-end examples are of the 1915 variety since there was a redemption program available to the public. In 1914, no such program existed which meant there was only one way to acquire the cards, right from the box of sticky Cracker Jacks, caramel stains and all. Jackson, one of the greatest hitters in baseball history, is pictured in full swing – a swing that helped him achieve a .356 career batting average.

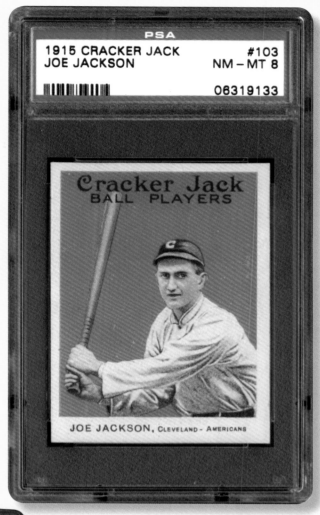

10

1934 Goudey Lou Gehrig (2)

These two specimens are the most popular Gehrig cards in the hobby, with #37 considered a sportscard classic. In 1934, Gehrig hit .363 with 49 home runs and 165 RBI, a tremendous but typical season for the legendary slugger. He even slugged .706! Despite winning the elusive Triple Crown that same season, Gehrig only managed to finish fifth in the MVP voting. These two Gehrig cards provide the foundation to this extraordinary set. The #37 card, a hobby favorite, shows a smiling Gehrig against a yellow background. It is one of the most attractive cards in the hobby and more difficult than the #61 card in the same set. That card, showing Gehrig with his bat from the waist up, is also very eye-appealing. On the reverse of the #37 card, is a quote from Gehrig that reads, "I love the game of baseball and hope to be in there batting them out for many years to come, fortune has been kind to me …" Just a few years later, Gehrig would be stricken with ALS. In a showing of class and dignity, Gehrig would give a speech that will never be forgotten on July 4, 1939. A tearful but grateful Gehrig uttered, "Today, I consider myself the luckiest man on the face of the earth." Those words echo in eternity.

11

1948-49 Leaf #8 Satchel Paige SP

This is, arguably, the toughest post-war card in the hobby and it features one of the greatest stars from the Negro Leagues. Eventually, Satchel Paige would be given the chance to pitch in the Major Leagues but it was well after his prime. It would have been awesome to watch a prime Paige work his magic against the best in the league. In 1948, at the age of 42, Paige started seven games, winning six of them and sporting an ERA of 2.48. Just imagine what he could have done at the age of 32! Paige was so popular that more than 72,000 fans came out to see him in his first home start in Cleveland after winning his first game on the road in Philadelphia. This two-time All-Star and former Negro League star was inducted into the Baseball Hall of Fame in 1971. This particular card, one of several scarce short prints in a terribly difficult set, suffers from poor print quality and focus. High-end copies are seldom found and, as of the date of this writing, no Leaf Paige has ever reached PSA Mint 9 status or better.

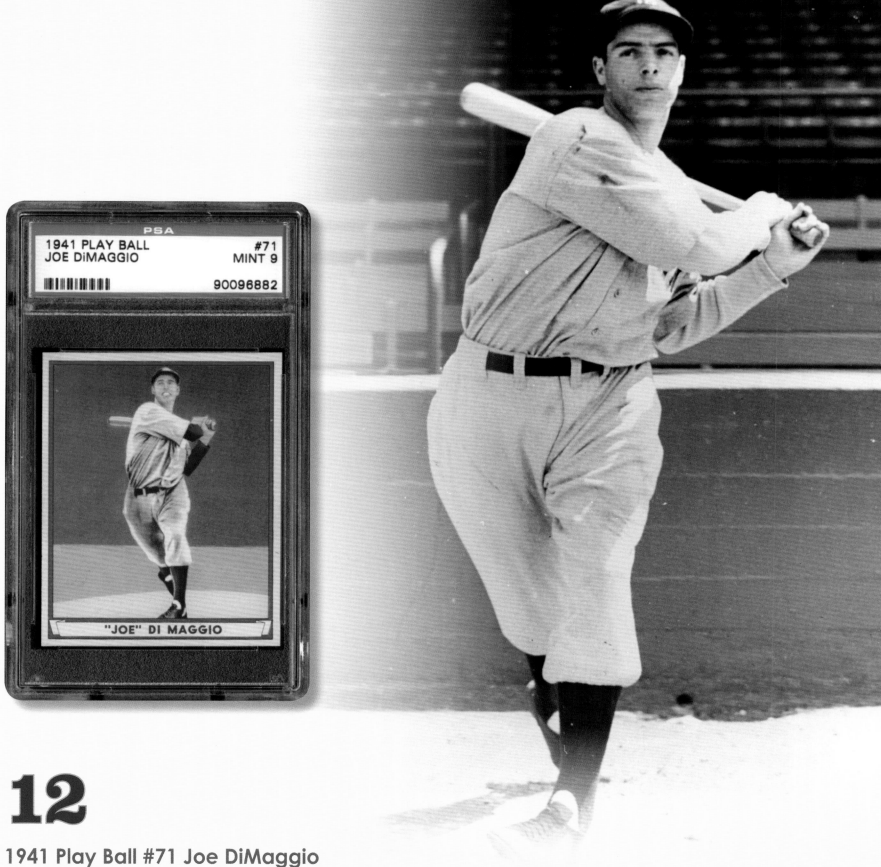

12

1941 Play Ball #71 Joe DiMaggio

This card is considered a true classic in the hobby and, while not his rookie, it is Joe DiMaggio's most popular card. The image is striking, showing *Joltin' Joe* finishing that great swing. In 1941, DiMaggio's swing never looked better as he established a new mark by hitting safely in 56 consecutive games. That same year, DiMaggio would also go on to win the AL MVP after finishing with a .357 batting average, 30 home runs and a league-leading 125 RBI, denying that sweet swinging lefty from Boston the award. It would be one of three MVP trophies for the Yankee legend. While DiMaggio's hitting streak may be his most memorable moment and a showing of ultimate consistency, his entire career mirrored this accomplishment. In 13 seasons with the Yankees, he made 13 All-Star teams. DiMaggio drove in 100 or more runs in each of his seasons with a minimum of 500 at bats. In the two seasons that DiMaggio failed to reach 100 RBI, he drove in 95 and 97 respectively. He was as dependable as they come. This card, the key to the 1941 Play Ball set, is a symbolic treasure.

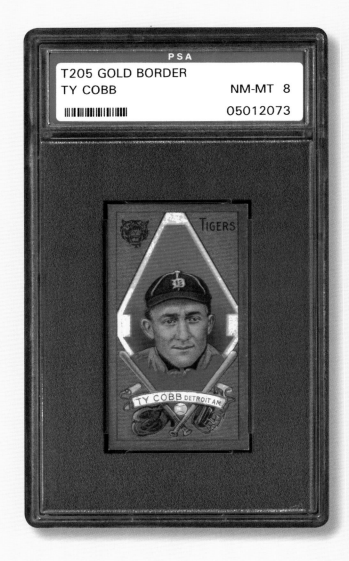

13

1911 T205 Gold Border Ty Cobb

This is the centerpiece to one of the most difficult sets ever manufactured. The T205 set is one of the more eye-appealing issues of the pre-war era, but the set offers a challenge even the most advanced collectors have often failed to take. The gold borders framing these gorgeous cards are extremely susceptible to chipping, revealing wear with the slightest touch. For those who seek high-grade material, the opportunities are few and far between. The cards can vary slightly in size but most examples measure somewhere in the 1⁷⁄₁₆" by 2⅝" size range. In 1911, Ty Cobb had one of his best seasons. He set career highs in batting (.420), hits (248), doubles (47), triples (24), RBI (127), runs (147) and slugging average (.621). Cobb led the league in each of those categories as well as in stolen bases with 83. This is a fitting tribute ... an extremely tough card for an extremely tough competitor.

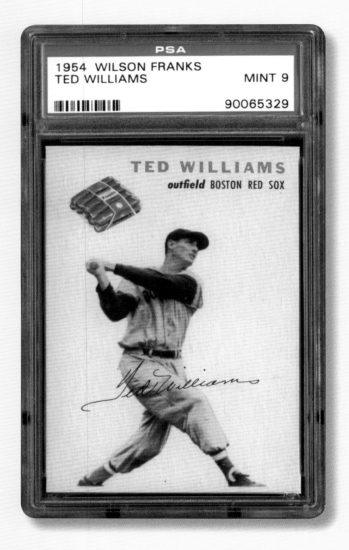

14

1954 Wilson Franks Ted Williams

This is not only the key to the set but it is the most important regional card ever produced during an era that produced many of the hobby's top regional issues. While it is certainly one of the toughest cards on the entire list and a true condition rarity, this issue is also very eye-appealing. These cards were inserted into packages of hot dogs, making it virtually impossible to locate high-end examples. In fact, most copies are found with very poor centering. The issue's extremely narrow borders leave very little room for error. The few high-end copies that have been found are believed to have escaped from the factory, prior to insertion into the packages of greasy franks, avoiding the likely damage to follow. This card measures approximately 2⅝" by 3¾". Ted Williams, a master with the bat and an exceptional military pilot, is featured on many of the most important cards in the hobby but, of all the great cards that picture this American hero, this is the most desirable.

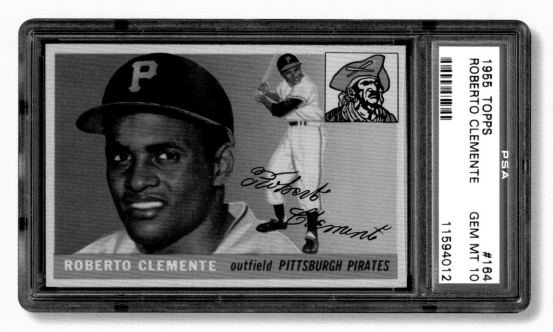

15

1955 Topps #164 Roberto Clemente

This is the only recognized rookie card of the legendary Pittsburgh Pirate. Roberto Clemente did not post numbers like Hank Aaron or Willie Mays but he was clearly one of the best outfielders of his generation. His fiery approach on the field and his generous ways off the field made him a special individual. This true five-tool player finished his career with a .317 batting average, 240 home runs and exactly 3,000 hits. He would have finished with more but, during one of his charitable missions to earthquake victims in Nicaragua, the plane Clemente was on crashed before arrival. Before his career was over, Clemente would make 12 All-Star appearances and win 12 consecutive Gold Gloves (1961-1972). This card, along with the Killebrew and Koufax rookies in the same set, is a key and tougher to find in high-grade than either of them. Finding well-centered copies appears to be one of the biggest challenges for the advanced collector.

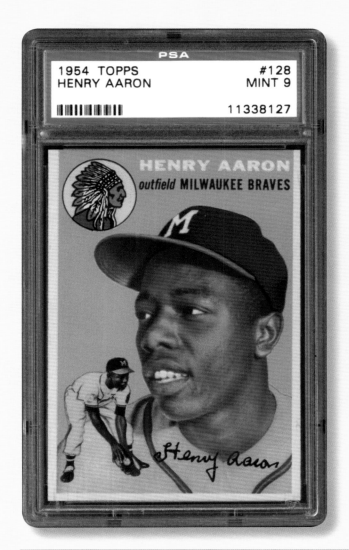

16

1954 Topps #128 Hank Aaron

This is the only recognized rookie card of *The Hammer*. Even though his career home run mark of 755 has now been eclipsed by Barry Bonds, Hank Aaron remains a symbol of class, consistency and grace. In 1954, Aaron's debut season, he hit a mere 13 home runs in 122 games. From that point on, Aaron hit no less than 20 homers in a season until 1975! His tremendous hand and wrist strength enabled him to turn on inside fastballs with incredible quickness. With all of his home runs, Aaron never struck out 100 times in a season and was an outstanding all-around player. During his career, he won three Gold Gloves, hit .305, amassed 3,771 hits, 2,297 RBI, scored 2,174 runs, stole 240 bases and won the NL MVP in 1957. Aaron made 24 All-Star appearances during his amazing career and was inducted into the Baseball Hall of Fame in 1982. This card is one of the true classics in the hobby. While not nearly as tough as some of the other vintage cards on the list, finding well-centered, high-end copies can be a challenge. This card is the heart and soul of the 1954 Topps set and the image is unforgettable.

17

1935 National Chicle #34
Bronko Nagurski

This is the most valuable football card in the hobby. Bronko Nagurski, owner of one of the truly classic names in sports, was one of the charter members of the NFL Hall of Fame in 1963 and a force to be reckoned with on the field. Nagurski didn't use deception or trickery to avoid defenders, he simply ran over them. Steve Owen, of the New York Giants, once said of Bronko, "The only way to stop Nagurski is to shoot him before he leaves the dressing room." Ernie Nevers, a Hall of Famer himself added, "Tackling Bronko is like tackling a freight train going downhill." The image on this card shows Nagurski charging like a bull during a time when players wore very little padding. It's not often that you feel sorry for the guy doing the tackling but, in this case, bringing down Nagurski must have been a dangerous job. As a member of the Chicago Bears (1930-1937), he helped lead his team to several division titles and two NFL championships. He also excelled as a defensive lineman during an era where players were accustomed to playing both sides of the ball. In 1993, the Football Writers Association of America created the Bronko Nagurski Trophy, which is awarded to the best defensive player in college football. As part of the tough high-number run in a terribly difficult set, this card remains the symbol of gridiron cardboard.

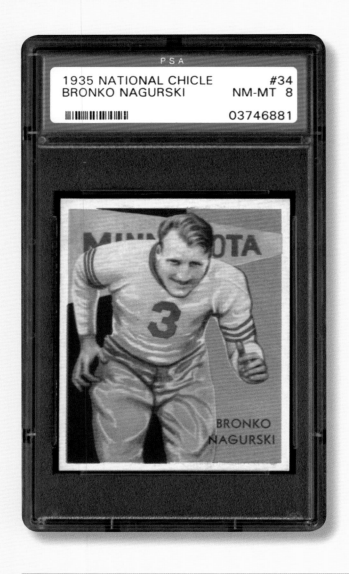

18

1948 Bowman #69 George Mikan

This is a classic card of basketball's first marquee player. George Mikan is more responsible than any player of his generation for making basketball a nationally recognized sport. On the face of this card, Mikan is pictured storming towards the basket with relentless fury. At 6'10", 245 pounds, Mikan was the game's first dominant big man, paving the way for legends like Bill Russell and Wilt Chamberlain. He led his team, the Minneapolis Lakers, to five championships in six years. It was the first time that the word "Dynasty" was used to describe a professional basketball team. Mikan averaged 23.1 points per game during his career, leading the league on three separate occasions. He retired as basketball's career-scoring leader. Mikan was named to the first four NBA All-Star teams from 1950 to 1953. After his playing days, Mikan was inducted into the Basketball Hall of Fame in 1959 and came back to the game as the ABA's first commissioner in 1967. This card measures approximately 2¹⁄₁₆" by 2½" and, like most 1948 Bowmans, is often found off-center with toning along the edges, making it tough to locate in high-grade. The cards are also found hand-cut as some uncut sheets made their way into the hobby years ago.

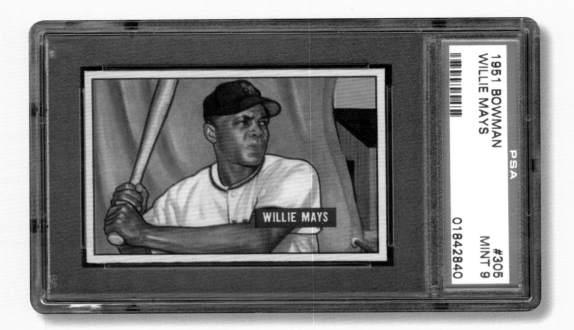

19

1951 Bowman #305
Willie Mays

This is the only recognized rookie card featuring *The Say Hey Kid*. Willie Mays was, perhaps, the greatest all-around player the game has ever seen. He could match Mickey Mantle and Hank Aaron in power, field and throw like Roberto Clemente and run like Lou Brock. In 1951, Mays started off in a horrific slump, but broke out of it with a home run against fellow Hall of Famer Warren Spahn. Mays finished the year with a .274 batting average, 20 home runs and 68 RBI, giving fans a glimpse of what was to come. After being named NL Rookie of the Year, Mays would reach great heights as he became the first player to reach 500 home runs and 3,000 hits. Mays also made 24 All-Star Game appearances, a record that still stands today. Mays, a two-time NL MVP, was inducted into the Baseball Hall of Fame in 1979. This card, along with the Mantle rookie, is one of two major keys to the set and is arguably tougher than *The Mick's* rookie in high-grade.

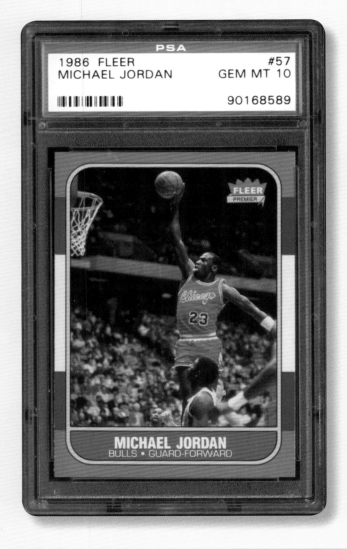

20

1986 Fleer #57 Michael Jordan

This is the most recognizable basketball card and the most important modern card from any sport in the entire hobby. It's hard to believe that this NBA legend was actually cut from his high school team as a sophomore, but it's true. Just a few years later, Michael Jordan would make the game-winning basket in the NCAA Finals for North Carolina. The legend of "Air" Jordan was just beginning. Jordan won six NBA titles, eight scoring titles, five regular-season MVPs, six Finals MVPs, three All-Star Game MVPs and one Defensive Player of the Year award. In fact, Jordan was named to the All-Defensive First Team nine times, a record. This 14-time All-Star and former NBA Rookie of the Year (1985) scored 32,292 points and averaged 30.1 points per game in his career. While Jordan did make a brief comeback as a member of the Washington Wizards, he will always be remembered as the man who led the Chicago Bulls to glory. This card, the most heavily counterfeited card in the hobby, is susceptible to chipping and edge wear due to the multi-colored borders.

1869 Peck & Snyder Cincinnati Red Stockings (2)

This card, featuring the first professional team in the game, is considered by many hobbyists to be the first true baseball card. Managed by Harry Wright, the Red Stockings would dominate their opposition in 1869, giving ample reason for the New York area sporting goods company (Peck & Snyder) to create such a card. A sepia photograph is mounted on the front with a large ballplayer cartoon and advertisement on the reverse. These cards came in two different sizes, one measuring approximately 4³/₁₆" by 3⁵/₁₆" (large) and the other measuring 3¹⁵/₁₆" by 2³/₈" (small). From the classic uniforms to the boot-like shoes, the photograph captures the birth of our great pastime at the professional level. Can you imagine playing baseball without gloves? That is exactly what these pioneers had to do. This card symbolizes the beginning of the hobby that millions of collectors have come to enjoy ever since.

1887 N172 Old Judge Cap Anson (2)

This selection comes from one of the great issues in our hobby, perhaps the most important 19th Century set in existence. Packed in Old Judge and Gypsy Queen Cigarette packs, these cards had to survive more than one hundred years travel to reach collections today. The cards also exhibit a slight variance in size as they were cut inconsistently. The series, which extended from 1887-1890, includes well over 3,000 different cards. Some individual players have more than a dozen variations in the set in the form of different poses, team affiliation or text on the cards. There are two Cap Anson cards of note. While both are highly desirable and tough, the *In Uniform* variation takes scarcity to another level. With only a handful of known copies, this Anson card has been seen in person by only a few and actually handled by even fewer. Even low-grade copies have fetched $50,000 or more on the rare occasion the card has been offered for sale. Anson, during his 27-year career, would reach a .300 batting average 24 times and hit .380 or better three times. He even showed occasional power, becoming the first man to club three consecutive homers in one game during the Dead Ball Era. This is, without question, the most desirable issue featuring baseball's first superstar player.

1888 N28 Allen & Ginter Cap Anson

This card features the 19th Century's most popular player in a set containing figures from a variety of subjects. This visually appealing card, which measures approximately 1½" by 2¾" in size, is not as scarce as the Old Judge issue from the same year, but the addition of color increases the collector demand. The reverse of each card features a checklist for the set, so don't be surprised if you find examples with handwritten notations on the back. Cap Anson was the first player to reach 3,000 career hits, although there is dispute about his exact total. Some historians claim his career hit total to be in excess of 3,400 while others claim it was closer to 3,000. Anson also had a career batting average of .333 and led the league in RBI 8 times, totaling 2,076 for his career. He was considered an innovative manager, being the first to require spring training for members of the team in order to get them into shape for the upcoming season. For all of his accomplishments, the Veteran's Committee inducted Anson into the Baseball Hall of Fame in 1939.

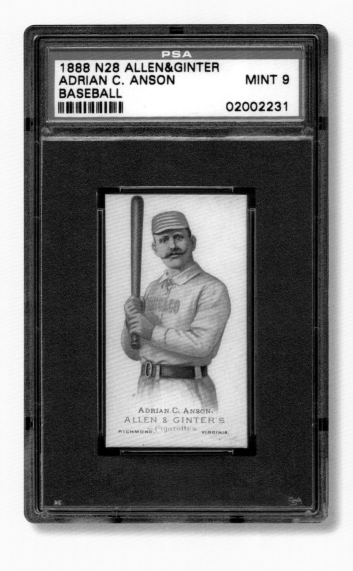

1888 N162 Goodwin Champions Cap Anson

This is, arguably, Cap Anson's most visually appealing card on the list due to the increased use of color and its attractive design. While not quite as difficult as the Old Judge issue, this great 19th Century card is tougher than the aforementioned Allen and Ginter N28 issue. Like the 1887 N172 Old Judges, these cards were inserted into packages of Old Judge and Gypsy Queen Cigarettes and, like the N28s, they feature a checklist along the reverse of each card. The full color cards, which measure approximately 1½" by 2⅝" in size, feature a variety of athletes including boxers and college football players. This particular card was one of eight baseball players included, and it is one of four Hall of Fame baseball players in the issue. Anson, who was considered the best overall hitter and run producer of his era, had his best season in 1881 when he led the league with a .399 batting average. He also led the league in hits and RBI that year. At the time of his retirement, Anson was the all-time leader in several categories including, but not limited to, career hits and runs scored. He also remains the all-time Cubs leader in hits, RBI and runs scored at the time of this writing. This card is a great example of how trading cards can serve as tiny, artistic time capsules, giving collectors a chance to catch a glimpse of baseball's early stages.

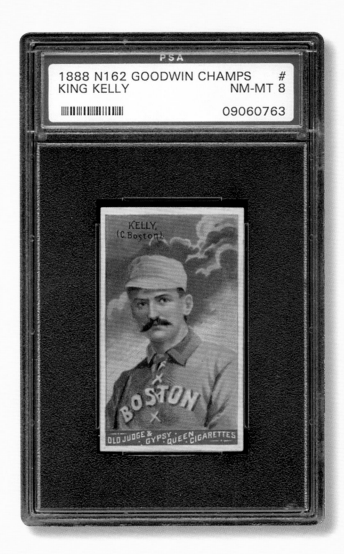

1888 N162 Goodwin Champions King Kelly

This beautiful card features one of baseball's first entertainers. Part of several pennant–winning teams, King Kelly led the league in batting twice, hitting .354 in 1884 and .388 in 1886. Kelly also led the league in runs scored three times with totals of 120, 124 and 155 from 1884 through 1886. Kelly was also an outstanding base stealer, although accurate stolen base statistics were not kept during that era. While certainly a solid player, hitting .308 during the course of his career, it was Kelly's colorful character that made him a standout during the era. Everything about Kelly was flamboyant, from the way he dressed to the way he played. Kelly was even known to occasionally drink during the game. He was such a popular character that, just before the 1887 season, the Chicago White Stockings sold Kelly to the Boston Beaneaters for a record sum at the time, a whopping $10,000. My, how things have changed! After acting as a player/manager for a few years, Kelly retired from the game after the 1893 season. The Veteran's Committee inducted Kelly into the Baseball Hall of Fame in 1945.

1902-11 W600 Sporting Life Cabinets Honus Wagner (In Uniform)

This is one of the most ornate cards ever produced and it captures Honus Wagner is his classic portrait pose. *Sporting Life*, a weekly newspaper out of the Philadelphia area, created these early masterpieces between 1902 and 1911. The cabinet-style cards contain highly desirable portraits. Taken by legendary photographer Carl Horner, these photos were mounted on and surrounded by a thick cardboard frame. Many of the images seen in this set were used to design the T206 set, including this spectacular Wagner card. Each card, measuring approximately 5" by 7½" in size, was placed inside a large envelope and offered to the public via a redemption program or for purchase. It is hard to imagine but the cards were sold for a mere 10 cents each! The cards were offered individually, so it has been difficult for hobby experts to compile a master checklist for the series. During the time they were issued, the style of the card frames and the images changed. In fact, there are some examples that picture the players in street clothes while others capture the players in their uniform. Honus Wagner was one of them, with the *In Uniform* variety being the more desirable of the two. During the time this issue was released, Wagner was in his prime. From 1902-1911, Wagner never hit less than .320 in a single season, peaking at .363 in 1905.

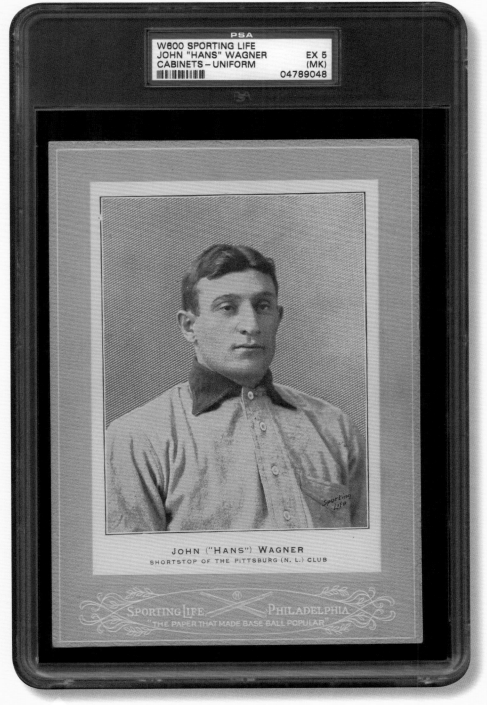

1909 E92 Dockman and Sons Christy Mathewson

This is, arguably, the most beautiful card to ever capture Christy Mathewson. The horizontal pre-war masterpiece depicts the great pitcher releasing the ball against a multi-colored background, including a lush green pasture and partially cloudy sky as the sun illuminates the setting. This gum-card set actually contains 40 total cards, including those of Honus Wagner and Cy Young, although the backs for the cards claim to be one of 50. The image seen of this Mathewson card was actually used on multiple occasions in a variety of candy issues from the time period. As an interesting side note, Mathewson's name was actually misspelled on this card (Matthewson) with an extra "t" in the middle of his last name. The error was never corrected. As with most early candy issues, this card is extremely difficult to find and seldom found in a grade of PSA EX-MT 6 or better.

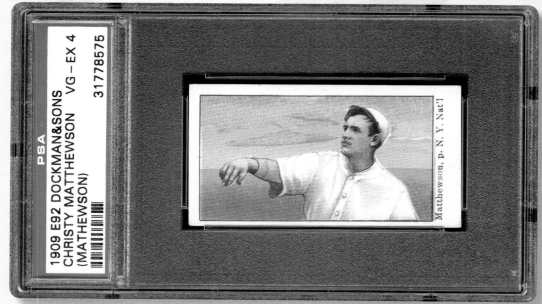

1909 E95 Philadelphia Caramel Honus Wagner

This is one of the most popular pre-war candy issues in the hobby, and this Honus Wagner card is one of two major keys to the set, along with the one featuring Ty Cobb. This 25-card set was issued by the Philadelphia Caramel Co., based in Camden, New Jersey. Each card contains a checklist of the entire set on the reverse, a feature that made this particular issue unique among similar sets of the time period. These tiny relics, measuring approximately 1½" by 2⅝" in size, are extremely difficult to locate in mid-grade or better with most examples exhibiting heavy creasing and wear throughout. In 1909, Wagner hit .339 with 100 RBI and 35 stolen bases in what amounted to an average year for the Hall of Fame shortstop, who was enshrined after receiving more than 95% of the vote on the very first ballot in 1936.

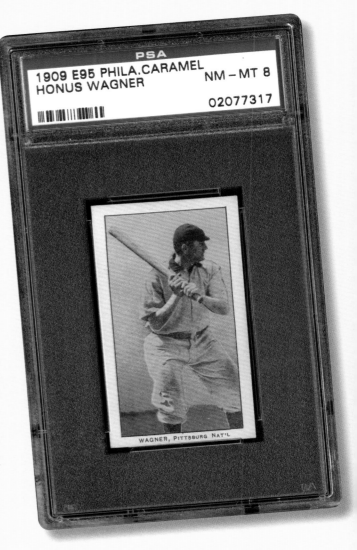

1909 T204 Ramly Cigarettes Walter Johnson

This card is as visually stunning as it is rare. The T204 cards, which measure approximately 2" by 2½" in size, were distributed with Ramly and T.T.T. brand Turkish tobacco cigarettes. The black and white portrait of Walter Johnson is surrounded by gold embossed borders, providing a beautiful frame for this antique gem. Since chipping and wear along the edges are so easily seen, beware of examples that have been recolored in order to cover the damage. There are a few rarities in the 121-card set, but this *Big Train* card is the key. With 12 seasons of 20 or more victories, including two with more than 30, many baseball historians consider Johnson to be the most dominating pitcher of all time. His greatest season on the mound, and perhaps the greatest season by any pitcher, took place in 1913 when Johnson went 36-7 with a 1.14 ERA. During that same campaign, Johnson led the league in strikeouts and posted 11 shutouts. Of all the great Johnson cards on this list, this one is certainly the most challenging.

1909-11 American Caramel E90-1 Joe Jackson

Considered by many hobbyists to be Joe Jackson's official rookie, this card resides in one of the most popular pre-war candy sets of all time. While this set is filled with the great players of the era like Ty Cobb and Honus Wagner, and some great rarities like the Mike Mitchell short print, this first issue of *Shoeless Joe* is far and away the most desirable card in the set. Packaged with hard caramel candy treats, these cards vary slightly in size but normally fall into the 1½" by 2¾" size range. Even though the backs of the cards claim to be one of 100 subjects, there are well over 100 known cards in the set. On August 25, 1908, Joe Jackson made his debut for the Philadelphia Athletics and he got off to a relatively slow start. A few years later, Jackson was considered one of the great hitters in the game. Jackson received his nickname (Shoeless) long before he made his professional debut. While working for a textile mill as a teenager, Jackson played for the mill's baseball team. Jackson removed his cleats after suffering a painful blister during a game. He proceeded to the plate without his shoes. While on base, hecklers started mocking him for not wearing them. The nickname stuck and the rest is history. This card, simple in design with Jackson leaning on his trusty bat against a purple backdrop, is one of only a handful of Jackson cards available. It is clearly his most valuable.

1909-11 T206 White Border Ty Cobb (4)

This is one of two legendary cardboard quartets featured in this book along with the 1933 Goudey Babe Ruth group. The T206 set, arguably the hobby's ultimate issue, features beautiful stone lithography. The cards, which measure approximately 1⁷/₁₆" by 2⁵/₈" in size with some slight size variations, exhibit simply terrific artwork throughout. The four Ty Cobb cards all differ in popularity, scarcity and appearance. The majority of collectors find the portraits the most desirable poses in the set. With Cobb, there are two different portraits to choose from. *The Green Portrait* is by far the toughest of the elite group, followed by the *Bat on Shoulder, Bat off Shoulder* and *Red Portrait* in order of scarcity. On the *Red Portrait*, there are wide variations in color, with some showing a deep red while others have an orange background. In addition, keep in mind there are a variety of backs that can be collected with Sweet Caporal and Piedmont being the two most common.

1909-11 T206 White Border Joe Doyle "Hands Over Head" variation

This is one of the key rarities in the T206 set and it is, truthfully, the hardest to find of the bunch. Joe Doyle may not be the most recognizable name in baseball history but this rarity is one of the most valuable cards in the entire hobby. Doyle pitched for five seasons in the major leagues, compiling a modest 22-21 record to go along with a solid 2.85 ERA. He began his career with the New York Highlanders of the American League and was pitching for them when the T206 set was introduced. That is where the problems begin. Joe Doyle was pictured on a T206 card, in a windup pose, except he was listed as playing for "N.Y. NAT'L" to the right of his last name. Doyle, as mentioned earlier, was a member of a New York team but it was an AL team. Larry Doyle, a second baseman, played for the New York Giants of the NL. The mistake was clear and it seems as if the error was corrected ("NAT'L" removed) quickly since only a handful of uncorrected copies are known at this time. For the collector of T206 cards or great rarities, this card remains more challenging than the Sherry Magee, Eddie Plank or Honus Wagner cards of the same set.

1909-11 T206 White Border Walter Johnson (2)

This is, perhaps, the most popular issue to feature *The Big Train*. During the early part of the 20th Century, Walter Johnson's dominance was staggering. With 417 total victories and a career ERA of 2.17, his numbers are remarkable. Johnson was the first of five men to be elected to the Hall of Fame in 1936 along with Babe Ruth, Ty Cobb, Christy Mathewson and Honus Wagner. Wow! What a select group. While the Johnson Portrait is certainly more popular, the *Hands at Chest* variation is considered to be more difficult. This is due, in large part, to *The Southern Find*, which accounts for most of the high-grade Johnson Portraits that exist today.

1909-11 T206 White Border Sherry Magie (Magee)

This is one of the three big rarities in the T206 baseball set along with the Honus Wagner and Eddie Plank cards. It is also, perhaps, the most famous error card in the entire hobby. Sherry Magee was an excellent major leaguer, finishing his 16-year career with a .291 batting average and 1,176 RBI during the Dead Ball Era. In fact, he led the NL in RBI on four separate occasions and finished among the league leaders in home runs several times, but his solid performance is not what makes this card so desirable. Magee's name was initially spelled incorrectly as "Magie" and then quickly corrected, with the corrected version printed in much higher abundance than the coveted error. Although it is subject to debate, most hobbyists feel this card is a must if you want to truly complete the T206 set.

1909-11 T206 White Border Christy Mathewson (3)

This great trio features one of baseball's best hurlers. Four times in his illustrious career, Christy Mathewson won 30 or more games with a career-high of 37 in 1908. Mathewson would achieve much of his success with the use of a specialty pitch that was most likened to a screwball. This pitch would fade away from lefties and nip the outside corners on right-handed hitters. With a career ERA of 2.13, it is clear that this pitch was very difficult to hit. Mathewson, like other top HOF players in the set, has more than one pose to choose from. *The White Cap* variation is considered to be the most difficult of the three Mathewson cards, but the Portrait is the most popular. In addition, the Mathewson Portrait is one of the toughest HOF portraits in the entire set to find in high-grade.

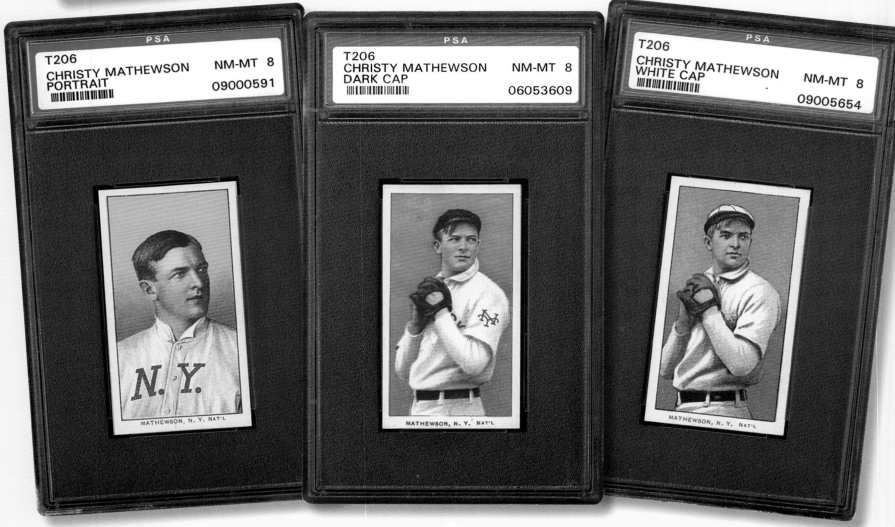

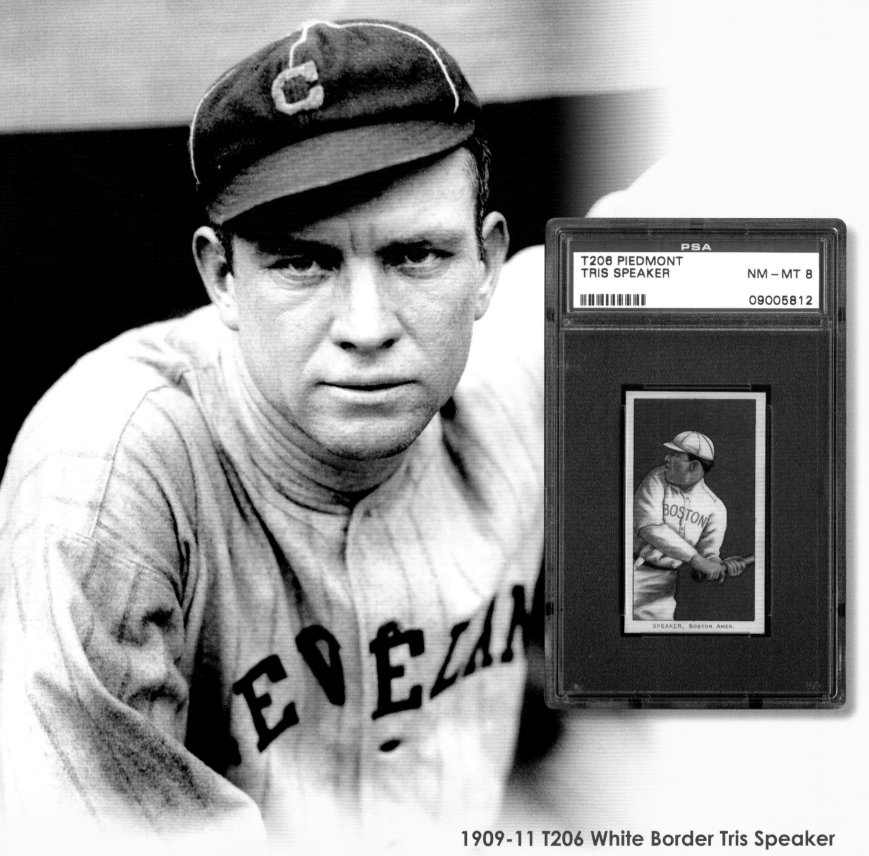

PSA

T206 PIEDMONT
TRIS SPEAKER

NM – MT 8

09005812

SPEAKER, BOSTON AMER.

1909-11 T206 White Border Tris Speaker

This is the only card in the set to feature the great centerfielder. Known as the *Grey Eagle*, Tris Speaker collected more than 3,500 career hits and was considered by most historians to be the premier defensive outfielder of the era. His .345 career average places Speaker in the top five hitters of all-time and his 792 doubles rank first in the category. For his exploits, Speaker was elected to the Hall of Fame in 1937. This card – acknolwedged by many as his rookie card – shows Speaker ready to strike the ball with his lethal bat, a fitting tribute to one of baseball's greatest offensive machines.

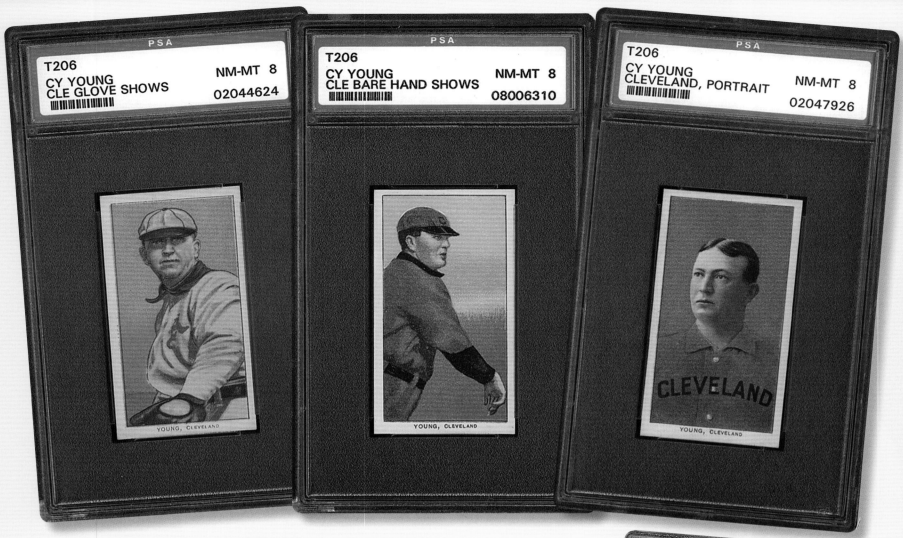

1909-11 T206 White Border Cy Young (3)

When it comes to durability and winning, this man set the standard, a standard that may never be approached. While most experts do not consider Cy Young to be the most dominant pitcher in history, his 511 career wins are simply mind-boggling. Just think for a second. You would have to win 20 games per year, every year, for 25 consecutive years to reach 500. As if winning 500 wasn't tough enough, you would still need to win 11 more games to reach Young! Young completed 749 games and pitched 7,354 innings in his career, both all-time records. Young's three no-hitters and a career ERA of 2.63 just add to his legacy, and his name graces the MLB award for pitching excellence. Young has three cards to choose from within the T206 set and, with the exception of the super rarities, all three cards are considered tougher than most other Hall of Fame cards in the set. Along with the Mathewson, the Young Portrait is one of the tougher portraits in the T206 set to find in high-grade.

1909-11 T206 White Border Ty Cobb (Ty Cobb Back)

While the extreme rarity of this card precludes it from being considered as part of the T206 set, overall, it remains one of Ty Cobb's most desirable cards. Cobb, already featured on four different T206 cards mentioned earlier on this list, appears a fifth time. Technically, this card is a mere variation of the Red Background Cobb, appearing virtually identical on the front. The reverse, instead of containing one of the tobacco brands associated with the issue, is labeled "Ty Cobb, King of the Smoking Tobacco World" in large letters. The face of the card, while identical in image, was given a slightly glossier coating to protect the card from staining since it was originally distributed inside of Ty Cobb tobacco tins, a desirable collectible in itself. At the time of this writing, there were less than 15 known examples of this great rarity, making this card technically tougher to find than the three notable rarities in the set, including the famed Honus Wagner.

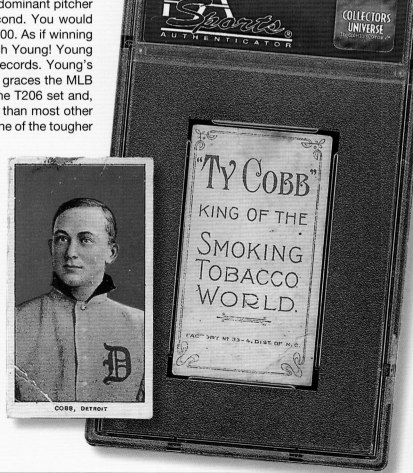

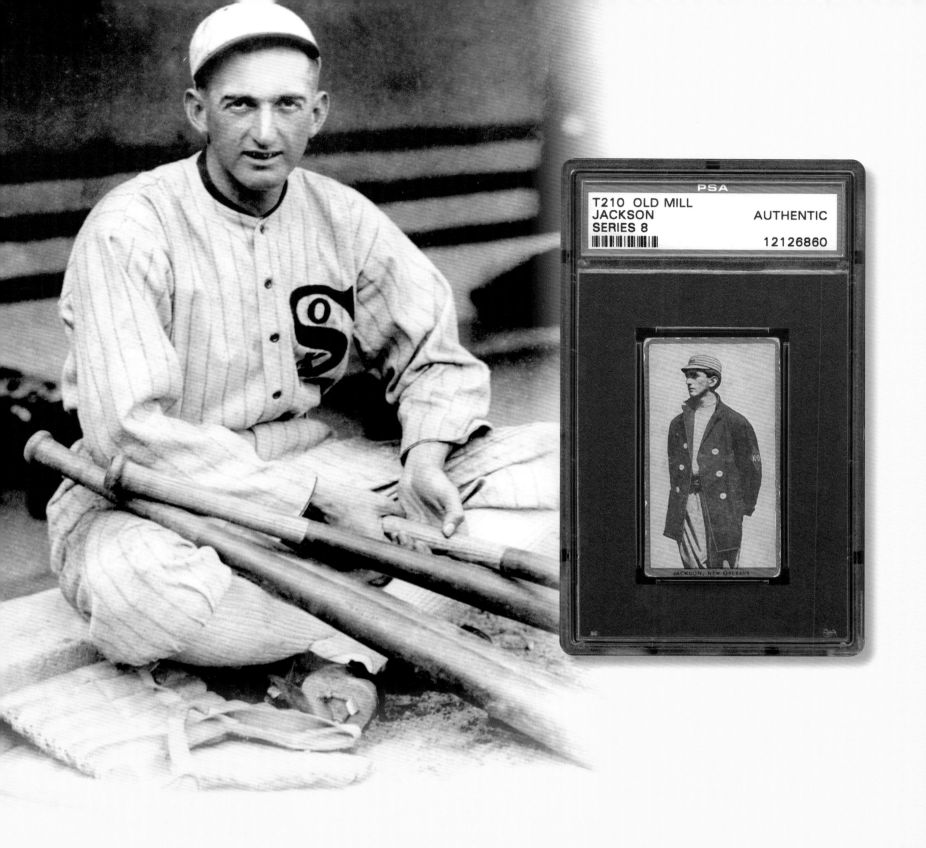

1910 T210 Old Mill Joe Jackson

    This is one of the great rarities of the pre-war era and remains one of only a handful of cards manufactured during Joe Jackson's playing days. This extremely tough card features Jackson as a member of the New Orleans Pelicans, a minor league team, in between his stints with the Philadelphia Athletics and the Cleveland Naps. Despite being pictured as a minor leaguer, many collectors prefer the image of Jackson on the T210 Old Mill card over the E90-1 American Caramel card because he clearly is more recognizable in the facial region and the pose itself is more striking. The set, which consists of hundreds of minor leaguers, many of whom you and I have never heard of before, is centered on this Jackson card. The set itself has never been hugely popular for that very reason, but this card has remained a treasure for those seeking the best of the best. In addition to the inherent rarity of the card, with only a handful of known copies in the hobby, the surrounding red borders are very sensitive and prone to wear. This card measures approximately 1½" by 2⅝".

1911 T205 Gold Border
Walter Johnson

This is one of the key star cards to an ultra-tough set. The ingenuity and talent that went into creating these cards is something special. As we said with the aforementioned Cobb card in the *Top 20*, this set is even more daunting than it is beautiful. In 1911, Walter Johnson enjoyed a typical "Train-like" season. He would lead the league with 36 complete games and six shutouts en route to 25 total victories, a career high at that point. This was the beginning of a very strong run for Johnson, who would win 33 and 36 games, respectively, during the next two seasons. This card captures *The Big Train*, the first truly dominant power pitcher in his prime.

1911 T205 Gold Border
Christy Mathewson

This is one of *Matty's* toughest and most desirable cards. Christy Mathewson was a dominant pitcher and a fan favorite. His life story is a study in triumph and tragedy. The card shows a smiling Mathewson, a smile that would fade much too quickly as he passed away in his mid-40s from accidentally inhaling poison gas during World War I. While some of his greatest seasons were behind him, including three consecutive seasons of 30 or more victories (1903-05), 1911 was another excellent campaign. In 1911, Mathewson led the league in ERA (1.99) while posting a 26-13 record, which included 29 complete games.

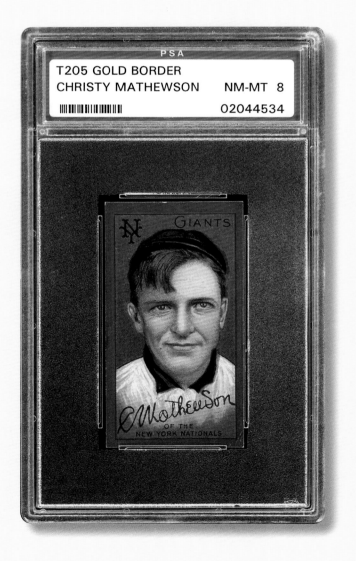

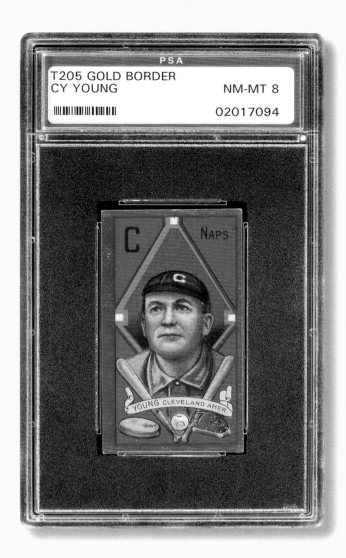

1911 T205 Gold Border Cy Young

Along with Ty Cobb, Walter Johnson and Christy Mathewson, this is one of four major keys to the T205 set. Seldom seen in high grade, these cards are extremely desirable. In 1911, Cy Young came to the end of his illustrious career. Limited to 18 starts overall (7 with Cleveland and 11 with Boston), Young would win a total of seven games between two clubs. He did manage to throw two shutouts and complete 12 of his final 18 games, a testament to his incredible durability. In 1956, MLB chose to name their annual award for pitching excellence after Young, an honor that will continue to keep his name in the minds of future generations of baseball fans and collectors. With 15 seasons of more than 20 victories, including five seasons of 30 or more, it is easy to see why his name graces this significant trophy.

1911 T201 Mecca Double Folders Johnson/Street

This Walter Johnson card is one of the keys to an extremely innovative set that features other legends like Ty Cobb and Christy Mathewson. The T201 issue introduced an entirely new concept by including two different players on a card with a factory fold about 2/3 of the way up the horizontal design. That fold allowed the collector to interchange the torso of each player with the same set of legs on the front by folding the upper image back and forth. The set features eye-catching pastel artwork and more than a dozen Hall of Famers. There are 50 total cards in the set, representing 100 total individuals. These cards measure approximately 2⅛" to 2³/₁₆" by 4¹¹/₁₆". Johnson was in the middle of his prime in 1911, going 25-13 with 207 strikeouts and an ERA of 1.90. This card, one of three major keys in the set, is very condition sensitive with paper wrinkles and edge wear as the leading obstacles.

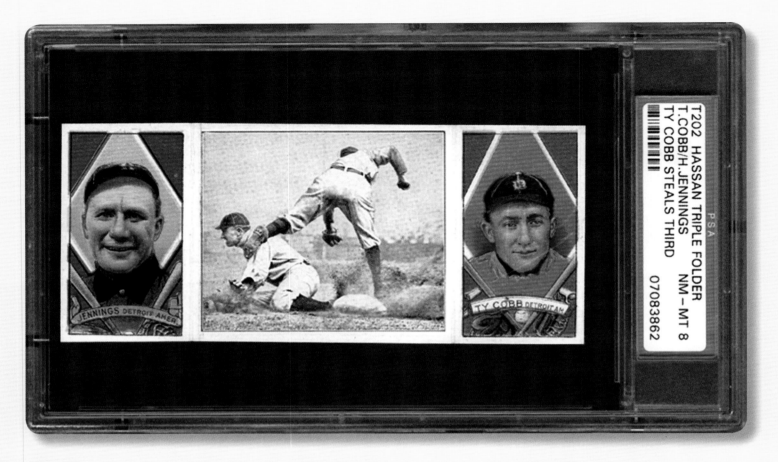

1912 T202 Hassan Triple Folders Ty Cobb Steals 3rd (w/Jennings)

This is one of six cards to feature Ty Cobb in the 132-card set – a set which is considered by many to be one of the most visually appealing productions in the hobby. Colorful portraits of Hall of Fame players Hughie Jennings, the manager of the Detroit Tigers at the time, and Ty Cobb, frame the classic black and white Charles Conlon image in the center of the card. In addition to being considered one of the greatest sports photographs of all-time, the image is widely regarded as the photo that best exemplifies Cobb's intensity and style of play. The amazing action shot captures Cobb crashing into third base below Jimmy Austin of the St. Louis Browns. Cobb slides with a menacing look on his face as the infield dirt flies into the air. This card, along with the other five that feature Cobb, is considered the key to the set. Each portrait, appearing to be a virtual replica of the images used in the T205 Gold Border set, contains biographical information on the reverse while the center image contains a description of the action taking place on the back. The cards, which measure approximately 5¼" by 2¼" in size, are very condition sensitive. Since the cards were designed to be folded, the perforations that divide the card into three sections can often produce paper wrinkles. Those wrinkles can hinder the grade of the card depending on their severity.

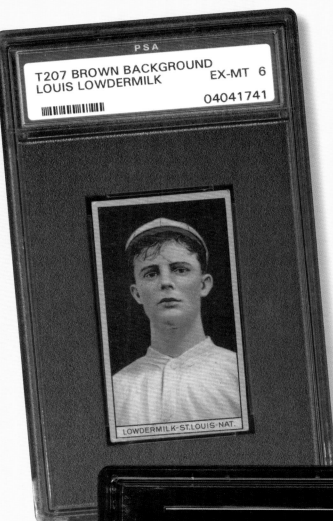

1912 T207 Brown Background Louis Lowdermilk

This is the key to the T207 set and one of the great rarities in the hobby. Most casual baseball fans and collectors will not recognize this man's name. Louis Lowdermilk was a left-handed pitcher with the St. Louis Nationals for a mere two seasons and compiled a less than impressive 4-5 record during that time. While his career was not memorable, this card certainly is. As one of three major rarities in the set, along with cards of Irving Lewis and Ward Miller, this Lowdermilk has long been regarded as one of the hobby's most desired and elusive cards. Interestingly enough, and sometimes typical of great rarities, there is no clear explanation as to why these three cards are so rare. Some speculate that their lack of popularity may have resulted in lower production or lower retention of these cards. In any event, the cards are very scarce, with the Lowdermilk leading the way. There are several Hall of Fame cards and other important cards in the set like those of Walter Johnson, Tris Speaker and Buck Weaver, but Lowdermilk remains the key. This card, which measures approximately 1⁷/₁₆" by 2⁵/₈", resides in a very condition sensitive set and is a great find in any grade.

1913 T200 Fatima Team Card Cleveland Americans

This is one of the most interesting pre-war issues ever manufactured and this card picturing *Shoeless Joe* Jackson (in the upper left) during his prime is one of the keys to the set. In 1913, Jackson hit .373 and was only a couple of years away from joining the Chicago White Sox, the last Major League team he would ever play for. The T200 set contains 16 total team cards, eight from the American League and eight from the National League. The cards, which measure approximately 2⁵/₈" by 4¾" in size, were produced with a high-gloss surface on thin paper stock. Each card contains an offer for a 1913 Fatima Premium, which is a larger version of the team card. In exchange for 40 Fatima cigarette coupons, a premium could be yours. The premiums measure approximately 21" by 13" in size and are very difficult to find. Also pictured is Napoleon Lajoie, who was a member of the team and can be seen near the bottom right in the photo. In addition, this photo pictures Ray Chapman, the only player in history to suffer a fatal injury on the field. Chapman was struck in the head by a Carl Mays fastball in 1920 and died as a result of the impact.

1914 Baltimore News Babe Ruth

This is one of the great rarities in the hobby and, fittingly, it features *The Sultan of Swat*. While it's true that Babe Ruth became a legend as a result of his mighty stick, scouts were drawn to his arm. On the face of the card, Ruth is captured as a minor league pitcher for the Baltimore Orioles of the International League. The reverse contains a schedule for the team. The Baltimore News set is comprised of cards that picture players from the two local teams, the aforementioned Orioles and the Terrapins of the Federal League. It wouldn't be long before Ruth was on the mound for the Boston Red Sox and quickly became the finest lefty in the league. At the time of this writing, there are less than 10 known copies of this legendary card. The copies that have been discovered are generally in low-to-mid grade condition due to the very condition sensitive borders and paper stock. The cards, which measure approximately 2⅝" by 3⅝" in size, can be found with either blue or red borders. In any grade, this pre-rookie card is a find of a lifetime.

1914/15 Cracker Jack #30 Ty Cobb

This is one of the true classics in our hobby and one of Ty Cobb's best looking cards. The striking image of Cobb, glaring fiercely at the viewer, is laid against a deep red backdrop. In terms of pure eye-appeal, this card ranks high on the list. The Cracker Jack issue is one of the hobby's all-time favorites, with the 1914 set being significantly tougher than the 1915 issue because of the absence of a redemption program that year. In the case of Cobb, as with the vast majority of cards in the set, the cards are almost identical each year. The two key differences are the 1915 cards have a reverse that is turned upside down and the 1914 cards were printed on a thinner paper stock. This key card, arguably, captures Cobb's intensity better than any other issue.

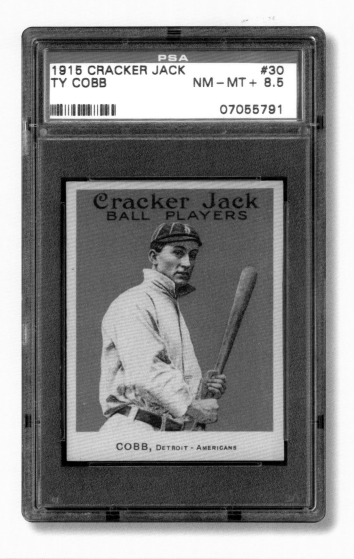

1914/15 Cracker Jack #57 Walter Johnson

When it comes to most star cards from the famed series, the players are shown in a portrait-style pose. In the case of Walter Johnson, Cracker Jack decided to make an exception by depicting the legendary pitcher in his memorable windup, ready to unleash an overpowering fastball. After posting back-to-back 30-win seasons (33 and 36 respectively), Johnson won 28 games in 1914 and 27 in 1915 to lead the league. In fact, in an amazing showing of consistency, Johnson won at least 20 or more games every year from 1910-1919. With the supreme importance of the set coupled with the unique pose, this Cracker Jack card is certainly one of the 12-time strikeout king's best.

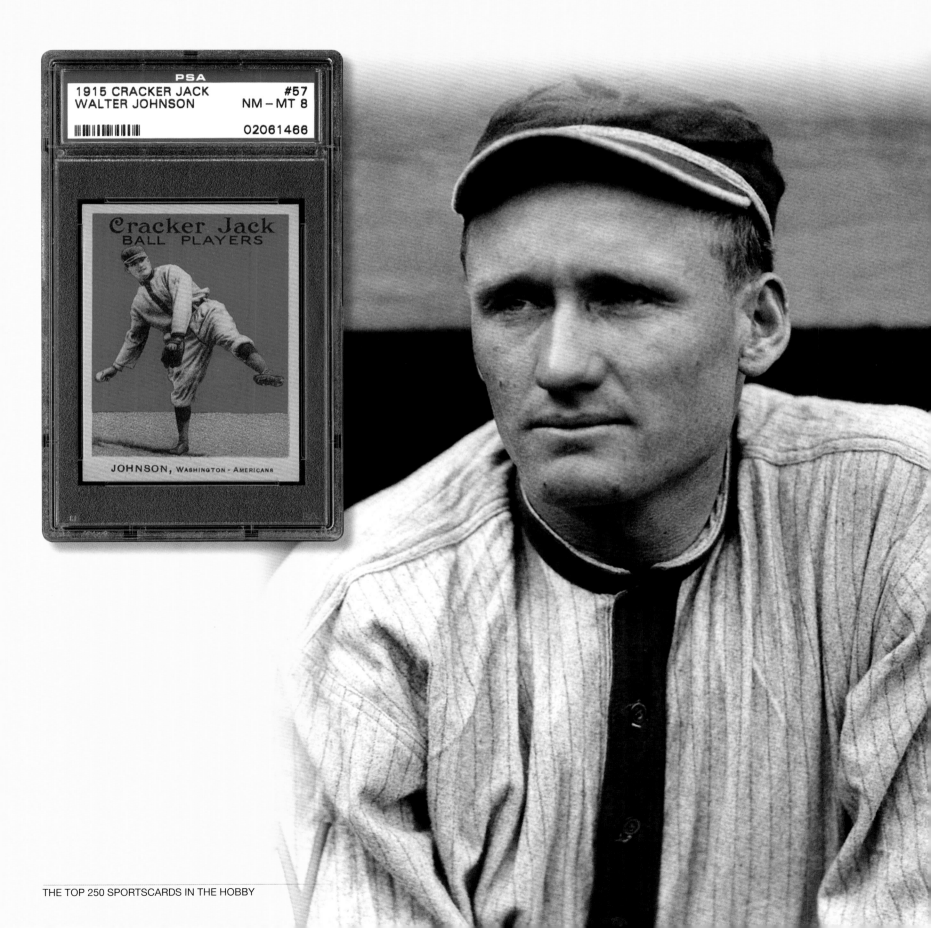

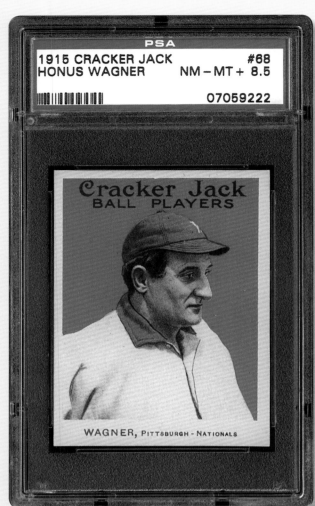

1914/15 Cracker Jack #68 Honus Wagner

While Honus Wagner may be best known for his T206 baseball card and not his athletic prowess, the fact remains that he set the standard for offensive excellence at the shortstop position. Wagner, owner of eight NL batting titles, finished his career with a .327 average, 3,415 hits, 1,732 RBI and 722 stolen bases. When you look throughout history, very few shortstops have ever put up serious offensive numbers. So, when you consider the few who have been able to do so and compare them to Wagner, a greater appreciation for the Pirate legend emerges. Before Ernie Banks, before Cal Ripken, Jr., before Derek Jeter and before A-Rod, there was Wagner. This stunning card captures Wagner nearing the end of his career as a player, and what a career it was.

1914/15 Cracker Jack #88 Christy Mathewson (2)

In a set filled with difficult and eye-appealing cards, Christy Mathewson may take first prize. As noted earlier, the 1914 and 1915 Cracker Jack sets are virtually identical in set composition and in appearance but there is one major exception. In 1914, Mathewson was depicted in an action pose, in mid-delivery much like the Walter Johnson card from the same set, but that is where the similarities end. First, the 1914 Mathewson card is a horizontal one, which makes it different from all the other key cards in the set. Second, Mathewson is the only player featured in both sets to have two entirely different poses as his 1915 card is of the portrait variety. Finally, while no logical explanation has ever surfaced, the 1914 Mathewson is one of the great rarities in the hobby and clearly the most difficult card to find in the set. The 1915 Mathewson card, which pales in comparison to the 1914 in terms of rarity, is considered one of the most visually appealing cards in its respective set.

1915/1916 (M101-5) Sporting News #86 Joe Jackson

This is one of the few Joe Jackson cards available in the marketplace that dates to his playing days, prior to his ban from the league. It remains the second most valuable card in the entire set – a set featuring the rookie card of the greatest player in baseball history, Babe Ruth. This tough black and white issue, available via mail to those who requested it at that time, is subject to a host of condition obstacles, namely consistently poor centering. There is some debate over what year these cards were actually produced, 1915 or 1916, but that controversy has not affected the value of the cards in any way. The surface of these cards exhibit a glossy coating, appearing to be slightly laminated. As a result, cracking along the surface is not uncommon on this issue. This controversial player is pictured in a classic batting pose and, while it is not as popular as his Cracker Jack issue, this card is no less difficult to find.

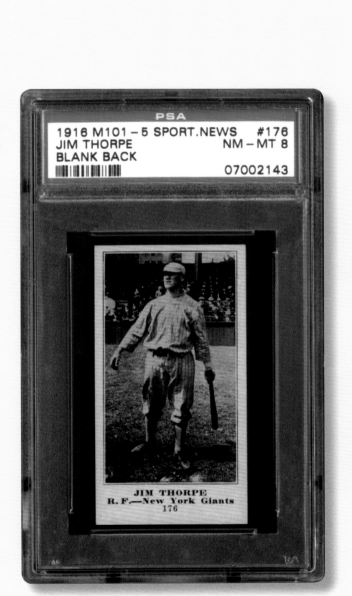

1915/1916 (M101-5) Sporting News #176 Jim Thorpe

This is the only mainstream card to feature Jim Thorpe as a professional baseball player. Thorpe, one of the greatest all-around athletes in sports history, was inducted into the Pro Football Hall of Fame in 1963. While Thorpe wasn't nearly as successful on the baseball field, he hit a respectable .252 during his major league career, which spanned 289 total games from 1913-1919. Nevertheless, Thorpe's importance in history remains. He paved the way for two-sport stars like Bo Jackson, Brian Jordan and Deion Sanders of the modern era. This card is rarely offered publicly due to its difficulty and it is one of only a few standouts in the set.

1932 US Caramel #11 Rogers Hornsby

This is one of the toughest cards in the set and it features the greatest right-handed hitter of the era, maybe ever. Rogers Hornsby was able to hit for average and power during a time when few baseballs cleared the fences. He had a .358 career batting average, including a season when he hit an amazing .424, which remains the NL record. That would be one of three times Hornsby would hit .400 or better. As a result, Hornsby won seven batting titles, six of them consecutively from 1920-1925. The legendary hitter also clubbed 301 homers, leading the league twice in that department. His well-rounded skills at the plate enabled Hornsby to win two Triple Crown Awards and two MVPs en route to his Hall of Fame induction in 1942. This card remains one of the keys to this super difficult and important set, which includes great athletes from a variety of sports. This card measures approximately, 2½" by 3". While there was a find of 1932 U.S. Caramel cards several years ago, no Hornsby cards were discovered, making this card extremely tough to locate in high-grade.

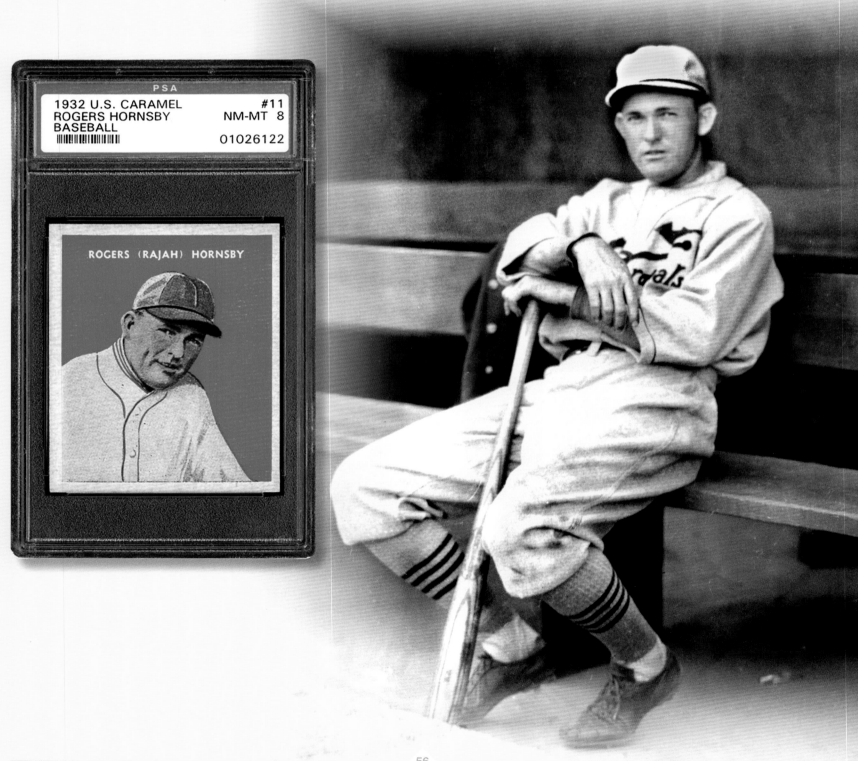

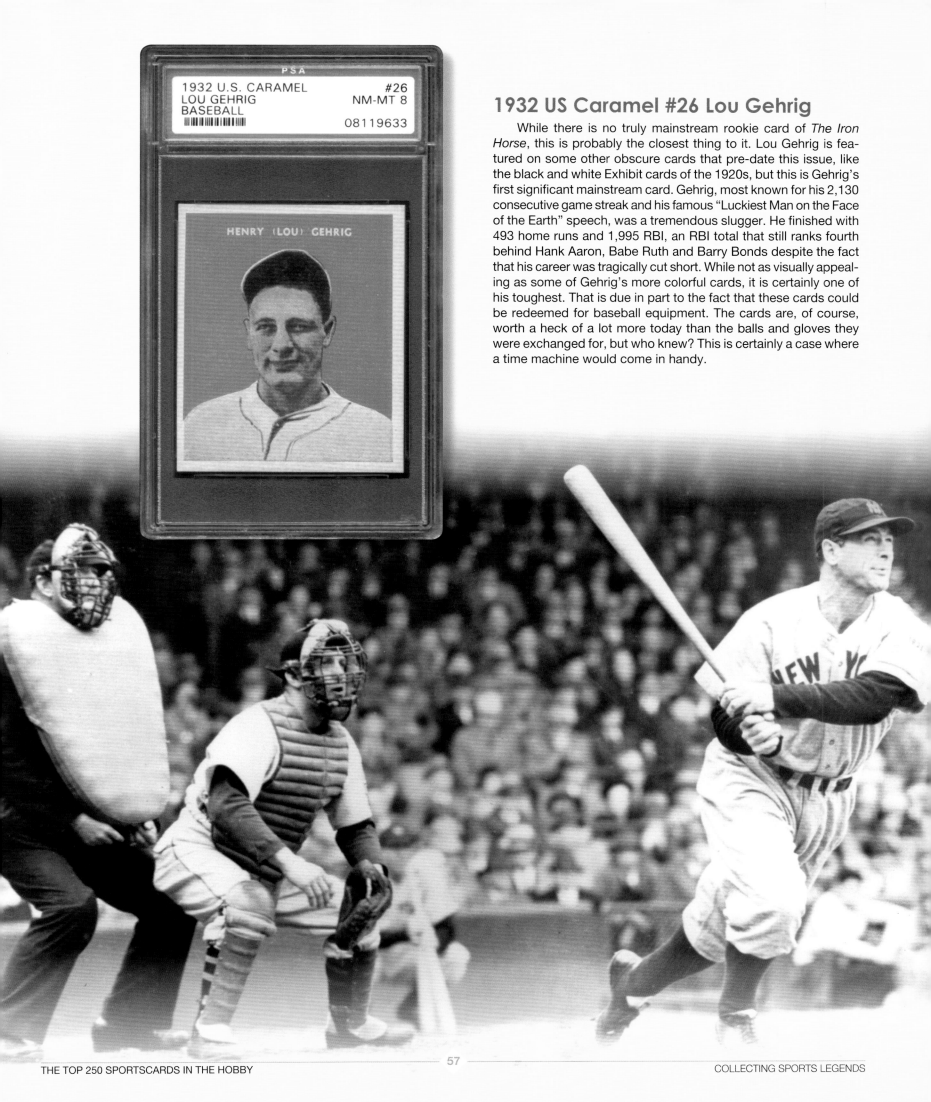

1932 US Caramel #26 Lou Gehrig

While there is no truly mainstream rookie card of *The Iron Horse*, this is probably the closest thing to it. Lou Gehrig is featured on some other obscure cards that pre-date this issue, like the black and white Exhibit cards of the 1920s, but this is Gehrig's first significant mainstream card. Gehrig, most known for his 2,130 consecutive game streak and his famous "Luckiest Man on the Face of the Earth" speech, was a tremendous slugger. He finished with 493 home runs and 1,995 RBI, an RBI total that still ranks fourth behind Hank Aaron, Babe Ruth and Barry Bonds despite the fact that his career was tragically cut short. While not as visually appealing as some of Gehrig's more colorful cards, it is certainly one of his toughest. That is due in part to the fact that these cards could be redeemed for baseball equipment. The cards are, of course, worth a heck of a lot more today than the balls and gloves they were exchanged for, but who knew? This is certainly a case where a time machine would come in handy.

1932 US Caramel #32 Babe Ruth

This is the last card and most valuable card in a very challenging set. During the 1920s, Babe Ruth was depicted on several candy issues, but many of them are considered obscure today. This particular card captures Ruth during a season that added to his almost unbelievable legacy. During the World Series, Ruth hit the famous "Called Shot" in Game 3 against the Chicago Cubs after letting the first two strikes go by without removing the bat from his shoulder. Some dispute the authenticity of the event claiming Ruth never actually pointed to the bleachers in centerfield. They say Ruth may have been merely waving his hands in anger at the Chicago bench. The Chicago players were really giving him a hard time, ragging on Ruth relentlessly. Whether or not he called the shot, Ruth shut up the Chicago dugout quickly when he finally swung his mighty bat. A tape measure blast into the centerfield bleachers will do that.

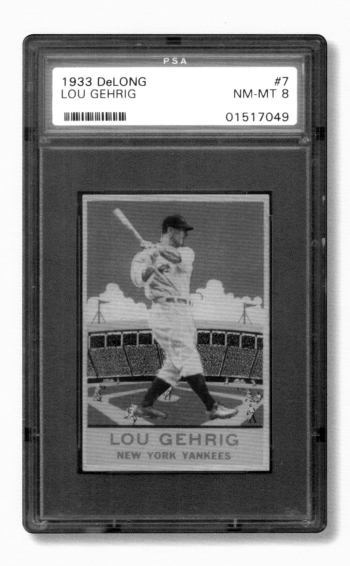

1933 Delong #7 Lou Gehrig

This extremely difficult card is one of Lou Gehrig's best. In fact, it may be the toughest Gehrig card on the entire list. In 1933, Gehrig had a typical Gehrig-like year. He hit .334 with 32 homers, scored a league-high 138 runs and drove in 139 more. To put Gehrig's RBI prowess in perspective, his 1933 total was the 9th best total of his career. For most Hall of Famers, 139 RBI would be a career high. For Gehrig, it was below his average. The card measures approximately $1^{15}/_{16}$" by $2^{15}/_{16}$". This card suffers from a host of condition obstacles. The cards are often found off-center due to the narrow borders that frame the image. The cards may also suffer from severe toning along the edges. Some degree of mild toning is acceptable to most collectors, especially if the toning does not hinder the overall eye-appeal of the card.

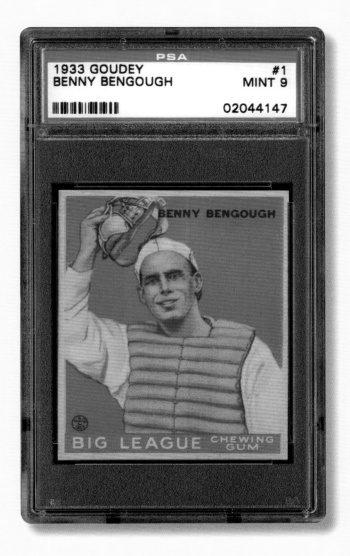

1933 Goudey #1 Benny Bengough

This is the first card in one of the most celebrated baseball card sets in hobby history. The 1933 Goudey baseball set is not only visually stunning but it also contains an amazing star selection throughout. In several cases, some of the best names in the game appeared on more than one card in the set, providing the set with tremendous mainstream appeal. To the contrary, the guy who plays leadoff man to this great Goudey lineup is a name that most casual baseball fans fail to recognize. Benny Bengough's claim to fame in baseball was playing part-time catcher for the New York Yankees during one of their historic runs in 1920s. From 1923-1930, Bengough played with Babe Ruth and Lou Gehrig during their prime years, which included being a member of the legendary 1927 Yankee squad. While he never reached stardom on the field, this Bengough card has become a star in the word of collecting. This card, which measures approximately $2^3/_8$" by $2^7/_8$" and is often found off-center, is part of the extremely tough low-number series and was the subject of much abuse over the years. As with most low-number cards from the set, this card is often encountered with some degree of "foxing," or small brown spots from paper aging. This Bengough card represents one of the toughest holes to fill for the high-grade collector of this historic set.

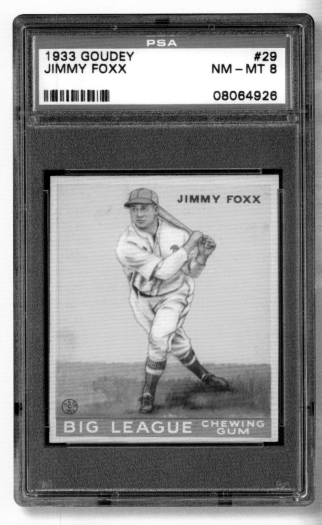

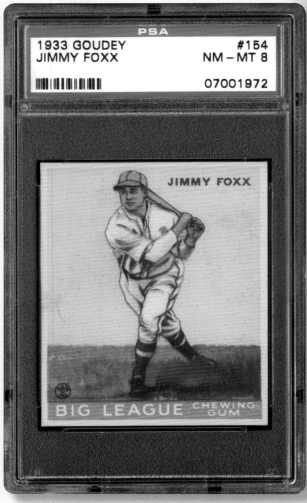

1933 Goudey Jimmy Foxx (2)

During the 1920s and 1930s, most of the headlines were focused on the slugging duo in New York, Lou Gehrig and Babe Ruth. But there was a man who was as powerful as either of them. His name was Jimmie Foxx. In 1933, Foxx showed just how powerful he was. After hitting .356 with 48 homers and 163 RBI, Foxx earned the Triple Crown and the AL MVP. If you can believe it, Foxx's numbers were actually better the prior season. During that season, he hit .364 with 58 homers and 169 RBI en route to being named the AL MVP. Foxx is represented twice in this important set on #s 29 and 154. The #29 Foxx is considered the tougher of the two, but both suffer from the typical condition obstacles associated with the set such as toning and bleeding on the reverse. The bleeding resulted from the uncut sheets of cards occasionally being laid on top of each other before the ink was dry, leaving ink residue on the backs of some of the cards. In addition, even though the cards are virtually identical on the front, each card is distinguishable in color and image detail.

1933 Goudey Lou Gehrig (2)

Like Jimmie Foxx, Lou Gehrig is represented twice in this wonderful set. Unlike Foxx, it is Gehrig's high number that it actually more difficult. Card #160 is seen far less frequently than his #92 card and rarely seen in PSA NM-MT 8 or better. In addition, it is usually found with whiter borders and a lighter blue coloration than the #92 card. Along with the common condition obstacles associated with the issue, both Gehrig cards often suffer from a general lack of eye-appeal from subpar focus and color. While these two Gehrig cards are not quite as popular as the two from the 1934 Goudey set, they are keys to the set and have been, arguably, underappreciated for some time. From his first full season in 1927 through 1932, Gehrig posted RBI totals of 175, 142, 126, 174, 184 and 151. Not even Babe Ruth himself could match Gehrig in that regard.

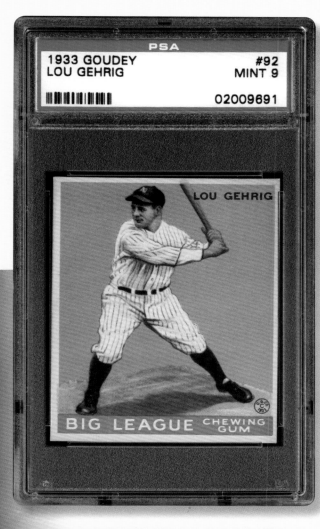

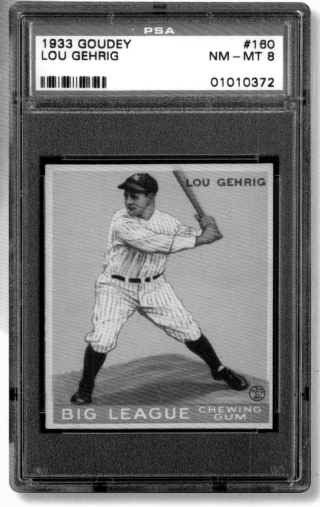

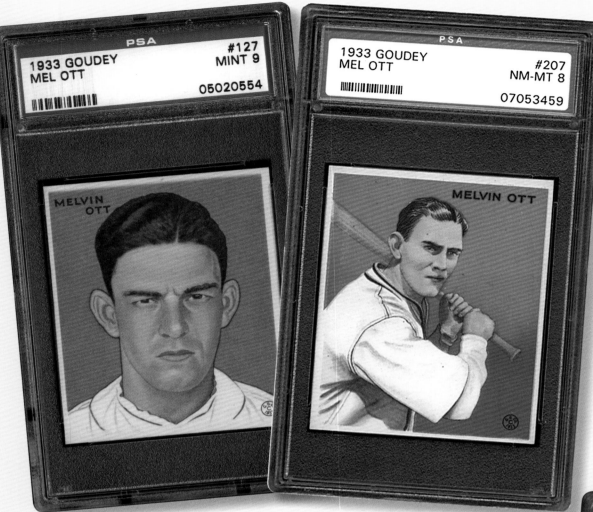

1933 Goudey Mel Ott (2)

While Mel Ott did not fit the description of a prototypical power hitter, his tenacity and unique swing helped him reach the elusive *500 Home Run Club*. With an uncanny ability to pull the ball, Ott was able to take advantage of the short porch in right field at the Polo Grounds, crushing 511 homers in his career. It was only 257 feet down the line! At the time of his retirement, Ott was the NL leader in career RBI (1,860), runs scored (1,859) and walks (1,708). Featured on two different cards in the set, #s 127 and 207, you can see the mean glare on Ott's face. The high-number Ott is the more difficult of the two cards and very difficult to find well-centered. With the stunning red background, it is also more visually appealing, yet both are important cards. Ott was inducted into the Baseball Hall of Fame in 1951.

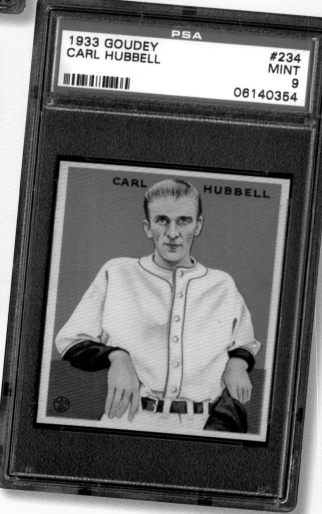

1933 Goudey Carl Hubbell (2)

These are two key cards of baseball's first left-handed screwball specialist. Carl Hubbell was a very deceptive pitcher and his screwball was devastating at times. How devastating? In the 1934 All-Star Game, Hubbell struck out Babe Ruth, Lou Gehrig, Jimmie Foxx, Al Simmons and Joe Cronin consecutively. Hubbell would also go on to win 253 games in his career, including five straight seasons of 20 or more from 1933-1937. Along the way, Hubbell would win two MVPs, once in 1933 when he went 23-12 with a 1.66 ERA, and again in 1936 when he went 26-6 with a 2.31 ERA. Unfortunately, Hubbell's specialty pitch did him in as he underwent surgery to repair his pitching elbow. He was never quite the same. The Goudey set features two different cards of the great pitcher, both exhibiting great eye-appeal. The #230 (Pitching Pose) card is considered the tougher of the two and is rarely seen in high-grade. Hubbell was elected to the Hall of Fame in 1947.

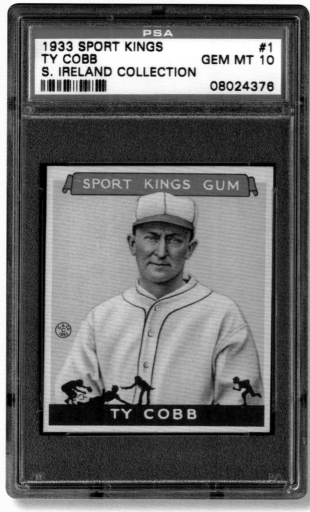

1933 Goudey Sport Kings #1 Ty Cobb

This is the first card and a key to one of the most desirable sportscard sets ever produced. Filled with athletes from a variety of sports, Ty Cobb was chosen to begin the set and one of only three baseball players included. Babe Ruth and Carl Hubbell were the other two. Many people forget that Cobb actually received more support than Ruth when the Hall of Fame first opened its doors in 1936. This set features figures from sports like baseball, basketball, billiards, boxing, football, golf, hockey, swimming and even dog sledding. That's right, dog sledding. This is a very diverse set and that is part of its charm, along with its great design. This card, in addition to being subject to handling abuse as the first card in the set, can often suffer from a lack of eye-appeal if the yellow background is faint in appearance. This gem, despite being produced after Cobb's playing days, is one of his most important cards.

1933 Goudey Sport Kings #2 Babe Ruth

The Sultan of Swat took position number two in this tremendous set, yet when it comes to demand, he remains number one. While Babe Ruth has four different cards to choose from in the Goudey baseball set, here, there is only one. This card, in terms of difficulty, is comparable to the #149 Ruth in the Goudey baseball set. It is rarely offered in PSA NM-MT 8 or better condition and is often found centered towards the bottom or exhibiting a slight angular cut. After 12 home run, 11 walk, 13 slugging percentage and 8 run scoring titles in his career, Ruth was certainly "The King" of his era. In fact, many people forget that he also hit for average since Ruth is so well know for hitting homers. In 1923, Ruth almost reached .400 for the season with a .393 average. This is one of Ruth's most desirable cards.

1933-36 Zeenut Joe DiMaggio

This is the first issue to ever picture Joe DiMaggio as a professional and it remains an extremely elusive card. DiMaggio began his career in the Pacific Coast League where he made an immediate impression with his bat. In 1932, DiMaggio made his pro debut by playing in a mere three games but he would get the chance to play a full season in 1933, finishing with a .340 average, 28 home runs and 169 RBI. DiMaggio would hit safely in an amazing 61 consecutive games that year, five more than his MLB record of 56 in 1941. In 1934, DiMaggio appeared on two different Zeenut PCL cards, in a batting pose and throwing pose. Every card in the series (1933-1936) had Joe's name mispelled on the front as "DeMaggio" and his two brothers, Dom and Vince, suffered the same fate on their cards. Many of the cards, which measure approximately 1¾" by 3½" intact, featured a perforated coupon at the base of the card that could be redeemed for premiums. The expiration date along the base helps in determing the year of release since no season information was included on the cards, making it hard to pinpoint the exact year of release.

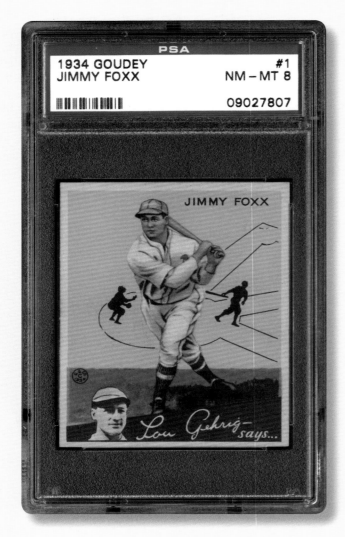

1934 Goudey #1 Jimmy Foxx

This is, without question, the most important card to ever feature Jimmie Foxx. Foxx, nicknamed *The Beast* for his menacing look, would often intimidate opposing pitchers by rolling up his sleeves to reveal his imposing arms. Ironically, Foxx was also known for being one of the most personable players in the game. As the greatest right-handed slugger of his generation, Foxx crushed 534 home runs and was elected to the Hall of Fame in 1951. Foxx also became the first player in history to win three MVP Awards (1932, 1933 and 1938). In 1934, Foxx hit .334 with 44 home runs and 130 RBI, a typical season for the mild mannered slugger. While the 1933 Goudey issue is clearly the more significant set of the two, the 1934 issue is, arguably, more visually appealing. This card measures approximately 2⅜" by 2⅞". This is the first card in the set, making it extremely tough to locate in high-grade.

1934 Goudey #6 Dizzy Dean

This is a collector favorite and one of the keys to a historically important set. Dizzy Dean, a colorful character, was one of the best pitchers of his era. He would win the MVP in 1934 after posting a 30-7 record with an ERA of 2.66 for the St. Louis Cardinals as a member of the team's *Gas House Gang*. Dean, after several decades have passed, stands as the last National League pitcher to reach 30 victories in a season. Despite an injury that caused Dean to leave the game prematurely, his career mark was 150-83 with 154 complete games. After breaking his toe in the 1937 All-Star Game, Dean altered his delivery, which led to permanent damage in his arm. For his efforts, Dean was inducted into the Baseball Hall of Fame in 1953. This card is considered one of the best looking cards in the set, showing Dean in a classic pitching pose.

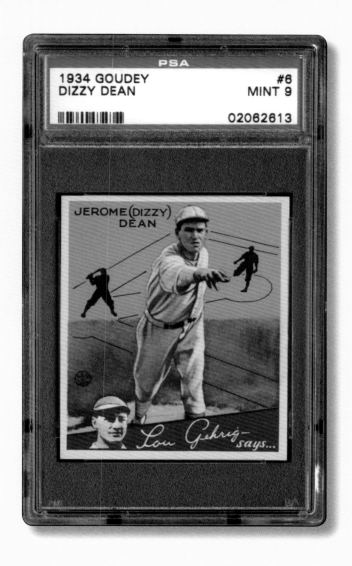

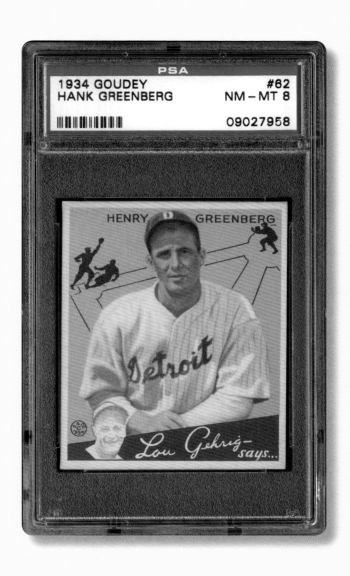

1934 Goudey #62 Hank Greenberg

This card features one of the most prolific sluggers in baseball history and it is his most visually appealing issue. Hank Greenberg had some incredible seasons for the Detroit Tigers and, despite missing nearly four years to military service, he left a permanent mark on the game. Greenberg posted career-highs of 183 RBI in 1937 and 58 homers in 1938, numbers that put him amongst the greatest sluggers in the game. In only nine full seasons, Greenberg amassed 331 homers and 1,276 RBI. He was named MVP twice, once in 1935 and again in 1940, and was inducted into the Baseball Hall of Fame in 1956. You will notice that Greenberg shares the front of the card with another great slugger of the era, Lou Gehrig, who appears on every card in the set. In an interesting twist, Greenberg almost ended up with the Bronx Bombers over in New York. He was offered a contract to join the team but they wanted him to play somewhere other than first base. They already had Gehrig in that slot, so Greenberg decided to sign on with Detroit. Both first basemen went on to terrorize pitchers throughout the league and make history in the process.

1934-36 Diamond Stars #1 Lefty Grove

This is the first card in a very tough, yet overlooked prewar set. Lefty Grove was a dominant pitcher in his day. Many baseball experts feel Grove may be the best left-handed pitcher in baseball history. Grove finished his career with a 300-141 record, resulting in an astonishing winning percentage of .680, which is the highest of any pitcher to win 300 or more games. From 1927-1933, Grove won 20 or more games each and every season, including an incredible season where he went 31-4 with a 2.06 ERA. While he will be remembered primarily for being the ace of the Philadelphia Athletics, Grove did have a few productive seasons with the Boston Red Sox before his retirement. Grove was inducted into the Baseball Hall of Fame in 1947. Measuring approximately 2³⁄₈" by 2⁷⁄₈" and rarely offered in high-grade, this is one of the toughest #1 cards in the hobby.

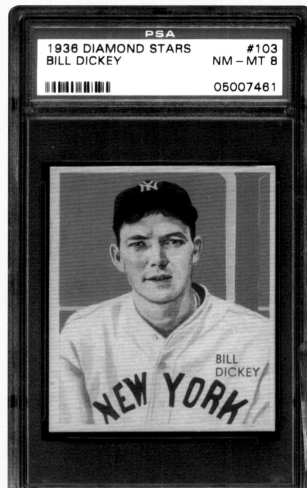

1934-36 Diamond Stars #103 Bill Dickey

This is one of Bill Dickey's most desirable cards, residing in the tough high-number series of the beautiful Diamond Stars issue. As a player, Dickey was one of the best catchers to ever play the game. He also was one of the fiercest. After a collision at the plate in 1932, Dickey broke the jaw of Carl Reynolds with one punch. Dickey hit .313 with 202 home runs and 1,209 RBI in his career, a career that included a four-year streak where he reached at least 20 homers and 100 RBI (1936-1939). In 1936, Dickey hit .362, which remains the highest single-season batting average for a catcher (tied with Mike Piazza – 1997). Dickey won seven World Series championships as a player with the New York Yankees and was a master at handling pitchers. In fact, Dickey was brought back to the Yankees in 1949 to mentor another Hall of Fame catcher, Yogi Berra. This eight-time All-Star was inducted into the Baseball Hall of Fame in 1954. This card, along with 11 others in the high-number series, was not originally issued with the set. The company decided to add the 12 cards later to complete it since they promised the public 108 total cards. Each card in the series, including this Dickey card, is very scarce compared to the rest of the cards.

1938 Goudey Joe DiMaggio (2)

This is the mainstream rookie issue of *Joltin' Joe*. Joe DiMaggio ranks right up there with Babe Ruth, Lou Gehrig and Mickey Mantle as one of the most celebrated New York Yankee legends in history. DiMaggio's popularity went beyond the game of baseball; he was an American Icon. In 1938, DiMaggio had a typical DiMaggio-like season by hitting .324 with 32 home runs and 140 RBI. The set features two different DiMaggio cards, the #250 (without cartoons) and #274 (with cartoons). The #274 card is considered slightly more difficult to find than the #250 DiMaggio but both are tough to locate in high-grade. In fact, the #250 card is actually tougher to find in high-grade despite being easier to locate overall. This issue is plagued by poor centering, print defects and toning, which is the biggest condition obstacle in the set. This is one of only a handful of issues to depict the great Yankee centerfielder during his playing days.

1938 Goudey Bob Feller (2)

These two cards represent the only mainstream rookie offerings of one of base-ball's most feared pitchers. If Bob Feller had not missed nearly four full seasons due to military service, who knows what his career numbers would look like. Feller was a classic, right-handed power pitcher who had a fastball that went unmatched in his day. With 266 career victories, a 3.25 ERA, over 2,500 strikeouts and three no-hitters to his credit, Feller was a dominant force on the mound. In 1938, Feller was 19 and embarking on his first full season on the hill. During that year, he posted a 17-11 record with a league-high of 240 strikeouts. He would lead the league in that category six more times in his career with a high of 348 in 1946. While both of these cards (#s 264 and 288) are difficult to find in high-grade, as is typical of the issue, the high-number version is the tougher of the two.

1939 Play Ball #26 Joe DiMaggio

Joe DiMaggio's first Play Ball card is one of the keys to the set, along with the Ted Williams rookie card. In 1939, DiMaggio would continue to excel at the plate and in the field. He would lead the league in hitting with a .381 batting average, smack 30 homers and drive in 126 runs. This would be his fourth consecutive season with 100 or more RBI. After such a fantastic season, DiMaggio would be named AL MVP for the first time. He would win a total of three MVPs in his career – a career that led DiMaggio to the Hall of Fame in 1955. This Play Ball issue, while simple in its black and white format, offers one of the more recognizable and classic images of the Yankee legend. While not one of DiMaggio's more difficult cards, poor centering and stray print marks are two condition obstacles to be wary of. This card measures approximately 2½" by 3⅛".

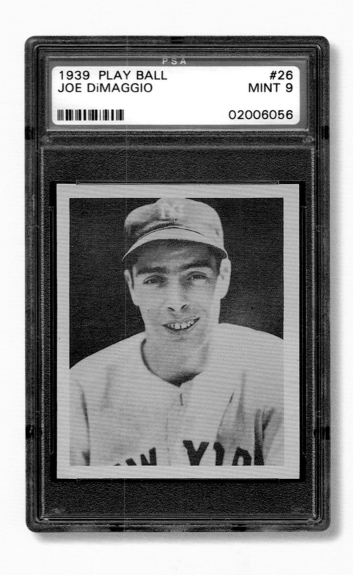

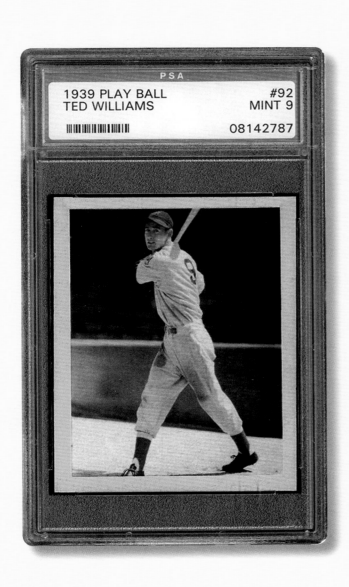

1939 Play Ball #92 Ted Williams

This is the only recognized rookie card of the *Splendid Splinter*. Fittingly, Ted Williams is pictured finishing his legendary swing with his famous number (9) visible on the back of his jersey. From day one, Williams wanted to be known as the greatest hitter who ever lived. Are you going to argue with him? Despite missing nearly five full seasons of his prime due to military service, Williams posted a .344 batting average, a .483 on-base average (the highest of all time). He owns the second highest slugging average of all-time at .634 and crushed 521 homers. There's no question that Williams would have challenged Babe Ruth's career home run mark of 714 before Hank Aaron had he not missed so many games. To put Williams and his hitting prowess in context, just imagine a player who consistently hits for a higher average than perennial batting champs like Wade Boggs and Tony Gwynn, yet also powers the ball over the fence at a faster rate than Mickey Mantle or Mike Schmidt. This classic card is not the most difficult issue to feature Williams but, as his only true rookie, it is extremely important.

1940 Play Ball #1 Joe DiMaggio

This is the first card in a very condition sensitive issue, loaded with Hall of Fame players. This DiMaggio card is one of three major keys to the set, along with the Ted Williams and Joe Jackson cards. In 1940, DiMaggio would have another stellar season. He led the league with a .352 batting average, drilled 31 homers and had 133 RBI. This would be DiMaggio's fourth consecutive season of 30 or more homers and fifth with 100 or more RBI. He was a model of consistency on the field. One of DiMaggio's most impressive career statistics is the fact that he only struck out a total of 369 times, yet he still managed to club 361 homers – an almost 1:1 ratio, which is unheard of in baseball. This card, as with all the cards in the set, has to deal with varying degrees of toning. If severe, it can damage the overall eye-appeal quite a bit. As the #1 card in the set, it is very elusive in high-grade and it pictures DiMaggio in his classic batting pose.

1940 Play Ball #225 Shoeless Joe Jackson

This card represents the final tribute to one of baseball's most intriguing figures. In 1940, Play Ball decided to fill their set with a combination of current players and retired stars. Joe Jackson, long since banned from baseball after the 1919 Black Sox scandal, remains one of three keys to the set. When Jackson was banned from baseball, the fans were deprived of watching one of the greatest hitters in history. In Jackson's first full season, he hit .408. In his last full season, Jackson hit .382, which obviously shows that the legendary hitter was still going strong at the time of the ban. Even though this card was not produced during his playing days, with so few Jackson cards to collect, this one enjoys solid demand.

1941 Play Ball #14 Ted Williams

This is one of the *Splendid Splinter's* most popular cards and it commemorates a special season. In 1941, Ted Williams hit an amazing .406! What is more remarkable is the way he chose to end the season. Going into the last day of the season, Williams could have taken himself out of the lineup since he had already reached .400, thus preserving his accomplishment. Instead, Williams insisted on playing in the doubleheader that day. It was a major risk for Williams but he ended up going 6 for 8, raising his average to .406. He would finish the season with 37 homers, 120 RBI, 145 walks and a .553 OBP. Astonishingly, despite such a historic season, Williams finished second to Joe DiMaggio in the MVP voting. This card suffers from a few condition obstacles, including poor centering, toning and subpar color as many examples appear washed out.

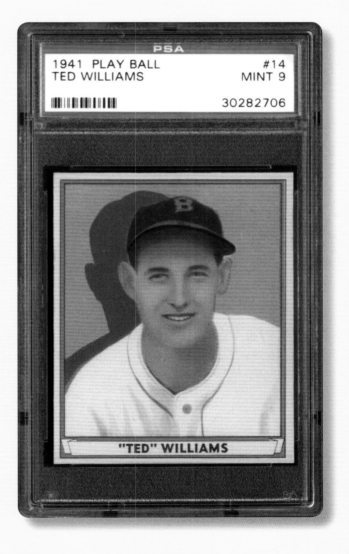

1941 Play Ball #54 Pee Wee Reese

This is the only recognized rookie card of the Brooklyn Dodger favorite. Pee Wee Reese, Brooklyn's starting shortstop for over a decade, excelled on defense and was one of the leaders in the clubhouse. In fact, he was able to rally his troops around Jackie Robinson after a less than warm reception. Though he was not a powerhouse on offense, Reese finished in the top 10 of the NL MVP voting eight different times. After his playing career came to an end, Reese was hired as the head of player recruitment for the H&B Bat Company because he was so well liked throughout the league. Even though it took some time, Reese was inducted into the Baseball Hall of Fame in 1984. This card is the most significant rookie card in the entire Play Ball set and considered more difficult than many of the other keys in the set.

1948 Bowman #6 Yogi Berra

This is the only recognized rookie card of the legendary Yankee backstop. Yogi Berra was known as much for his colorful personality as he was for his ability with the bat and glove. His memorable quotes have been referenced time and time again, but it was his ability to win that made him special. During his time with the Yankees, as the leader behind the plate, Berra helped them reach the World Series 14 times, winning 10 championships. It's no wonder that Berra remains the all-time World Series leader in hits and games. In 1948, Berra would play in 100 games for the first time in his career, hitting .305 and driving in 98 runs. After this performance, Berra became a mainstay for over a decade. This card measures approximately 2¹/₁₆" by 2½" and is one of a few key Hall of Fame rookies in the set.

1948 Bowman #36 Stan Musial

This is one of two recognized rookie cards of *Stan the Man* who was, without a doubt, one of baseball's greatest hitters. Along with the Yogi Berra rookie, this card is one of two major keys to the black and white 1948 Bowman set, their first baseball production. In 1948, seven years after his Major League debut, Stan Musial hit .376 with 39 home runs and 131 RBI. His batting average and RBI marks led the league, but he was also the leader in runs scored (135), hits (230), doubles (46), triples (18), OBP (.450) and slugging percentage (.702). Most of those figures were career-bests for Musial, who was named NL MVP for the third time in his career. While his 1948-49 Leaf issue is considered more difficult overall, the 1948 Bowman Musial is more popular.

1948-49 Leaf #1 Joe DiMaggio

This is the first card and one of the most visually appealing cards in a terribly difficult set. This also marked the second time that Joe DiMaggio was chosen to lead-off a major set from the 1940s. The first time was when DiMaggio was at the top of the 1940 Play Ball set. The 1948-49 Leaf set is filled with important cards, including ones featuring Babe Ruth, Satchel Paige, Ted Williams, Bob Feller and rookies of Warren Spahn, Stan Musial and Jackie Robinson, to name a few. The 1948 and 1949 seasons were both productive for DiMaggio. In 1948, he would hit .320, while leading the league with 39 homers and 155 RBI in only 153 games. In 1949, DiMaggio would miss about half of the season, but he came back to hit .346 with 14 homers and 67 RBI in only 76 games. This is one of DiMaggio's toughest cards to find in high-grade, residing in the often abused, number-one slot. This card measures approximately 2³⁄₈" by 2⁷⁄₈". In addition, many Leaf DiMaggio cards are found off-center.

1948-49 Leaf #3 Babe Ruth

This is the last major card to feature Babe Ruth and, while it was technically manufactured after his playing days, the card is not treated as such. On June 13, 1948, Ruth made his last appearance at Yankee Stadium. Weakened by cancer, Ruth could barely stand, leaning on a bat to keep him steady on his feet. On August 16, 1948, the world lost *The Sultan of Swat* for good. In its own way, this card represents a final farewell to the greatest slugger in baseball history. To put Ruth's sheer domination into perspective, consider this ... Babe Ruth hit more home runs, by himself, than every entire team in the American League in both 1920 and 1927. This particular issue is very condition sensitive. Poor centering has always been a problem with this Ruth card as well as wide variances in print quality. You will notice dramatic differences in color and clarity as you analyze more copies of this classic card.

1948-49 Leaf #4 Stan Musial

This is one of two recognized rookie cards to feature the legendary hitter, with this Leaf card being the tougher of the two. The card, which is often plagued by distracting print lines, is also considered more visually attractive with the use of color as opposed to the black and white Bowman issue. Stan Musial is one of a few players that exemplified consistency. How consistent was he? In one of the more striking statistics on record, Musial had the same amount of hits at home (1,815) as he did on the road, totaling 3,630 hits. Musial finished his career with a .331 batting average, 475 home runs, 1,951 RBI, 1,949 runs scored, 725 doubles, 177 triples and a .559 slugging percentage (a figure higher than both Mantle and Mays). Along the way, Musial won three NL MVP awards in 1943, 1946 and 1948. This seven-time NL batting champion was inducted into the Baseball Hall of Fame in 1969.

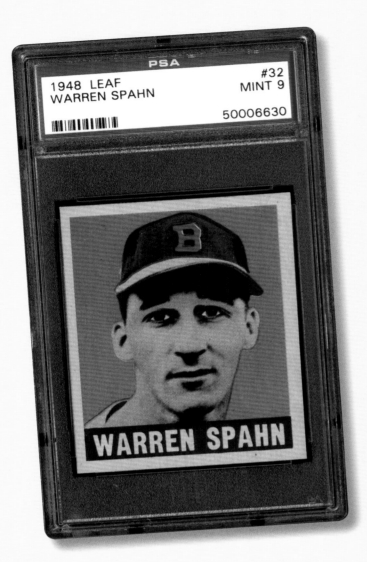

1948-49 Leaf #32 Warren Spahn

This is one of only two recognized rookie cards of baseball's all-time leader in wins for lefties. Sandy Koufax and Steve Carlton threw harder and Lefty Grove may have been more dominating, but no other lefty was as durable as Warren Spahn. He won 20 or more games 13 times in his career and compiled a total of 363 victories, even though he didn't win a single game until he was 25 years old. Along the way, Spahn earned the Cy Young Award in 1957 and was elected to 14 All-Star teams, a record for pitchers. In 1973, Spahn was elected to the Hall of Fame after recording a career ERA of 3.09, a career that spanned 21 years. This particular card, one many hobby experts consider to be underrated, is considerably more difficult than his 1948 Bowman rookie and is one of the better looking cards in the set.

1948-49 Leaf #76
Ted Williams

This card is the first post-WWII issue to feature Ted Williams and it is one of the keys to a tough set. The 1948 Leaf card shows Williams finishing his magical swing and, if found centered and bright, is one of the more visually appealing cards in the set. In 1948, Williams hit a league-high .369 with 25 home runs and 127 RBI, but he would outdo himself one year later. In 1949, while his average fell slightly to .343, Williams pounded 43 homers and finished with 159 RBI, both AL bests. Williams would earn the 1949 AL MVP for his outstanding performance, the second of his career after winning the first in 1946. This Leaf card is one of Ted's toughest, with print quality and poor centering being the two biggest condition obstacles.

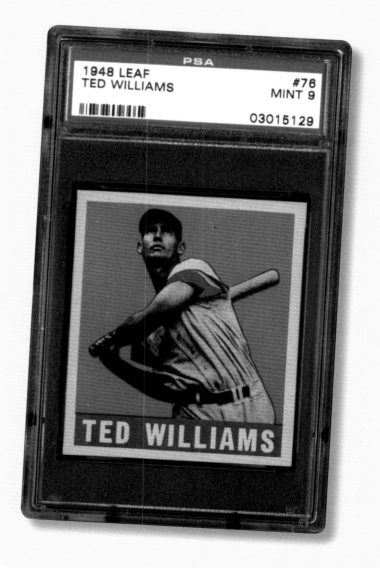

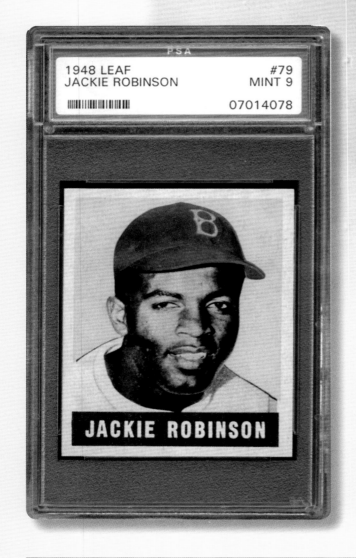

1948-49 Leaf #79 Jackie Robinson

This is the only true rookie card of baseball's first African-American representative and hero to all. You cannot say enough about the importance of this man or this card. As a result of Jackie Robinson's contribution, the game of baseball is a better one today, showcasing players from all over the globe. He endured racist taunts and hate mail long before the likes of Hank Aaron and Ken Griffey, Jr. stepped onto the field. In 1947, Robinson would immediately make an impact by coming away with the NL Rookie of the Year Award at the age of 28. Two years later, in 1949, Robinson would have his finest year by hitting .342 (a league-high) with 203 hits, 124 RBI, 122 runs scored and 37 stolen bases. This card, in addition to being one of the keys to the Leaf set, is also one of the issue's more difficult cards. It usually suffers from poor print quality and color. Black print defects can severely hinder the eye-appeal in the light background, and the background itself often exhibits a faint or dull yellow color. Even though Robinson would put up impressive numbers in his brief MLB career, it was his everlasting impact on the game and society that makes this card such an important piece.

1948-49 Leaf #93 Bob Feller

This is one of *Rapid Robert's* earliest cards and maybe his most difficult. In 1948 and 1949, Bob Feller won 19 and 15 games respectively while leading the league in strikeouts in 1948. Feller had just posted back-to-back 20 win seasons in 1946 and 1947, cementing himself as the premier power pitcher of the era. Fans and collectors have always been drawn to power, with both hitters and pitchers. Along with Walter Johnson, Bob Gibson, Nolan Ryan and Roger Clemens, Feller exemplified right-handed power pitching. This card is as tough to find in high-grade as it was to hit the man it pictures. The Leaf Feller is one of several short-printed cards in the set and is rarely seen in high-grade. The two biggest issues with this card, in addition to its scarcity, are print quality and poor centering. Dark print defects plague the yellow background and even high-grade copies appear unfocused near his face. This is a terribly problematic card.

1949 Bowman #84 Roy Campanella

This is the only recognized rookie card of the legendary Brooklyn Dodger catcher and a key to the set. In 1949, Roy Campanella played his first full season. After hitting .287 with 22 home runs, the Dodgers decided to make Campy a regular for years to come and he became a perennial All-Star (1949-1956). Campanella was also a three-time NL MVP (1951, 1953 and 1955) as he led the Dodgers to several pennants. His RBI total of 142 in 1953 remains the standard for catchers. Losing some of his playing career to time spent in the Negro Leagues, Campanella's career was further cut short by a horrible car accident that left him paralyzed in 1958. This card is a key rookie, along with cards of Richie Ashburn and Duke Snider, in the Bowman set. This card measures approximately 2¹/₁₆" by 2½". Border toning, poor centering and lackluster color appear to be the leading condition obstacles with this card, a card that pictures one of the greatest backstops in history.

1949 Bowman #224 Satchel Paige

This is one of only a handful of Satchel Paige cards to collect, and it is one of the keys to the set. In 1948, Paige signed with Cleveland and, though his MLB career was brief, he gave us a glimpse of what could have been with some outstanding performances. In 1949, well past the age of 40, Paige finished the season with four wins, five saves and an ERA of 3.04. In 1965, at the age of 59, the Kansas City A's brought Paige back for one last appearance. He pitched three scoreless innings against the Boston Red Sox, giving up one hit to fellow Hall of Famer Carl Yastrzemski. This two-time (1952-1953) All-Star had such great longevity that he was able to pitch against the likes of Josh Gibson and a young Yaz – amazing! This card, one of only three mainstream Paige cards from his playing days remains a classic and is subject to the same condition obstacles as most 1949 Bowmans.

1949 Bowman #226 Duke Snider

This is the only recognized rookie card of one of baseball's most popular figures from the 1950s. There was Mickey, Willie and The Duke, three great centerfielders, all playing in New York at the same time. Who was the best? Well, conventional wisdom would lead you to either Mantle or Mays, but consider this ... no player hit more home runs than Duke Snider from 1950-1959 ... no one. In 1949, Snider hit .292 with 23 home runs and 92 RBI in his first full season at the plate. After that performance, Snider earned the starting spot and joined the heart of the Dodger lineup for years. This card, picturing the outstanding slugger at the beginning of his historic run, is one of Duke's most important issues.

1950 Bowman #98 Ted Williams

This is the first Bowman card to feature the *Splendid Splinter*. In 1950, Bowman decided to add this legendary slugger to the set after two years of absence. The timing couldn't have been better as Bowman enhanced its design with a full-color presentation. Ted Williams is shown finishing his majestic swing, looking skyward. That season, Williams would hit .317 with 28 home runs and 97 RBI. While that doesn't sound typical for Williams, keep in mind that he did that in just 89 games! Along with Jackie Robinson, this Williams card is one of two major keys in the set. This particular card may not be Ted's toughest card to find in high-grade, but it is a difficult card to find centered with such narrow borders providing the frame. This card measures approximately 2^{1}/$_{16}$" by 2½". Keep in mind that this card is notorious for having a print line that extends from the roof of the stadium towards his cap. Since this is a common defect for the card, it will not detract from the overall grade.

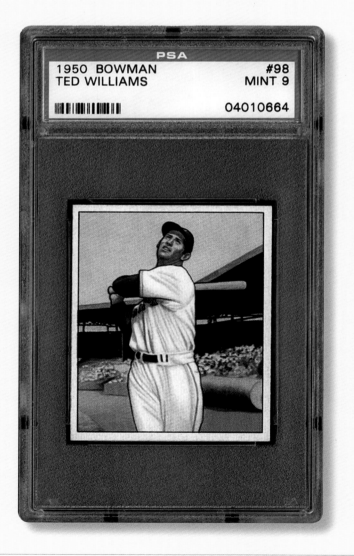

1950-51 Toleteros Josh Gibson

This is the only known vintage trading card to ever feature Negro League superstar Josh Gibson. No one seems to know exactly what Gibson's numbers were during the course of his career but one thing is certain, no matter what the records do or do not show, he is regarded as the premier slugger in Negro League history. Unfortunately for Gibson and baseball fans across the country, he was never allowed to play in the Major Leagues and, just three months before Jackie Robinson would officially break the color barrier in 1947, Gibson died from a stroke at the age of 35. Gibson caught for the Pittsburgh Crawfords and then the Homestead Grays, hitting tape measure home runs and showcasing his cannon-like arm throughout the league. In 1972, Gibson was inducted into the Baseball Hall of Fame. This card, which captures the legend during a winter league stint in the off-season, is extremely scarce with only about a dozen copies known at this point in time. This card measures approximately 1¾" by 2½". Collectibles such as autographs and original photos of Gibson exist in miniscule numbers, leaving collectors with few buying opportunities. With such a limited amount of vintage Gibson collectibles available, this card is of extreme importance.

1951 Bowman #1 Whitey Ford

This is the first card in a very popular set, and it features the only recognized rookie card of a New York Yankee legend. A seemingly happy Whitey Ford is pictured on the face of this important rookie card and, as the ace of the Yankee staff during a dominant period, he had plenty of reasons to smile. Ford used a variety of pitches and great control to baffle opposing hitters. In fact, Ford holds one of the highest winning percentages of all time at .690 for pitchers with 200 or more victories. His 10 victories and 2.71 ERA in World Series play earned Ford the reputation of being a "Big Game" pitcher. In 1950, Ford made his debut after being called up halfway through the season. He went 9-1 with a 2.81 ERA. Ford would miss the next two seasons to service in the military but came back as a starting pitcher in 1953. Ford's best season came in 1961, when he compiled a 25-4 record with 209 strikeouts and an ERA of 3.21 en route to winning the Cy Young Award. This eight-time All-Star was inducted into the Baseball Hall of Fame in 1974. This card, being the first in the set, was subject to a great deal of handling and is also difficult to find well-centered. This card measures approximately 2¹/₁₆" by 3⅛".

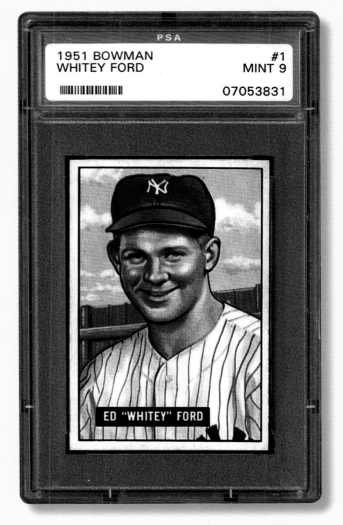

1951 Topps Major League All-Stars Robin Roberts SP

This is one of three major rarities in the set and the only one to feature a Hall of Famer. In 1951, before the introduction of the groundbreaking 1952 Topps set, this issue was released during the same year as the Topps Blue and Red Back sets along two other special sets, the Connie Mack All-Stars and 1951 Topps Teams. This set of current All-Stars contained 11 total cards but three cards were never issued to the public. These three cards were those of Jim Konstanty, Robin Roberts and Eddie Stanky. Despite never being officially released by Topps, a few examples escaped from the factory, providing collectors with three extraordinarily rare cards. These cards, which measure 2¹⁄₁₆" by 5¼," were made with a die-cut design so the players featured could be popped out from the background in an upright position. Since the cards were intended to be folded, finding nice examples is virtually impossible. Roberts won 286 games in his career and finished with 2,357 strikeouts and an ERA 3.41. This seven-time All-Star was inducted into the Baseball Hall of Fame in 1976, and this card is clearly his most valuable issue.

1952 Bowman #1 Yogi Berra

This is the first card in the set, and it features 1951 AL MVP and Yankee favorite Yogi Berra. The 1952 Bowman set, while not as popular as their previous offering, is filled with stars and beautiful artwork. In 1952, Berra hit .273 with 30 home runs (a career-high for Berra) and 98 RBI, an excellent follow-up season to his MVP performance in 1951. In fact, his home run *and* RBI totals eclipsed the totals from the prior year. This 15-time All-Star was one of the more remarkable contact hitters in baseball history. On several different occasions, Berra managed a higher number of home runs than strikeouts, a statistical oddity in baseball. This card measures approximately 2¹⁄₁₆" by 3⅛". In addition to troublesome centering and staining on the reverse, this card is subject to degrees of toning along the edges, a fate suffered by many Bowmans of the era. In fact, there are actually two different versions of this card seen in the marketplace. One has brighter colors and whiter borders, the other exhibits more subdued color and toned paper. This is typical for most low-numbered cards in the set.

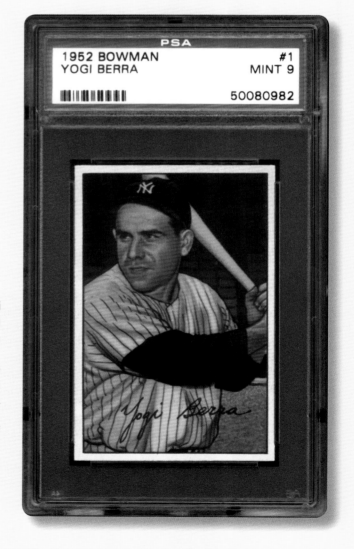

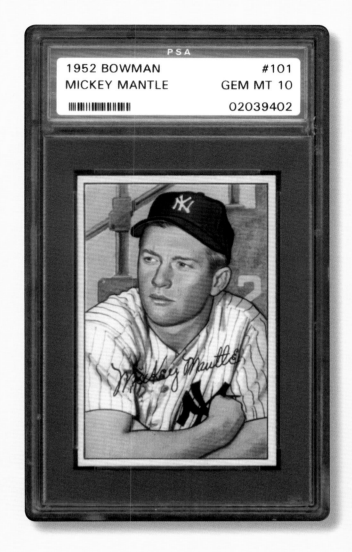

1952 Bowman #101 Mickey Mantle

This is a very important second-year issue of Mickey Mantle; it is also one of his best looking cards. In 1952, Mantle gained a little more experience, and it showed at the plate, as he hit .311 with 23 home runs and 94 runs scored. It would be the first time Mantle would appear in the All-Star Game as well. The very next year, Mantle would begin a run of nine straight seasons of 100 runs scored or more as a part of the powerful Yankee lineup. This particular card is one that has seemingly been overlooked throughout the years. With so much attention given to his classic 1952 Topps card, a card with a larger format and part of a much more intriguing set, the Bowman Mantle remains underappreciated. The gap in market value between the two cards has become astronomical, giving collectors a more affordable alternative with this great card.

1952 Bowman #196 Stan Musial

This has often been considered one of the most visually attractive cards in the hobby and it was the first full-color issue to feature *Stan the Man*. In 1952, Stan Musial hit .336 with 105 runs scored, had 194 hits and a .538 slugging average, leading the National League in each category. He added 21 home runs and 91 RBI that same year. Fittingly, Musial was depicted with his favorite weapon on this card, his bat. This three-time World Series champion was one of the toughest outs in the game. Preacher Roe, his teammate, summed it up by explaining the best way to pitch to Musial. "I throw him four wide ones and try to pick him off at first," Roe explained. Another aspect to consider is Musial's likability. He has always been considered one of the more personable players in history, resulting in a large fan base. This colorful issue, while not Musial's toughest, may be his most popular card. The image is certainly a classic by any standard.

1952 Bowman #218 Willie Mays

This is one of Willie's toughest cards and a key to the set. Much like the Mickey Mantle card from the same issue, this high-number card appears to have been overlooked for quite some time. While not as popular as his 1952 Topps card, it is certainly more difficult to find in high-grade. The disparity in market value is not as great as it is between the two Mantle cards from the same year, but the Bowman Mays can often be acquired for about half the price of the Topps issue. In regards to Mays as a player, one of the most impressive aspects of his game was the combination of power and speed. In 1955, Mays became the first player in NL history to hit 50 or more homers and steal 20 or more bases in a single season. At different points in his career, Mays was so well-rounded as a player, he won titles in batting, home runs, runs scored, stolen bases and fielding. This card is difficult to find well-centered and absent of border toning, which plagues many cards in the set.

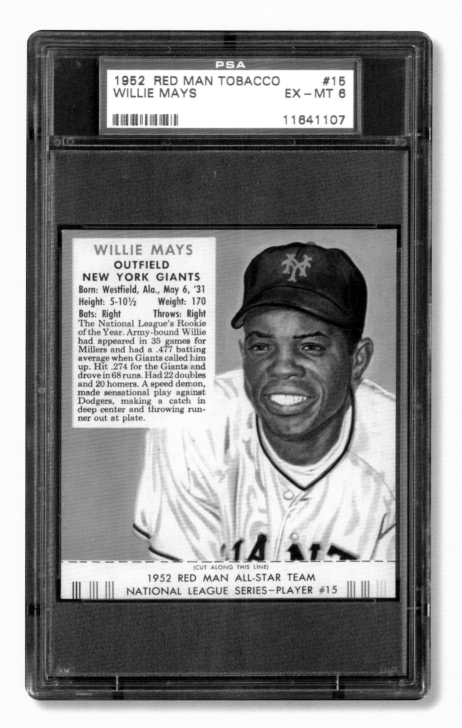

1952 Red Man Tobacco #15N
Willie Mays

This is one of the keys to the inaugural Red Man Tobacco issue. Along with cards of Ted Williams and Stan Musial, this Willie Mays card remains a standout in a colorful set. Furthermore, unlike Williams and Musial, who both had been in the league for more than a decade and were depicted in several previously issued cards, this Mays card was issued in his second year in the league. The Red Man cards, sealed in plastic, were located outside pouches of their tobacco product. These large cards, which measure 3½" by 4", contained a perforated tab along the bottom edge. These tabs functioned as coupons for consumers who wanted to redeem them for a baseball cap. In most cases, the tabs were removed in a haphazard manner by those seeking the Red Man Tobacco gift. Today, the cards that have the tab intact are considered more desirable and sell for a premium over those missing the tab. Red Man Tobacco issued sets for four consecutive years (1952-1955), but the 1952 cards are clearly considered the toughest of the four series. Due to the manner in which they were packaged, the aforementioned tab dilemma and the fact that each card has colored borders, these cards are very condition sensitive.

1952 Topps #1 Andy Pafko

This is the most important #1 card in the postwar era. Andy Pafko may not be a household name in the world of sports, but he is a very big name amongst baseball card collectors. Pafko, who managed to hit .285 and club 213 home runs in his career, is the lead-off man for the 1952 Topps set. There are a very limited number of non-star cards on this *Top 250* list, but this is clearly the most significant of the bunch. This card measures approximately 2⅝" by 3¾". Finding this card well-centered and in high-grade is extremely tough but, several years ago, a collector had the find of a lifetime. After buying an unopened 1952 Topps pack, this collector had a decision to make. Does he preserve the pack in unopened form or take the huge risk of opening it? With only five cards inserted into each pack and a ton of condition problems associated with the issue, the chance of pulling anything of significant value was slim to none. He decided to do it anyway and after removing the top two cards in the pack, the Pafko card revealed itself. Tucked in the middle of the five-card pack, it was immaculate, eventually grading PSA Gem Mint 10 and selling for $83,970. Of course, that card is worth much more today. To this day, this is the only example to grade higher than PSA NM-MT 8. What a find!

1952 Topps #191 Yogi Berra

This is one of the more difficult cards in the 1952 Topps set to find in high-grade and, quite possibly, Yogi Berra's most important card. Berra's personality and charm often overshadowed just how great he was on the field. One of his most impressive statistics and perhaps the most telling is the fact that Berra received MVP votes in 15 different seasons. Berra, who led his Yankee team to 14 World Series appearances, established WS records in games (75), at-bats (259), hits (71), singles (63), doubles (10), games caught (63) including catching the only perfect game in WS history (thrown by Don Larsen in 1956). In another surprising statistic, Berra led the Yankees in RBI for seven consecutive seasons (1949-1955) despite playing with super sluggers Joe DiMaggio and Mickey Mantle. This 15-time All-Star was elected to the Hall of Fame in 1972. Finding a well-centered example of this important Berra card is a real chore.

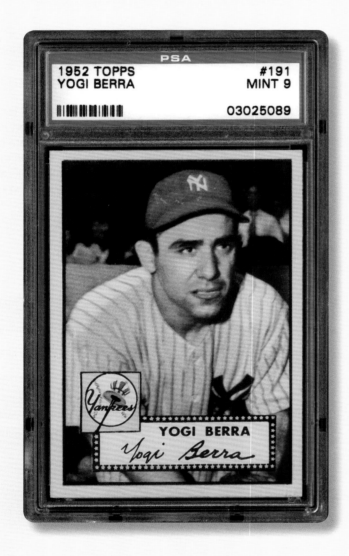

1952 Topps #261 Willie Mays

This is the first Topps card to feature Willie Mays, coming only one year after his Bowman rookie offering. Some players create moments for themselves that are remembered for eternity, and Mays was one of them. In 1954, during the World Series against Cleveland with the score tied at 2-2, Vic Wertz drove a pitch from reliever Don Liddle about 450 feet to centerfield. With runners on first and second, it appeared as if Cleveland was going to take the lead after Wertz made contact. With Mays playing shallow, it was believed that no one could catch up to this majestic drive, but Mays never gave up. He started running like a sprinter the moment the ball was hit and miraculously outran the ball, making an improbable over-the-shoulder catch and firing the ball back into the infield to preserve the tie. The Giants would go on to win the game 5-2, and the image of Mays making what is now referred to as *The Catch* will forever be remembered. This card, while not Willie's toughest, is prone to tilt or diamond cuts resulting in centering problems.

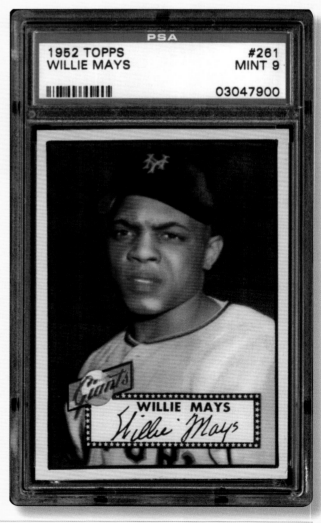

1952 Topps #312 Jackie Robinson

This is one of Jackie's best looking cards in one of the hobby's most important issues. In 1952, Robinson hit .308 with 19 home runs, 24 stolen bases, 104 runs scored and a league-high .440 OBP. These are outstanding numbers for a second baseman. One of Robinson's more impressive statistics is the fact that he only struck out 291 times with nearly 5,000 at-bats in his career, which shows he had serious bat control. It's too bad fans didn't get to see Robinson for a full career in MLB. There's no question Robinson could have put up huge numbers, especially at his position. Because of his long-lasting impact on the game, MLB retired his number (42) in 1997 on the 50th anniversary of his debut for the Brooklyn Dodgers. This card captures a joyous Robinson, who always found a way to smile despite enduring so much torment from hateful folks. All we can do as collectors is continue to appreciate what he did and thank him for helping make the game better.

1952 Topps #314 Roy Campanella

This classic card features a man who was deprived of a lengthy MLB career due to racism and serious injury. During the 1950s, Roy Campanella struggled with injuries to his hand, but that didn't stop him. A nearly fatal car accident did. After the accident, almost 100,000 fans came out to honor Campanella during an exhibition game in the spring of 1959. He was a beloved player and this showing of support proves it. In 1952, Campanella would hammer 22 homers and drive in 97 runs in a solid season. One year later, he had the best season of his career. Campanella was awarded the NL MVP (one of three in his career) after hitting .312 with 41 homers, 142 RBI (a league-high) and he slugged .611. This is one of the finest single-season performances by any catcher. With this card, pay close attention to the yellow background, which can be faint and subject to dark print defects at times.

1952 Topps #407 Eddie Mathews

This is the last card in the 1952 Topps set and the only recognized rookie card of slugging third baseman Eddie Mathews. If the last card in the 1952 Topps set featured an average player, it would be special simply due to the inherent difficulty of the card. Since it features a member of *The 500 Home Run Club* and one half of the most prolific home run duo of all time, the card is extraordinary. No, that duo wasn't Lou Gehrig and Babe Ruth; it was Hank Aaron and Eddie Mathews. In 1952, Mathews debuted with 25 home runs, but his encore was even better. With only one year under his belt, Mathews pounded 47 homers, hit .302, drove in 135 runs and was named runner-up in the NL MVP voting. This nine-time All-Star led the league in homers twice and hit 30 or more home runs in nine consecutive seasons en route to his Hall of Fame induction in 1978. Since Bowman did not include Mathews in their 1952 offering, all the focus turns to this card – a card that is very tough to find centered since it was located near the bottom corner of the sheet.

1953 Bowman #33 Pee Wee Reese

In terms of imagery, this card is one of the classics of our hobby. The image of Pee Wee Reese leaping in mid-air to avoid a runner and desperately trying to break up the double play is one that stands alone in card collecting. Years ago, hobbyists used to refer to this card as a reverse negative since it appears as if the runner is diving headfirst, running from third to second base. The runner could have been simply barreling into second, with the runner merely appearing to be headed in the wrong direction. Whatever the case may be, Reese and Jackie Robinson would "turn two" often as teammates in Brooklyn. This image was taken in spring training and if you take a close look, you will notice that no other players or spectators can be seen in the background. This card measures approximately 2½" by 3¾". The biggest condition obstacles for this card appear to be poor centering and focus. Since the image is so crucial to the importance of this card, be sure to look for focused copies.

1953 Bowman #93
Billy Martin/Phil Rizzuto

This is one of the first multi-player baseball cards ever produced, and it features two of the most popular New York Yankee figures in baseball history. Billy Martin, a second baseman and 1956 All-Star who played from 1950-1961, was also the fiery manager of the New York Yankees after his playing career, a position he held on five different occasions. Despite leading the Yankees to back-to-back World Series appearances in 1976 and 1977, Martin is best known for his animated arguments with umpires. Phil Rizzuto, a shortstop and broadcaster who called the game on the radio and television for 40 years, was nicknamed *The Scooter* by teammate Billy Hitchcock while playing in the minor leagues. After watching Rizzuto, who possessed short legs, run around the bases, Hitchcock described Rizzuto's technique as "scootin" as opposed to running. From 1941 to 1956, Rizzuto won 10 AL titles in 13 seasons with the powerful Yankees and quickly became a fan favorite. Rizzuto, an outstanding defensive player throughout his career and owner of several World Series records at the shortstop position, hit .273 in his career. His best season came in 1950, when Rizzuto hit .324 and scored 125 runs as the leadoff man for New York. He was named AL MVP that year after finishing second to Ted Williams the prior year. This five-time All-Star was inducted into the Baseball Hall of Fame in 1994. This card is one of two multi-player cards in the extremely popular 1953 Bowman Color set, with poor registration, print defects and sub par centering as the leading condition obstacles.

1953 Bowman Black and White #39 Casey Stengel

This is the key card in the very tough 64-card Bowman set. In 1953, Bowman produced what many hobbyists consider to be one of the greatest sets ever issued, the 160-card 1953 Bowman Color set. What some collectors forget is Bowman also issued a much smaller, yet tougher, black and white set. This set, which lacks the star power of its colorful cousin, contains five total Hall of Famer cards, but none are more important than the one featuring Casey Stengel. Stengel, a solid player who hit .284 for his career from 1912-1925, is best known for his managerial excellence and reign over the New York Yankees. From 1949-1960, Stengel managed the Yankees and helped lead them to 7 World Series titles. It was a team filled with stars like Yogi Berra, Whitey Ford and Mickey Mantle, but it was Stengel who made the decisions for the Bronx Bombers. Stengel, who also had managerial stints with the Brooklyn Dodgers (1934-36), Boston Braves (1938-1943) and New York Mets (1962-1965), was inducted into the Baseball Hall of Fame in 1966 by the Veteran's Committee.

1953 Stahl-Meyer Franks Mickey Mantle

This is one of Mickey Mantle's most elusive cards, and it resides in one of the key regional issues of the era. In 1953, this New York-based meat company decided to issue one of nine cards into packages of their hot dogs. In their first trading set, they chose to manufacture three cards from each of the three New York area teams: the Dodgers, Giants and Yankees. Stahl-Meyer, who issued three different trading cards sets from 1953-1955, included some of the brightest stars from each of those teams, such as Duke Snider and Monte Irvin, but none of those stars shined brighter than Mickey Mantle, the key to the inaugural issue. These white-bordered cards, which measure approximately 3¼" by 4½" in size, were cut with diagonal corners, and the fronts were designed with a wax coating. In addition, these cards are not only very difficult to locate, but are extremely condition sensitive. This Mantle card is rarely seen and it remains one of the missing links to collections based on the Yankee legend.

1953 Topps #1 Jackie Robinson

This card features Jackie Robinson, a true American hero, and is one of the most significant #1 cards in the hobby. We have discussed the importance of some of the other prominent #1 cards throughout this book and, while it may not be nearly as valuable as some, it is extremely important. In 1953, Jackie Robinson put together an outstanding year, hitting .329 with 95 RBI and 109 runs scored. It was offensive production like this that helped elevate Robinson to Hall of Fame status in 1962. This card measures approximately 2⅝" by 3¾" and is subject to several condition obstacles, but two are the most noteworthy: poor centering and chipping along the black bottom edge. With wear so visible along that edge, it becomes very difficult to locate high-end copies of this key Robinson card. Many of the high-grade copies of this card originated from a few Canadian finds during the 1980s and 1990s.

1953 Topps #82
Mickey Mantle

This is one of Mickey Mantle's most important cards and one of two major keys, along with Willie Mays, to this popular Topps set. In 1953, Mantle was productive but still a few years away from becoming a superstar. He hit .295 with 21 home runs, 92 RBI and 105 runs scored. This card, which can be found with booming eye-appeal as a result of a "find" many years ago, is tough to locate in high-grade. The red bottom border is subject to chipping, as expected, and the card is very tough to find well-centered. Since the image provides a close-up view of Mantle, beware of print defects that encroach on Mantle's face. This could be an eyesore to many collectors. While the Bowman issue from the same year is popular in its own right, the Topps Mantle is clearly the more popular of the two.

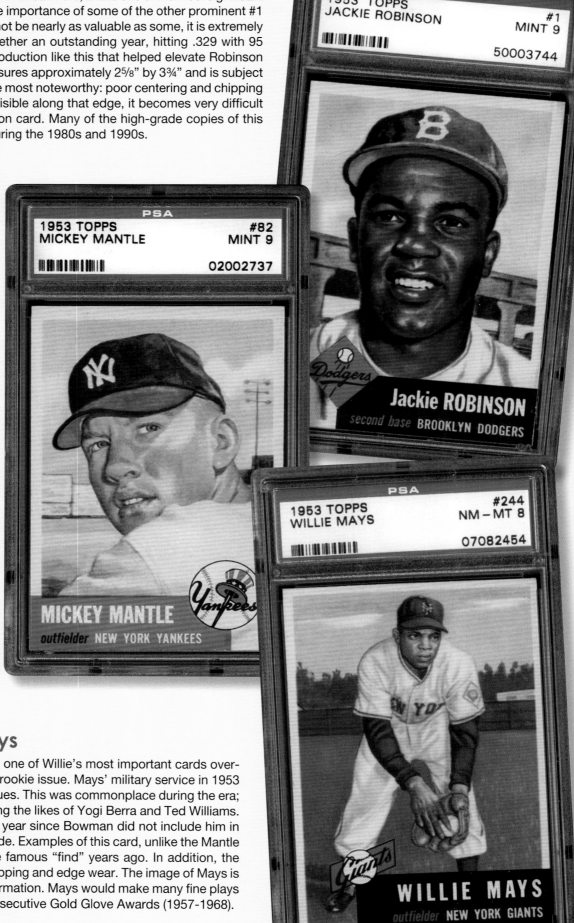

1953 Topps #244 Willie Mays

This is the key to the 1953 Topps set and one of Willie's most important cards overall, ranking second behind his 1951 Bowman rookie issue. Mays' military service in 1953 prevented him from playing in the Major Leagues. This was commonplace during the era; many superstars missed playing time, including the likes of Yogi Berra and Ted Williams. This card, Willie's only mainstream issue that year since Bowman did not include him in their set, is extremely tough to find in high-grade. Examples of this card, unlike the Mantle card from the same set, were not part of the famous "find" years ago. In addition, the black bottom border is very susceptible to chipping and edge wear. The image of Mays is a classic, holding his hands in basket catch formation. Mays would make many fine plays with the glove over his career, earning 12 consecutive Gold Glove Awards (1957-1968).

1954 Bowman #66 Ted Williams

This card not only comes with a great story, but it is also widely considered to be one of the most significant cards in the postwar era. Ted Williams, under exclusive contract with Topps at the time, was slated to be card #66 in the Bowman set. Pulled from production early due to the contract dispute, his card was eventually replaced by one of Jim Piersall, creating a legendary rarity for collectors. While the card is not quite as scarce as once thought, it is clearly one of the legendary hitter's best cards. In 1954, with only 117 games under his belt, Williams hit .345 with 29 homers, 136 walks, a .513 OBP and he slugged .635. This card measures approximately 2½" by 3¾" and is subject to several condition obstacles, with poor centering being commonplace. In addition, dark print defects are often found in the background sky, around Ted's face. Keep in mind that no Williams examples were found in the 1954 Bowman unopened wax "find" several years ago.

1954 Dan Dee Mickey Mantle

This is one of Mickey Mantle's toughest and most attractive cards overall. In 1954, collectors were faced with another dilemma, similar to the one affecting Ted Williams. This time, the opposite occurred. While Mantle was included in the 1954 Bowman issue, he was left out of the Topps production. In 1954, Mantle hit .300 with 27 home runs, 102 RBI and he scored a league-leading 129 runs. It was the first of many big seasons from *The Mick*. This card, along with the 1954 Wilson Franks Ted Williams, is one of the most important regional issues ever manufactured. Since these cards were inserted into bags of potato chips, oils from the chips often soiled the cards. This card measures approximately 2½" by 3⅝". In addition, most of the cards exhibit 60/40 centering, or worse, and the edges will sometimes have varying degrees of perforations. The perforations are natural, but they can be severe. While they do not detract from the technical grade, some collectors do not like the appearance.

1954 Red Heart Stan Musial SP

This is one of the toughest cards in the entire set. It features Stan Musial, who was absent from both the Bowman and Topps sets in 1954. The Red Heart Dog Food set has long been a favorite amongst collectors due to its vibrant colors and manageable size. The 33-card set was broken into three groups, each showcasing a different color in the background, blue, green and red. The red background series – which includes this Musial card – have always been considered the toughest of the three groups. This short printed card measures approximately 2⅝" by 3¾" and is also commonly found off-center. This makes high-grade copies tougher to come by, even though the set is relatively easy to locate in high-grade overall. There are two key reasons for the relative ease in acquiring nice examples. First, the cards could be obtained via mail as part of a redemption program. Second, and perhaps most importantly, the cards could still be obtained from the company for approximately 20 years after they were initially released, until the early 1970s! Along with Mickey Mantle, this Musial card is a key to the set but much tougher to locate in high-grade.

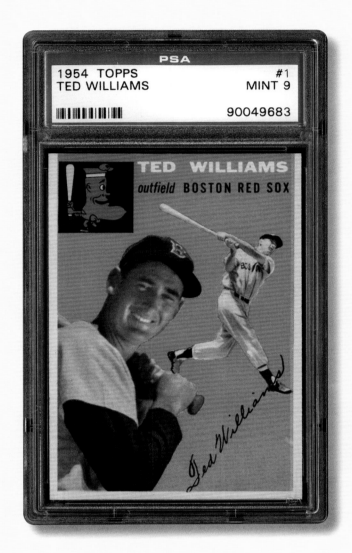

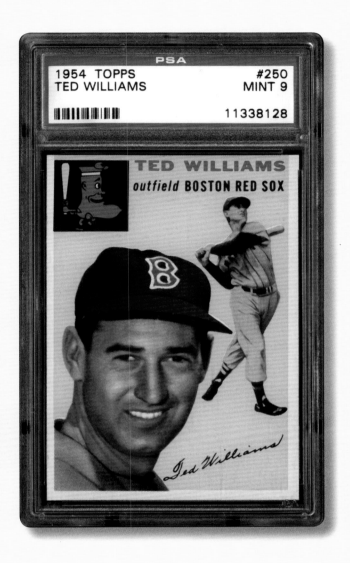

1954 Topps Ted Williams (2)

In 1954, Ted Williams was chosen to "bookend" the set for Topps. This classic set is filled with Hall of Fame rookies and a great selection of star cards, despite the absence of Mickey Mantle and Stan Musial. But these two Williams cards stand out. The #250 card was long believed to be the tougher of the two, but that theory has changed since the advent of Population Reports for graded cards. These cards measure approximately 2⅝" by 3¾". Both cards are commonly found off-center with some degree of chipping along the green reverse. The presence of chipping, as long as it is not severe, will not detract from the overall grade of the card. Since the #250 card has a bright yellow background, be wary of print defects that may hinder the eye-appeal.

1954 Topps #94 Ernie Banks

This is the only recognized rookie card of *Mr. Cub*, a 500 Home Run Club member. Along with the likes of Michael Jordan and Walter Payton, Ernie Banks is one of the most significant figures in Chicago sports history. Known for his undying enthusiasm, Banks became well-known for his battle cry…"Let's play two!"…expressing his love of the game. In 1954, Banks gave the Cubs a taste of his power with 19 homers, but he more than doubled his output the next year with 44 big flies. Banks, much like Hank Aaron, used his lightning-quick wrists to drive the ball out of Wrigley Field and he did that 512 times in a variety of ballparks. Banks won back-to-back NL MVP's in 1958-1959, hit 40 or more homers in five different seasons and even won a Gold Glove in 1960 en route to his Hall of Fame induction in 1977. This card is one of the keys to the set and is considered more difficult than the Hank Aaron rookie card. It is hard to find well-centered and the white background can be a haven for print defects.

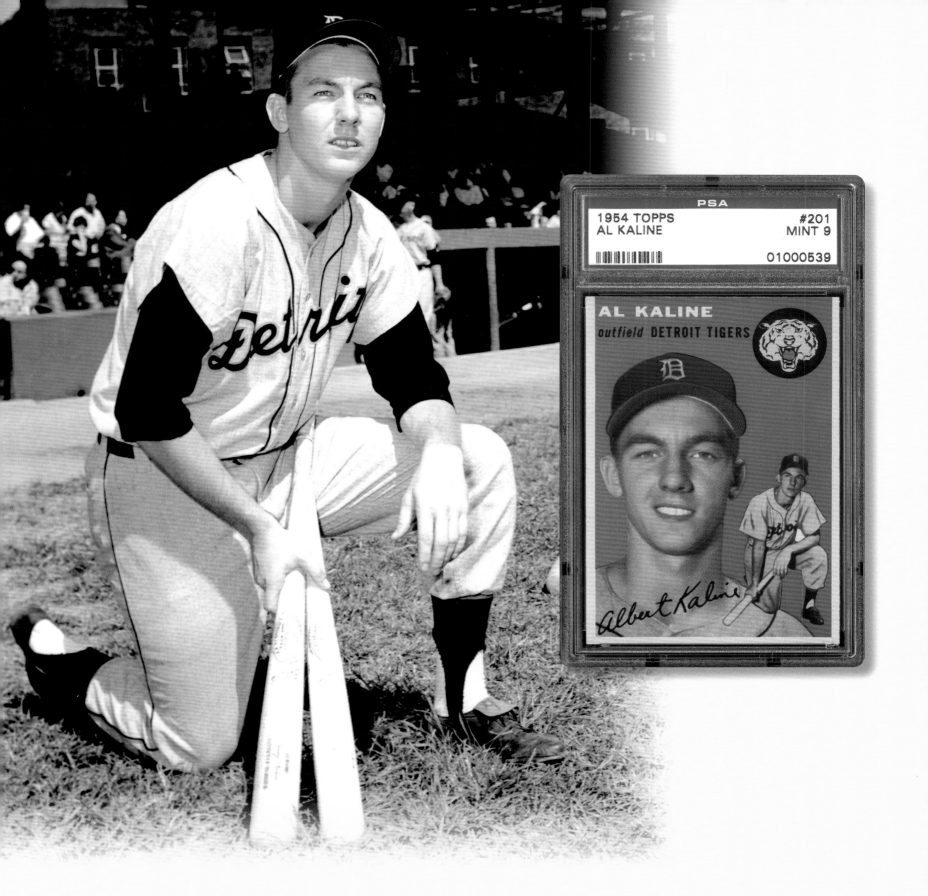

1954 Topps #201 Al Kaline

    This is the only recognized rookie card of the Detroit Tiger legend. Al Kaline, while he tends to be underappreciated by many, was simply an outstanding all-around player. In his career, Kaline won 10 Gold Gloves, collected 3,007 hits and crushed 399 home runs. In 1954, Kaline only hit four homers and drove in 43 runs but, the very next year, Kaline broke out. At the tender age of 20, Kaline amassed 200 hits, belted 27 homers, had 102 RBI, scored 121 runs and led the league with a .340 batting average, becoming the youngest man in history to do so. Kaline, named to 15 All-Star teams, hit .379 with two homers and 8 RBI in the 1968 World Series, helping the Tigers win a championship after years of franchise mediocrity. This card is one of three major rookies in the set, along with those of Hank Aaron and Ernie Banks. In some cases, you will see a variance in color in the background, ranging from a cherry-red to an almost orange color.

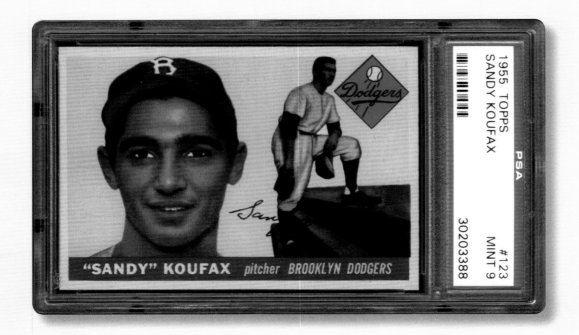

1955 Topps #123 Sandy Koufax

This is the only recognized rookie card of, arguably, the most dominant lefty in baseball history. Sandy Koufax's career ended prematurely due to injury but, before it was all said and done, he showed the world his spectacular stuff. After going 36-40 in his first six years in MLB, Koufax found his groove. Koufax would go on to lead the NL in ERA for five straight seasons and, during that run, he went 111-34 with four no-hitters, three Cy Young Awards and one NL MVP. In 1965, Koufax would throw a perfect game and strike out 382 batters, an NL record and one behind the all-time record held by Nolan Ryan at 383. Known as a clutch performer, Koufax had a World Series ERA under 1.00 and was named MVP twice in the Fall Classic (1963 and 1965). After battling arthritis in his pitching arm, Koufax was forced to retire at only 30 years of age. He ultimately became the youngest man ever elected to the Hall of Fame in 1972. This card measures approximately 3¾" by 2⅝", is one of the true classics on the list and a key to the set. It is tough to find well-centered and void of print defects in the yellow background.

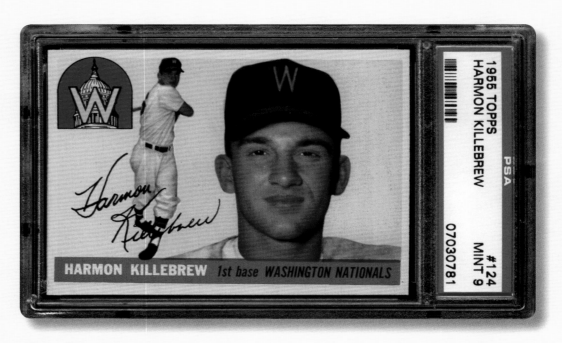

1955 Topps #124 Harmon Killebrew

This is the only recognized rookie card of super slugger Harmon Killebrew, one of the most personable players in the game. Known as *Killer,* this man was the symbol of brute power. Much like Mickey Mantle, Killebrew was responsible for many tape-measure drives in his career, a career that saw him clout 573 homers. Even though Killebrew made his debut in 1954, he did not play a full season until 1959 and he certainly made the most of it. Killebrew clubbed 42 homers and drove in 105 runs! Overall, he crushed 40 or more homers in eight different seasons, leading the league six different times. Killebrew's finest season came in 1969 when he hit 49 home runs, had 140 RBI and was named AL MVP. Killebrew, an 11-time All-Star, was inducted into the Baseball Hall of Fame in 1984. This card is one of three key rookies in the set. Like the Sandy Koufax card in the same set, poor centering and print defects are the two biggest condition obstacles.

1955 Topps #210 Duke Snider

This is the last card in the tremendously popular 1955 Topps baseball set, and it features Brooklyn Dodger slugger Duke Snider. In 1955, the Dodgers finally came away with a championship after defeating the rival New York Yankees. Snider was a key to the Dodger lineup filled with notable names. He enjoyed, perhaps, his best season at the plate. Snider hit .309 with 42 home runs, slugged .628, and led the league with 136 RBI and 126 runs scored. Snider would hit 40 home runs or more in five straight seasons (1953-1957) en route to his Hall of Fame induction in 1980. Always considered one of the more likable players in baseball history, Snider has always been a fan favorite. This particular card is the toughest of all the 1955 Topps cards on the list, with poor centering and print defects as the two leading condition obstacles.

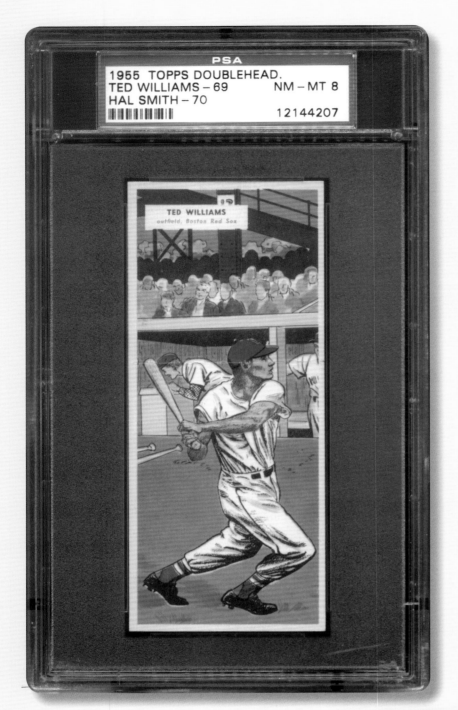

1955 Topps Double Headers #69 Ted Williams

This is the key card in this classic throwback set. The 1955 Topps Double Headers set is filled with a nice selection of stars, including the likes of Hank Aaron and Jackie Robinson, but the one featuring *Teddy Ballgame* is the most desirable of all. In 1955, Ted Williams hit .356 with 28 home runs and 83 RBI in just 98 games. He also had a slugging average of .703! This 66-card issue shares a very similar design to the 1911 T201 Mecca Double Folders, where two players can be interchanged with one set of legs, depending if the card is unfolded or folded. The 132 subjects in the set, which closely resemble the same group selected to start the regular Topps set from 1955, have short bios on the reverse of each card. These cards, which measure approximately 2$\frac{1}{16}$" by 4$\frac{7}{8}$" in unfolded form, are very condition sensitive. They contain very narrow white borders, which result in many copies exhibiting poor centering, due to the folds, many of these cards suffer from paper wrinkles along the reverse.

1956 Topps #135 Mickey Mantle

This is, quite simply, one of Mickey Mantle's most attractive and popular cards. On this card, Mantle is captured grinning ear-to-ear. And you would be too if you had a season like he did in 1956. Mantle captured the elusive Triple Crown by leading the league with a .353 batting average, 52 home runs and 130 RBI. Mantle also led the league with 132 runs scored and a .705 slugging average. This card is certainly the key to the 1956 Topps set, which lacks any serious rookie card power. This card measures approximately 2$\frac{5}{8}$" by 3$\frac{3}{4}$". There are two variations of this card, one with a white back and one with grey back. While the white backs are tougher to find and sell for a premium, the grey backs are usually seen with superior eye-appeal. Even though this card is not one of Mantle's more difficult issues, it is challenging to find centered, and some 1956 Topps cards are found with severe rough-cuts. The existence of rough-cuts do not tend to hinder the technical grade of the card, but some collectors do not like the appearance.

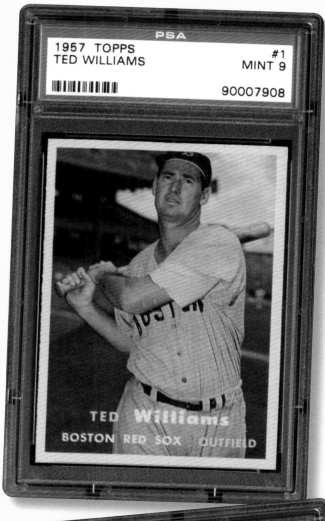

1957 Topps #1 Ted Williams

This is the first card in the ever-popular 1957 Topps set. Ted Williams was no stranger to being selected as the leadoff man for a Topps baseball card issue. He would be chosen three times by Topps (1954, 1957 and 1958), resulting in a tough but very desirable card for collectors. Even though Williams was coming to the end of his phenomenal career, he could still crush at the plate. In 1957, Williams hit .388 with 38 home runs, a .526 OBP and a .731 slugging average. His .388 mark led the league at 39 years of age. Williams would finish second in the MVP voting to Mickey Mantle, and many believe that Williams should have come away with more awards during his career. Williams' poor relationship with the media certainly didn't help his cause. One year later and at the age of 40, Williams would win another batting title by hitting .328. This card measures approximately 2½" by 3½" and like many 1957 Topps cards that are found with a tilted image and lackluster eye-appeal, this card is also tough to find well-centered.

1957 Topps #18 Don Drysdale

This is the only recognized rookie card of one of the most feared pitchers in baseball history. Don Drysdale combined with Sandy Koufax to form one of the toughest pitching duos. Both pitchers had great stuff and threw hard, but at 6'5" and 200-plus pounds, Drysdale was the more physically intimidating of the two. Drysdale, who compiled a career record of 209-166 with an ERA of 2.95, had his best season in 1962. After leading the league with 25 wins, 232 strikeouts and 314.3 innings pitched, Drysdale was awarded the Cy Young. In 1968, Drysdale set a record for throwing 58 consecutive scoreless innings. That record was eventually broken by Orel Hershiser in 1988, when he finished with 59. Drysdale ended his career with 2,486 strikeouts and 49 shutouts to his credit. This eight-time All-Star and career Dodger was inducted into the Baseball Hall of Fame in 1984. Drysdale, who worked as a broadcaster for more than 20 years, died suddenly in 1993 from a heart attack while on the road for the Los Angeles Dodgers. This card is difficult to find well-centered and void of print defects, as are most 1957 Topps cards.

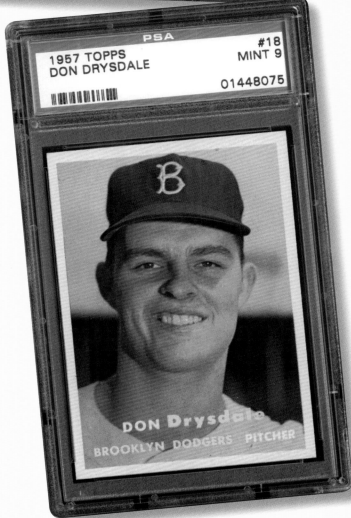

1957 Topps #35 Frank Robinson

This is the only recognized rookie card of Frank Robinson, the first man to ever win the MVP in both leagues. Robinson, who excelled in nearly every facet of the game, is regarded by many to be one of the most underrated players in baseball history. Robinson finished his career with a .294 batting average, 586 home runs, 2,943 hits, 1,812 RBI, 204 stolen bases, and he became the first African-American manager in MLB history. In addition to his two MVP awards, one in 1961 for the Cincinnati Reds and again in 1966 for the Baltimore Orioles, Robinson also won the elusive Triple Crown and was named World Series MVP in 1966. Robinson also jacked 38 home runs in his rookie campaign in 1956. That figure remained the MLB rookie record until 1987, when Mark McGwire clubbed 49 as a member of the Oakland A's. After his tremendous career, Robinson was inducted into the Baseball Hall of Fame in 1982. This card is tough to find well-centered and void of white print marks, known as print snow, in the background.

1957 Topps #302 Sandy Koufax

This classic Sandy Koufax card is one of the keys to the 1957 Topps set. In 1957, Koufax was still learning to harness the talent that made him the most dominant pitcher during the 1960s. Koufax compiled a 165-87 mark with a 2.76 ERA before an arm injury brought his sparkling career to an end. During the three seasons in which he won the Cy Young Award (1963, 1965 and 1966), Koufax also won the pitching version of the Triple Crown by leading the league in wins, strikeouts and ERA each season. This four-time All-Star also was the first pitcher in baseball history to finish his career averaging more than a strikeout per inning at 9.28. This particular card can be very visually appealing, but it is subject to some condition obstacles such as poor centering and print snow, which is common for the 1957 Topps baseball issue.

1957 Topps #328 Brooks Robinson

This is the only recognized rookie card of one of baseball's most popular players. Nicknamed *The Human Vacuum Cleaner*, Brooks Robinson is considered by many to be the finest defensive third baseman in the history of the game. With 16 consecutive Gold Gloves (1960-1975), an almost unthinkable streak of defensive excellence, it's easy to see why. His spectacular performance in the 1970 World Series, which helped the Orioles defeat the Cincinnati Reds, was unforgettable. Robinson was also named to the All-Star team in 15 straight seasons (1960-1974). For all of his defensive genius, Robinson was a solid hitter. In his finest season, Robinson hit .317 with 28 home runs and 118 RBI, helping earn him the 1964 AL MVP. Robinson finished his career with 268 home runs and 2,848 hits, along with two World Series championships en route to his Hall of Fame induction in 1983. This card is a key, along with the Sandy Koufax card from the same set, and is subject to very similar condition obstacles with a slight variance in color from example to example.

1957 Topps #407 Yankee Power Hitters

This is a great card showcasing the two men who were at the heart of the Yankee lineup during their amazing championship run. These two New York legends have enough rings between them to start a jewelry store. In addition, these two combined for a total of six AL MVPs during that awesome run. This card was included on the list for several reasons, but one stands out more than any other. This card represents the first time that two superstars were featured on a combo card in a major Topps set. The practice of issuing combo cards became commonplace after the 1957 Topps issue was released. It created an entirely new collecting craze. This card clearly started it all and it couldn't have featured two more significant or popular players from the era. Like most cards in the set, poor centering and print defects are two keys to look out for when searching for high-grade examples.

1958 Bell Brand Sandy Koufax

This is one of the most important regional sets ever manufactured, featuring the most popular pitcher in Dodger history. In 1958, Bell Brand decided to commemorate the Dodger franchise move from Brooklyn to Los Angeles. They inserted one of ten unnumbered cards into their bags of corn and potato chips. The cards, which measure about 3" by 4" in size, are surrounded by a light green border. The border was designed to appear like a wooden frame around the sepia-tone image of the player featured. After taking one year off, Bell Brand continued to issue Dodger trading cards in 1960, 1961 and 1962, but this first issue is unmistakably the most desirable of the group. It is also considered the most condition sensitive due to its colored edges and slightly larger size. In 1958, Sandy Koufax was yet to begin an unprecedented streak of pitching excellence, one that elevated him to legendary status. At the end of his career, Koufax held the opposition to a .205 batting average and compiled four no-hitters, the most ever until Nolan Ryan surpassed him about two decades later.

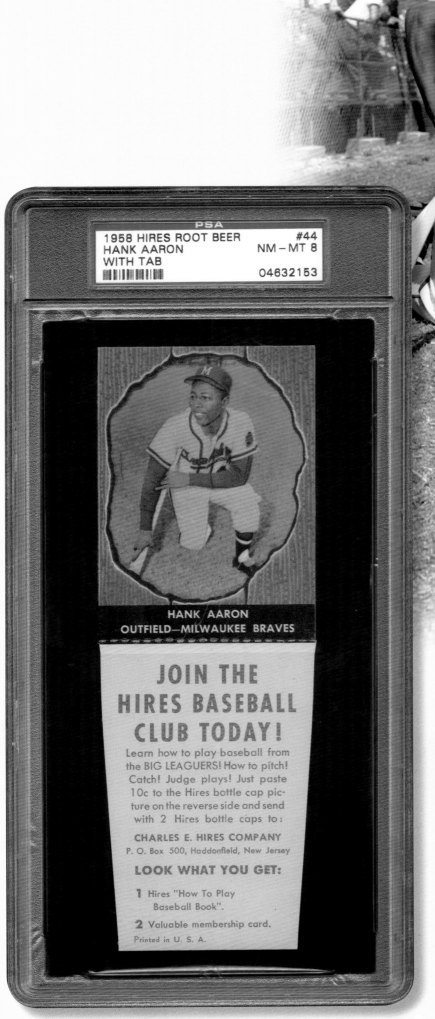

1958 Hires Root Beer #44 Hank Aaron

This is one of the keys in a very popular, yet condition sensitive regional set. Finding any of these cards intact and in nice condition today is a real chore as each one had to endure two main obstacles. First, the large tabs found at the base of each card promoted the Hires Baseball Club and were designed to be removed. In addition, the tabs helped prop each card up within the six-packs of root beer. These cards, which measure approximately 2⅜" to 2⅝" in width by 3⅜" to 3½" in length without the tab can extend another 3½" in length with the tab attached. Most price guides only provide values for these un-numbered cards without the tabs since intact examples are so tough to find. In 1958, Hank Aaron hit .326 with 30 home runs and 95 RBI, helping lead the Braves to another World Series appearance. He even won his first Gold Glove in the process. This Aaron card, which is surrounded by fragile brown and black edges in the non-tab portion, is one of two major keys to the 66-card set.

1958 Topps #47 Roger Maris

This is the only recognized rookie card of the former single-season home run champion. Roger Maris is, of course, best known for his great 1961 season, a season commemorated on his 1962 Topps card. What many people forget is that Maris, while his career numbers are modest, was more than just a one-season wonder. After playing for the Cleveland Indians and Kansas City Athletics his first two seasons, Maris joined the powerful New York Yankees. From that point forward, he became a fan-favorite in the Bronx. In his first full season in New York, Maris led the league in RBI, slugging percentage and was awarded the Gold Glove for his outfield play. With such an outstanding performance, Maris was named AL MVP for the first time in his career. He would win the AL MVP again the very next year with his record breaking 61 home run season. This four-time All-Star finished with 275 homers in his career, a career that ended in St. Louis. As a member of the Cardinals, Maris helped them win back-to-back pennants, including a World Series championship in 1967. Maris hit .385 with one homer and 7 RBI in the series. This card is one of the keys to the 1958 Topps set and difficult to find well-centered.

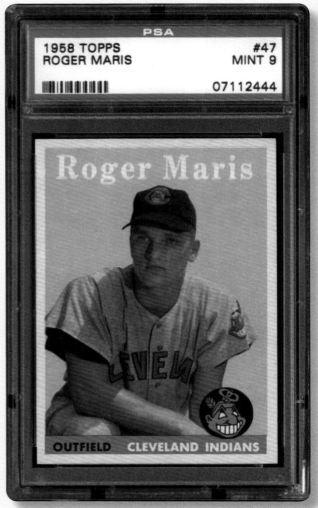

1958 Topps #418 World Series Batting Foes

This is the only card to ever feature Hank Aaron and Mickey Mantle together. With a total of 1,291 home runs between the two, this card packs a lot of power. Aaron reached his mark with a quick bat and consistency while Mantle made his mark with brute strength. In 1957, both men were named MVP of their respective leagues, but it would be Aaron who walked away with a World Series championship as the Milwaukee Braves defeated the New York Yankees in seven games. Aaron would shine at the plate by hitting .393 with 11 hits, three home runs and 7 RBI. It would be Aaron's lone championship during his long career. This card has a few condition obstacles, as do most 1958 Topps cards due to their design, but the leading obstacle would be faulty print. Many of these cards are found with a plethora of print defects, especially in the background behind the two stars, causing eye-appeal problems that hinder the grade.

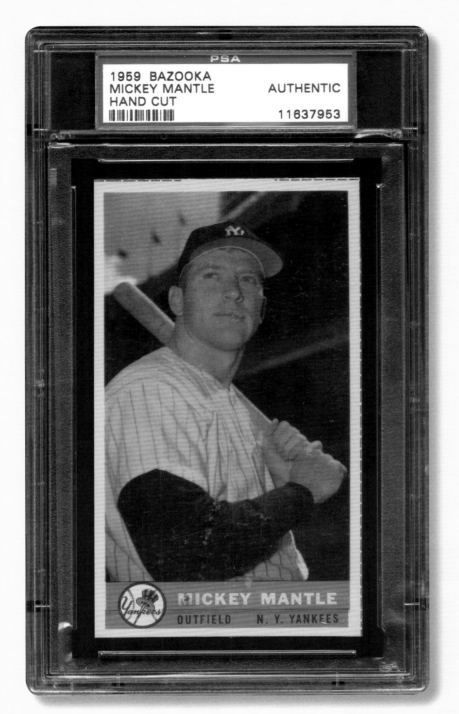

1959 Bazooka Mickey Mantle

This is the key to the first and most popular Bazooka baseball issue in the hobby. This unnumbered, 23-card set featured some of the game's greatest players including this man, Mickey Mantle, the most desirable card in the gum series. Printed on the bottom of Topps bubble gum boxes, these cards are extremely condition sensitive. The cards were framed by a dotted line to give the collector guidance if they chose to remove the cards from the box. If the blank-backed cards were cut along the lines provided, they would measure approximately $2^{13}/_{16}$" by $4^{15}/_{16}$". Cards cut outside the lines are considered more valuable than those cut inside the dotted lines. Often times, it was very difficult to remove the cards from the box safely, as many of the cards were poorly located, leaving very little room to cut around the edges. Due to their scarcity, complete boxes are highly desirable. Of the 23 cards in the set, 14 are considered short prints as they were released at a later date and in lower quantities than the nine cards that preceded them. In 1959, Mantle would hit .285 with 31 home runs and 104 runs scored. This Mantle card dominates this colorful Bazooka production and is extremely difficult to locate.

1959 Fleer #68 Ted Signs for 1959

This is the key card in a unique issue devoted entirely to Ted Williams. This was Fleer's first offering and they chose a pretty special player to launch their product. Fleer was able to sign Williams to an exclusive contract for the duration of his career, depriving Topps collectors of Williams cards from 1959-1961. This 80-card set, tells the story of one of the more interesting individuals to ever walk onto the field. From fishing to military duty, the cards cover a variety of subjects. This card was pulled from production early due to an alleged contract dispute with Buck Harris (the other man depicted on the card), resulting in a higher degree of scarcity. The card, while not overly difficult to locate in PSA NM-MT 8 or better, is often found with subpar centering and blunt corners due to the way these cards were cut and packaged. This card was also heavily counterfeited at one time, dating back to the 1970s. From his game-winning home run in the 1941 All-Star Game to slugging one over the fence in his final career at-bat, Williams had a flair for the dramatic. In 1966, after leaving baseball fans with so many memorable moments, Williams was inducted into the Baseball Hall of Fame.

1959 Topps #514 Bob Gibson

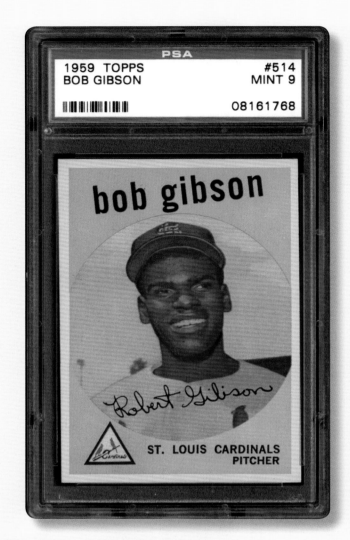

This is the only recognized rookie card of one of baseball's most intimidating pitchers. It was simple … a batter should not disrespect Mr. Gibson. If the batter chose to show up the nasty right-hander, the next pitch would be near his ear. For right-handed batters, Bob Gibson was a nightmare. With a devastating slider, Gibson won 20 or more games in seven different seasons (twice winning 19 games) with two Cy Young Awards (1968 and 1970) and one NL MVP (1968) to his credit. During his MVP season, Gibson turned in what many consider the greatest single season pitching performance of all-time. Gibson went 22-9 with 13 shutouts and a microscopic ERA of 1.12. That same year, Gibson would fan 17 Detroit Tigers in Game One of the World Series, a record that still stands as of the writing of this book. He would finish his career with a 251-174 record, 3,117 strikeouts and an ERA of 2.91. This eight-time All-Star and nine-time Gold Glove winner was inducted into the Baseball Hall of Fame in 1981. This card is tough to find well-centered and the light pink background is often plagued with print marks.

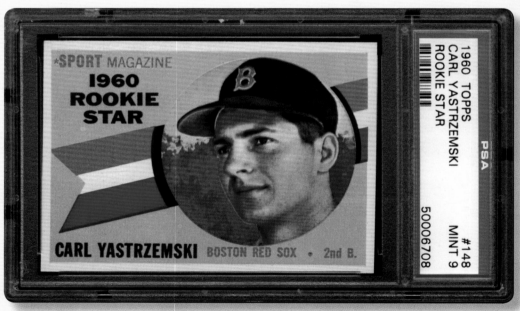

1960 Topps #148 Carl Yastrzemski

This is the only recognized rookie card of this legendary Boston Red Sox outfielder. Carl Yastrzemski, affectionately referred to as *Yaz*, had one of the most difficult jobs in baseball in the early 1960s. He would have to replace, perhaps, the greatest hitter who ever lived – Ted Williams. While no one could replace a legend like that from an offensive standpoint, Yaz came as close as anyone could have hoped. The powerful slugger finished his career with 3,419 hits, 452 home runs and 1,844 RBI, making him the first AL player in history to reach 3,000 hits and 400 home runs. Along the way, this 18-time All-Star would win three batting titles and seven Gold Gloves. He also remains the last man to win the elusive Triple Crown. In 1967, *Yaz* hit .326 with 44 home runs and 121 RBI, earning him that distinction as well as the AL MVP. After playing 23 years with the Red Sox, *Yaz* retired in 1983 and was ultimately inducted into the Baseball Hall of Fame in 1989. This card is one of two major rookies in the 1960 Topps set along with the Willie McCovey rookie and, despite a find of 1960 cello packs several years ago, it remains a daunting task to find well-centered copies that are void of black print marks along the face of the card.

1962 Topps #1 Roger Maris

This is the first card in the super tough 1962 Topps set, and it might be Roger Maris' most important card. While this is not his rookie card, the 1962 Topps Maris captures the Yankee legend at his peak. Maris is, naturally, known for his great 1961 campaign when he battled Mickey Mantle in a home run chase, eventually surpassing Babe Ruth on the final day of the season with home run number 61. This condition sensitive card, which is surrounded by fragile brown borders, commemorates that season with the 1961 statistics along the reverse of the card. In addition, Maris is pictured with the Yankees as opposed to the Cleveland Indians, the team he played for during his rookie campaign. Finally, while both cards are tough to locate in high-grade, the image on the 1962 Topps card may be his best. In 1961, Maris was named AL MVP for the second consecutive year. In addition to his record-setting 61 home runs, Maris hit .269 with 142 RBI and 132 runs scored. No, Maris will never be inducted into the Baseball Hall of Fame, but his impact on the game will never be forgotten.

1962 Topps #387 Lou Brock

This is the only recognized rookie card of the former all-time stolen base leader and current 3,000 Hit Club member. Lou Brock began his career with the Chicago Cubs in 1961, but it was in St. Louis where he emerged as a star. Brock was sent packing to the Cardinals in 1964 after Chicago management became frustrated with his development. For the remainder of the 1964 season, Brock hit .348 and stole 38 bases, leading the Cardinals to a World Series championship. He would lead them to another title in 1967 alongside teammates Bob Gibson and Roger Maris. Brock possessed outstanding speed and was an excellent overall hitter as evidenced by his .293 career batting average and 3,023 hits. Brock held the record for stolen bases in a single season (118 in 1974) and career (938) until Rickey Henderson surpassed both marks. In fact, Brock led the league in steals eight times in his career. After 19 seasons in the league, Brock retired in 1979. This six-time All-Star was inducted into the Baseball Hall of Fame in 1985. This card is seldom found in PSA NM-MT 8 or better condition due to extremely fragile brown borders that reveal the slightest hint of wear.

1963 Topps #537 Pete Rose

This is the only recognized rookie card of baseball's all-time *Hit King*. While this set also contains a great rookie card of Pittsburgh slugger Willie Stargell, the Pete Rose rookie is clearly the key to the colorful set. Despite being banned from baseball and precluded from Hall of Fame consideration, what Rose accomplished on the field has never been questioned. Rose, while clearly not the most physically-gifted player of his era, showed unrivaled heart and determination to reach unthinkable heights. Just imagine what it would take to reach 4,256 hits, his career total. During his career, Rose would hit .300 or better in 14 different seasons and reach or surpass 200 hits 10 times. After being named NL Rookie of the Year in 1963, Rose would win the NL MVP in 1973 as part of Cincinnati's *Big Red Machine*. In 1978, Rose would hit in 44 consecutive games, resulting in the second longest hitting streak in baseball history. Rose was named to 17 All-Star teams in his career at five different positions, a career that continued until 1986 when he made his final appearance. This card, which is often found with print defects and poor centering, has a blue colored border along the top that is very susceptible to chipping. One of the hobby's first major scandals involved a hoard of counterfeit Rose rookies that surfaced during the hobby boom of the 1980s. Even his cards can't escape controversy!

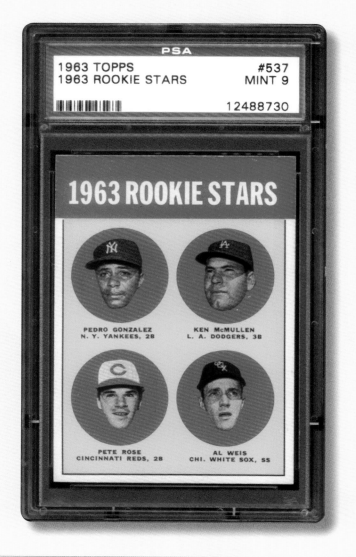

1964 Topps Stand-Up Carl Yastrzemski SP

This might be the toughest card in the very popular and colorful 1964 Topps Stand-Up set. In 1964, Topps issued a 77-card set that was intended to be more like toys than trading cards. The cards were designed to be popped and then folded, allowing the collector to prop these blank-backed cards up for display. Each player is shown against the dual-colored background, with the bottom half in green and the upper half in yellow. In particular, the green portion of the card is very susceptible to chipping and wear. This Carl Yastrzemski card is one of 22 short prints in the set, each of which is substantially tougher to find than the rest of the cards. While the set includes a tremendous star selection, featuring the likes of Hank Aaron, Roberto Clemente, Sandy Koufax, Mickey Mantle and Willie Mays, the Yastrzemski card is the one that torments most set builders. In 1964, Yastrzemski hit .289 with 15 home runs and was just a couple of years away from his peak, where he hit at least 40 homers and drove in at least 100 RBI in three out of four seasons (1967-1970).

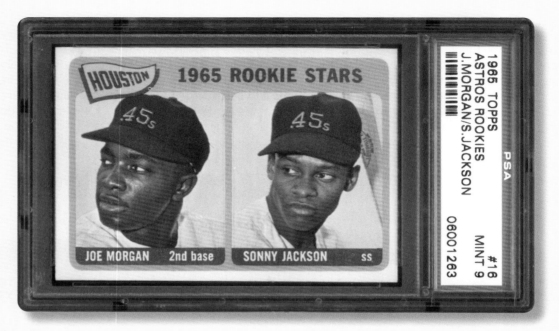

1965 Topps #16 Joe Morgan

This is the only recognized rookie card of who many baseball historians consider to be the best second baseman in history. Joe Morgan started his career in Houston with the Colt .45s but, after being traded in 1972, he became a star as a key component to *The Big Red Machine* in Cincinnati. Morgan showcased his rare blend of power and speed from the second base position, helping lead the Reds to back-to-back World Series titles in 1975 and 1976. In fact, Morgan captured the NL MVP in each of those seasons. Morgan finished his career with a .271 batting average, a .392 on-base percentage, 268 home runs, 2,517 hits, 689 stolen bases and five consecutive Gold Gloves to his credit (1972-1976). This 10-time All-Star was inducted into the Baseball Hall of Fame in 1990. After retiring from the game in 1984, Morgan started a career in broadcasting the following year with his former team, the Cincinnati Reds. Since 1990, Morgan has been teamed up with Jon Miller for ESPN baseball broadcasts and has won two Emmy Awards for sports analysis during that time. This Morgan rookie is often found off-center and chipping along the colored reverse can also detract from the overall grade of the card.

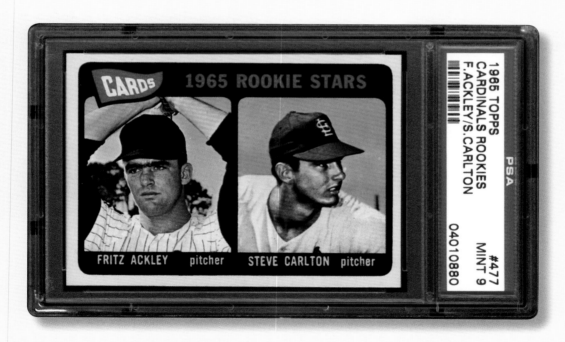

1965 Topps #477 Steve Carlton

This is the only recognized rookie card of one of baseball's most dominant lefties, Steve Carlton. *Lefty* combined the overpowering stuff of Sandy Koufax with the longevity of Warren Spahn. He finished with 329 victories, 4,136 strikeouts and a 3.32 ERA, pitching over 5,000 innings. Carlton won 20 or more games in six different seasons, including a 27-10 season for the last place Philadelphia Phillies in 1972. Carlton also had 310 strikeouts, 30 complete games and an ERA 1.97 that year, one of the greatest pitching performances of all time. He remains the only pitcher in baseball history to win the Cy Young as a member of a last place team. This was one of four Cy Young Awards that Carlton earned in his career (1972, 1977, 1980 and 1982). This 10-time All-Star was elected to the Hall of Fame in 1994. This card is not overly difficult to find in PSA NM-MT 8 condition, but it does have its share of condition obstacles such as reverse chipping along the colored edges and poor overall print quality.

1966 Topps #126 Jim Palmer

This is the only recognized rookie card of the greatest pitcher in Baltimore Orioles history. Jim Palmer, with his seemingly effortless delivery, baffled batters from 1965 to 1984, helping his team win several pennants along the way. In 1971, Palmer was one of four Orioles pitchers to win at least 20 games in the same season. Palmer remains the only pitcher in baseball history to win a World Series game in three decades, 1966, 1970-71 and 1983. Palmer won three Cy Youngs in his career, including back-to-back awards in 1975 and 1976. In his 19-year career, Palmer finished with a 268-152 record, an ERA of 2.86, 2,212 strikeouts and 53 shutouts to his credit. This included eight seasons of 20 wins or more for the dominant Baltimore mainstay. Palmer was also an outstanding fielder and was honored with the Gold Glove Award on four separate occasions. This six-time All-Star was inducted into the Baseball Hall of Fame in 1990. After his playing days, Palmer has enjoyed a successful broadcasting career. This card is difficult to find well-centered as many cards from this set suffer from tilts.

1967 Topps #569 Rod Carew

This is the only recognized rookie card of one of baseball's best hitters of the 1960s and 1970s. Rod Carew, while not a powerhouse at the plate, was a master technician with the bat, hitting .328 during the course of his career. Using an extremely unique batting stance and lightning quick reflexes, Carew would pepper the entire field with line drives. A tremendous bunter and blessed with terrific speed, Carew used many tools to reach 3,053 total hits. Carew won seven batting titles in all and after batting .388 in 1977, he was named the AL MVP. Carew stole 353 bases in his career, including 17 steals of home, a rare occurrence in the game. This 1967 NL Rookie of the Year was named to the All-Star team each and every year between 1967 and 1984, only missing selection in his final year (1985). In 1991, Carew was inducted into the Baseball Hall of Fame. This card has two main condition obstacles to note, poor centering and dark print defects along the face of the card.

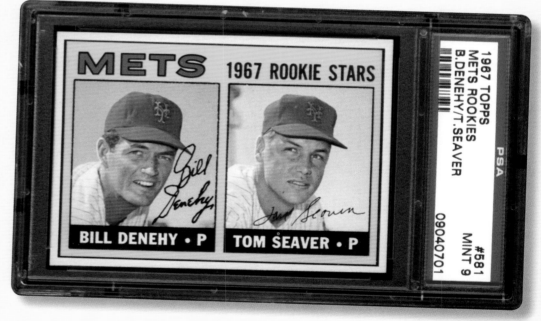

1967 Topps #581 Tom Seaver

This is the only recognized rookie card of *Tom Terrific*. This three-time Cy Young Award winner won 311 games in his career, had an ERA of 2.86 and a .603 winning percentage. By using his legs to generate power, Tom Seaver used his fine fastball to strike out 3,640 batters in his career, including 10 seasons of 200 or more and a single game-high of 19. In 1967, Seaver finished with 16 victories and a 2.76 ERA in his first big league season for the New York Mets. He was named NL Rookie of the Year for his efforts. A couple of years later, Seaver went 25-7 for the *Amazing Mets* of 1969, winning his first Cy Young Award and helping the Mets win their first World Series championship. When it came to Hall of Fame voting, this 12-time All-Star was named on 98.8% of the ballots in 1992, an all-time record. Despite being part of the high-number series in the set, this card is not particularly difficult by vintage card standards, but finding well-centered copies can be tough due to the narrow borders.

1968 Topps #177 Nolan Ryan

This is the only recognized rookie card of baseball's *strikeout king*. Nolan Ryan was a physical marvel. Still able to throw in the mid-90s well into his 40s, Ryan baffled hitters for four decades. In 1993, his pitching arm finally gave out when he suffered a sudden elbow tear, ending his career. Ryan finished with 324 wins, a 3.19 ERA, 5,714 strikeouts and seven no-hitters. His strikeout total is one of those records that seems unbreakable. Consider this. If you struck out 250 batters for 20 consecutive seasons, that would get you to 5,000. You then would have to add another 714 strikeouts to tie Ryan. It defies logic! This humble cowboy from Texas never had the chance to pitch for a great team, resulting in an unspectacular won/loss record of 324-292. This eight-time All-Star and owner of dozens of MLB records was inducted into the Baseball Hall of Fame in 1999. This card, one that also pictures another fine pitcher in Jerry Koosman, is not overly tough to find in PSA NM-MT 8 condition, but collectors should look for well-centered copies and be aware of chipping along the colored reverse. In addition, due to the print design along the borders, corner wear may be hard to detect at first glance.

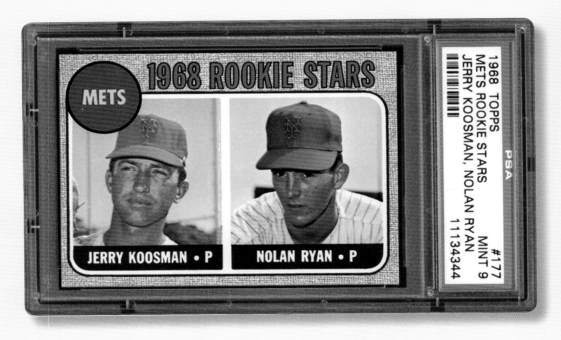

1968 Topps #247 Johnny Bench

This is the only recognized rookie card of whom many consider to be the greatest catcher in baseball history. Captain of Cincinnati's *Big Red Machine*, Johnny Bench, who possessed a rocket arm and a lethal bat, offered a rare combination of stellar offense and defense from the catcher position. Behind the plate, Bench won 10 consecutive Gold Gloves from 1968-1977 and baserunners throughout MLB feared his arm. With the bat, Bench led the league in home runs twice and RBI three times, a rarity for a catcher. In fact, Bench drove in more runs than any other player during the 1970s. This 1968 Rookie of the Year was named NL MVP twice (1970 and 1972). In fact, his 1970 season is considered one of the best ever by a catcher. At the age of 22, Bench became the youngest player ever to capture the MVP, hitting .293 with 45 home runs and 148 RBI. This 14-time All-Star put an exclamation point on his career during his final home game in 1983. On Johnny Bench Night at Riverfront Stadium, Bench homered and threw out the only runner who attempted to steal in front of a sell-out crowd. Bench was ultimately inducted into the Baseball Hall of Fame in 1989. This key 1968 Topps card, in terms of difficulty, is much like the Ryan rookie and subject to similar condition obstacles.

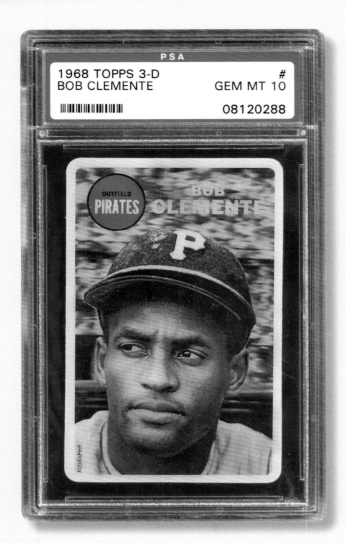

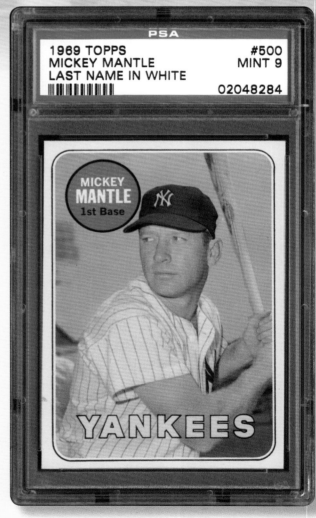

1968 Topps 3-D Roberto Clemente

This is, perhaps, the toughest Roberto Clemente card in the hobby and the key to an extremely tough set. This Topps issue was actually a Test Set that was never intended for distribution, resulting in the scarcity we see today. While there were other good players included in the set, Clemente was the only true superstar. When this card was produced, Clemente was coming off one of his best seasons. In 1967, Clemente hit .357 with 209 hits (both league-highs), 110 RBI and 103 runs scored. One year earlier, Clemente won the NL MVP. Overall, Clemente won four NL batting titles (1961, 1964, 1965 and 1967), two World Series championships (1960 and 1971) and he was still going strong in 1972 (.312 batting average) before he perished in a plane crash bound for Nicaragua. Clemente's throwing arm is still regarded as one of the most powerful and accurate of all time, as he gunned down nearly 300 runners from right field in his career. This card measures approximately 2¼" by 3½" and, due to its unique design, is subject to some unique condition obstacles, namely cracking along the plastic-coated surface. The grade of the card will suffer depending on the severity of the crack with most cards being downgraded to PSA EX-MT 6 or lower. The reverse printing also was inconsistent, with some examples exhibiting tilted or unfocused print, but the existence of this defect will not hinder the grade in a major way.

1969 Topps #500 Mickey Mantle White Letter

This is the last card and one of the most difficult cards to feature Mickey Mantle. The 1969 Topps White Letter variations are just plain tough, affecting just a small group of cards within the #s 400-511 in the massive set. The unaffected cards were printed with the player's surname in yellow while these variations were printed in white. It remains a mystery as to why these cards were produced in this manner. Was it a mere mistake or error in printing? Was it intentional in hopes of generating more interest in the product? No one seems to know for sure, but it resulted in one of the great cards of the 1960s. One of the beauties of this card is that the reverse contains statistics from Mantle's entire career. In Mantle's last season, after injuries had taken their toll on the great slugger, he managed to hit 18 home runs, bringing his career total to 536. Like most of the cards in the set, many of these Mantle cards are found with poor centering and print defects, but finding one of these White Letter prizes at all is a real challenge.

1969 Topps Super #28 Reggie Jackson

This is a key rookie card of one of baseball's great performers and it resides in one of the most popular Topps sets in hobby history. This glossy, full-color set includes many of the greatest sluggers to ever take the field. Hank Aaron, Willie Mays and Mickey Mantle were all starting to wind down their careers, but it was just the beginning for a brash, outspoken outfielder from the Oakland A's. Let's face it – baseball is a form of entertainment and no one during his era entertained fans more than Reggie Jackson. Everyone knew when Jackson was coming to the plate. Fans either loved him or hated him but, no matter how they felt about him, they couldn't ignore him and his awesome power. How about his unforgettable performance in Game 6 of the 1977 World Series? Jackson crushed three home runs on three pitches to help the New York Yankees beat the Los Angeles Dodgers. Jackson finished his career with 563 home runs, 1,702 RBI and five World Series titles to his credit. Jackson won his first and only MVP as part of the Oakland A's in 1973 but was named MVP of the World Series twice in 1973 and 1977. This 14-time All-Star was inducted into the Baseball Hall of Fame in 1993. This Topps Super issue measures approximately 2¼" by 3¼" and, while not considered condition sensitive due to their rounded-corner design, they are far less plentiful than any regular Topps issue. This is one of two key Jackson rookies issued by Topps as he also appeared on a regular 1969 Topps card, one that is deceptively tough in high-grade.

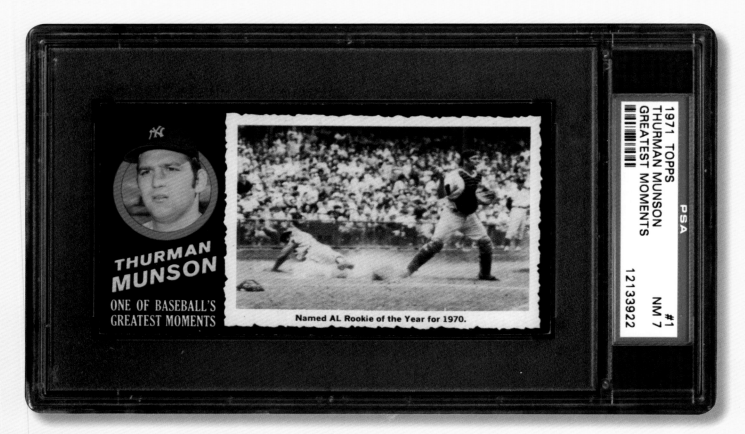

1971 Topps Greatest Moments #1 Thurman Munson

This is the first card in one of the most condition sensitive sets of the era. This great Topps issue, which features many of the game's best players from the period, contains 55 cards throughout. Each card captured a notable accomplishment in a large format, with each card measuring 2½" by 4¾". Thurman Munson, the first Yankee captain since Lou Gehrig, was selected to start the set. After being named the AL Rookie of the Year in 1970, Munson remained the starting catcher for the Yankees until he perished in a plane crash on August 2, 1979 at the age of 32. This seven-time All-Star was named the AL MVP in 1976 after hitting .302 with 17 home runs and 105 RBI. That same year, Munson hit an unthinkable .529 in the World Series, but the Yankees fell to the Cincinnati Reds and Johnny Bench in the end. Munson was also an excellent defender, winning the Gold Glove Award three years in a row (1973-1975). He finished his career with a .292 batting average but, more importantly, he was beloved by his teammates and fans. This card, one that is surrounded with fragile black borders, is often found off-center, making it one of Munson's toughest cards overall.

1973 Topps #615 Mike Schmidt

This is the only recognized rookie card of the best third baseman of all-time and the key to the 1973 Topps set. There have been some outstanding third basemen throughout the years. Eddie Mathews, Brooks Robinson and George Brett are some of baseball's best, but none of them can match Mike Schmidt overall. Schmidt was the premier home run threat of his era with eight home run titles and 548 total homers over the course of his career. As a defensive player, Schmidt won 10 Gold Gloves, breaking numerous fielding records along the way. On the bases, Schmidt stole 174 bags, a skill that went unnoticed due to his powerful bat and stellar glove. This 12-time All-Star won three NL MVP awards in his career (1980, 1981 and 1986) and drove 1,595 runs. Schmidt also led the Philadelphia Phillies to six NL titles during the 1970s and 1980s before being inducted into the Baseball Hall of Fame in 1995. This particular card is subject to three main condition obstacles: poor centering, print defects and reverse chipping along the black edges.

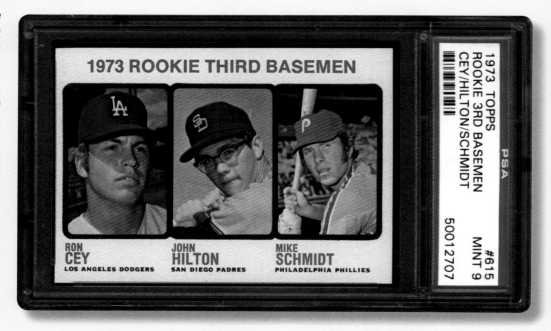

1975 Topps #228 George Brett

In a set filled with HOF rookie cards like those of Robin Yount and Gary Carter, the George Brett card stands apart in one of the most popular sets of the modern era. Known for his intensity and clutch hitting, Brett let his bat do the talking. In 1980, Brett rose to stardom by making a run at .400. He ended the season at .390 and drove in 118 RBI in just 117 games. Brett was named the AL MVP. It was Brett's second batting title. In fact, Brett became the first player ever to win batting titles in three different decades (1976, 1980 and 1990). In 1985, Brett's brilliant regular season and postseason play helped the Kansas City Royals to their first World Series title in franchise history. This 13-time All-Star finished his career with a .305 batting average, 317 home runs and 3,154 total hits after singling up the middle in his final career at-bat. The 1975 Topps set is one of the tougher issues of the decade. The multi-colored borders are not only fragile, but the abundance of color in the design created even more opportunities for stray print marks. The issue is also susceptible to image tilts, resulting in poor centering. The standard card measures approximately 2½" by 3½". Keep in mind that Topps produced a more limited mini version measuring approximately 2¼" by 3⅛" the same year.

1979 Topps #116 Ozzie Smith

This is the only recognized rookie card of *The Wizard* and a post-1970 condition rarity in PSA Mint 9 or better. Ozzie Smith, while certainly a competent hitter and excellent base runner, made a name for himself by showcasing his stellar glove at shortstop. He began his career with the San Diego Padres in 1978 and remained there until 1982, when he was traded to the St. Louis Cardinals. Smith joined a team that was built on defense, pitching and speed. In his first year, Smith helped the Cardinals to a World Series title. In 1985, Smith hit a rare, game-winning home run against Tom Niedenfuer of the Los Angeles Dodgers that helped the Cardinals reach the series again. This would be one of the most memorable moments of Smith's career. In 1987, he would once again help lead his team to the World Series with, perhaps, his best season. Smith hit .303 with 104 runs scored, 75 RBI, 40 doubles, 43 stolen bases and an OBP of .392. Smith finished his career with a .262 batting average, 2,460 hits and 580 stolen bases. This 15-time All-Star was inducted into the Baseball Hall of Fame in 2002. This card is usually found severely off-center, preventing most examples from ever reaching unqualified PSA Mint 9 status or better.

1980 Topps #482 Rickey Henderson

This is the key rookie card of baseball's greatest leadoff man. Rickey Henderson, who played an amazing 25 years, combined power and speed at the top of the lineup for nearly three full decades. Henderson finished his career with 1,406 stolen bases (#1 all-time), 3,055 hits, 2,295 runs scored (#1 all-time), 2,190 walks, a .401 on-base percentage and 297 home runs. In fact, he led off a game with a home run 81 times, the MLB record. This 10-time All-Star led the league in stolen bases 12 times and he still holds the record for stolen bases in a season with 130, a number that seems unreachable in today's game. In 1990, Henderson won the AL MVP as a member of the Oakland A's by hitting .325 with 28 home runs, 119 runs scored, 65 stolen bases and a .439 OBP. This card is fairly tough to find centered by modern standards and the 1980 Topps card was often cut in a manner that left the corners with a blunt appearance. In addition, print defects are found on this card from time to time but, since the image of Henderson was taken from a distance, the presence of such defects may not affect the eye-appeal quite as much as they would on a portrait-style image. Finally, this card has been counterfeited – so beware.

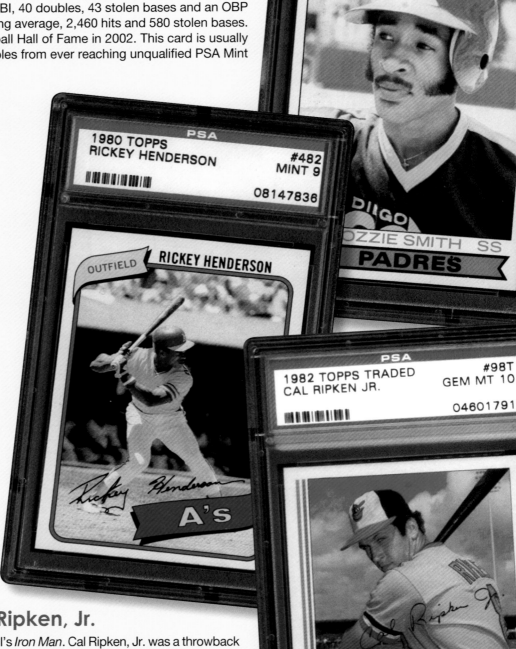

1982 Topps Traded #98T Cal Ripken, Jr.

This is the most desirable rookie card of baseball's *Iron Man*. Cal Ripken, Jr. was a throwback player. No one played harder and no one of his stature took as much time to please the fans like he did. Ripken could be seen signing autographs hours after the game, time and time again. While Ripken will be remembered most for his consecutive game streak of 2,632, he accomplished so much more. This two-time AL MVP (1983 and 1991) finished his career with 431 home runs, 1,695 RBI and 3,189 hits, a rare amount of offensive production for a man who played shortstop for most of his career. This former AL Rookie of the Year (1982) and two-time Gold Glove winner (1991 and 1992) was named to the All-Star team 19 times! For all of his impressive numbers and accomplishments, what separated Ripken from the rest was his consistent showing of class during an era defined by ego and selfish behavior. Ripken was ultimately inducted into the Baseball Hall of Fame in 2007. This card was produced with mediocre paper stock and the red reverse can be subject to chipping. It is also more limited than his regular Topps issue from the same year, which were issued in a separate boxed set.

1983 Topps #482 Tony Gwynn

This is the key rookie card of one of baseball's most consistent hitters. Tony Gwynn, the San Diego Padre favorite, is considered by many to be the best pure hitter of the last 30 years, and his numbers certainly support that belief. Gwynn won a total of eight NL batting titles (only Ty Cobb won more) and finished with a career batting average of .338. This 15-time All-Star made a run at .400 in 1994, but the season was cut short by a strike, leaving Gwynn and his fans wondering if he would have made it. In addition to his excellence with the bat, Gwynn was an outstanding baserunner with 319 stolen bases (he had a career-high of 56 in 1987) and fielder with five Gold Gloves for his work in right field. Gwynn was inducted into the Baseball Hall of Fame along with Cal Ripken, Jr. in 2007 and, like Ripken, Gwynn played his entire career with one team, a rarity in the modern era. While Gwynn does have other rookie cards in the Donruss and Fleer sets, this Topps issue is his most desirable. It is also rather difficult to find well-centered.

1984 Fleer Update #U-27 Roger Clemens

This is the most valuable rookie card of one of baseball's most dominant pitchers. *The Rocket* has been racking up wins and striking out batters for more than 20 years. Like his idol Nolan Ryan, Roger Clemens has shown incredible longevity for a power pitcher, evidenced by his nearly 4,700 strikeouts and 3.12 ERA during an era filled with offense. As of the time of this writing, Clemens was still going strong at 45 years of age for the New York Yankees. He has won more Cy Young Awards than any pitcher in baseball history (seven) and his 354 victories separate him from any pitcher from the 1980s to the present. The most remarkable part of his pitching record, perhaps, is the fact that he pitched during an era defined by offense. During his illustrious career, Clemens has recorded 20 strikeouts in a single game on two different occasions. This 11-time All-Star is well on his way to Cooperstown. This card, which was released with incredible buzz, was produced in very limited quantities in comparison to his other regular issue rookie cards in 1985. The cards, packed tightly in their set boxes, are sometimes found with reverse tearing near the corners.

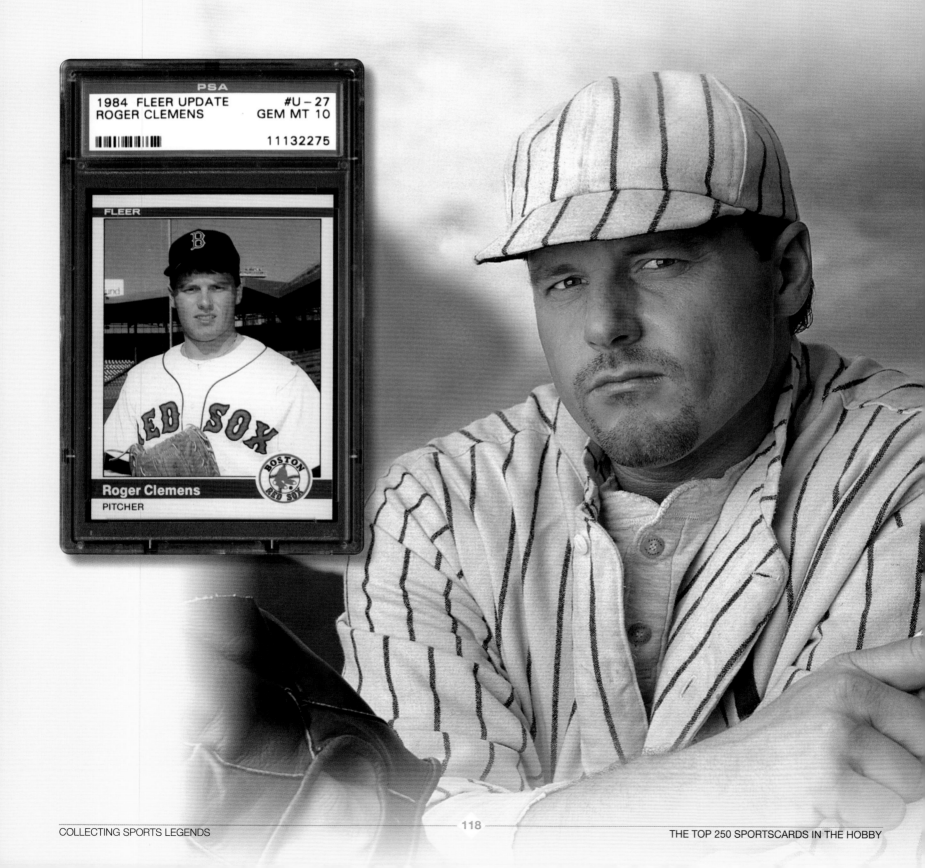

1987 Donruss #36 Greg Maddux

This is the most popular rookie card of the man who won more games in the 1990s than any pitcher in baseball. Greg Maddux did not possess the overpowering stuff that defined Sandy Koufax or Roger Clemens, but his ability to outthink hitters coupled with pinpoint control made him a star. In the beginning, Maddux did not appear to be a star in the making, going 6-14 with an ERA of 5.61 for the Chicago Cubs, but he was determined to show the world that he belonged. Maddux, still going strong today, has compiled 347 victories, 3,273 strikeouts and an ERA of 3.11 at the time of this writing. Maddux won four consecutive Cy Young Awards (1992-1995), going 75-29 with an ERA of 1.98 during that span. This eight-time All-Star has won 17 Gold Gloves, an all-time record, which ties with Brooks Robinson and Jim Kaat for the most at any position. When it comes to this rookie card, there are a couple of things to note. First, keep in mind there are two different versions, the wax pack and factory set cards. The factory set examples are slightly smaller than the wax pack version and are often found with blunt corners due to the cellophane wrapping they were tightly packaged in. Both versions are subject to chipping and edge wear along the black borders.

1987 Fleer #604 Barry Bonds

Where do we start with this guy and this card? Well, love him or hate him, Barry Bonds is one of the greatest players in baseball history. I am not talking about a top 50 or top 20 player; he is one of the very best of all time. The numbers and accomplishments are staggering. Bonds, who is still going strong as of the time of this writing, is a seven-time NL MVP (an all-time record), 14-time All-Star and eight-time Gold Glove winner. His sheer numbers are even more amazing. Bonds, a member of the 500-500 Club (home runs and stolen bases), holds records for single-season home runs (73), career home runs (762), career walks (2,558) and is at or near the top in many other single season and career categories. Currently, Bonds holds a .298 career average with 1,996 RBI, 2,935 hits and a .607 slugging percentage. There are other Bonds rookie cards available, with some that are actually tougher in high-grade or more limited in production, but this 1987 Fleer card is his most popular. Keep in mind, there is a Glossy version of this card. While the Glossy is scarcer, it is actually easier to find in Gem Mint condition than the regular issue Fleer card.

1989 Upper Deck #1 Ken Griffey, Jr.

This is the key rookie card of one of the best all-around players in baseball history. While Ken Griffey, Jr. has been overshadowed by Barry Bonds and hampered by injuries late in his career, he has accomplished some amazing feats. As of the writing of this book, Griffey was rapidly approaching 600 home runs, has 1,700-plus RBI and owned a career average right around .290. In addition to all of his offensive output, Griffey was a tremendous centerfielder, earning 10 consecutive Gold Gloves (1990-1999) and making some of the most spectacular catches ever caught on film. This 13-time All-Star was named AL MVP in 1997 after hitting .304 with 56 home runs, 147 RBI and 125 runs scored. Griffey would nearly duplicate these numbers the very next year with 56 home runs, 146 RBI and 120 runs scored in 1998. This card, one of the most symbolic cards of the modern era, is subject to one hidden flaw. Many Griffey rookies contain a factory wrinkle on the reverse, which can severely diminish the grade (usually no higher than a PSA EX-MT 6 if present) of an otherwise Mint card.

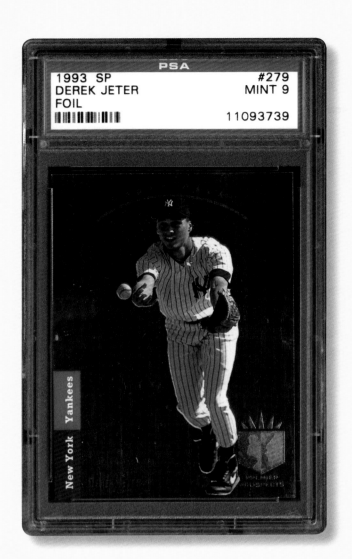

1993 SP #279 Derek Jeter

This is one of the toughest modern-era rookie cards to find in Mint condition, and it features New York Yankee favorite Derek Jeter. Unlike most of the baseball players on this list, Jeter did not make it because of his overwhelming numbers; he made it because of his grit, class, popularity and his ability to win. At the time of this writing, Jeter has a career batting average around .320 and is starting to close in on 3,000 hits with over 2,300 at the present time. Jeter has also displayed occasional pop in his bat, closing in on 200 career home runs in 2007, which is a rarity for a shortstop. On the defensive end, this eight-time All-Star has won three Gold Gloves. The captain of the Yankees has earned the right to be called a winner by leading his team to the postseason time and time again. His mark of 153 career postseason hits is an all-time record to go along with 17 postseason home runs. Jeter has also been an outstanding base runner during his career with more than 250 stolen bases to his credit. This card is clearly Jeter's most appealing rookie issue with one major condition obstacle: The dark edges, coupled with the foil coating, give this issue problems, with many of these rookie cards exhibiting wear from the moment they are removed from a pack.

1994 SP #15 Alex Rodriguez

Like the Derek Jeter card (above), this is one of the toughest modern-era rookies in the hobby. *A-Rod* is considered by many to be the best player in the game today and the greatest threat to not only the career home run mark held by Barry Bonds, but also every major offensive record on the books. Far ahead of the pace set by Barry Bonds or Hank Aaron, at the young age of 32, *A-Rod* appears to be well on his way to owning the record books. *A-Rod* is also one of the best overall players in the game, showcasing power, defense and speed. He already has in excess of 500 home runs (the youngest ever to reach that mark), a career batting average over .300 and more than 250 stolen bases, including a 40-40 season in 1998 where he hit 42 homers and stolen 46 bases in the same season. This three-time AL MVP (2003, 2005 and 2007) and 11-time All-Star has won two Gold Gloves along the way. This card is much like the 1993 SP Jeter rookie in that light wear from a combination of the design and packaging causes many of these cards to grade less than PSA Mint 9, even straight from the pack. Keep in mind that there is a Die-Cut version of this card that was produced in more limited numbers.

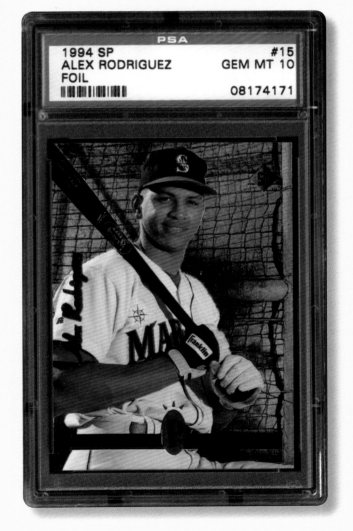

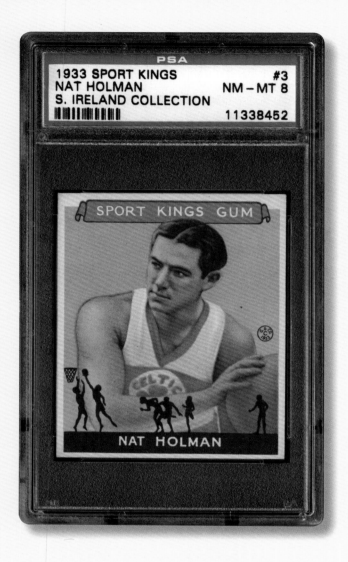

1933 Goudey Sport Kings #3
Nat Holman

This is one of the most important basketball cards in the hobby and one of the toughest cards in the set. During the 1920s, Nat Holman was one of the game's best ball handlers and shooters, in addition to being an innovator on the court as one of basketball's first great playmakers. He spent most of his career with the Original Celtics, a dominant team who won back-to-back American Basketball League titles in 1927 and 1928. Amazingly, Holman became the head coach of the City College of New York in 1920 while still very active as a player and remained in that position for 37 years. In 1950, Holman helped lead CCNY to the NCAA and NIT titles in the same season, a feat never before accomplished nor since, by any other college team. He finished his coaching career with a 421-190 record and officially retired in 1960. Holman was inducted into the Basketball Hall of Fame as a player in 1964. This card, positioned behind Ty Cobb and Babe Ruth in the wonderful 1933 Goudey Sport Kings set, is extremely difficult to locate in PSA NM-MT 8 or better condition, primarily due to consistently poor centering.

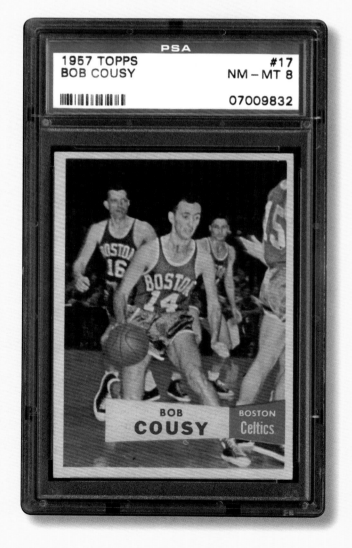

1957 Topps #17 Bob Cousy

This is the only recognized rookie card of basketball's *Houdini of the Hardwood.* Until Bob Cousy's arrival, basketball had been a methodical game with pre-planned plays and little spontaneity. Cousy changed the game with his unpredictable style and incredible passing game, exciting fans across the country. As the point guard for the Boston Celtics, Cousy led his team to six NBA Championships. He was named the league's MVP in 1956-1957 after averaging 20.6 points, 4.8 rebounds and 7.5 assists per game. In fact, he won eight consecutive assists titles during his career. This 13-time All-Star, winning the All-Star Game MVP twice (1954 and 1957), was named to 10 All-NBA First Teams and was inducted into the Basketball Hall of Fame in 1971. In terms of difficulty, the 1957 Topps issue is in a league of its own. These cards measure approximately 2½" by 3½" and are plagued with print problems and poor centering. In fact, during a small unopened vending find in Texas, more than 1,000 uncirculated cards were discovered. Of those 1,000-plus cards, only 50 or so were considered PSA NM 7 or better. These are really tough cards.

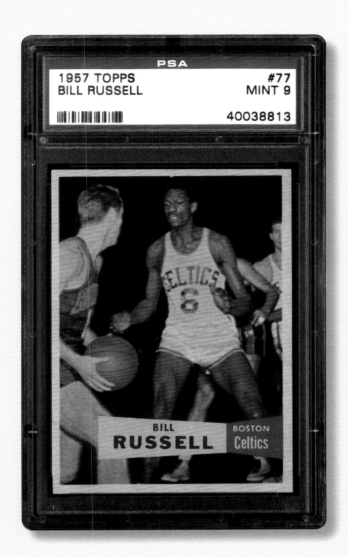

1957 Topps #77 Bill Russell SP

    This is the only recognized rookie card of the NBA's biggest winner. This is also the key to the 1957 Topps set, one of the toughest and most important basketball issues ever produced. In 13 seasons with the Boston Celtics, Bill Russell won 11 championships. Russell's focus on defense changed the way fans defined star players, making defensive play an art. While Russell did lead the league in rebounding four times, averaged 22.5 rebounds per game during his career and 15.1 points per game, his impact cannot be measured by statistics alone. This 12-time All-Star was awarded the MVP five times and was one of the finest shot blockers in NBA history. As an amateur, Russell won two NCAA titles and even won a Gold Medal during the 1956 Olympics. This legendary big man was inducted into the Basketball Hall of Fame in 1975. This rookie issue, as mentioned earlier, is extremely difficult in high-grade, with poor centering and print defects wreaking havoc on the card.

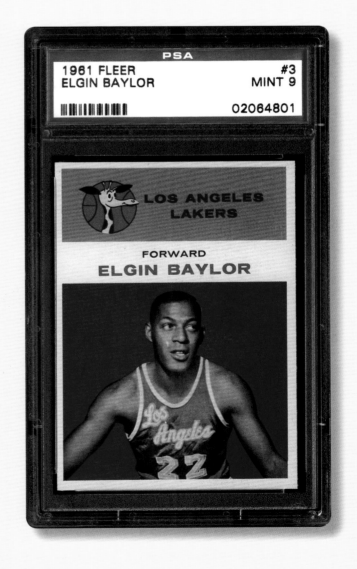

1961 Fleer #3 Elgin Baylor

    This is the only recognized rookie card of one of basketball's most exciting players during the 1960s. Elgin Baylor was fast, powerful and inventive. In today's game, powerful dunks and acrobatic shots fill the highlight reels but Baylor was the first to do it routinely. During his 14 seasons with the Los Angeles Lakers, Baylor averaged 27.4 points and 13.5 rebounds per game. This former NBA Rookie of the Year (1959) was an 11-time All-Star and named to the NBA All-First Team 10 times. What made Baylor, perhaps, most exceptional was his all-around ability on the court. During the 1962-63 season, Baylor finished the year ranked in the top five in scoring, rebounding, assists and free-throw percentage. It was the first time in NBA history that a player ranked so high in these four major categories. Baylor was inducted into the Basketball Hall of Fame in 1977. This card measures approximately 2½" by 3½". While there was a find of these inaugural Fleer basketball cards, even cards that originate from the find have condition obstacles such as poor centering and stray print defects. Keep in mind that every Baylor card contains a print mark on the right side of his face, so its existence will not hinder the grade.

1961 Fleer #8 Wilt Chamberlain

This is the only recognized rookie card of the most dominant basketball player to ever play the game. Who is the best player in basketball history? Well, some might say Michael Jordan or Magic Johnson but statistics don't lie. If you want pure dominance, dominance of "Ruthian" proportions, your choice has to be Wilt Chamberlain. At 7'1", 275 pounds, he simply dominated the smaller opposition. No one could stop him. Chamberlain was the only player in history to score 4,000 points in a season. He averaged 50.4 points per game during the 1961-62 season, holds the record for points in a single game with 100, the record for rebounds in a single game with 55 and he led the league in scoring for seven straight seasons. Furthermore, he led the league in rebounding in 11 of his 14 seasons and holds numerous other offensive records. This former NBA Rookie of the Year (1959-1960) was a four-time league MVP, and he led his team to six NBA Finals, winning two. Chamberlain was inducted into the Basketball Hall of Fame in 1978. This card is seen more often in high-grade than some of the other key rookies in the set, but it still falls subject to the same condition obstacles common to the issue.

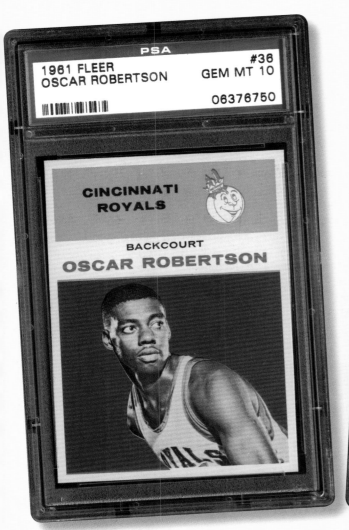

1961 Fleer #36 Oscar Robertson

This is the only recognized rookie card of basketball's most well-rounded legend. Oscar Robertson could beat his opponents in many ways, whether it was on the offensive or defensive end. In one of the most incredible single-season performances of all-time, Robertson averaged 30.8 points, 12.5 rebounds and 11.4 assists per game during the 1961-62 season. That's a triple-double for the entire year! In fact, he came within a whisper of repeating the feat on four separate occasions. At 6'5", 220 pounds, Robertson was a powerful guard and helped revolutionize the position. He was selected to the All-Star team in 12 of his 14 seasons, won one NBA title in 1970-71 and was named league MVP for his 1963-64 performance. Robertson, who finished his career with a 25.7 scoring average and 9.5 assists per game, was inducted into the Basketball Hall of Fame in 1980. This card is subject to the typical condition obstacles associated with the issue.

1961 Fleer #43 Jerry West

This is the only recognized rookie card of one of basketball's greatest shooters. Known for his ability to come through with the big shot, *Mr. Clutch* led the Los Angeles Lakers to the NBA Finals nine times in a 14-year span. When it was all said and done, West finished his career with a 27-point per game average and he was selected to the All-Star team in each of his 13 seasons. When he retired, West held the highest playoff scoring average in the history of the NBA at 29.1 points per game. He also became one of only three players to reach the 25,000-point mark. During the 1971-72 season, West helped lead the Lakers to the best record ever at 69-13, a record that was later broken by Michael Jordan and the Chicago Bulls at 72-10. During that season, West averaged 25.8 points per game and led the league in assists per game (9.7) en route to the NBA title. West was also named to the All-NBA First Team 10 times in his career. It is no wonder why the NBA used West's dribbling silhouette as part of their logo. This card is one of four keys in the 1961-62 Fleer set and is subject to the typical condition obstacles associated with the issue.

1968 Topps Test #5 John Havlicek

This is one of the keys to a very scarce test issue and the most valuable rookie card of a man they called *Hondo*. John Havlicek is considered by many to be the best sixth man in the history of the game. This former All-American from Ohio State led his team to the NCAA title in 1960, alongside teammates Jerry Lucas and Bob Knight. As a professional, Havlicek would play each of his 16 seasons with the Boston Celtics. During that time, he became the first player ever to score at least 1,000 points per year for 16 consecutive seasons. Havlicek, a 13-time NBA All-Star, won eight NBA championships in his career and finished with a total of 26,395 points (20.8 points per game). His finest scoring season came in 1970-71 when he scored 28.9 points per game. Havlicek, a prolific scorer, was also an excellent defensive player. Havlicek showcased his quick reflexes by stealing an inbounds pass with five seconds left in Game 7 of the 1965 Eastern Conference championship, which sealed the series for Boston. This card, which actually has Havlicek's name misspelled "Havilcek," is very scarce. It measures approximately 2½" by 3½", and many of the cards in the set suffer from poor centering.

1969 Topps #25 Lew Alcindor

This is the only recognized rookie card of the most prolific offensive player in NBA history. Lew Alcindor, later known as Kareem Abdul-Jabbar, perfected the sky hook, an offensive weapon that no one could stop during his reign. At 7'2", Jabbar would use his body to shield this graceful shot as he tossed the ball from his outstretched arm and into the basket. As an amateur, Jabbar led the UCLA Bruins to an unreal 88-2 record and 3 NCAA Championships. The Bruins, led by the big man, won an unimaginable 72 consecutive games during this run. As a pro, Jabbar won six NBA titles as a member of the Milwaukee Bucks and Los Angeles Lakers. This former NBA Rookie of the Year (1970) won six league MVPs (a record), two NBA Finals MVPs and was named to the All-Star team 19 times. After 20 seasons in the NBA, Jabbar retired in 1989. He was inducted into the Basketball Hall of Fame in 1995. This oversized card, measuring approximately 2½" by 4¹¹/₁₆", is vulnerable to more general wear due to its size, is difficult to find well-centered and has a white background that can be a haven for visible print defects.

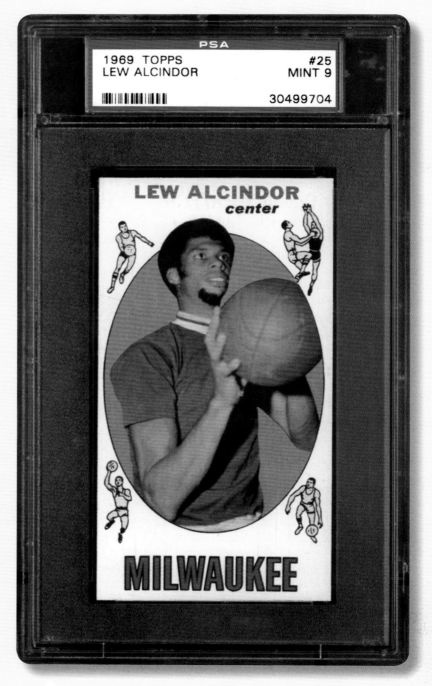

1970 Topps #123 Pete Maravich

This is the only recognized rookie card of one of the basketball's great entertainers. *Pistol Pete* was a crowd favorite. He mesmerized defenders with his incredibly quick hands and could fool just about anyone who stepped onto the court. As a collegiate player, Pete Maravich averaged a record 44.2 points per game, an average that was achieved without the benefit of the three-pointer! He also established records for single season points, career points, field goals and attempts. After a brilliant college career, Maravich went on to play 10 years in the NBA. He was named to the All-Star team for five of those seasons and led the league with 31.1 points per game in 1976-1977. During that season, Maravich scored a career-high 68 points against the New York Knicks. For his career, Maravich averaged 24.2 points per game and, more importantly, changed the game with his dazzling passes and acrobatic moves. He was inducted into the Basketball Hall of Fame in 1987. This card, like the Lew Alcindor rookie, is subject to similar condition obstacles due to its large design and narrow borders, which cause many examples to grade off-center.

1972 Topps #195 Julius Erving

This is the only recognized rookie card of one of basketball's most exciting players. *Dr. J.* was able to leap to incredible heights, dunking with power and grace long before the likes of Michael Jordan and Dominique Wilkins came along. After a short time in the ABA, Julius Erving was lured away to the NBA. In 16 total seasons (ABA and NBA combined), Erving scored 30,026 points, which was third on the career-scoring list at the time of his retirement. In fact, he was one of only five players in history to reach 30,000 points at the time of this writing. He was also named to the NBA All-Star team in each of his eleven seasons in the league. Twice named MVP of the ABA (1974 and 1976), Erving was named NBA MVP in 1981. After winning two ABA titles with the New York Knicks, Erving won his sole NBA title as a member of the Philadelphia 76ers in 1983. Erving was inducted into the basketball Hall of Fame in 1993. Due to the white borders and yellow background, this card has to contend with print defects more often than not. Keep in mind that there is a very common print dot that resides next to Erving's left elbow and its presence should not affect the overall grade of the card.

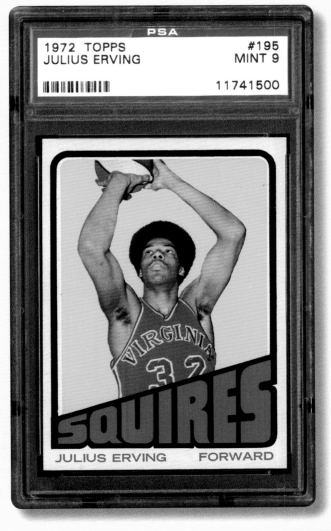

1980 Topps Larry Bird/ Magic Johnson

This is the key rookie card of the two most popular players of the 1980s. Larry Bird, a forward, and Magic Johnson, a point guard, had a competitive fire between them that started at the college level. After Bird led Indiana State to the NCAA Finals during the 1978-79 season, Magic and Michigan State ruined Bird's dream season by defeating Indiana for the title. From that point forward, the rivalry began. Bird would lead the Boston Celtics to three titles while Magic would lead the Los Angeles Lakers to five. Bird, a former NBA Rookie of the Year (1980), won three MVP Awards and was named to 12 All-Star teams in his career. Magic, whose career shared many similarities to Bird's, was named to the NBA All-Star team and was the league's MVP an equal number of times. Both men, of course, were inducted into the Basketball Hall of Fame, Bird in 1998 and Magic in 2002. Beyond their numbers and accomplishments, these two men were able to take the NBA to a new level of popularity. This three-player card, one that also includes Julius Erving, is notorious for having black print defects scattered across the front and is fairly difficult to find perfectly centered.

1992 UD #1 Shaquille O'Neal

This is the most popular rookie card of the most dominant center of the modern era. Before he laced up his shoes and walked out onto the NBA floor, everyone knew that Shaq was going to be something special. At 7'1", 300-plus pounds, Shaq moves like a small guard with the force of a small tank. Never before has the NBA seen such athleticism and coordination from a man of his size. After spending a few seasons with the Orlando Magic, Shaq headed to Los Angeles to play for the Lakers and helped them to three NBA titles. Shaq would then travel back to Florida to play for Miami where he helped bring the Heat their first NBA championship. This 1999-2000 NBA MVP was named Finals MVP three times as a member of the Lakers. Shaq, a former NBA Rookie of the Year (1992), has been selected to the All-Star team for 14 consecutive seasons. He averages 25.5 points and 11.5 rebounds per game over the course of his career – a career that appears to still be going strong as a member of the Phoenix Suns. Popular on and off the court, Shaq has a magnetic personality. This card, one that features a high-gloss surface and black edges, is very susceptible to wear.

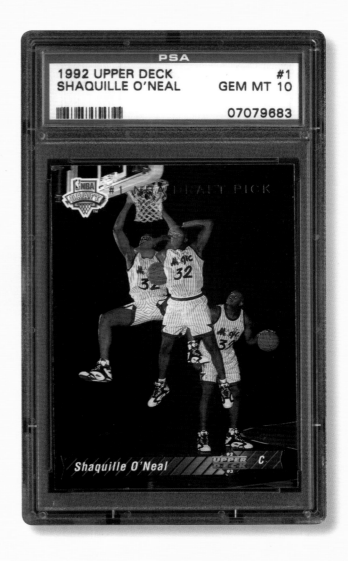

1996 Topps Chrome #138 Kobe Bryant

This is the most popular rookie card of the most devastating offensive and defensive machine since Michael Jordan. Kobe Bryant, like Shaq, was seemingly destined for greatness. As the first guard to ever be drafted straight out of high school, Bryant matured quickly in the NBA. From his high-flying dunks to his long distance bombs from all over the court, opposing players cringe at the thought of being asked to defend this guy. Along with Shaq and with a few years under his belt, Bryant helped lead the Los Angeles Lakers to three consecutive NBA titles from 2000-2002. Bryant has also been named to the All-Star team 10 times and was the back-to-back NBA scoring champion in 2006-2007, which included a career-high scoring average of 35.4 in 2006. Considered to be, perhaps, the best all-around player in the game, Bryant has also been named to seven All-Defensive Teams as either a 1st or 2nd Team selection. At only 29 years old, Bryant should have many more productive years ahead of him and a shot at several career records when it is all said and done. This high-gloss, chrome card is very susceptible to surface scratching and wear.

Football Cards

1933 SPORT KINGS #4
RED GRANGE   MINT 9
S. IRELAND COLLECTION
50005553

SPORT KINGS GUM

RED GRANGE

1933 Goudey Sport Kings #4 Red Grange

This is one of the best looking cards in a classic set, full of great athletes. Red Grange, with his extraordinary running ability, was able to help take football to a new level after a spectacular career at the University of Illinois. Grange, a three-time All-American, was known as *The Galloping Ghost* throughout his career. His tremendous speed and deceptive moves made him the biggest draw in the sport during the 1920s. As a junior in college, Grange ran for four touchdowns in the first 12 minutes against Michigan, totaling over 250 yards. As a senior, he graced the cover of *Time* in 1925, a year when Grange had his best overall performance. In one game, Grange ran for 363 yards on 36 carries. In his day, Grange piled up endorsements as the man who put football on the map. Grange was inducted into the Pro Football Hall of Fame in 1963. This card is subject to two major condition obstacles: edge toning and ink bleeding. When fresh, wet sheets of Goudey cards were laid on top of each other at the factory, the moist ink stuck to the reverse of the cards directly above. Unless the bleeding is severe, the presence of this defect should not hinder the grade significantly.

1933 Goudey Sport Kings #6 Jim Thorpe

This is one of the most visually appealing cards in the incredibly popular 1933 Goudey Sport King set. In 1950, Jim Thorpe was voted the greatest male athlete of the first half of the 20th Century. Here, Thorpe is depicted as a football player in a set that contains great athletes from a variety of sports. Thorpe was an All-American halfback at Carlisle in back-to-back years, 1911 and 1912. In 1915, the Canton Bulldogs signed Thorpe as a player and coach for $250 per game, an unheard of figure for a football player at that time. Thorpe was a huge attraction and helped propel football to the next level. The Bulldogs were dominant during the next few seasons with Thorpe on their side. Thorpe would end up playing for several teams during his career. In 1920, Thorpe became the first president of the American Professional Football Association, which later became the NFL. This American sport icon, who opened the doors for future two-sport stars like Bo Jackson, Deion Sanders and Brian Jordan, was inducted into the Pro Football Hall of Fame in 1963. This card is subject to the typical condition obstacles associated with the issue, including ink bleeding and toning along the edges.

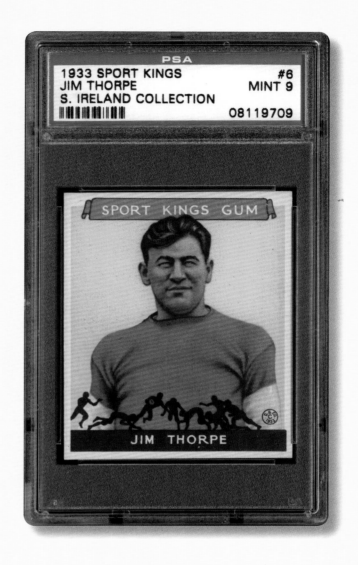

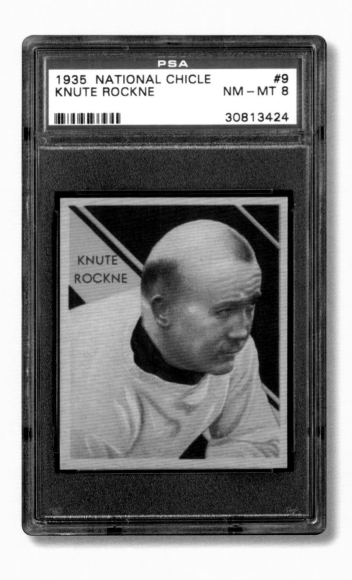

1935 National Chicle #9 Knute Rockne

This is one of the keys to an incredibly difficult set. Knute Rockne is simply the most popular coaching figure in football history – a history filled with several great coaches. While Rockne was known for being a perfectionist and the ultra-disciplinarian, his motivational speeches are what made him famous, and they came in all forms. After trailing at the half in one game, a disgusted Rockne stormed into the Notre Dame locker room with his players expecting a serious verbal lashing. Instead, Rockne calmed down and simply said, "Let's go girls." Needless to say, The Irish went on to victory. His famous "Win one for the Gipper" speech that inspired Notre Dame to upset Army, is one of his most memorable orations. Rockne finished his career with an astonishing 105-12-5 record, which included six National Championships (1919, 1920, 1924, 1927, 1929 and 1930) and five undefeated seasons. In 1931, right in the prime of his coaching career, Rockne perished in a plane crash. He was inducted into the College Football Hall of Fame in 1951. This card measures approximately 2⅜" by 2⅞" and it is, without question, one of the toughest on the list with poor centering as the most noteworthy condition obstacle.

1948 Leaf #1 Sid Luckman

This is not only a key rookie card, but it's the first card in a very tough set. Sid Luckman, with a powerful arm and mind, led the Chicago Bears to four NFL titles and five division championships during his career (1939-1950) and became the first successful T-formation quarterback. The Bears simply dominated teams during the 1940s. With Luckman's vast array of offensive plays, the Bears would absolutely destroy the opposition. They mauled the Washington Redskins 73-0 in the 1940 Championship Game. In a 56-7 victory, Luckman threw seven touchdown passes against the New York Giants during his 1943 MVP campaign. Later that same year, Luckman would throw for 276 yards, including five touchdown passes, in a 41-21 victory over the Washington Redskins in the championship game. For all of his success on the field, Luckman was inducted into the Pro Football Hall of Fame in 1965. This card measures approximately 2⅜" by 2⅞" and is subject to two major condition obstacles: very poor centering and print defects that riddle the bright-colored background behind the image of Luckman. There is also a wide variance in eye-appeal with this issue due to an inconsistent printing process. In addition, there are several color variations throughout the set.

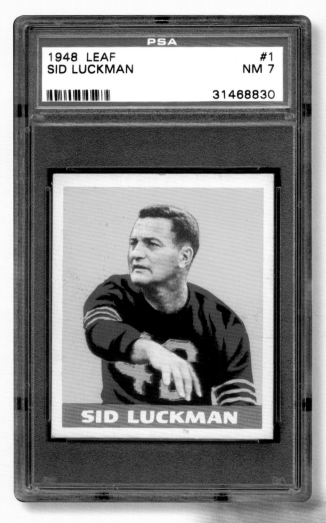
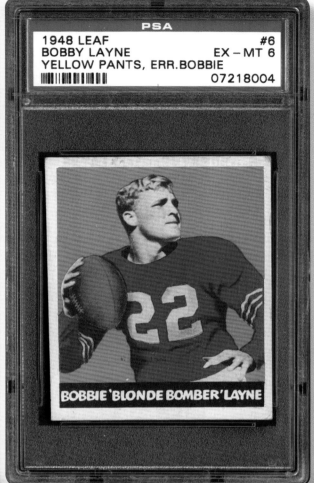

1948 Leaf #6 Bobby Layne

This is the only recognized rookie card of the *Blonde Bomber,* and it resides in a very difficult set. After a brilliant college career at Texas, setting several career passing records, Bobby Layne became known for his clutch drives late in regulation as a pro for four different teams, but his greatest success came as a member of the Detroit Lions. In fact, Layne's last-second touchdown pass during the 1953 title game gave his team the championship. Layne would lead Detroit to four division titles and three NFL titles during the 1950s. By the time his career was over, Layne threw for 26,768 yards and 196 touchdowns. At the time of his retirement, Layne was the all-time leader in attempts, completions, passing yards and passing touchdowns. In addition, many people forget that Layne, one of football's great all-time quarterbacks, also kicked field goals on occasion. Layne was inducted into the Pro Football Hall of Fame in 1967. This card, like all 1948 Leafs, is subject to a few major condition obstacles and this issue is one of the toughest on the list to find in high-grade.

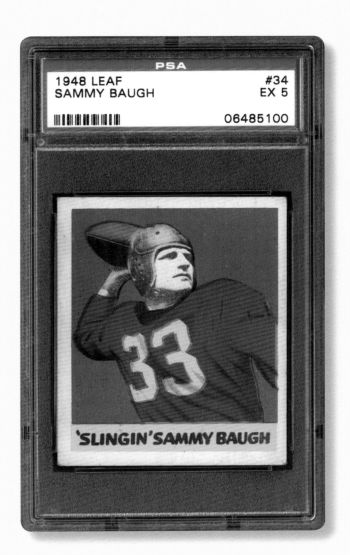

1948 Leaf #34 Sammy Baugh

This is the key card in the 1948 Leaf set and an important rookie card of a quarterback legend. In a set that contains a hoard of key rookie cards such as those featuring Hall of Fame legends Leo Nomellini and Chuck Bednarik, this card is the most desirable of all. After college, Sammy Baugh signed with the St. Louis Cardinals as a third baseman but quickly changed his mind and set his sights on football. *Slingin' Sammy* became one of the most accurate passers of all-time. He would lead the league in passing six times, using a combination of short passes and long bombs. Baugh led the Washington Redskins to five championship games and was one of the charter members of the Pro Football Hall of Fame in 1963. Like several other football players of the era, Baugh was extremely versatile. In 1943, Baugh led the league in passing, punting and interceptions! As a punter, Baugh is still considered one of the best ever. In fact, his single season punting average of 51.4 yards per punt remains the record today. He finished his career with 21,886 passing yards and 187 touchdowns. While Baugh does have a Bowman rookie card, this Leaf issue is considered slightly more desirable. This card is subject to the typical condition obstacles associated with the issue, including poor centering, print defects, toning and inconsistent print quality.

1950 Bowman #1 Doak Walker

This is one of two keys to the 1950 Bowman set, along with the Otto Graham rookie card. Doak Walker, a former All-American at Southern Methodist University, was a player with many talents. He lettered in three different sports: baseball, basketball and football. On the football team, he played running back, defensive back, place kicker and punter, in addition to other positions. He even returned kicks and threw passes on occasion. Awarded the Heisman Trophy in 1948 as a junior, Walker's abilities on the football field did not go unnoticed. As a professional, Walker made an immediate impact with the Detroit Lions even though many scouts felt he was too small for the league. Walker was named the NFL Rookie of the Year and led the league in scoring, a feat he would repeat in 1955. During Walker's brief six year career in the league (1950-1955), the Lions won three division titles and two NFL championships (1952 and 1953). This five-time Pro Bowl selection was inducted into the Pro Football Hall of Fame in 1986. This card measures approximately 2¹/₁₆" by 2½" and is terribly difficult to locate in high-grade due to poor centering and general wear issues, being the first card in the set and subject to much handling abuse.

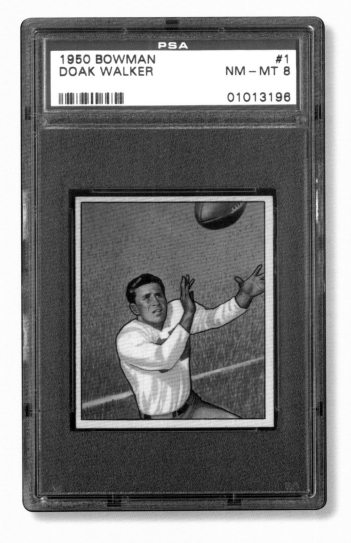

1950 Bowman #5 Y.A. Tittle

This card, one of the keys to the 1950 Bowman set, features one of the game's greatest quarterbacks. Y.A. Tittle, a number-one draft pick in 1948, never won a championship but he had an outstanding career. As the quarterback for the Baltimore Colts, San Francisco 49ers and New York Giants, Tittle would pass for 33,070 yards and 242 touchdowns. Tittle would also be named Player of the Year twice in his career, winning the award in back-to-back seasons (1962 and 1963). During those MVP campaigns, Tittle would throw for 33 and 36 touchdowns respectively, including one game when he threw for seven touchdowns against the Washington Redskins in 1962. After being traded to New York and labeled "over the hill" by the media, Tittle would lead the Giants to three Eastern Division titles. This six-time Pro Bowl selection was inducted into the Pro Football Hall of Fame in 1971. This card, like most Bowman cards of the era, is subject to three main condition obstacles: poor centering, reverse staining and print defects in the sky background.

1950 Bowman #45 Otto Graham

This important rookie card is one of the keys to the 1950 Bowman set. Otto Graham was the starting quarterback for the Cleveland Browns from 1946-1955. Even though Graham's passing numbers are very impressive, it was his ability to win that made him a football legend. In a brief 10-year career, Graham led the Browns to six division and three NFL Championship crowns. During that time, the Browns compiled an amazing record of 105-17-4. Graham was named All-League in 9 of his 10 seasons and was twice named the NFL MVP. His finest title-game performance came in 1954 when Graham threw for three touchdowns and ran for three more in a 56-10 destruction of Detroit. When his career came to a close, Graham finished with 23,584 yards passing, 174 passing touchdowns and 44 rushing touchdowns before being inducted into the Pro Football Hall of Fame in 1965. This card is subject to the typical condition obstacles of the issue, including staining along the reverse that tends to penetrate the cardboard and downgrade the card.

1950 Topps Felt Backs Joe Paterno

This is the only trading card to depict Joe Paterno as a player, and it is the key to the difficult 1950 Topps Felt Backs set. This tiny card, which measures approximately 7/8" by 1 7/16," features the legendary and popular Penn State football coach as a player during his time at Brown University. Each card in the set features a star college player laid against one of five different color backgrounds blue, brown, green, red or yellow. The reverse of each card features a small felt pennant, representing the school of the player depicted on the front. While there are 100 different players included in the set, there are an additional 25 color variations. The set features four players who eventually gained entry into the Pro Football Hall of Fame, including Lou Creekmur, Leo Nomellini, Ernie Stautner and Doak Walker, but Paterno remains the key. Since 1966, Paterno has guided Penn State to 22 bowl victories, the most of any coach in college football history. Paterno also holds the distinction of being the only coach to have won each of the four major bowls, Fiesta, Orange, Rose and Sugar at least once as well as the Cotton Bowl. Paterno, who won two NCAA Championships (1982 and 1986), was inducted into the College Football Hall of Fame in 2007. This card, which has a very fragile blue border and background, is an extreme football card rarity.

1951 Bowman #4 Norm Van Brocklin

This is the key to the 1951 Bowman set and it features a legendary quarterback. Norm Van Brocklin was not the most graceful, scrambling quarterback the game has ever seen, but could he ever throw. In his 12 years at quarterback, Van Brocklin led the league in passing three times, throwing for a total of 23,611 yards and 173 touchdowns. He was also one of the league's best punters, leading the league twice in that department, averaging over 40 yards per punt for his career. Van Brocklin would win NFL championships with the Los Angeles Rams and the Philadelphia Eagles in 1951 and 1960, respectively. In 1951, in one of the best performances of his career, Van Brocklin threw for 554 yards. The 1960 championship was especially satisfying for Van Brocklin as he led a perennial loser to the title after the Rams sent him packing. For his efforts, Van Brocklin was named NFL MVP that year. This nine-time Pro Bowl selection was inducted into the Pro Football Hall of Fame in 1971. This card measures approximately 2 1/6" by 3 1/8" and is subject to the typical condition obstacles associated with early Bowman football issues, such as poor centering and reverse staining.

1951 Bowman #20 Tom Landry

This is the only recognized rookie card of legendary coach Tom Landry. Landry was a solid defensive back, finishing with 32 interceptions in only 80 games as a pro. While he is depicted on this beautiful Bowman card as a player, it was his innovative coaching that made him famous. For 29 straight seasons, Landry called the shots for the Dallas Cowboys with his unshakable demeanor along the sidelines. During his reign, the Cowboys won 13 Division titles, five NFC titles and two Super Bowls in 1971 and 1977. After a horrific start in 1960 and a few more subpar seasons, Landry and the Cowboys began an unprecedented run of excellence. From 1966-1985, for 20 consecutive seasons, the Cowboys would finish better than .500. This is, quite possibly, Landry's most impressive accomplishment. His overall record, regular season and postseason record combined, was 270-178-6 during his incredible career. He was inducted into the Pro Football Hall of Fame in 1990. This card, while not quite as valuable as his 1952 Bowman Large and Small issues, is his official rookie. Like most Bowmans of the era, this card is tough to find well-centered, absent reverse staining and print defects.

1952 Bowman Large and Small #1 Norm Van Brocklin

This is the first card in one of the most important football sets ever produced. Norm Van Brocklin had the uncanny ability to perform under pressure. In the 1951 NFL Championship game, he threw a famous 73-yard bomb to receiver Tom Fears to win the game and defeat the Cleveland Browns. That year, Van Brocklin didn't even lead his team in passing, despite some great single-game performances. This was a result of the coach's decision to platoon Van Brocklin with Bob Waterfield. After his retirement, Van Brocklin decided to try his hand at coaching. In 1961, he signed to become the head coach of the Minnesota Vikings and, in 1968, Van Brocklin became the head coach of the Atlanta Falcons. In both cases, the results were mediocre at best but he did help Atlanta to its first winning season during his tenure. The Large version measures approximately 2½" by 3¾" while the Small version measures approximately 2¹/₁₆" by 3¹/₁₈". This tough, short-printed card is one of the toughest football cards on the list to find in high-grade. Being the #1 card in the set, it was subject to substantial abuse over the years.

1952 Bowman Large and Small #16 Frank Gifford

This is the only recognized rookie card of this all-purpose football great. Like most players from the era, Frank Gifford played both sides of the ball, and he did it extremely well. After being named All-American at USC after his senior year, Gifford was selected in the first round by the New York Giants and went on to have an outstanding career in the NFL. This eight-time Pro Bowl selection was named the NFL's Player of the Year in 1956 when he helped lead the Giants to a league championship over the Chicago Bears. On the offensive end, Gifford amassed 367 total receptions, helping him reach 9,862 total yards. One fact that really helps illustrate Gifford's great versatility as a player was that he was selected to the Pro Bowl at three different positions during his career. Gifford was inducted into the Pro Football Hall of Fame in 1977. This card, which resides in one of the most important football sets of all time, is difficult to find well-centered. Both the Large and Small versions are subject to similar condition obstacles.

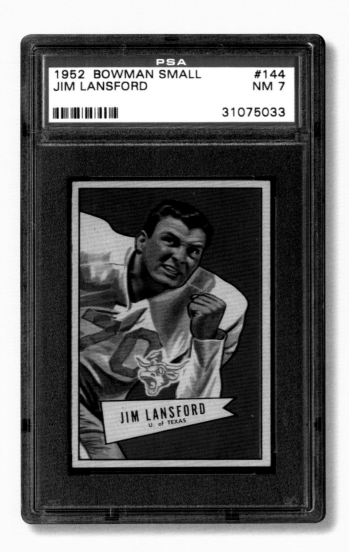

1952 Bowman Large and Small #144 Jim Lansford SP

This card is the most notorious condition rarity in the football card hobby. Along with the 1952 Topps #1 Andy Pafko and a mere handful of other cards, this is one of the only non-star cards to make this prestigious list. This is the final card in, perhaps, the most beautiful football card issue ever produced. The large design, detailed artistry and bold colors make this Jim Lansford card as eye-appealing as it is difficult. Lansford, a tackle for the Dallas Texans in the NFL following his collegiate career at the University of Texas, is depicted with fierce intensity as he charges down the field. This card captures the spirit of the game and also exemplifies the visual strength of this classic football set. This tough, short print was subject to great abuse through the years from handling and storage, much like the #1 Norm Van Brocklin of the same set.

1954 Bowman George Blanda #23

This is the only recognized rookie card of the great quarterback and the key to the 1954 Bowman set. When it comes to longevity, George Blanda is football's equivalent to Nolan Ryan in baseball or Gordie Howe in hockey, playing for an amazing 26 seasons as a quarterback and place kicker. By the time he retired, Blanda was the all-time leader in points with 2,002 after playing in 340 games. As a quarterback, he threw for a total of 26,920 yards and 236 touchdowns, which included seven in one game in 1961. As a kicker, Blanda connected on 335 field goals and 943 extra points. Blanda will probably be best remembered for his 1970 performance with the Oakland Raiders. During that season and at the age of 43, Blanda had a string of five consecutive games with a last-second score to either win or tie the game (four wins and one tie.) He led the Raiders to the AFC Championship Game, becoming the oldest quarterback to do so. Blanda retired at the age of 48, just before the 1976 season. In 1981, he was inducted into the Pro Football Hall of Fame. This 1954 Bowman issue, measuring approximately 2½" by 3¾" is not quite as difficult as some of the other 1950s football sets, but is difficult to find well-centered in PSA NM-MT 8 or better condition.

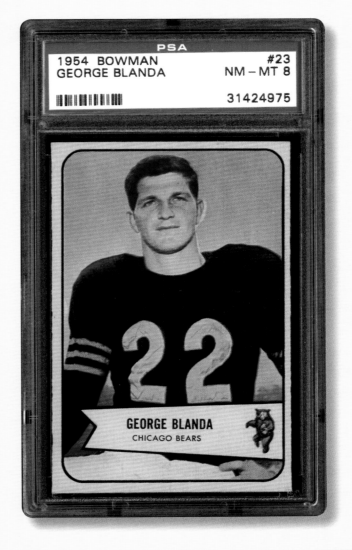

1955 Topps All-American #37
Jim Thorpe

This is the key football card of, perhaps, the greatest pure athlete of the 20th Century. Jim Thorpe, who won Olympic gold medals in the pentathlon and decathlon, signed with the Canton Bulldogs in 1915. While Thorpe did play professional baseball and basketball, football is where he made the biggest impact as a professional. Thorpe, due to his amazing athletic ability, was extremely versatile on the field. He could pass, throw, kick and tackle with anyone in the game. He helped lead the Bulldogs to championships in 1916, 1917 and 1919. More importantly, his popularity helped in taking the team's attendance to record levels, bringing increased attention to the sport. He even helped coach the team, in addition to playing, between 1921 and 1923. Thorpe was inducted into the Pro Football Hall of Fame in 1963. This card is part of the one of the most visually appealing card issues on the entire list. It measures approximately 2⅝" by 3⅝". The card, while not quite as difficult as some of the earlier Bowman and Leaf issues, is tough to find well-centered and absent of distracting print defects.

1955 Topps All-American #68 Four Horsemen

This is one of the keys to the 1955 Topps All-American set and one of the most popular cards in the entire hobby. Knute Rockne, legendary coach for Notre Dame University, was a believer in the brains over brawn theory on the field. The Four Horsemen, which made up the backfield for the Fighting Irish, epitomized Rockne's philosophy and became a dominant force. Elmer Layden, Jim Crowley, Harry Stuhldreher and Don Miller made up the fearsome foursome, nicknamed after the four horsemen of the apocalypse by Grantland Rice, a sportswriter for the *New York Herald Tribune*. Despite being smaller than most of their opponents, these four helped lead their team to the Rose Bowl in 1925, defeating Stanford 27-10. In fact, Notre Dame went a perfect 10-0 that year. During the three years these four teammates played together, Notre Dame only lost twice in 30 games, both times falling to Nebraska. This card is difficult to find well-centered and, due to the large amount of white and yellow on the face of the card, print defects are very detectable.

1955 Topps All-American #97 Don Hutson

This is the only vintage issue to ever feature the greatest receiver of the 1930s and 1940s. At the beginning, many football scouts questioned Don Hutson's ability to succeed at the professional level due to his lanky build. The former All-American from Alabama quickly erased any doubt. As a member of the Green Bay Packers, Hutson led the league in receiving in eight of his 11 seasons. In fact, at the time of his retirement, Hutson held 18 NFL records. This two-time NFL MVP (1941 and 1942) finished his career with 99 touchdowns, 488 career receptions and 7,991 receiving yards. Hutson's career touchdown mark stood for more than 40 years, and his career reception total was nearly double that of his closest rival. Hutson also played kicker and safety, intercepting 30 passes in his career. With his unique combination of kicking and receiving talents, Hutson would lead the league in scoring for five straight seasons (1941-45). Hutson was inducted into the Pro Football Hall of Fame in 1963. While Jerry Rice, statistically, is considered the greatest receiver in NFL history, many experts feel Hutson was more dominating during his era. This card, which is a tough short print, is difficult to find well-centered.

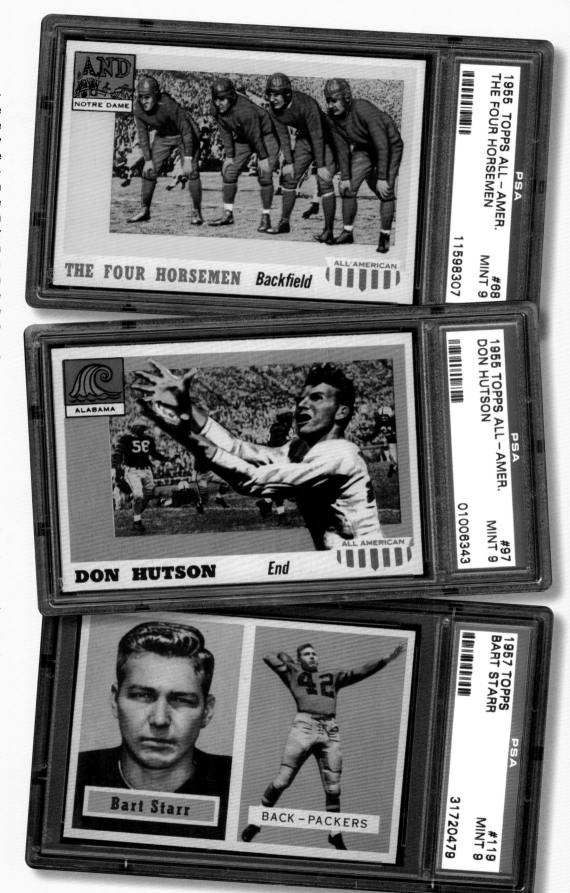

1957 Topps #119 Bart Starr

This is the only recognized rookie card of this perennial winner and one of three keys to the 1957 Topps set. From 1956-1971, Bart Starr would lead the Green Bay Packers to six division, five NFL (1961, 1962, 1965, 1966 and 1967) and two Super Bowl titles (1967 and 1968). Moreover, Starr was named MVP of Super Bowls I and II. During the regular season, Starr was named MVP once, in 1966, and was a three-time passing leader. Starr threw for 24,718 yards and 152 touchdowns in his career, which included an impressive 57.4 completion percentage. Perhaps his most impressive accomplishment is the fact that after losing to Philadelphia in 1960, the Packers never lost another postseason game with Starr as their quarterback. After his playing days, Starr served as an assistant coach and then the head coach of the Packers for several years. This four-time Pro Bowl selection was inducted into the Pro Football Hall of Fame in 1977. This card, which resides in the tough high-number series in the set, measures approximately 2½" by 3½" and is very difficult to find in high-grade with poor centering, print defects and lackluster eye-appeal as the leading condition obstacles.

1957 Topps #138 Johnny Unitas

This is the only recognized rookie card of the legendary quarterback and one of the keys to the 1957 Topps set. Believe it or not, Johnny Unitas struggled to make it into the NFL when he was cut by the Pittsburgh Steelers in 1955. After being given a chance with the Baltimore Colts as a free agent in 1956, Unitas made the most of his opportunity. By the time his career ended, Unitas held virtually every major quarterback record. Unitas threw for 40,239 yards, 290 touchdowns, completed 2,830 passes, passed for 300 or more yards 26 times and had a 47-game streak with at least one touchdown pass. His most memorable moment came in 1958 when Unitas led the Baltimore Colts to a title. He made a late drive in regulation to tie the game and then, in sudden death overtime, he drove the Colts down the field again for the 23-17 win. This three-time NFL MVP (1959, 1964 and 1967) and 10-time Pro Bowl selection was inducted into the Pro Football Hall of Fame in 1979. This card, which is tough to find in high-grade, is subject to the typical condition obstacles associated with the issue.

1957 Topps #151
Paul Hornung

This is the only recognized rookie card of this former number-one draft pick and Hall of Fame member. Paul Hornung was a multi-talented athlete who could do just about anything on the field. At Notre Dame, Hornung won the Heisman Trophy in 1956 as a quarterback but showed amazing overall versatility. He could throw, kick, catch and run, all with excellence. At the professional level with the Green Bay Packers, Hornung was a fine halfback and kicker. In fact, his point total of 176 in 1960 remains the NFL record despite the league adding more regular season games since his historic performance. He would lead the league in scoring three years in a row, winning two NFL MVP Awards in 1960 and 1961. In addition, Hornung is one of only a handful of players to win the Heisman and NFL MVP. Hornung set the record for most points in a championship game with 19, a record achieved against the New York Giants in a 37-0 demolition in 1961. This two-time Pro Bowl selection was inducted into the Pro Football Hall of Fame in 1986. This card resides in the tough, high-number series and it subject to the typical condition obstacles associated with the issue.

1958 Topps #62 Jim Brown

This is the only recognized rookie card of football's most feared fullback of all time. After lettering in three different sports at Syracuse (basketball, football and lacrosse), Jim Brown was selected by the Cleveland Browns as their number-one pick. This three-time NFL MVP (1957, 1958 and 1965) simply turned defensive lines into Swiss cheese from 1957-1965. This former 1957 NFL Rookie of the Year would lead the NFL in rushing in all but one year during his entire career. He also rushed for 1,000 or more yards in seven seasons despite the fact that there were only 12 games on the schedule during the early stages of his career. Brown retired at the age of 30 after a mere nine seasons, but remains the all-time leader in yards per carry with 5.2. No running back in history with 1,000 carries or more has challenged that mark. This 9-time Pro Bowl selection was inducted into the Pro Football Hall of Fame in 1971. After his playing days, Brown decided to try his hand at acting. His most memorable role came in the 1967 movie *The Dirty Dozen* alongside Charles Bronson, Lee Marvin and Donald Sutherland. This card, one that is found often with print defects, is also susceptible to poor centering and reverse chipping along the red edges.

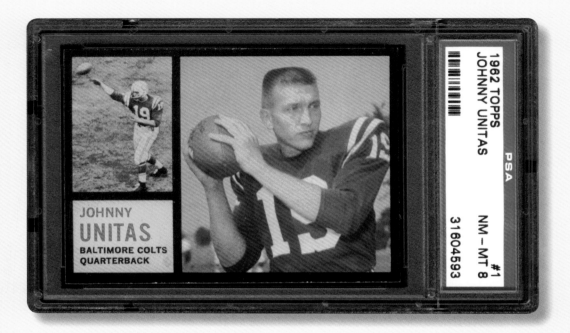

1962 Topps #1 Johnny Unitas

This is the first card in the super tough, black-bordered 1962 Topps set. This former Louisville Cardinal was drafted in the 9th round by Pittsburgh, 102nd overall. Johnny Unitas was quickly released by the franchise and never given an opportunity to throw a single pass for the Steelers. Do you think the Steelers regret that decision? Unitas went on to become one the NFL's greatest quarterbacks and he was certainly the best of his era. Beyond all of his accomplishments and tremendous statistics, Unitas was an inspiration for athletes and fans alike. Unitas did not possess some of the physical gifts that many of his contemporaries had, but he never gave up and maximized his potential. In Super Bowl III, while he was sidelined all year with a bad arm, Unitas was brought into the game in the 4th quarter to see if he could rally his troops. While they lost the game to Joe Namath and the New York Jets, Unitas threw for more yards in one quarter than the starting quarterback did in the previous three quarters, putting the Colts on the scoreboard with their lone touchdown. This card, with its fragile black borders, is extremely tough in high-grade and is often the victim of re-coloring by card doctors.

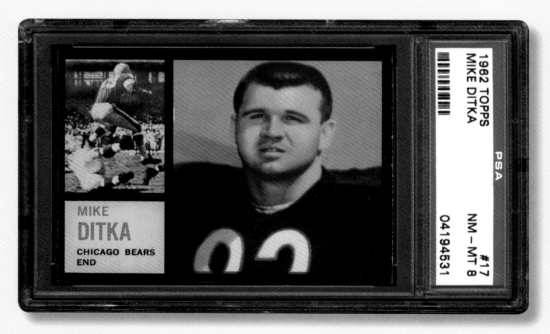

1962 Topps #17 Mike Ditka

This is the only recognized rookie card of a legendary tough guy and former Chicago Bears coach. The slicked-back hair, the mean stare and the nickname *Iron Mike* all point to one man, Mike Ditka. While most modern-era fans remember Ditka best for his leadership of the Chicago Bears, Ditka redefined the position of tight end as a player. In fact, he would become the first tight end to ever be inducted into the Pro Football Hall of Fame in 1988. Ditka's offensive numbers, coupled with his devastating blocking ability, made him a standout. Ditka finished with 427 receptions, 5,812 yards and 43 touchdowns as a pro. In 1963, Ditka led the Chicago Bears to a championship as a player and, 23 years later, he did it again as head coach for the same team. One of Ditka's last great moments as a player came in 1971 when the five-time Pro Bowl selection scored the final touchdown in the Super Bowl as a member of the Dallas Cowboys. The Cowboys went on to win that game 24-3 over the Miami Dolphins. As the head coach of the Bears for 11 years, Ditka was twice named the NFL Coach of the Year by the Associated Press (1985 and 1988). This card is subject to the typical condition obstacles associated with the issue, namely chipping and wear along the fragile black edges.

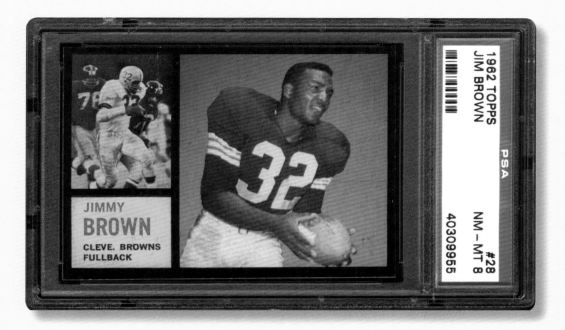

1962 Topps #28 Jim Brown

This is one of Jim Brown's most important cards, and it resides in one of the most condition sensitive sets in the hobby. This three-time Pro Bowl MVP capped off his great career with a three-touchdown performance in the 1966 game. This former 1957 NFL Rookie of the Year averaged more than 100 yards rushing per game and remains to be the only player in history to do so. Despite leaving the game at such a young age, Brown finished his career with 12,312 yards rushing and 262 receptions for 15,459 total yards. Amazingly, with all the physical contact and punishment absorbed at that position, Brown never missed a game in his entire career. Brown's 1963 season rushing record of 1,863 yards stood for two decades. He also rushed for 106 touchdowns in his career and caught 20 more. This black-bordered card, one of the most valuable cards in the set, is subject to the typical condition obstacles for the issue, including chipping along the black borders.

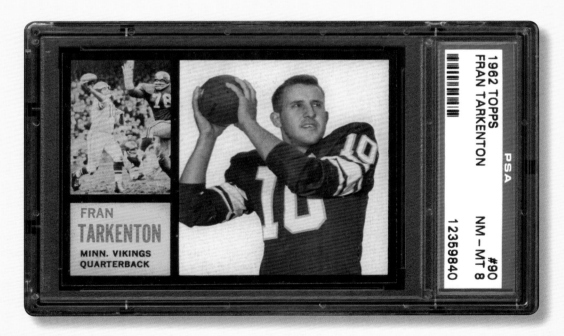

1962 Topps #90 Fran Tarkenton

This is the only recognized rookie card of one of the NFL's most prolific passers. It didn't take long for Fran Tarkenton to make an impact on the field. In his very first game in 1961, Tarkenton threw four touchdown passes for the Minnesota Vikings. By the time his career came to a close, Tarkenton threw for more yards than any other quarterback in NFL history. He finished with 6,467 attempts, 3,686 completions, 47,003 yards passing and 342 touchdowns. These were all records at the time of his retirement. Even though Tarkenton amassed tremendous passing statistics, he was probably best known for his scrambling ability. Tarkenton used his quick feet to rush for 3,674 yards and 32 touchdowns. This nine-time Pro Bowl selection, who also played for the New York Giants, was inducted into the Pro Football Hall of Fame in 1986. While Tarkenton led the Minnesota Vikings to the Super Bowl three times during his final years, he never came away with a victory in the big game. After his playing days were over, Tarkenton did enjoy some success on television, which included a key hosting role on the hit show *That's Incredible*. This card is subject to the typical condition obstacles for the issue, including chipping along the black edges.

1965 Topps #122 Joe Namath

This card is considered one of the true classics of the hobby and is the only recognized rookie of *Broadway Joe*, a man who may have been even more popular off the field. This card is, arguably, the most recognizable football card in the entire hobby. Joe Namath is best remembered for his guaranteed win in Super Bowl III when his team was a near 20-point underdog against the Baltimore Colts. Namath's New York Jets went on to defeat the Colts in a major upset 16-7 and the great quarterback was named MVP after passing for 209 yards. One year earlier, in 1967, Namath became the first quarterback to amass 4,000 passing yards in a season. Despite his constant battle with injuries, Namath finished his career with 27,663 passing yards and 173 touchdowns. This former 1965 AFL Rookie of the Year and 1974 NFL Comeback Player of the Year was inducted into the Pro Football Hall of Fame in 1985. This card, due to its large format, measuring approximately 2½" by 4¹¹/₁₆", is subject to general wear from handling abuse and, as a result of its narrow borders, is also difficult to find well-centered. Keep in mind that some of these examples are found with a distinct print mark on his left hand. Hobbyists refer to this as the "Butterfly" variation, although it appears to have no affect on the market value of the card.

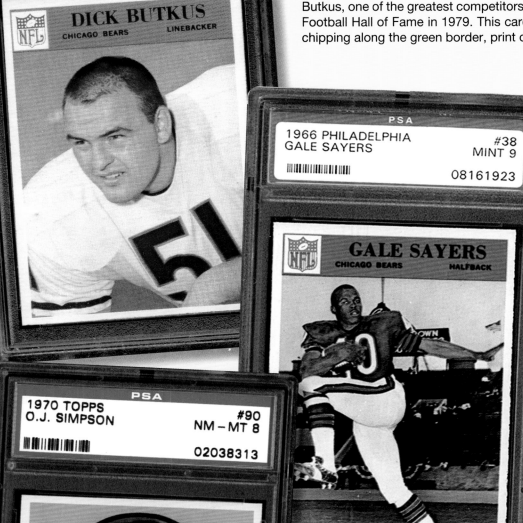

1966 Philadelphia #31 Dick Butkus

This is the only recognized rookie card of the greatest linebacker to ever play the game. If you like brutal, if you like mean, if you like tough, then you like Dick Butkus. Even his name sounds mean. Many opposing players had their life flash before their eyes when they saw Butkus coming at them with a head full of steam. His 22 interceptions and 27 fumble recoveries were NFL records at the time of his retirement in 1973. In nine total seasons, Butkus was selected to the Pro Bowl eight times, a real testament to his consistency of play. This former 1965 first-round draft pick was forced to retire after suffering a serious knee injury. Butkus, one of the greatest competitors this game has ever seen, was inducted into the Pro Football Hall of Fame in 1979. This card is very difficult to find in high-grade, with reverse chipping along the green border, print defects and poor centering common to the issue.

1966 Philadelphia #38 Gale Sayers

This is the only recognized rookie card of one of the most dazzling running backs in NFL history. Before there was Walter Payton, a man by the name of Gale Sayers wowed Chicago Bears fans with his electric running game. From his incredible punt returns to his magical moves, Sayers brought excitement to the game. In his first season as a pro, Sayers set rookie records in touchdowns (22) and points (132), making an immediate impact on the sport. This four-time Pro Bowl selection finished with 9,435 combined net yards, 4,956 rushing yards and 336 points scored. In 1969, Sayers was named the NFL Comeback Player of the Year after recovering from a serious knee injury. When his career came to an end, Sayers was the all-time leader in kickoff returns, ultimately being inducted into the Pro Football Hall of Fame in 1977. This card is subject to the typical condition obstacles associated with the issue and is very difficult to find in PSA NM-MT 8 or better condition.

1970 Topps #90 O.J. Simpson

This is the only recognized rookie card of one of football's greatest running backs, at both the collegiate and professional levels. I have to admit, I really didn't want to include this card on the list because of obvious reasons. However, O.J. Simpson's performance on the field and the importance of this card simply overpower the controversy outside of the game. This former two-time All-American and 1968 Heisman Trophy winner from USC entered the NFL with as much fanfare as anyone in the history of the sport. His breakout season came in 1973 when Simpson became the first player in history to rush for 2,000 or more yards in a season, finishing with 2,003 in only 14 games for the Buffalo Bills. In 1975, Simpson would rush for 1,817 yards and 23 touchdowns, a record number of scores at the time. Simpson would lead the league in rushing four times and amass 11,236 rushing yards in his 11-year career. Simpson would add 2,142 yards receiving and 76 career touchdowns as well. This six-time Pro Bowl Selection was inducted into the Pro Football Hall of Fame in 1985. This card, the key to the 1970 Topps set, is often found with poor centering and print defects along the face of the card, which can hinder the grade.

1971 Topps #156 Terry Bradshaw

This is the only recognized rookie card of perennial winner Terry Bradshaw. After being the first pick in the 1970 NFL Draft, Bradshaw got off to a shaky start in the pros. There were huge expectations of the Pittsburgh quarterback and it was obvious that the pressure was getting to him but, after a few seasons, Bradshaw came into his own and led his team to postseason-play year after year. Bradshaw led the Steelers to eight AFC Central titles and four Super Bowl championships during his 14-year career. He also amassed 27,989 passing yards, threw for 212 touchdowns and rushed for 32 more. This former 1978 NFL MVP was also named MVP twice in the Super Bowl (XIII and XIV). In fact, at the time of his retirement, Bradshaw held several Super Bowl passing records. This three-time Pro Bowl selection was inducted into the Pro Football Hall of Fame in 1989. Now a popular broadcaster, Bradshaw remains in the limelight. This card, surrounded by a solid red border, is susceptible to chipping and edge wear along the front.

1972 Topps #200 Roger Staubach

This is the only recognized rookie card of Dallas Cowboy legend Roger Staubach. This 1963 Heisman Trophy winner needed patience at first, serving several years in the Navy before getting an opportunity to play in the NFL in 1969, at the age of 27. After two seasons as a backup, Staubach burst onto the scene in 1971. In his first full season at quarterback, Staubach led the league in passing, was named the NFL Player of the Year and won the Super Bowl MVP. During his career, Staubach would lead the league in passing four times and lead the Cowboys to six NFC Championship games and four Super Bowls, winning two (VI and XII). At the time of his retirement, he finished his career with 22,700 yards, 153 touchdowns and the greatest career quarterback rating of all-time (83.4). Staubach was also excellent on his feet, rushing for 2,264 yards and 20 touchdowns, averaging 5.5 yards per carry. Staubach's "Hail Mary" pass in the 1975 play-off game against the Minnesota Vikings is still considered one of the most exciting plays in NFL history. This card, while not particularly difficult in high-grade, is clearly one of the keys to the set.

1976 Topps #148 Walter Payton

This is the only recognized rookie card of the running back they called *Sweetness*. Don't be fooled by the smile on his face. Walter Payton was a fierce competitor who only smiled after running over defenders on his way to the goal line. Walter Payton ran with grace, power and made it all seem effortless. During his 13 years with the Chicago Bears, Payton would set multiple rushing records. He finished his career as the all-time rushing leader with 16,726 yards, 3,838 carries and 110 rushing touchdowns. He also held the highest single game mark of 275 yards rushing. As a receiver, he caught 15 more touchdown passes, had 492 total receptions and 4,538 yards. Payton's combined net yards (21,803) made him the all-time leader in that category as well. This nine-time Pro Bowl selection and two-time NFL MVP (1977 and 1985) was inducted into the Pro Football Hall of Fame in 1993. In a show of amazing durability, Payton only missed one game his entire career, playing in 186 consecutive games after missing one during his rookie year. Payton's life ended way too soon as he died at the young age of 45 in 1999. This card, while not overly difficult in high-grade, is tough to find perfectly centered, making a PSA Gem Mint 10 example elusive.

1981 Topps #216 Joe Montana

This is the only recognized rookie card of quarterback legend Joe Montana. Montana did not possess the greatest arm strength or the quickest feet, but what he did possess was extreme intelligence and poise, leading the San Francisco 49ers to countless victories during the 1980s. When Montana and the 49ers were at their best, they didn't simply defeat their opponents, they destroyed them. During 14 seasons with San Francisco, Montana led his team to 10 postseason berths, eight division championships and four Super Bowl victories. Montana was also named Super Bowl MVP on three different occasions, which is still an NFL record. In fact, Montana set many passing records, including several in the postseason. He finished his career with 40,551 yards passing, 273 touchdown passes and an astonishing quarterback rating of 92.3. This eight-time Pro Bowl Selection was inducted into the Pro Football Hall of Fame in 2000. This card, which is not too difficult to find in high-grade, does suffer from condition obstacles such as poor centering and print defects.

1982 Topps #434 Lawrence Taylor

This is the only recognized rookie card of one of the greatest defensive players in NFL history. Lawrence Taylor's career was not controversy-free due to his repeated struggles with drug addiction during and after his playing career, but L.T. used his amazing combination of strength and speed to redefine the linebacker position as a member of the New York Giants. During a 10-year stretch with Taylor dominating on the defensive end, the Giants reached the playoffs six times and won two Super Bowls (1986 and 1990). During that 1986 season, Taylor was named the NFL MVP after recording a career-high 20.5 sacks. In fact, he became the only defensive player in history to win the NFL MVP unanimously. Taylor was also named the NFL Defensive Player of the Year for the third time in 1986. The first two awards came in 1981 and 1982. Taylor finished his career with 132.5 sacks, which ranked second all-time at the time of his retirement. This 10-time Pro Bowl selection was inducted into the Pro Football Hall of Fame in 1999. This card, while not one of the more difficult entries on the list, is very tough to locate in PSA Gem Mint 10 condition and is the most valuable card in the 1982 Topps football set.

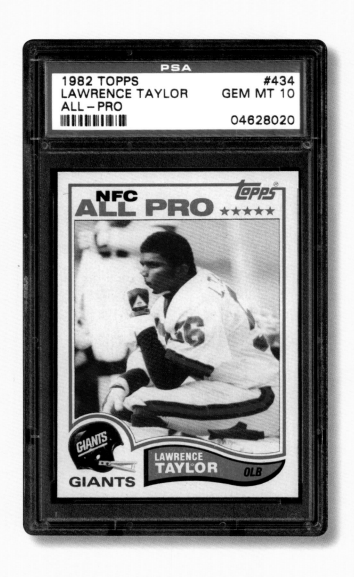

1984 Topps #63 John Elway

This is the only recognized rookie card of legendary comeback specialist John Elway. Elway knew how to rally his team to victory, using a rocket arm and excellent mobility. In fact, with 47 fourth-quarter comebacks to his credit, Elway stands alone in the record books. For seven straight seasons, Elway would pass for at least 3,000 yards and rush for 200 more. He also was named NFL MVP in 1987 and AFC Player of the Year in 1993. After eight playoff berths, 7 AFC Western Division titles and four AFC championships, Elway and the Broncos won back-to-back Super Bowls (XXXII and XXXIII). In the first Super Bowl victory, Elway led his team past the heavily-favored Green Bay Packers 31-24. In the second one, Elway captured Super Bowl MVP honors after throwing for 336 yards in a 34-19 triumph over the Atlanta Falcons. It was Elway's last game and a great way to end such a spectacular career. Elway finished with 51,475 passing yards and 300 touchdowns. This nine-time Pro Bowl selection was inducted into the Pro Football Hall of Fame in 2004. This card, one that has been heavily counterfeited, suffers from print defects which can prevent the card from reaching PSA Gem Mint 10 status.

1984 Topps #123 Dan Marino

This is the only recognized rookie card of one of the NFL's most prolific passers. Dan Marino made his presence felt immediately in the NFL. In his first season, Marino led the AFC in passing and started the Pro Bowl en route to being named the NFL Rookie of the Year. In his second year, Marino left football fans in awe and was named NFL MVP. He finished with 362 completions, 5,084 yards, 48 touchdown passes and led the Miami Dolphins to the Super Bowl. Despite losing the game, Marino set Super Bowl records for attempts and completions. When it was all said and done, Marino shattered numerous career passing records. At the time of his retirement, Marino was the most prolific passer in NFL history. He finished with 4,967 completions in 8,358 attempts, 61,361 yards passing and 420 touchdowns. One of Marino's most remarkable accomplishments might be the fact that he passed for at least 300 yards in a game on 63 different occasions. This nine-time Pro Bowl selection was inducted into the Pro Football Hall of Fame in 2005. This card, one that has been heavily counterfeited like the Elway rookie card from the same set, suffers from similar condition obstacles, making PSA Gem Mint 10's elusive.

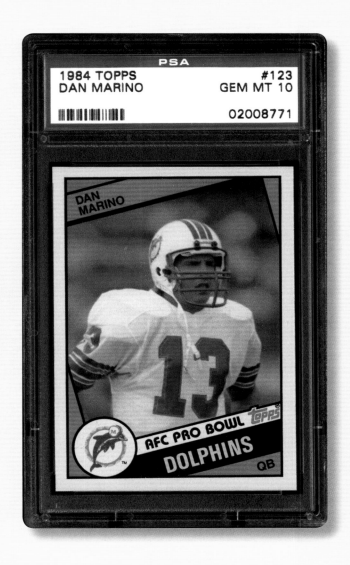

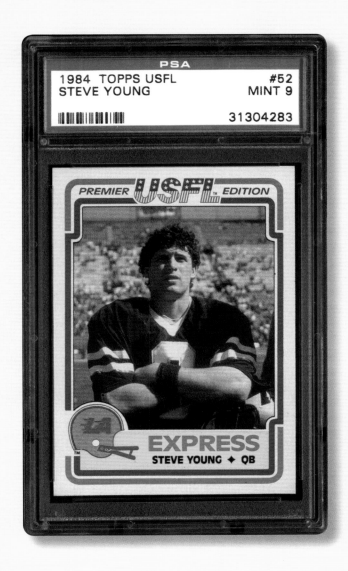

1984 Topps USFL #52 Steve Young

This is the key rookie card in one of the most significant post-1980 football issues. Some of the best players in the NFL got their start in the rival USFL, including Hall of Fame players Jim Kelly, Reggie White and Steve Young. All three have important rookie cards in this set but Young's is the most desirable. Young, after playing for Brigham Young University, signed with the Los Angeles Express of the now-defunct league. After just a couple of seasons, the USFL folded, giving Young a chance with the Tampa Bay Buccaneers. Young got off to an atrocious start and, after a couple of seasons, he was sent to San Francisco to serve as the backup quarterback to Joe Montana. In 1991, Young finally got the chance to start and the rest is history. Young went on to win six NFL passing crowns and was named NFL MVP twice (1992 and 1994). Young's finest season came in 1994 when he set a new standard for quarterbacks with a then-record 112.8 passer rating by completing 324 passes out of 461 attempts. Young compiled 3,969 total yards and 35 touchdowns that year. In his career, Young threw for 33,124 yards, 232 touchdowns and rushed for 43 more. At the time of this writing, Young still holds the all-time record for career passer rating at 96.8. This seven-time Pro Bowl Selection and three-time Super Bowl Champion was inducted into the Pro Football Hall of Fame in 2005. This card is one of the toughest post-1980 cards to locate in PSA Gem Mint 10 condition.

1986 Topps #161 Jerry Rice

This is the only recognized rookie card of the NFL's greatest wide receiver. Montana to Rice ... Young to Rice ... these are phrases that most football fans of the 1980s and 1990s are familiar with. San Francisco fans loved to hear it and opposing fans cringed at the thought. Jerry Rice holds virtually every major receiving record, both regular season and postseason, in NFL history. Rice retired as the all-time leader in many categories including, but not limited to, receptions (1,549), receiving yards (22,895), touchdown receptions (197), all-purpose yards (23,540), touchdowns (208), single-season receiving yards (1,848), seasons with 1,000 or more receiving yards (14, 11 consecutive), games with at least 100 receiving yards (76) and consecutive games with at least one reception (274). This 13-time Pro Bowl selection was part of three Super Bowl championship teams as a member of the San Francisco 49ers. For 20 years, Rice reigned as the best at his position and is on his way to the Hall of Fame. This card has to contend with one major condition obstacle, which is chipping along the green borders, making it very tough to locate true PSA Mint 9 or better specimens.

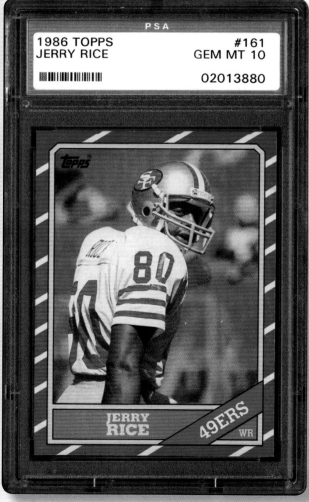

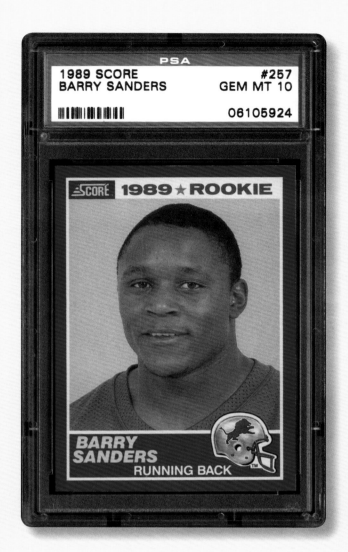

1989 Score #257 Barry Sanders

This is a key rookie card featuring the most dominant running back of the 1990s. Barry Sanders, despite a shocking retirement from the game in 1999, had a 10-year run of epic proportions with the Detroit Lions. For 10 straight seasons, Sanders rushed for at least 1,000 yards (the first man to accomplish the feat), proving that he was not only quick and powerful, but durable as well. Keep in mind that Sanders kept that streak alive despite missing five games in 1993. Sanders would also become the third player in NFL history to rush for at least 2,000 yards when he finished with 2,053 yards in 1997 on 6.1 yards per carry. Sanders was awarded the NFL MVP that same year. His career rushing total of 15,269 yards currently ranks third behind Emmitt Smith and Walter Payton, but Sanders had a better yards per carry average than either of them at 5.1. He also scored 99 touchdowns in his career. This 10-time Pro Bowl selection and former Heisman Trophy winner was inducted into the Pro Football Hall of Fame in 2004. This card, like the aforementioned Jerry Rice rookie, is susceptible to chipping along the green borders.

1990 Score Update #101T Emmitt Smith

This is the most popular rookie card of football's all-time leading rusher. Emmitt Smith did not posses the flash of Barry Sanders or the grace of Walter Payton, but he did possess grit and consistency. In 1991, Smith would begin a streak of 11 straight seasons with at least 1,000 yards rushing, peaking with 1,773 yards and 25 touchdowns in 1995. Smith's touchdown mark would establish a new single season record that year. Holder of many NFL rushing records, Smith became the first man in NFL history to have five consecutive seasons of 1,400 rushing yards or more (1991-1995) en route to his unthinkable career total of 18,355. In addition, Smith remains the all-time leader in rushing touchdowns with 164. This eight-time Pro Bowl selection and former NFL MVP (1993) was a three-time Super Bowl champion as a member of the Dallas Cowboys. Smith, who performed well in postseason play, holds several key playoff records, including rushing touchdowns and rushing yards. This card, which is susceptible to chipping along the colored borders, was only available through the factory as part of a complete set. The packaging caused many of the Smith rookies to fall short of PSA Mint 9 quality.

1991 Topps Stadium Club #94 Brett Favre

This is the key rookie card of one of the most popular quarterbacks to ever play the game. Brett Favre is one of the game's classic tough guys, starting an amazing 237 consecutive regular season games for the Green Bay Packers. Favre led the Packers to back-to-back Super Bowls in 1996 and 1997, winning the first against the New England Patriots and losing the second as the Denver Broncos pulled the upset. During that time, Favre became the first player ever to be named the NFL MVP in three consecutive seasons (1995-1997). At the time of this writing, Favre ranks first all-time with 5,377 career completions, 442 touchdown passes and 160 career victories. During the 2007-2008 season, Favre became the all-time leader in passing yards, (61,655) surpassing the 61,361 yards mark set by fellow quarterback legend Dan Marino. This nine-time Pro Bowl selection and owner of several NFL records is well on his way to the Pro Football Hall of Fame. By the way, who can forget his cameo appearance in the hit comedy *There's Something About Mary*? Even though his 1992 Stadium Club card is more valuable, the 1991 issue remains his true and most popular rookie. The card is subject to wear at the tips of the corners due to the colored design, but it is available in high-grade.

1998 SP Authentic
#14 Peyton Manning

This is, arguably, Peyton Manning's best overall card and a key for anyone assembling a collection of great quarterback rookies. Manning is well on his way to the Pro Football Hall of Fame and, since the departure of some of the other legendary quarterbacks mentioned on this list, he has been the league's most prolific passer. At the time of this writing, Manning has already set several passing records and his career is still going very strong. Manning established the single-season touchdown pass mark with 49 in 2004 (since eclipsed by Tom Brady) and has thrown for 4,000 yards or more in a season, a record seven times. During that 2004 season, Manning threw for 4,557 yards and had a 121.1 passer rating, which broke Steve Young's previous record of 112.8, on his way to being named NFL MVP for the second consecutive year. In 2007, after reaching the playoffs several times but coming up short of a title, Manning led the Indianapolis Colts to a Super Bowl championship by defeating the Chicago Bears 29-17. This eight-time Pro Bowl selection was also named Super Bowl MVP to cap off another outstanding year. Currently, Manning only trails Steve Young in career passer rating on the all-time list. This card is one of the tougher post-1980 entries on the list with corner and edge wear as the biggest condition obstacles.

Hockey Cards

1910 C56 #8 and #12 Art Ross

This is the only recognized rookie card of one of hockey's toughest players and innovators. As a player, Art Ross was an excellent defenseman and a member of two Stanley Cup championship teams, the Kenora Thistles and the Montreal Wanderers. In 167 regular season games, Ross scored 85 goals in addition to being tenacious on defense. After retiring as a player, Ross tried his hand at officiating for a brief time and then coaching for the Boston Bruins in 1924. He also served as the team's general manager. Ross remained a part of the Bruins, either coaching or managing, until 1954. During that time, the Bruins won three Stanley Cups (1929, 1939 and 1941) and finished at the top of the regular season standings 10 times. Ross remains the all-time Bruins leader in coaching victories. While working for the Bruins, Ross argued for the use of a synthetic puck instead of the natural rubber pucks to improve the consistency of play. He also helped implement the B-shaped goal, replacing the square goal, a goal that would produce dangerous rebounds. In 1947, the NHL created the Art Ross Trophy, an award given to the top goal scorer. Ross was part of the inaugural Hockey Hall of Fame class in 1945. This card measures approximately 1½" by 2⅝" in size and, like all early tobacco hockey cards, is very condition sensitive. The corners and edges are very fragile, so it is not unusual to see examples with some degree of chipping to the top layer of paper.

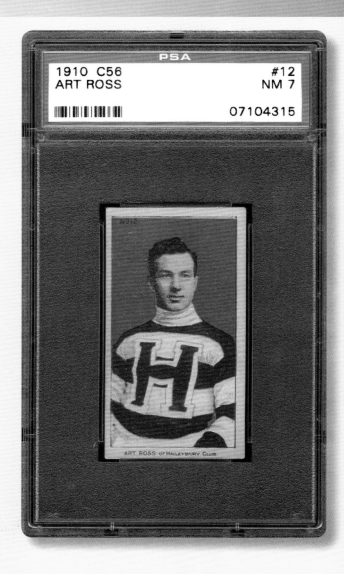

1910 C56 #15 Cyclone Taylor

This is the only recognized rookie card of hockey's first true superstar. Frederick "Cyclone" Taylor, a defenseman, earned his nickname by being an explosive skater on the ice. In 1907, Taylor signed with the Ottawa Senators and led them to the Stanley Cup in 1909. After an alleged dispute with management, Taylor left to join the Renfrew Creamery Kings of the National Hockey Association. There, Taylor averaged nearly one goal per game during two seasons before the team folded. The Vancouver Millionaires of the Pacific Coast Hockey Association were able to acquire Taylor and he remained there from 1913 to 1921. As a forward, Taylor averaged more than a goal per game during his stay. In 1915, Taylor won his second Stanley Cup and, in 1917, he scored an amazing 32 goals in just 18 games. In fact, Taylor finished his career with an average of more than one goal per game with 194 goals in 186 regular season games. From 1900 to 1918, Taylor was named to the First All-Star team each and every year, a remarkable accomplishment. Taylor was inducted into the Hockey Hall of Fame in 1945, its inaugural class.

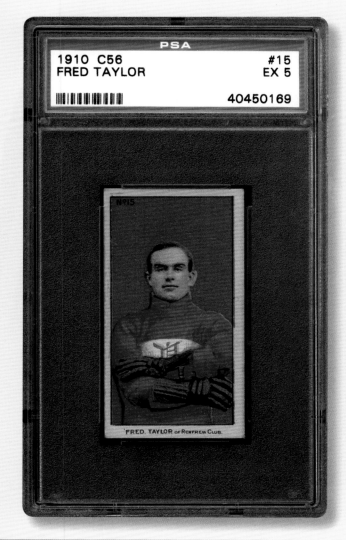

1911 C55 #38 Georges Vezina

This card, which measures approximately 1½" by 2½", is the only recognized rookie card of the man whose name is synonymous with goal-tending excellence. Georges Vezina is to hockey goalies what Cy Young is to baseball pitchers when it comes to personal achievement. At the end of each season, the best goalie in the league is presented with the award that bears Vezina's name. From the beginning, it was clear that Vezina was something special. In his rookie campaign of 1910, Vezina led the league in goals-against average and repeated the feat the very next year. He also led the Montreal Canadiens to their first two Stanley Cups in 1916 and 1924. During training camp for the 1925 season, Vezina fell ill and was diagnosed with advanced tuberculosis. Vezina passed away in 1926 but, prior to that season, the NHL created the Georges Vezina Trophy to recognize the game's best goalie and honor the man who set the standard at the position. Fittingly, the first recipient of the award was Vezina's replacement, George Hainsworth. Vezina finished his career with a goals-against average of 3.49, a figure that is even more impressive when you consider that goalies were not allowed to go down to their knees to gain control of the puck at that time. Vezina was part of the inaugural Hockey Hall of Fame class of 1945.

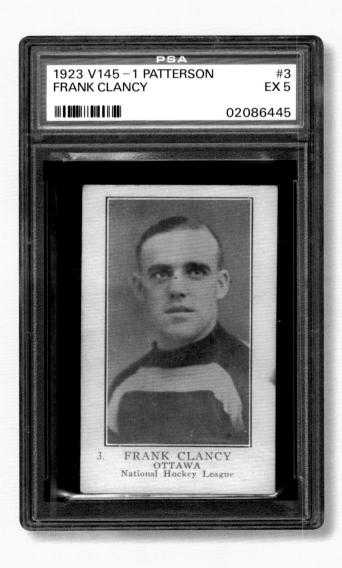

1923 V145-1 #3 King Clancy

This is the only recognized rookie card of one of the hockey's most likable, yet competitive players. At only 150 or so pounds, King Clancy was not the biggest man on the ice but he was certainly one of the toughest. Clancy, a defenseman, began his career with the Ottawa Senators and helped lead them to two Stanley Cups in 1923 and 1927. In 1930, the Toronto Maple Leafs acquired the energetic defender in hopes that Clancy could help the team reach championship form and that's exactly what he did. In 1932, Clancy helped bring the first Stanley Cup to Toronto and he did it during the first year at Maple Leaf Gardens. Clancy retired from the game during the 1936-37 season after scoring 136 goals in his career. He then tried his hand at coaching, refereeing and management during the next few decades. In fact, Clancy worked in the Toronto front office during the 1960s when the Maple Leafs won four Stanley Cups. This four-time All-Star was inducted into the Hockey Hall of Fame in 1958 and, each year, a current player is awarded the King Clancy Trophy for his charitable efforts in the community. This issue, which contains 40 blank-backed cards, measures approximately 2" by 3¼" and is very difficult to locate in high-grade. The paper stock is quite thin on this sepia-toned issue, making the cards very susceptible to paper wrinkles and creasing.

1923 V145-1 #15 Howie Morenz

This is the only recognized rookie card of one of hockey's fastest players and its first true superstar. Howie Morenz, often referred to as "The Babe Ruth of Hockey," began his career with the Montreal Canadiens as a center in 1923 and won a Stanley Cup his very first season as a professional. He would go on to win two more Stanley Cups with the team in 1930 and 1931. Morenz, a master puck handler and prolific scorer who finished his career with 270 regular season goals, was awarded three Hart Memorial Trophies in his career as the NHL's MVP and twice led the league in scoring. His career-high came during the 1929-30 season when he scored 40 goals in only 44 games. When Morenz began to lose his trademark speed, he was sent to the Chicago Black Hawks and then the New York Rangers before returning to Montreal for one last run. Unfortunately, his return was cut short due to a severely broken leg suffered during a home game on January 28, 1937. Just a few weeks later, shockingly, Morenz would pass away as a result of blood clots from the injury. Morenz, a member of the inaugural Hockey Hall of Fame class in 1945, was mourned by thousands of fans outside of Montreal's Forum. This card is considered one of the most valuable in the set, only taking a back seat to the Bert Corbeau short print rarity.

1933 O-Pee-Chee V304A #3 Eddie Shore

This is the only recognized rookie card of one of hockey's most intimidating forces. After playing a few seasons in the Western Canada Hockey League, Eddie Shore joined the NHL as a member of the Boston Bruins in 1926. Shore quickly gained the reputation as a temperamental tough guy who had no problem getting physical on the ice. Just a few years into his career, Shore would help the Bruins to their first Stanley Cup in 1929. Ten years later, in 1939, the Bruins repeated the feat. After a brief retirement from the game, Shore made a limited comeback with the Bruins and was then traded to the New York Americans but, at that point, his NHL days were numbered. Shore, an eight-time All-Star, won the Hart Memorial Trophy as the league's most valuable player a total of four times in his career, the most ever by a defenseman. In 1947, Shore was inducted into the Hockey Hall of Fame after scoring 105 regular season goals and bruising countless players in his 14 seasons in the NHL. This issue, which measures approximately 2⁵/₁₆" by 3⁹/₁₆" in size, was the first of five O-Pee-Chee sets distributed in the 1930s.

1937 V356 World Wide Gum #95 Connie Smythe

This is the only mainstream hockey card to honor one of hockey's great executives. While Connie (or Conn) Smythe never laced up the skates as a professional, he remains one of the most significant figures in hockey history. As one of hockey's more colorful characters, Smythe helped build the New York Rangers and Toronto Maple Leafs. As part of the latter, Smythe would become a legend, as Toronto emerged as a dynasty under his watch. Smythe was the principal owner of the team from 1927 to 1961. Between 1945 and 1951, Toronto won five Stanley Cups. They won 11 total Stanley Cups in all. As a showing of respect, the NHL introduced the Conn Smythe Trophy in 1965, an award given to the most valuable player in the Stanley Cup playoffs. In addition, one of the NHL's four divisions is actually named after him – the Smythe Division. Finally, not only is Smythe a member of the Hockey Hall of Fame, he actually oversaw its construction in 1961. This card, which measures approximately 2³/₈" by 2⁷/₈" and is somewhat difficult to find well-centered, is part of a 135-card set filled with Hall of Fame rookie cards.

1951 Parkhurst #4 Maurice Richard

This is the only recognized rookie card of one of hockey's most prolific scorers. Maurice "The Rocket" Richard of the Montreal Canadiens, with surprising strength and tremendous quickness, was able to get the puck past many goalies during his career. In fact, Richard would finish his career with 544 regular season goals (becoming the first player to reach 500), which included a season of 50 goals in 50 games (1944-45). That feat would not be repeated again until 1981! Richard also scored 82 postseason goals along the way. At the time of his retirement, Richard had set 17 NHL records, including the aforementioned 50/50 accomplishment. In addition to Richard's offensive excellence, he also was part of eight Stanley Cup championship teams and earned one Hart Trophy (1947) in his career. This 14-time NHL All-Star and former team captain was inducted into the Hockey Hall of Fame in 1961. This card measures approximately 1¾" by 2½" and suffers from a host of condition obstacles, including poor centering, subpar paper stock and ink bleeding, much like 1930s Goudey baseball issues.

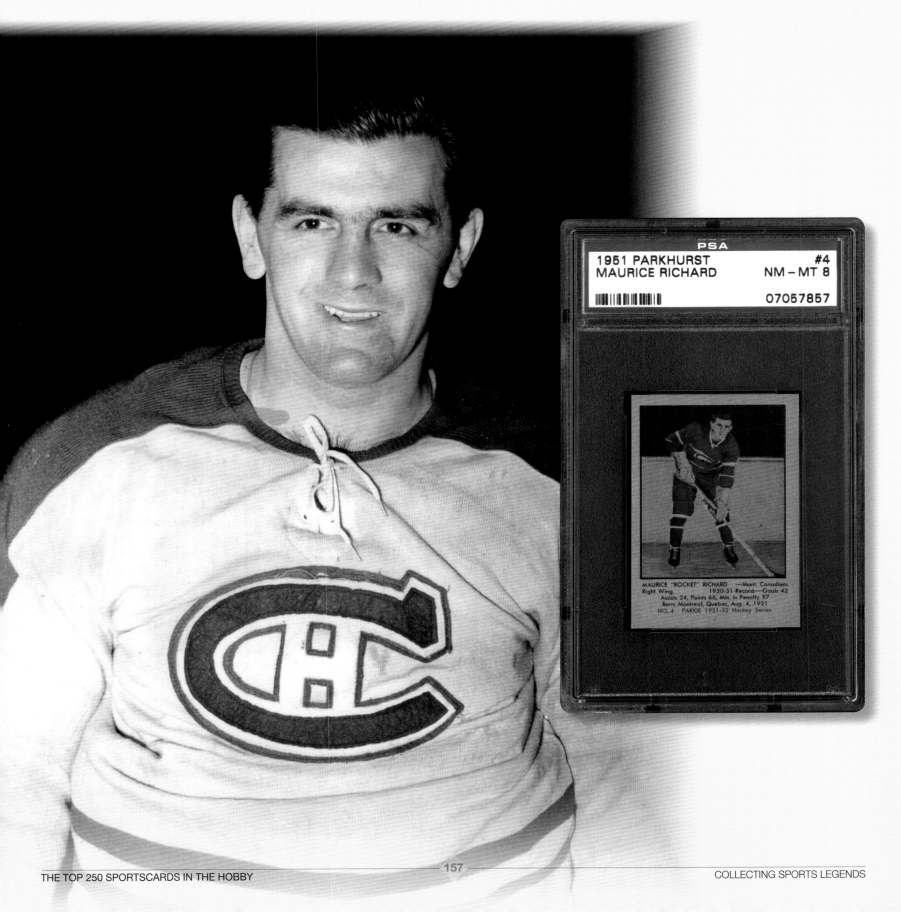

1951 Parkhurst #61 Terry Sawchuk

This is the only recognized rookie card of one of hockey's greatest goalies. Terry Sawchuk overcame multiple injuries during his career to become a mean force in front of the net. In fact, Sawchuk had 103 regular season shutouts in his career, a mark that no other goalie has approached since. In his first five years as a pro, Sawchuk led the league in wins and was named to the NHL All-Star team each year. He had a streak of five consecutive seasons with a goals-against average of under 2.00 and retired as the all-time wins leader with 447, a record that stood for 30 years. While Sawchuk was unstoppable on the ice, his temper would do him in. After a bout with depression over his failed marriage in 1970, Sawchuk allegedly started a fight with his teammate Ron Stewart. During the fight, Sawchuk fell over a barbecue pit and was severely injured. During surgery to repair his liver, a blood clot caused his heart to stop, killing him. This four-time Stanley Cup champion and three-time Vezina Trophy winner was inducted into the Hockey Hall of Fame in 1971, a year after his death. This card, which is tough to locate in high-grade, is subject to the condition obstacles common to the issue.

1951 Parkhurst #66 Gordie Howe

This is the only recognized rookie card of *Mr. Hockey* and the key to the set. Gordie Howe, who made his debut at the age of 18 in 1946, held virtually every offensive record until a guy named Wayne Gretzky came along. Along the way, Howe ranked in the top five in scoring for 20 straight years and scored at least 23 goals per season for 22 straight years. Howe's ability to sustain such a high level of play for so long made him a wonder, much like Nolan Ryan in the baseball world. Howe came away with six Hart Trophies as the league's MVP and played in 23 NHL All-Star games during his amazing career. From 1948-1955, Howe led the Detroit Red Wings to seven consecutive first place finishes during the regular season, a feat that has not been achieved since. After 26 NHL seasons and 32 overall (NHL and WHA combined), Howe finally walked away from the sport, setting numerous records in the process. This card suffers from the typical condition obstacles associated with the issue and is very elusive in PSA NM-MT 8 or better condition.

1953 Parkhurst #27 Jean Beliveau

This is a tough, key rookie card featuring a perennial winner. Jean Beliveau or *Le Gros Bill* (nicknamed after a popular French song of the day) was a player that combined size, strength, grace, instinct and precision stickhandling. At 6'3", 205 pounds, he represented the prototype for all future hockey players. Amongst Beliveau's most notable accomplishments are 507 goals scored, 712 assists (1,219 total points), 10 NHL All-Star selections, two Hart Trophies, one Art Ross Trophy, a Conn Smythe Trophy and 10 Stanley Cup Championships with the Montreal Canadiens. He retired as the NHL's leading postseason scorer with 79 goals in 162 playoff games. Beliveau, who served as a team captain for the final 10 years of his career, was inducted into the Hockey Hall of Fame in 1972. This card resides in a set considered one of the most beautiful postwar issues in the hobby, from any sport. This issue measures approximately 2½" by 3⅝" and is subject to a few different condition obstacles with the most notable being toning along the edges. While some degree of toning is acceptable to most hobbyists, if severe, the defect can hinder the eye-appeal dramatically.

1954 Topps #8 Gordie Howe

This is the key card to the inaugural hockey set from Topps. The beautiful colors and classic images in this set, coupled with its difficulty in high-grade, make the 1954 Topps hockey cards extremely desirable. Gordie Howe, during the course of his career, seemed to get better with age. He scored more goals after the age of 30 than before, including a season where he scored 44 goals at the age of 41. After spending six seasons in the WHA, Howe returned to the NHL for one last season in 1979 with the Hartford Whalers at the age of 51; and he still managed to play in all 80 games, scoring 15 goals! Howe did make an appearance in one game for the Detroit Vipers during the 1997-98 season, but it was more of a publicity stunt than anything else. He finished with 801 regular season goals and 1,049 assists in the NHL, with another 174 goals and 334 assists in the WHA. Amongst his many awards, Howe earned six Art Ross Trophies. This card measures approximately 2⅝" by 3¾" and is very tough to locate in high-grade with chipping to the bottom blue border being the most notable condition obstacle.

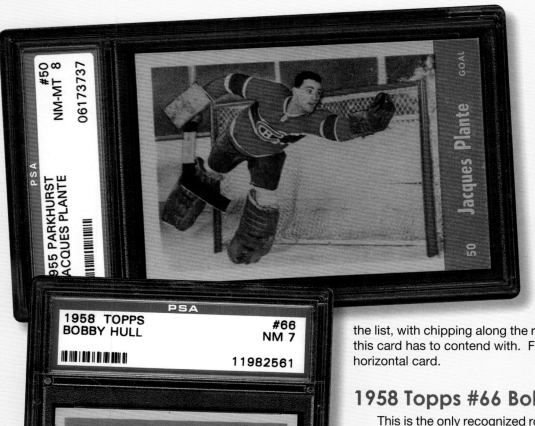

1955 Parkhurst #50 Jacques Plante

This is a key rookie card of one of hockey's greatest goalies. "Jake the Snake" Plante was an intense, focused athlete. His daring style was innovative as he often left the safety of the net to gain control of the puck, an uncommon practice during that time period. Plante also was the first NHL goalie to wear a mask regularly in the early 1960s. By the end of his career, Plante's accomplishments were abundant. Plante won seven Vezina Trophies (1956-1960, 1962 and 1969) for his work as a goalie and one Hart Trophy as the NHL MVP in 1962. Plante, who was named to the NHL All-Star Team seven times (three First Teams and four Second Teams) led the league in goals-against average eight times, a record for goalies. Plante, who played for several teams in his 17-year career, was inducted into the Hockey Hall of Fame in 1978. This 1955 Parkhurst issue measures approximately 2½" by 3⁹⁄₁₆" in size and is one of the tougher 1950s hockey issues on the list, with chipping along the red-bottom border representing just one condition obstacle this card has to contend with. Finding well-centered copies is also a true challenge on this horizontal card.

1958 Topps #66 Bobby Hull

This is the only recognized rookie card of the *Golden Jet* and the key to the 1958 Topps set. Bobby Hull was one of the most powerful slapshot artists the sport has ever seen, being clocked routinely in the 115-120 mph range and giving goalies across the NHL nightmares. His unreal power helped him achieve seven scoring titles, five 50-goal seasons, 12 All-Star selections and two Hart Trophies in back-to-back seasons (1965 and 1966) as the league's MVP. While Hull was part of only one Stanley Cup Championship team (1960-61 Chicago Blackhawks), he did win three Art Ross Trophies (1960, 1962 and 1966) and one Lady Byng Trophy (1965) en route to his Hockey Hall of Fame induction in 1983. Hull was also an anti-violence advocate for the sport during the 1970s and is partially responsible for the decrease in violence within the sport today. This card, which measures approximately 2½" by 3½", has one major condition obstacle, poor centering. Many of the Hull rookies are found with 70/30 centering or worse. This Hull card was placed in the bottom corner of the 1958 Topps uncut sheet, resulting in the centering issue. As the last card in the set, the Hull rookie has long been considered a condition rarity.

1966 Topps #35 Bobby Orr

This is the only recognized rookie card of hockey's most legendary defenseman. With blazing speed and tenacity, Bobby Orr always seemed to be around the puck. Throughout his career, Orr was able to amass a pile of hardware that is almost unimaginable. This included, but it wasn't limited to, three Hart Trophies, two Art Ross Trophies, two Conn Smythe Trophies, one Calder Trophy and eight Norris Trophies! In terms of sheer numbers, Orr's track record defies logic. It took Doug Harvey 18 years to break the record for assists by a defenseman. It took Orr a mere 7½ years to break that same mark. For six straight years, Orr reached at least 100 points, scoring at least 30 goals in each season, except one when he scored 29. In fact, Orr holds the records for most points and most assists by a defenseman at 139 and 102 respectively, both set during the 1970-71 season. This nine-time NHL All-Star selection and two-time Stanley Cup champion was inducted into the Hockey Hall of Fame in 1979. This card, like cards from the 1955 Bowman baseball set, is surrounded by brown borders and susceptible to chipping. Also, keep in mind there should be some room between his name and the bottom border in order for the card to be considered well-centered top-to-bottom.

1979 O-Pee-Chee #18 Wayne Gretzky

This is the key rookie card of hockey's greatest player. When people talk about the greatest athletes in sports, you often hear names like Babe Ruth, Muhammad Ali and Michael Jordan, but one could make a great argument that none of them dominated their sport the way Wayne Gretzky dominated hockey. At the time of this writing, Gretzky held more than 60, that's 60, NHL records from regular season, playoff and All-Star play. Some of the remarkable accomplishments from Gretzky's career include: finishing with 894 goals and 1,963 assist (2,857 points), 15 NHL All-Star selections (8 First Team and 7 Second Team squads), nine Hart Trophies as the league's best player, 10 Art Ross Trophies, two Conn Smythe Trophies and five Byng Trophies. Wow! Gretzky was also part of four Stanley Cup Championship teams with the Edmonton Oilers. His regular season records of 92 goals, 163 assists and 215 total points seem unreachable. In fact, he is the only player in history to reach 200 points in a season and he did it four times. He was, naturally, inducted into the Hockey Hall of Fame in 1999. This card, which is tougher than its Topps counterpart, has to contend with a few major condition obstacles including chipping along the blue border, print defects and severe rough-cuts, making PSA Mint 9 or better examples very hard to come by. In addition, the centering on this card is often found in the 60/40 or worse range.

1985 O-Pee-Chee #9 Mario Lemieux

This is the most important rookie card of, arguably, hockey's most gifted player. Mario Lemieux's size and skill made him the most feared player in the league and the heir-apparent to Wayne Gretzky as the NHL's best player. Lemieux had to deal with his share of adversity during his career, which included a few nagging injuries and a battle with Hodgkin's disease. The lingering effects of radiation treatment and chronic back problems forced Lemieux to retire. Despite all of the problems Lemieux faced, he was still able to pile up some very impressive numbers and achieve what few have done. He finished with 690 goals scored and 1033 assists (1,723 points) in his career. Lemieux won many awards in his career including, but not limited to, the NHL Rookie of the Year, six Art Ross Trophies, three Hart Trophies, two Conn Smythe Trophies, one Calder Trophy and one Masterton Trophy. This nine-time NHL All-Star selection and two-time Stanley Cup champion was inducted into the Hockey Hall of Fame in 1997. This card, while tougher than its Topps counterpart, is not particularly difficult overall, but marginal centering and slight rough-cuts may prevent the card from reaching PSA Mint 9 or better status.

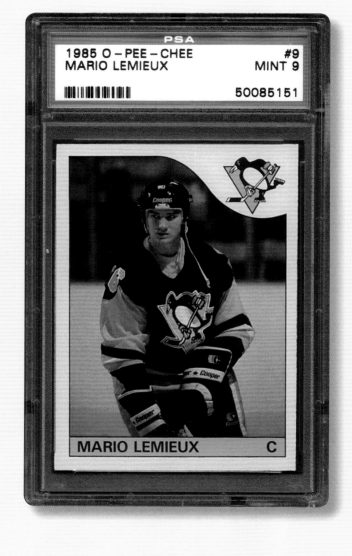

1986 O-Pee-Chee #53 Patrick Roy

This is the key rookie card of hockey's all-time header in victories. Patrick Roy made an immediate impression as a professional. In his rookie year (1985-86), Roy took over as the starting goalie and carried the Montreal Canadiens to the Stanley Cup, winning the Conn Smythe Trophy for his great postseason performance. In 1993, Roy and the Canadiens won another Stanley Cup with the elite goalie coming away with his second Conn Smythe Trophy. In 1995, Roy was sent to the Colorado Avalanche and, just a few months into his stay, he won a third Stanley Cup. During the 2000-2001 season, Roy surpassed Terry Sawchuk's career win record, finishing with an unthinkable 551 victories. That same year, Roy would win his fourth Stanley Cup and second one with the Avalanche, winning his third Conn Smythe Trophy along the way. During the 2002-2003 season, Roy became the first goalie to play in 1,000 NHL games, finishing with a record 1,029. Roy is also the all-time leader in playoff wins with 151. This 11-time All-Star and three-time Vezina Trophy winner was inducted into the Hockey Hall of Fame in 2006.

Boxing Cards

1888 N28 Allen & Ginters John L. Sullivan

This is the first boxing card of major importance, featuring the first modern heavyweight champion. With his huge crossed arms, John Sullivan looks like a guy you would not want to mess with. Born in Boston, Sullivan became a professional fighter in 1878 after gaining a fierce reputation as *The Boston Strong Boy.* Four years later, Sullivan would win the bare-knuckle heavyweight championship by knocking out Paddy Ryan in 9 rounds, holding that title until his death. Starting in 1882, some of Sullivan's matches were fought with gloves under new boxing rules. The last bare-knuckle championship bout was held in 1889. During that fight, Sullivan pummeled Jake Kilrain after 75 rounds of pure pain. That's right, 75 rounds! In 1892, Sullivan fought James Corbett for the heavyweight championship of the world under the new "glove" rules. Corbett knocked out Sullivan in 21 rounds and that remained the only blemish on his career record. This card, which measures 1½" by 2¾", was packed inside boxes of Allen & Ginter cigarettes, causing many of these cards to exhibit discoloration around the edges and reverse. In addition, keep in mind the reverse of these cards have checklists on them so beware of handwritten notations on the back.

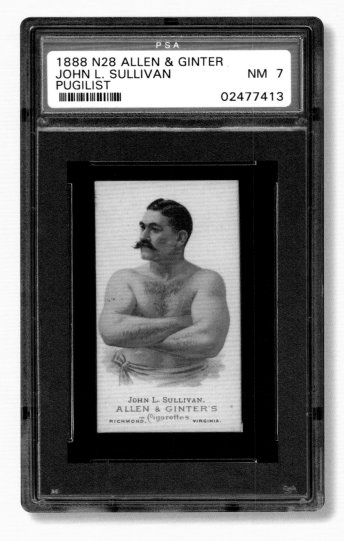

1911 T9 Turkey Red Cabinets #76 Jack Johnson

This is the key to one of the most significant vintage boxing issues in the hobby and it features, possibly, the best heavyweight boxer of his generation. Jack Johnson was as controversial outside of the ring as he was dominant inside of it. He became the first African-American heavyweight champion of the world on December 26, 1908 when he beat Tommy Burns in Sydney, Australia on a 14th round TKO. Up against a variety of opponents and a society that had trouble accepting him as the champion, Johnson refused to relinquish his crown, taking on all comers and remaining socially defiant in a racially hostile society. During his reign, Johnson soaked up the spotlight and took advantage of it by earning a substantial living on endorsements and enjoying an eccentric lifestyle. Johnson held the heavyweight title until April 5, 1915 when he was beaten by Jess Willard via 26th round knockout. Johnson, a member of the International Boxing Hall of Fame (1990), was a master technician who was virtually impossible to hit cleanly, possessing excellent speed and power. This card is a true condition rarity and even more desirable than Johnson's beautiful 1910 T218 issue. With its large size, measuring approximately 5¾" by 8" and showcasing brown borders, these giant cardboard relics were very difficult to preserve through time.

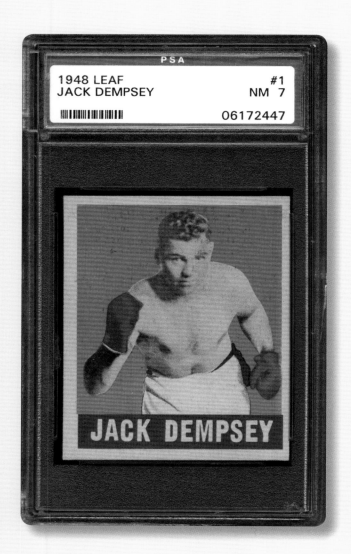

1948 Leaf #1 Jack Dempsey

This is the first card in a very tough set featuring *The Manassa Mauler*. Jack Dempsey epitomized toughness and helped take boxing to new levels of popularity during the 1920s. On July 4, 1919, Dempsey brutalized Jess Willard to claim the heavyweight title. Willard, the man responsible for ending Jack Johnson's reign as the champ, was left with broken ribs, a broken jaw and even partial loss of hearing as a result of Dempsey's punches. This damage was inflicted after only three rounds! Many fighters would meet a similar fate at the hands of Dempsey. In 1926, Dempsey would finally lose his title after facing a determined Gene Tunney in front of the largest crowd in boxing history, a crowd in excess of 120,000. In the rematch, Dempsey would knock Tunney down in the 7th round, but he failed to retreat to a neutral corner, giving Tunney extra time to recover and beat the 10-count. Tunney would end up winning by decision that day. Dempsey would finish his career with a 60-6-8 record with 50 wins coming by way of knockout. He was inducted into the International Boxing Hall of Fame in 1990. This card, as the first card in the set, is a true condition rarity. In addition, many of the cards in the set suffer from poor centering, toning, print defects and terrible registration. This card is as tough as the man it features.

1948 Leaf #48 Joe Louis

This is a key card of the man they called *The Brown Bomber*. Jackie Robinson is often given credit for breaking color barriers in sport and changing the way many viewed African-Americans in society, but it was Joe Louis who may have made the biggest impact of all. Louis was, without a doubt, the first African-American athlete to gain widespread acceptance and reach superstar status in a segregated society. He was a hero to all races and handled himself with dignity and grace during a time when racial lines were drawn. Louis held the heavyweight title for 12 years, a record that has yet to be approached in the sport. His reign was filled with great moments but the most memorable of all came when he avenged his loss to Germany's Nazi hero Max Schmeling. As the United States drew closer to World War II and with Hitler using Schmeling as the symbol of racial superiority, the pressure on Louis was immense. With the entire world listening, Louis destroyed Schmeling with a right hand, knocking him out in 124 seconds on June 22, 1938 in front of 70,000 plus at Yankee Stadium. The legend of Joe Louis was complete. He finished with a 68-3 record, including 54 knockouts. Louis was inducted into the International Boxing Hall of Fame in 1990. This card is subject to the typical condition obstacles associated with the issue, including poor centering, print defects, toning and subpar registration.

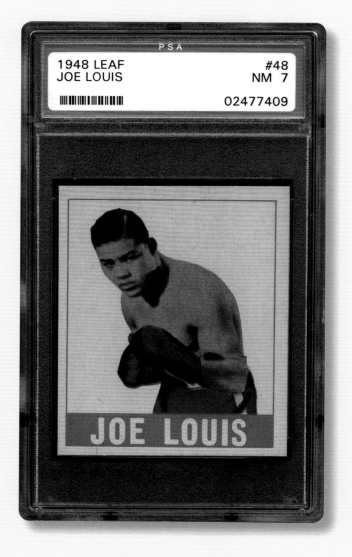

To a
fighter
a
Joe

1948 Leaf #50 Rocky Graziano

This card is the ultimate boxing rarity – boxing's equivalent of the T206 Honus Wagner, but clearly tougher. Rocky Graziano, the former middleweight champion of the world and one of the era's most powerful punchers, is best remembered for his three classic duels with Tony Zale. Despite losing to Zale twice, the three battles resulted in some of the greatest action ever witnessed at the professional level, including seven knockdowns between the two boxers. This trilogy cemented Graziano's reputation as a fierce brawler. He finished his career with 67-10-6 record, including 52 of his victories coming by way of knockout. Graziano was inducted into the International Boxing Hall of Fame in 1991. This card is one of the scarcest on the entire list and in the hobby, with only a handful of examples known at the time of this writing. Why is this card so rare? No one seems to know for sure, but the leading theory amongst hobbyists is that there was a contractual dispute between the parties. Whatever the reason may be, all we can do is wish you luck in finding one.

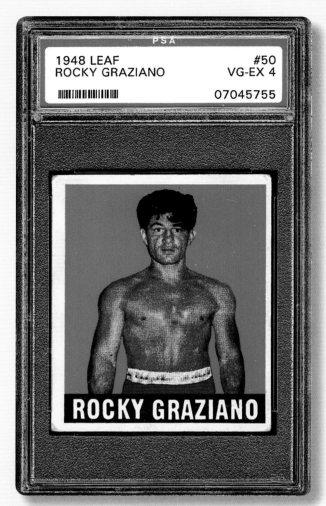

1951 Topps Ringside #32 Rocky Marciano

This is a key card of boxing's only retired, undefeated heavyweight champion. Rocky Marciano always wanted to play baseball and had dreams of catching for the New York Yankees growing up. After being told he lacked the skills needed for the position, Marciano turned to boxing. Even there, most trainers and scouts felt he lacked the physical gifts necessary for success in the sport. Marciano was shorter, slower and less graceful than most fighters. What some scouts failed to see was Marciano's enormous heart and the incredible power in his right hand. In addition, his ability to absorb punishment was inhuman. Marciano was willing to take three or four punches as long as he could land just one of his own. In 1952, Marciano would get his chance to fight for the heavyweight championship against Joe Walcott. After being knocked down in the first round and way behind on the scorecards after 12 rounds, Marciano landed a thunderous right hand in the 13th that knocked Walcott into another dimension and out. After winning the title, Marciano would defend it six times and retire with a perfect 49-0 record with 43 knockouts, including a knockout of his idol, Joe Louis. Marciano was inducted into the International Boxing Hall of Fame in 1990. Tragically, Marciano would perish in a plane crash in 1969 at the young age of 46. This card measures approximately 2$\frac{1}{6}$" by 2$\frac{15}{16}$" and, while not as tough as cards from the 1948 Leaf boxing issue, is difficult to find well-centered and the key to the popular set.

Golf Cards

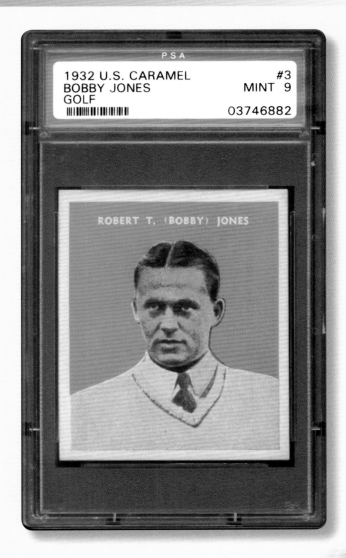

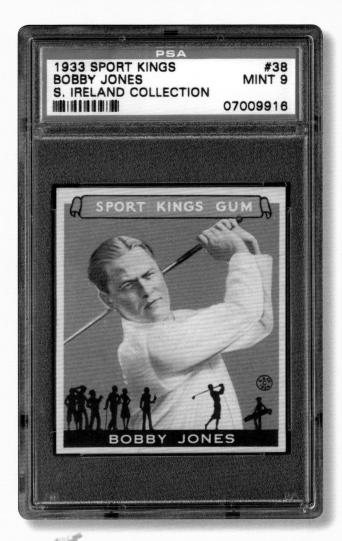

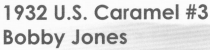

1932 U.S. Caramel #3 Bobby Jones

This is a key card featuring golf's first true superstar. This frail, temperamental boy turned into a well-liked golf champion by the time he was in his early twenties. When Bobby Jones retired at 28, he had experienced more than most grandfathers. After finding his groove and winning the 1923 U.S. Open, Jones never looked back, winning 13 Majors in only 20 attempts. He only trails Jack Nicklaus and Tiger Woods in that category. In 1930, Jones would become the only man to ever win golf's version of the Grand Slam (U.S. and British Opens as well as U.S. and British Amateurs). Furthermore, Jones didn't just win, he embarrassed his competition. In fact, during a 36-hole playoff in the 1929 U.S. Open, Jones beat Al Espinosa by 23 strokes! In 1974, Jones was inducted into the World Golf Hall of Fame. This card resides in one of the toughest sets on the list, contending with severe toning and a host of other issues. Keep in mind that these cards could be redeemed for baseball equipment at the time, removing many of the cards from circulation. Had it not been for a "find" of these cards in the 1980s, no high-grade copies may exist.

1933 Goudey Sport Kings #38 Bobby Jones

This is the single most important golf card in existence and a key to the extremely popular 1933 Goudey Sport Kings set. During the 1920s, sports in America were thriving and led by some of the greatest names in history. Baseball had Babe Ruth, boxing had Jack Dempsey, football had Red Grange and golf had Bobby Jones. Between 1923 and 1929, Jones was an unstoppable force on the golf course, showing amazing poise for a man in his early-20s. During that time, Jones won a total of 13 Majors, a record number that stood for more than 40 years. Some of the great golfers of the era, such as Walter Hagen and Gene Sarazen, never won a British Open or U.S. Open while Jones was active. Keep in mind that most professional golfers do not reach their peak until they are well past 30 and Jones retired from the game at 28. The image on this card is a classic. The smooth swing, the slicked-backed hair and the intensity in his eyes make the card a hobby favorite. This card, which is subject to the typical condition obstacles associated with the issue such as bleeding and toning along the edges, is not quite as tough as his 1932 U.S. Caramel issue, but the card is considered more visually appealing.

1998 Champions of Golf/Masters Collection Tiger Woods

This is a modern condition rarity in PSA Mint 9 or better featuring the most popular active athlete since Michael Jordan. No golfer of the modern era is more responsible for the increased interest in the sport, especially with the youth, than this man. In 1996, Tiger Woods entered the professional ranks and never looked back. In 1997, Woods would win his first Major, The Masters, winning by a record margin and becoming the youngest ever to win the event at only 21 years of age. At the age of 24, Woods became the youngest player ever to win a Career Grand Slam after his British Open victory in 2000. With his second Masters victory in 2001, Woods became the first golfer in history to hold all four Majors at the same time. At the time of this writing, Woods has won an astonishing 88 professional tournaments, 64 of those being official PGA Tour events. So far, Woods has been named the PGA Tour Player of the Year a record nine times and is still going strong. This 2½" by 4¾" card, which was placed at the bottom of the set, was shrink-wrapped in a very tight fashion. This caused most of the Woods cards to experience corner damage in the form of blunting or lifting. In addition, the card is surrounded by fragile black borders. Remember there is a sheet-cut version of the card and it is not nearly as desirable as the factory issue.

Miscellaneous Cards

1933 Goudey Sports Kings #45 Babe Didrickson

On a list dominated by male athletes and a hobby dominated by male collectors, this *Babe* stands alone. It is hard to comprehend how dominant Mildred "Babe" Didrickson was, possessing more all-around skills than the legendary Jim Thorpe. She excelled at a variety of sports including, but not limited to, track and field, basketball and golf during a time when women were discouraged from participating in athletics. In fact, she was such a powerful hitter as a teen that boys nicknamed her *Babe* after the larger than life slugger from New York. She was rumored to have hit five home runs in a single game. Didrickson won two Gold Medals in the 1932 Olympics and, in 1938, she competed in the Los Angeles Open on the men's PGA Tour. This feat would not be attempted by another woman for nearly 60 years. Against women, in the amateurs and professionally, Didrickson dominated, winning 16 straight amateur tournaments and 31 total tournaments in the professional ranks. She was inducted into the World Golf Hall of Fame in 1951 and the LPGA Hall of Fame in 1967. Didrickson helped pave the way for the great female athletes of today. She was a true one-of-a-kind. This card is subject to the typical condition obstacles associated with the issue, including toning along the edges and poor centering.

Building a Dream

A Look at Collecting the
Top 30 Complete Sets in the Hobby

By Brian Bigelow

The following pages deliver a wealth of imagery and a spectacular group of memories. Thirty of the industry's most popular, enduring and nostalgic productions were chosen for presentation in this "All-Time" lineup of collecting treasures. Each one is shown and described as a suitably cherished effort. The selections highlight complete sets of baseball cards, football cards, basketball cards and hockey cards, as well as cards whose productions cover a mixture of sports. The sight and the thought of these classics are splendid, but they give rise to fundamental questions such as how, exactly, is a collector transformed from a casual pack-buyer at one stage into a devoted set-builder in the next and how are these marvelous galleries constructed, catalogued and recorded?

Memories are precious to card collectors. Most enthusiasts can recall their very first contact with the hobby. For the majority, the introduction took place with a single, unopened and unfamiliar wax pack.

Before that package's wrapping was disturbed by the new owner, the concepts of collecting and trading cards – let alone buying and selling them – were not yet relevant. The first pack is a purely sensory experience and the initial sight of the cards can be a life-shaping event.

Typically, the attributes of a pack's cardboard collectible that merit instant attention are the most superficial ones. The buyer is apt to respond, right away, to the sight of a player's picture, quickly noting whether he is a famous star, a lesser figure or a total unknown. The athlete's team and its uniform are the details that are processed next (along with, perhaps, the front of the card's color scheme, franchise-logo graphics and border design), and then the back of the card is examined. There, the viewer finds information that is generally presented in the form of text, statistics and the like. All of these acts of comprehension take place in merely a second or less; it's an oh-so-brief interval that can still be enough to ignite a long-burning flame.

At some undefined point in the acquaintance-making session that takes place between a card pack and its buyer – the unsuspecting purchaser who may, after all, have simply wanted a piece of gum – a subtle revelation occurs. The cards' new owner discovers the pieces are *numbered*. If it's 1962, for instance, and Stan Musial is the face greeting the fortunate person who parts the folds of the green Topps Company wrapper, it will eventually be apparent that a pair of numerals – "50" – sits inside a small, baseball-styled circle at the cardback's upper left corner. This "50" doesn't seem to have any special significance, yet it occupies a spot that's hard to overlook. The idea dawns rather quickly that this prized *Stan the Man* piece is part of a sequence, and the intellect, unbidden, wishes for additional information.

If Musial was hiding inside a five-cent pack (the premium size that contained more than one card), further details were close at hand, as his packmates would have carried similarly placed identifiers: "32" John Roseboro, "21" Jim Kaat, "75" Milt Pappas, and – an entirely different thing here – "53," on a card that showcases Mickey Mantle, Roger Maris and the American League's other home run leaders for 1961!

Clearly, a pattern was taking shape. These numbers held designated positions in a mysterious sequence and their presence was triggering the urge to investigate further. Naturally, it's just one small step from that point – the inevitable – trying to obtain *all* of the numbers. The new goal was to obtain the full array of card subjects and having every one of them in hand simultaneously.

More clues became available with the purchase of additional packs. Inside one of those would likely have been the cards' *Rosetta Stone*, a piece that answered many questions: the Checklist ("22") for 1962 Topps' Series 1.

Among its orderly roster were numbers "1" Roger Maris, "5" Sandy Koufax, "45" Brooks Robinson, and many more, extending all the way to number 88. Eighty-eight different cards soon became the brand-new hobbyist's objective, "…got to get them all," and more packs were bought with this goal in mind.

As subsequent pack-buys were made and examined, a couple of new wrinkles emerged that complicated the seemingly straightforward business of assembling all of the cards. Card #22 in the 1962 Topps set is sometimes found displaying numbers 121 through 176 on its back, instead of the proper span between #33 and #88. Not only did the "Wrong Back" Checklist fail to list the issue's subjects in proper order, it gave a frustrating "sneak preview" to the novice enthusiast. No matter how many packs were opened on the heels of the Checklist's revelation, it was, at that moment, impossible to obtain "150" Al Kaline or "170" Ron Santo. They were in a series that had yet to go on sale, and it would take a while for the collector to become wise to Topps' "come-on" method of promoting upcoming segments of its product.

Having stuck with it to this point, however, a buyer was usually hooked. The prospect of completing a full set of cards became a challenge and a fascination. Trading ("swapping") began to occur as would-be-completists tried to overcome their respective set's deficits by exchanging duplicates. Before long, the avocation naturally spread among individuals who discovered that they had this "set-building" preoccupation in common.

A fan's passion for building sets derives from the systematic behavior of looking for a multitude of numbers and placing them in order. It is an activity that separates "collectors" from undirected gatherers or accumulators. Accordingly, a card maker's idea of placing sequential numbers on cards was perhaps the most significant development in the collecting hobby. With card numbers in place, the quest for completion is elementary. So, the compulsion of set-building begins the moment a collector is first exposed to cards. Once the seed of interest is planted, the drive to nurture its growth is demonstrably insatiable!

Although the incentive to put together sets can be provoked by simple curiosity about the card numbers, motivation is sustained by results. A complete set from any era acts as a time capsule, allowing the viewer to re-experience events that were current at the time the assembly was created. Full sets enable nostalgic tours of the 1950s, thoughtful recollections of the 1960s, or more recent reminiscing about the 1970s. Revisiting an early 1960s set brings to mind that period's then-new multi-player cards, its League Leaders, its Team cards and, in general, the season's activities in their most favorable light. A 1975 Topps set, with its gaudy, color-edged motif, just *looks* like a 1970s production, and it's a delight to view. But these more contemplative satisfactions aren't immediately apparent to the person who's just bought a first pack, and they're well down the road for someone who's barely had time to notice the card numbers!

The lesson brought to bear by the 1962 Topps baseball cards ("a checklist isn't always what it seems to be") has corollaries in other years' collectibles too. Most types of cards have their own quirks that, depending upon one's point of view; make the effort to collect them especially vexing or rewarding.

For example, logic dictates that the star players in a set would be the most desirable. Although that notion is frequently true, it's just as often contradicted by exceptions. Certain entries are short printed in various issues, as press-sheet layout and other considerations caused specific cards to be produced in smaller quantities than others. Production figures alone, in cases like these, mandate that cards like the 1963 Topps #470 Tom Tresh (an "SP") will be inherently tougher to find – and thus more "valuable" to a set-builder – than the same-year, same-series depiction of Hall of Famer Orlando Cepeda (#520). The "SP" phenomenon occurs repeatedly in set collecting, as does the circumstance in which "High Numbers" (those portions of a set released near the end of a season) are made in lesser abundance than the earlier, preceding groups. No sport's or topic's cards are immune from these built-in scarcities. They are a challenge in *any* set-building arena!

Sometimes, the manufacturer isn't to blame. In years gone by, before cards were perceived to hold actual "value," discarding duplicate "common cards" of undistinguished players was a routine part of a set-builder's housecleaning. Years later, many of those "commons" deemed unnecessary and disposable at their time of issue are actually the same pieces hungered for by advanced collectors seeking to assemble high-grade sets.

Condition constitutes another matter of some gravity among set-builders. If one aspires to complete a full set, doesn't it make sense that an attractive, uncirculated-looking set of all the cards would be best of all? As collecting evolved and the appearance of cards became a factor in their desirability, "condition rarity" became widely understood to apply to those cards that were always a chore to find in high-grade. The first and last cards in a set, due to rubber-banding and in-order stacking, are especially susceptible to damage. Number one cards like the 1952 Topps Andy Pafko, 1953 Topps Jackie Robinson and 1966 Topps Willie Mays are condition rarities, as are such last cards as the 1954 Topps #250 Ted Williams and 1967 Topps #609 Tommy John. Many of those first and last cards, like Pafko, can be very tough to find for the condition-conscious collector.

Modern times have brought about sophistication in many pursuits, and so it is with trading cards and set-building. These cards are much more elaborate

than in past years, and the manner in which they're collected has seen dramatic improvement. Years ago, devotees of set-building relied on word-of-mouth, casual contact and a few dealers to gain information about set-building projects and to acquire missing cards. Today, the PSA Set Registry allows precise comparison between collectors' holdings (conferring "bragging rights" at the same time) and reveals which cards are notably scarce. By studying the PSA Population Report data, participants can identify condition rarities and adjust their collecting strategies to elevate the priority of those items in the search for material.

In order to do justice to each card issue, it was necessary to select a very finite, too-limited number of sets for this "All-Time" listing. They were chosen on the basis of inherent, enduring appeal and widespread appreciation that each one inspires among hobbyists. It must be noted that these 30 sets are a cultural art form's highlights, not its full extent. More than a century of trading card production has yielded numerous issues that are truly fantastic. Isolating an elite few for "All-Time" honors requires methods of necessity that leave many great sets on the sidelines.

The enjoyment realized from completing sets of cards is evident to anyone who has tried it, and it's a definite force among those who have succeeded. Finishing a year's worth of cards entitles the hobbyist to look over a gallery in full bloom, with stars and memorable commons displayed together in a neat, inclusive continuum. It's fun to collect single cards, but there's closure in sets and satisfactory completion is often regarded as a beginning, rather than an end, with a hobbyist preparing for their next collecting challenge.

Background

The genre of objects known to modern hobbyists as "baseball cards" didn't just spring fully developed from the mind of a creative businessman. Rather, the concept that yielded trading cards evolved in a somewhat roundabout way. Seen in retrospect, it was all quite logical and wonderfully quaint.

Prior to tobacco companies becoming involved with cards in the late 1880s, the idea of collecting paper items centered around pieces of advertising that were handed out to the public by retailers or otherwise distributed in a person-to-person fashion. By intent, these usually colorful and elaborate "trade cards" were sufficiently attractive that individuals would become enamored with their content and paste them into scrapbooks for safekeeping. Maintenance of scrapbooks was an established, genteel avocation of the day. Many young ladies, in particular, held on to calling cards, decoratively lithographed die-cut novelties, and church or school awards in their own personally constructed volumes. By adding trade cards to this mix, advertisements were preserved – and viewed repeatedly – by a book's owner.

And so it was that cards produced by corset vendors, haberdashers, stove makers, and even funeral homes earned places of honor in Victorian-era scrapbooks. At some point, soon after this collecting trend took hold, a number of manufacturers – notably those engaged in the thread, sewing machine and coffee industries – produced cards in series. This practice engaged customers' interest in acquiring a defined array of cards that possessed a certain common theme. It further ensured that a card collector remembered a brand's name and sought out that specific business to the exclusion of its competitors. This development, in a time when word-of-mouth endorsements and actual visits to storefronts were primary means of facilitating commerce, was simply ingenious.

Makers of tobacco, upon taking notice that a new leisure-time habit was being indulged in by the populace, recognized that they already had – within every pack sold – a means of distribution, as well as actual cards. Insert-piece stiffeners made of thick cardboard were housed inside every package of hand-rolled cigarettes, and Goodwin & Co. of New York was among the first to place advertising upon this previously unadorned surface.

Goodwin, maker of "Old Judge" and "Gypsy Queen" cigarettes, experimented with the addition of its corporate byline to the inserts and, for good measure, to attract its customers' attention, the company placed black and white photographs on the cardboard slabs as well. The two primary themes for these photos' subjects were deliberately selected to be consistent with smokers' keenest interests, namely… what else? … girls and sports.

And so it became, that as a smoker emptied a pack, he found a picture inside. Many of them featured well-known stage actresses, and many more still, showcased athletes who participated in the 19th Century's National Pastime.

The "Old Judge" ballplayers – seen on blank-backed cards measuring roughly 1⁷⁄₁₆" by 2½" and assigned the designation the N172 issue in *The American Card Catalog* – became immensely popular and ultimately served as the cornerstone manifestation of "baseball cards." The N172 issue wasn't the first baseball card series but it constitutes the largest entity of its kind even to this day, and it reveals a marvelously comprehensive view of those who played the game during the period.

Composition

There is no N172 "set," as such, because the production's full extent has never been confirmed. The cards are not numbered and the manufacturer provided no formal listing of subjects. (To do so would have been self-defeating – by acknowledging that a collection could be "completed," it could be inferred that further buying to obtain more cards wasn't necessary – and it's also likely that many photographs were added or withdrawn on the spur of the moment during the issue's four-year period of distribution.) What *is* known is that more than 500 player entries have been documented and counting variations in pose, team association, photo cropping and caption spelling, the documented total of different cards exceeds 3,000 designs.

Old Judges are now well over a century old, and the cards' photography has in many cases faded or become less distinct with the passage of time. Most surviving examples exhibit a sepia-hued toning (which in some instances is almost pink in color) and their quality of focus varies widely. Still, the relics are undeniably captivating. The series features distinguished portraits, full-length standing poses and creative studio shots that show a fielder or batter poised to deal with a baseball, which is clearly suspended from a studio ceiling! Old Judge pioneered the multi-player card, wherein two athletes typically shared a carefully contrived "action" scene; managers, umpires, and team mascots (both human and canine) were also addressed by the release.

Most conspicuous among the issue's content in the eyes of many present-day collectors is the presence in the N172 issue of numerous Hall of Fame players. For the majority of these Cooperstown enshrinees, very few, if any other period collectibles, provide these stalwarts' career-contemporary, photographic likenesses. The N172 issue was a vastly inclusive effort, and it's not surprising that virtually all of the 19th Century greats are revealed in at least a few of its portrayals. Cap Anson, Dan Brouthers, Connie Mack and Harry Wright appear in only two or three poses apiece, but many others such as Charles Comiskey, Buck Ewing, Hoss Radbourn, Amos Rusie and John Ward can be found in five to ten varieties per man. Yet another (non-Hall) figure of interest to many, and who has been observed in at least five poses, is center fielder and future evangelist Billy Sunday.

Key Features and Rarities

Some Old Judges are one-of-a-kind pieces, and embody the very definition of rarity. Others have been observed in multiples over the years, yet as demonstrated by the zealously coveted Hall of Famers, enjoy demand scarcity that enhances their value and mystique.

The N172 issue is home to a plethora of often-obscure and very scarce nuances in detail, a fact that creates fertile ground for the specialist collector. And through the ongoing process of cataloging and information gathering, new rarities are discovered on an occasional basis. In terms of already-documented challenges, the "Spotted Ties" subset (containing player portraits of the 1887 Champions, with the cards so nicknamed by their subjects' distinctive neckwear) and the excruciatingly tough California League entries – which were probably limited to then-sparsely populated West Coast areas in their distribution – are noteworthy prizes for the devoted N172 enthusiast.

Bottom Line

In addition to filling an invaluable role as a visual chronicle of baseball's fabled 19th Century era, Old Judge's gallery stands as a primary building block for the collecting hobby. The sight of one or several of The N172 issue's photographic collectibles (more accurately described as *antiques)* serves to transport the viewer on an emotional journey into history. The modern cards that owe much of their origin to Old Judge may someday have the same effect upon future generations, but as the most extensive early issue of its size and scope, The N172 issue can be regarded as the sort of phenomenon that only occurs once – and irrevocably nudges and shapes the culture into which it is introduced.

Background

Those who participate in the modern collecting hobby have trouble envisioning a civilization without baseball cards. It must be remembered that "tobacco cards" sprang up more than 20 years after the Civil War, and packs of confection containing "gum cards" are within the grand scheme of the collectibles world a very recent development.

During the hobby's prehistory, the American Flag bore fewer stars than it does today. The Wild West was still rugged frontier country, and mass media consisted of little more than big cities' daily newspapers. It was in this environment – in the late 1880s – that the Allen & Ginter Co. of Richmond, Virginia, decided to add a bit of visual spice to the manner in which its product was presented.

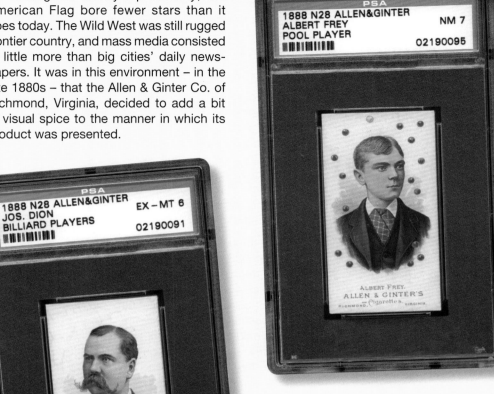

The manufacturer elected to modify and substantially enhance the appearance of the 1½" by 2¾" cardboard rectangles it had been using to stiffen its 10-packs of hand-rolled cigarettes. The stiffener was a utilitarian object – acting to ensure the integrity of a pack's smokes during packing, shipping and distribution – and it was also the ideal mechanism for placing advertising directly into customers' hands. Allen & Ginter wasn't the first to employ a cardboard device to accomplish these purposes, but the nature of its particular efforts are such that one of them lands squarely in "all-time" territory.

A&G concocted an especially appealing series of 50 cards carrying pictures of the greatest, most legendary sporting icons of the time – including ten of baseball's most prominent stars – and gave the group an imposing title: "The World's Champions." Instead of drab, thick-paper stock, or even the sepia-toned photographs displayed by some competing tobacco firms, the Champions featured beautifully lithographed *color* images of individual athletes from a variety of disciplines. These charming and sublime illustrations acted as tiny but distinguished portrayals, and undoubtedly served to acquaint smokers with superstars whose achievements were known, but whose faces were wholly unfamiliar. The cards' fronts also proclaimed the company's identity (in blue-inked printing, just below each subject's name) and the backs – in a gesture that may have contributed substantially to the brand-new notion of "collecting a set" – revealed all 50 of the release's topics in the form of a categorized checklist.

Later termed N28 in *The American Card Catalog*, Allen & Ginter's Champions production came to be a foundation piece for several hobby specialties and, in the process, delivers a significant glimpse of period Americana.

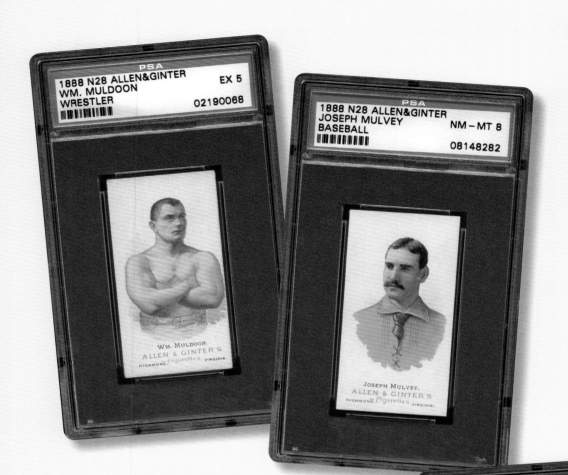

Composition

Although 50 cards comprise the entire N28 release, many enthusiasts consider its 10-player baseball component to be a fully legitimate set in its own right. A&G chose a power-packed lineup to represent the National Pastime in the N28 set: six of the players featured in the group have been enshrined in the Hall of Fame at Cooperstown. These include the time's foremost stars: Mike "King" Kelly, Tim Keefe and the great pitcher John Clarkson, as well as future owners/executives Cap Anson, John Montgomery Ward and Charles Comiskey. The quartet who rounded out the gallery – Charles Bennett, R.L. Caruthers, Capt. John Glasscock and John Mulvey – were other "name" players of the day who merited inclusion.

Although baseball was appropriately emphasized in the N28 set on the basis of popularity, the series was decidedly eclectic in character. Ten pugilists, (including John L. Sullivan), were depicted, as well as seven billiard players, two pool players, ten oarsmen and seven wrestlers. Finally, two key personalities who hold enduring fame, Buffalo Bill Cody and Annie Oakley, are present among the series' quartet of Rifle Shooters. It's easy to see how a consumer of A&G's products could have been easily captivated by the little inserts' stellar content!

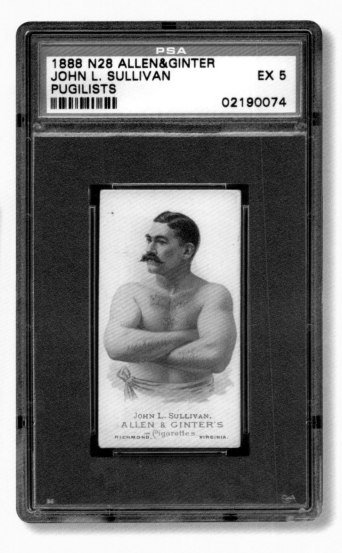

Key Features and Rarities

The N28 set contains no numerically derived rarities as such, because the issue's 50 subjects were presumably printed in equal quantities. The cards' availability in the hobby marketplace, however, acts to defy this logic-based supposition. The baseball subjects are the focus of such keen interest that they certainly *seem* to be more rare than the boxers or the billiardists, and the ballplayers values, not surprisingly, also imply premium status.

The baseball figures remain in constant, intense demand, and the other athletes have their devotees, too. But what's common to all N28s is the difficulty in obtaining them in a top-quality state of preservation. The set's composition encouraged "collecting," in principle, but a sense for "condition" was still many years away from even the most conscientious set-builder's mindset. "The World's Champions" collectibles, in prime, uncirculated shape are truly gorgeous paper antiques, and *those* are the most sought-after elements of the exquisite production.

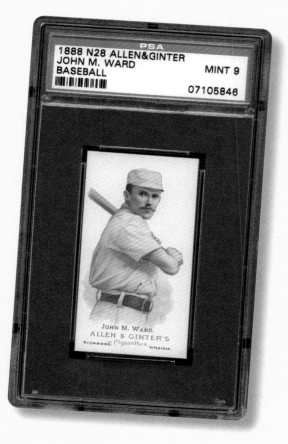

Bottom Line

The N28 set awakened the world to a different means of contact with its idols' images. Its basic premise – lovely characterizations of famous, worthy individuals – set a pace that was quickly followed by contemporary issues of the same type … and led to expansion into other topics. Allen & Ginter issued its own encore presentation adhering to the multi-sport theme (N29, the Champions "2nd Series") and the company's competitors, notably Goodwin and Kimball, quickly followed suit. The era's contemporary imitators of the N28 set validated the premise behind sports-themed trading cards, and the perpetuation of many of its features – not the least of which was the very idea of collecting cards in a systematic matter – underscored its importance.

Background

If someone thinks "tobacco card," that person immediately visualizes a T206. Issued during a three-year period throughout the heyday of the National Pastime just prior to World War I, these American Tobacco Company inserts – distributed in the packs of that monopolistic company's cigarettes – have been popular conversation pieces for nearly a hundred years. T206s defined the style, size and content of its era's baseball cards. The issue set a standard that would endure (and be copied) through a long interval of competition from early candy collectibles and anonymously made, cut-out pictures, which would last until the advent of "bubblegum" cards.

Never assigned a formal, all-encompassing title by its maker, the issue derives its T206 identity from a single line in Jefferson Burdick's definitive volume, *The American Card Catalog*. The reference reads, simply, "T206 - Baseball Series ... white borders ..." Serious hobbyists in modern times have tagged T206 with a nickname – "The Monster" – to affectionately acknowledge the difficulty of gathering all of its more than 520 entries.

Ubiquitous at the time of their distribution, T206's baseball depictions were just one of the themes ATC chose to promote and complement its Piedmont, Sweet Caporal, American Beauty, Polar Bear and other top-selling brands. Flags, birds, fish, soldiers, actresses and a host of additional topics are also well-represented in any vintage accumulation of small treasures from the early 1900s, but the baseball cards are, by far, the most memorable of those keepsakes.

The T206 cards' dimensions – about 1⁷⁄₁₆" by 2⁵⁄₈", and designed to conform to the packages they once shared with tobacco products – are "just right." They're perfect to accommodate the beautifully colored player images they convey, allowing an ideal amount of room for a caption detailing a subject's surname, team and league. A T206 card sits neatly in one's palm as the viewer looks at its athlete's features, and the card is easily overturned to allow scrutiny of the reverse-side advertising. Storage was easy, too. Many "old-time" collections have been found, often sorted into team groups by a family's great-grandfather, with cards still carefully housed in empty cigarette packs.

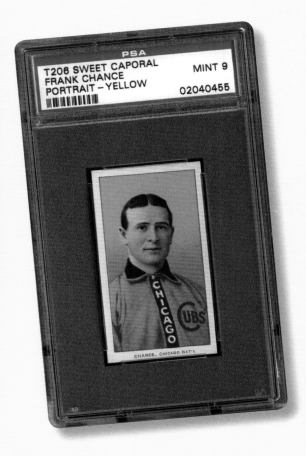

Composition

Much more than a single set of tobacco cards, T206s were actually the summary of several groups released within a three-year period encompassing the 1909 through 1911 seasons. As the issue advanced in longevity during its distribution, its content expanded to accommodate fans (and smokers) living outside relatively few major league cities during that time. Minor league players from a number of associations, and numerous towns from Minneapolis to Mobile, were soon included on the set's cumulative roster. Also, captions were updated on certain player cards to reflect changed allegiances as their subjects were traded, and poses were switched, presumably to keep the issue "fresh" – no one likes handfuls of duplicates! Perhaps to a greater degree than any other category of baseball cards, The T206 set acted as a living, breathing chronicle of the 1910 era's game and its personnel.

Finally, when American Tobacco moved along from production of the T206 issue in favor of newer cardboard innovations, it left behind a total of 524 distinctly different "White Border" player portrayals as a legacy to the modern collecting hobby. These include 390 cards that picture major league players (with multiple poses and captions for the same player counted separately) and 134 minor leaguers. The breadth of the series' lineup would be enough in itself to intimidate all but the most determined collectors. 500+ cards isn't the *real* challenge, though ... the true obstacle to completing the T206 set is its fabled rarities. Certain "key" players in the set – Wagner and Plank, to cite just two, are famously elusive, and few discussions of vintage baseball cards take place that don't gravitate toward these T206 depictions.

Key Features and Rarities

Regarded beyond anyone's reasonable doubt as the most famous baseball card in the world, T206's Honus Wagner entry enjoys renown and mystique like no other cardboard collectible. The legendary skills of the Pirates shortstop would be enough to propel Wagner's name to the top of an enthusiast's want lists, but the image of *The Flying Dutchman* – surrounded in its T206 incarnation by a distinctive orange background – occupies a niche in the card-collecting world that is incomparable and unique. Even the stories accounting for the Wagner's great rarity afford delicious intrigue, wild theories and abundant apocryphal tales, ranging from Wagner's reputed aversion to tobacco products, to the notion that he felt inadequately compensated for the use of his likeness. Wagner's T206 is a primary focus of card historians and its capture is a defining achievement for serious collectors. The card has been the theme of numerous articles and essays, has fueled countless hours of conversation and speculation, and holds an indisputable position as an icon of the sports-collecting hobby.

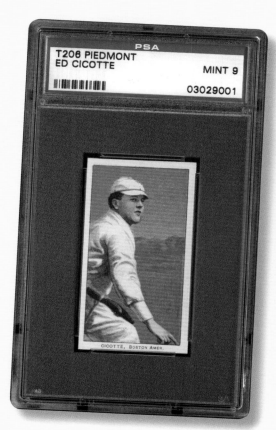

Wagner's fellow enshrinee, Philadelphia A's pitcher Eddie Plank, shares a heightened quality of rarity in the T206 set with his Pittsburgh colleague, and is viewed as the issue's second-most desirable depiction. Explanations for the Plank card's status are conjectural and range from the routine (opposition, once again, to association with tobacco) to the obscure, with the suggestion that a broken printing apparatus somehow affected only the Plank portrayal.

Those are the "Big Two," and these high-profile relics are as elemental in understanding the appeal of the T206 issue as they are in plotting the assembly of a full set in modern times. And, although Wagner and Plank are the most universally recognizable "flagship" scarcities in the crowd, there are others that will emerge at once during the aspiring T206 aficionado's first stages of research: Magee (with caption misspelled "Magie"), Demmitt and O'Hara (shown with St. Louis), Elberfeld, Brown and Smith. All are names that occur with predictable frequency on the wantlists of those enthusiasts who wish to conquer the classic White Borders.

One more aspect is the illumination of relative difficulty, with respect to T206 cards, that has focused on the cards' players. But citing the cardfront images of Wagner and Plank, et al, centers only on one dimension of the series' content. A whole new world is encountered when one addresses another facet of these personality-filled collectibles: the cards' *backs*.

As already mentioned, T206 cards were enclosed with a host of the different brand names that were encompassed under the American Tobacco Company's organizational umbrella, and the cards' stylishly conceived back-printing was tailored to suit the specific cigarettes with which the items were packaged. The majority of T206s bear reverse-side advertising touting the company's popular Piedmont, Sweet Caporal, Old Mill and Sovereign trademarks. Numbering 16 varieties in all, the hierarchy of scarcity ascends from those four names upward through such exotic types as American Beauty, Carolina Brights, El Principe de Gales and Hindu and nears its culmination with seldom-seen Hindu, Drum, Uzit and Lenox logos. The pinnacle of cardback difficulty is found in the ultra-rare "Ty Cobb" reverse design, wherein Cobb (who, incidentally, is the "Ty Cobb" back's only confirmed obverse subject) is termed "King of the Smoking Tobacco World." The vast number of back versions, when factored into an equation containing 524 distinct player illustrations on the cards' fronts, yields an exponential increase in the number of different T206s available to collect … a prospective life's work for the tobacco card hobbyist who wishes to face a serious and immensely rewarding challenge.

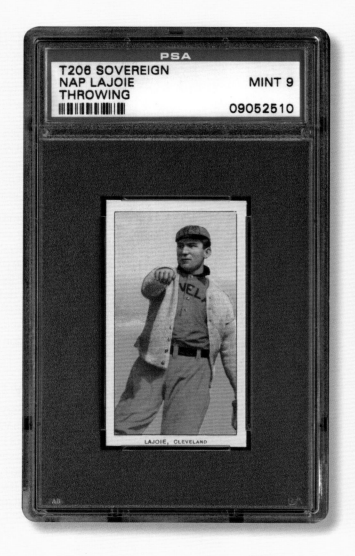

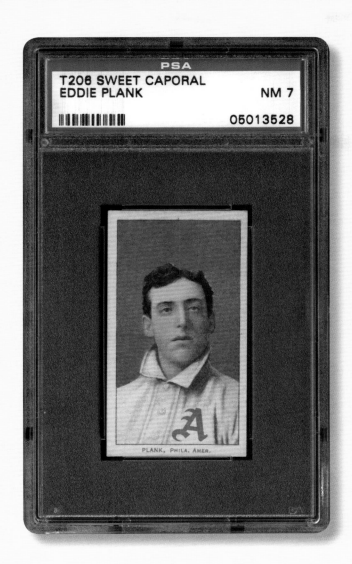

Bottom Line

Although examination of T206's extent and complexity tends to intimidate the reader, it's probably far too easy for the issue's inherent charm to be camouflaged by excessive detail. T206's famous and expensive Hall of Famers are certainly daunting in their own way, and mention of the set's rarities and their mysteries, and the obscure back designs, imply that an investment of scholarship is necessary to properly approach the White Border gallery. Incredibly, that's not the case.

True appreciation of these special collectibles, in its purest sense, doesn't rely upon any of those complicated aspects. An emotional fascination with baseball history is inevitably prompted by a close look at a single card … its colors, its subject's expression, the straightforward but simple arrangement of the front and the vintage printing on the back. The thoughtful observer grasps the set's flavor by looking at just one of its components … then a second, and so on. Before long, it's only natural that one "casually" seeks to gather the players comprising one's favorite team and, just that quickly, a fulfilling project has begun! T206's magic has been perpetuated in this fashion for almost a century and the spell, as many can attest, is irresistibly alluring.

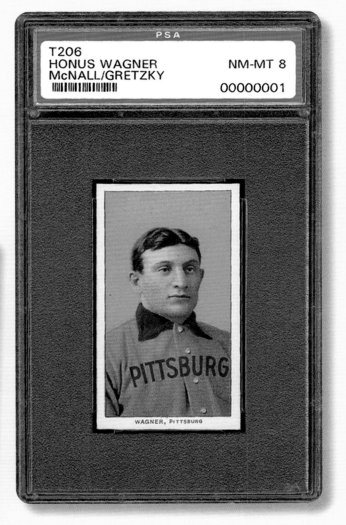

Background

Ask anyone who is involved in car sales, and they will confirm that it is important to keep a product fresh in the eyes of the buying public. Even if the old standby demonstrates continued success and its appeal remains as strong as ever, the time will come for it to *evolve*.

Another valid marketing axiom rests in the idea that, while change for the sake of refinement is usually a good thing, the finest points of a commodity's immediate predecessor shouldn't fall victim in the transition to an improved version. Product identity is a concept whose value has been acknowledged in countless winning sales endeavors, and ignored at great peril in many other, less favorable ones.

By 1911, the American Tobacco Company Group's cigarette brands had been the beneficiaries, for three years running, of the parent company's inspired and highly comprehensive T206 White Border baseball-themed insert cards. The stately little relics had achieved widespread acceptance among smokers who liked the concisely rendered, colorful novelties. Those clients responded positively to ATC's proven willingness to update its White Border series by adding new players, noting team-change information in captions, and even – to extend beyond its built-in big city content bias – including various Minor League and Southern League athletes.

One inescapable fact certainly dawned on ATC's product specialists as they contemplated making improvements to the T206 issue: a 1⁷/₁₆" by 2⁵/₈" cardboard rectangle (the card size mandated by the dimensions of the cigarette packs that would house the items) represents a very small area with which to work! When the company's new and improved Gold Border series made its debut, it became clear at once just how determinedly creative the designers had been when it came to bringing about positive change to an already-proven, much-appreciated venture.

Sublime portraits of individual players remained the emphasis of the revamped production, but with that key element in place and overall dimensions of the items' cardboard necessarily unchanged, that similarity to the cards' T206 forebearers became negligible. The primary modification – a feature that made ATC's modernized series stand out from anything that had ever been seen before – was its luscious, gold-colored borders.

T206's plain and discreet, white margins gave way to luminously metallic, shimmering ones. The Gold Borders were truly remarkable successors to their antecedents, but they brought more to the table than a simple change of peripheral hue. T205s – the lower number applied to the newer release in *The American Card Catalog's* definitive listings, simply because "Gold" comes before "White" alphabetically – replaced colorized, but straightforward, photo-based likenesses with illustrations that were lovingly artistic in character. Border graphics of varying types – usually incorporating team logo devices and arrangements of baseball equipment and placed in a specific manner that visually announced the league with which a subject was associated – enhanced each card's aesthetic. Facsimile signatures coursing across a portion of many ballplayers' depictions afforded another up-close touch. Furthermore, short biographies and statistical summaries were often added to the cards' backs.

The upgrade of the T206 set was an important undertaking to many, and clearly T205's designers had regarded the task in exactly that vein. The result of the timely revision of ATC's baseball insert production was a gift to the collecting hobby in the form of a fabulous, gold-enhanced gallery of the era's most storied ballplaying figures.

Composition

Although just 198 players are represented in the T205 set, there are, counting a few multiple poses and a number of legitimate variations, 209 different cards in the series. Hall of Famers abound in the release, with such stars as Ty Cobb, Walter Johnson, Addie Joss, Christy Mathewson, John McGraw and Cy Young appearing on T205 entries that are among each subject enshrinee's most coveted and prized career-contemporary collectibles from the era.

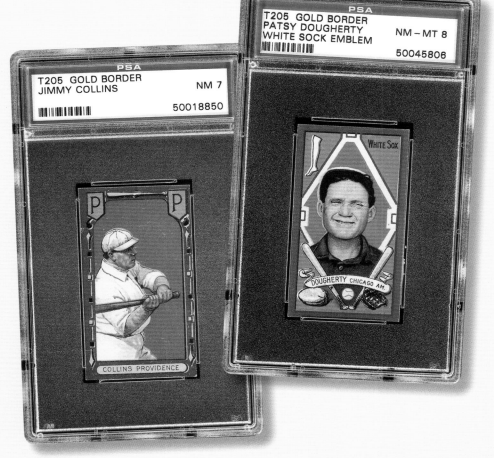

T205's National League player depictions are distinguished by no less than three obverse-side statements of team identity in the form of a decorative logo, a plain caption and a spelled-out legend. These, along with his black-inked signature and portrait, are settled inside its gold border, and back-dropped by one of a number of different colors that seem to have been selected entirely on the basis of their depth and intensity. American League ballplayers' treatments omitted their replica autographs, but added distinctively stylish embellishments like two crossed bats projecting upward from the design's bottom edge, basepaths framing the player's picture and gloves, balls, name-banners or other suitable elements as finishing touches. Finally, the issue's 12 Minor Leaguers – small in number and especially scarce – borrowed a special kind of gold-frame design from an American Tobacco Company non-sports release, its "Military Series." There's ATC's product identity in action, once again!

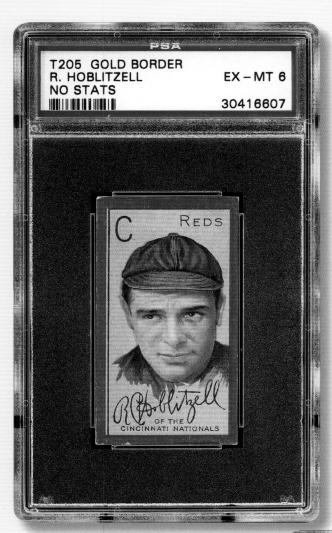

T205 GOLD BORDER
R. HOBLITZELL
NO STATS
EX – MT 6
30416607

T205 GOLD BORDER
MILLER J. HUGGINS
NM – MT 8
90362696

T205 GOLD BORDER
CHRISTY MATHEWSON
NM-MT 8
02044534

No discussion of T205 would be complete without mention of the features of the cards' backs. The manufacturer conceded valuable space, which, in T206, had been devoted entirely to promotion of its brands, to information pertaining to the player shown on a card's front. This feature included a formal name caption at the top, followed by a brief description of the athlete's career, and then in most cases, a couple of lines of statistical highlights from the 1908-10 seasons.

Key Features and Rarities

Arguably, the most enthusiastically desired T205 singles are those already mentioned, which feature the game's immortals: Cobb, Mathewson, Young and the others are keystone acquisitions for the finest collection.

T205 GOLD BORDER
TRIS SPEAKER
NM-MT 8
07000728

T205 GOLD BORDER
LEWIS McALLISTER
NM 7
50063171

Although none of T205's players, including the big names, are demonstrably more rare than others, the same cannot be said for its variations. Apparently, a bit of fine tuning of the Gold Borders' content on the part of its manufacturer resulted in several entries that can be counted upon to challenge modern-day hobbyists.

Since the cards do not bear numbers assigned by their makers – a convenient feature that did not become commonplace in trading cards until a generation later – early cataloguers of cards invented brief, handy terms to note readily identifiable attributes in each of T205's variations. For example, Hall of Famers Roger Bresnahan (who appears in "Mouth Open" and "Mouth Closed" versions, the former being more elusive) and Eddie Collins ("Mouth Open" and "Mouth Closed," with "Open" regarded as the toughie) lead the parade of the series' anomalies and are routinely described as noted. Another Cooperstown inductee, the St. Louis Browns' Bobby Wallace, can be found in *three* distinct T205 incarnations: "With Cap," "No Cap, 1 Line 1910 Stats" and the remaining "No Cap, 2 Lines 1910 Stats" version, which commands serious attention whenever an example surfaces.

A number of the issue's lesser lights have their quirks, too. The notorious Hal Chase exists in three varieties and Dick Hoblitzell is known in *four* types. E.B. Barger, Otis Crandall, Dolly Gray and David Shean are among the additional individuals who were presented in two different portrayals.

All of these variations are regarded as essential to the compilation of a truly complete T205 set and several of them, as noted, pose serious obstacles for the dedicated specialist.

As with T206, certain reverse-side advertisements can be thoroughly vexing for the person who wishes to assemble samples of the series' eclectic branding devices. The cardbacks' alliances range from ATC's old standards (Piedmont and Sweet Caporal, both of which are routinely seen) to such blindingly rare and obviously short-lived brands as Hindu and Drum. Eleven different cigarette brands in all can be found showcased on the backs of T205s, and constructing that group alone is tantalizing in its difficulty.

Several other depictions are considered condition rarities; that is, they're much harder than most T205 cards to locate in a quantifiably top-notch state of physical preservation. This aspect is subject to fluctuation and maturation – the latter being a process that will take place over time, as more T205s come to light and are submitted for evaluation by professional grading services.

Bottom Line

The American Tobacco Company faced a daunting task – improving upon its priceless T206 effort – and responded with the creation of a museum-quality array of new baseball collectibles. What could the company do for an encore to the White Borders? Some may have posed that question aloud, late in 1910, and ATC sure showed them. In the process, T205's maker gave force to the premise, which clearly would become important in later years, that baseball card productions should be renewed periodically, preferably on an annual basis and with bold, captivating new features. And it added yet another, vital chapter to America's legacy in trading cards as they specifically applied to the country's cherished National Pastime.

1911 T3 Turkey Red Cabinets Baseball

Background

Visually captivating though they were, the turn-of-the-century's small-sized tobacco cards left collectors anxious for more. Initially conceived by the manufacturer as "throw-away" pieces that would hold the buyer's attention for just a moment (long enough for quick notice of its ballplayer illustration, and for exposure to its back-printed advertising), baseball cards quickly became appreciated on a higher level. Smokers – many of whom had shown no prior inclination to "collect" anything – became enamored with the sublime little pieces in greater numbers than could have been expected. These people turned into the dedicated collectors of their time.

The marketing folks at the American Tobacco Company's Group of brands looked for a means to provide a suitable gesture to positively address the new-found propensity for collecting among its clientele. To that end, and to acknowledge the trend toward brand loyalty that had been reinforced by the cards' success, the amazing "Turkey Red" cabinet cards were introduced in 1910.

The Turkey Red cards, named after one of ATC's brands and eventually termed "T3" in *The American Card Catalog*, were unlike any baseball card production that had come before. The pieces utilized superbly well-detailed, lithographed player illustrations rendered in the purest colors and centered these on gigantic 5¾" by 8" thick cardstock pieces. Each one was a masterpiece, worthy of stand-alone display or as a component of an impressive gallery of the items. The visually inspiring effect of T3's (individual or aggregate) aesthetic properties simply cannot be overstated.

Obviously, something as supreme as a Turkey Red cabinet couldn't be distributed in a routine manner; these were for "preferred customers." To be sure that the appropriate consumers were being rewarded for their purchases, ATC

offered the cards through a mail-away, coupon-based promotion commencing in 1910 and extended through June, 1911. Ten coupons from the Turkey Red brand – or 25 from the (presumably cheaper) Old Mill or Fez packages – entitled the sender to choose a T3 from a checklist of 125 different depictions. (The series of 125 harbored 100 baseball designs, with the others – inclusive numbers 51 through 76 featuring pictures of boxers. The latter are seen as comprising a separate and distinct entity – T9.)

In addition to their undeniable physical glamour, T3s were significant as the first interactive production of its day. Buyers, for the first time in a generation, were given the option to select particular subjects for their collections. An enthusiast could assemble his holdings of favorite teams, particularly admired players, or entire leagues in a deliberate manner according to taste. In retrospect, it can be seen that ATC was quite clever to recognize the marketing value inherent in this sort of cooperation with its clients' wishes.

Composition

The T3 cards were designed with high-profile display in mind. Their images were breathtaking, and constituted sights that were ideal for sharing with a fan's like-minded acquaintances; the cards' physical size abetted this notion. Consistent with the collectibles' flamboyant appearance was their seriousness of content. Virtually all of the era's top stars are represented in the issue, with each one seen in a highly flattering portrayal. Ty Cobb, Walter Johnson, Mordecai Brown, Cy Young, Home Run Baker – these are just a few of the luminaries that could be had for a handful of coupons.

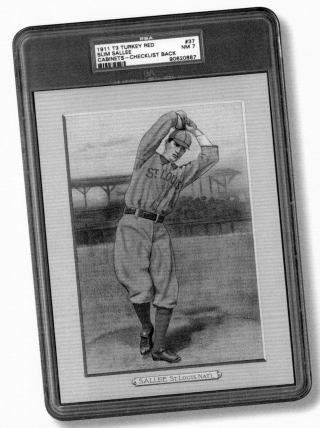

Also available were a number of generic scenes revealing ballplayers in glorified "action" scenes. Titles like #43's "Out At Third" and #44's "Trying To Catch Him Napping" must have been tempting selections for those coupon-holders who'd already captured their biggest-name favorites. Finally, various minor stars rounded out the set's total of 100 entries.

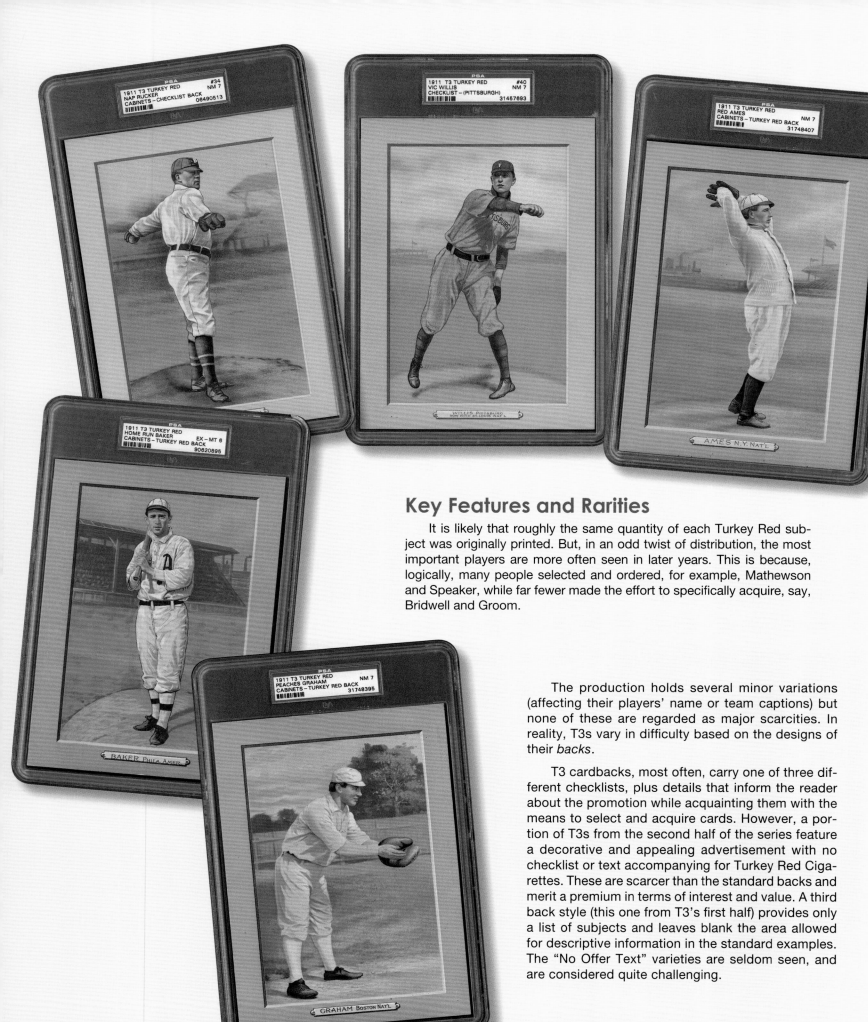

Key Features and Rarities

It is likely that roughly the same quantity of each Turkey Red subject was originally printed. But, in an odd twist of distribution, the most important players are more often seen in later years. This is because, logically, many people selected and ordered, for example, Mathewson and Speaker, while far fewer made the effort to specifically acquire, say, Bridwell and Groom.

The production holds several minor variations (affecting their players' name or team captions) but none of these are regarded as major scarcities. In reality, T3s vary in difficulty based on the designs of their *backs*.

T3 cardbacks, most often, carry one of three different checklists, plus details that inform the reader about the promotion while acquainting them with the means to select and acquire cards. However, a portion of T3s from the second half of the series feature a decorative and appealing advertisement with no checklist or text accompanying for Turkey Red Cigarettes. These are scarcer than the standard backs and merit a premium in terms of interest and value. A third back style (this one from T3's first half) provides only a list of subjects and leaves blank the area allowed for descriptive information in the standard examples. The "No Offer Text" varieties are seldom seen, and are considered quite challenging.

Bottom Line

The T3 set, arguably for the first time in the hobby's history, gave credence to the association of the word "magnificence" with trading cards. Those fabulous, high-quality collectibles carried the most formidable visual impact of any baseball relic produced to that point – and, perhaps since. Far from casual keepsakes, T3s' spellbinding manner of presentation started to bring about an elevated perception of the entire genre. In this special, early instance, a manufacturer's willingness to acknowledge and capitalize on the beauty of its cards worked to please the producer and buyers alike. And the modern hobby is yet another beneficiary nearly a century later.

Background

"… Buy Me Some Peanuts and Cracker Jack …" Baseball's cooperative relationship with the molasses-covered popcorn snack has been a long and comfortable one, predating the 1908 composition of the familiar song, "Take Me Out to the Ballgame." Culturally, consumption of the two national favorites is seen as an ideal pairing of indulgences – one for the spirit, one for the palate.

In 1914, Cracker Jack took the natural mutualism one step further. During that season – two years after Cracker Jack first introduced the gimmick of placing "a surprise" in each of its packages – the company inserted a brand new type of baseball card in its boxes. In comparison to the physically smaller, artistically restrained tobacco and candy cards already circulating during that era, the 1914 Cracker Jack cards were "dazzlers" in every sense of the word. They were creatively inspired, "delicious" collectibles, and a departure in style. The cards' visual demeanor was reflective of their association with a different sort of product – one that had a palpable "ballpark" orientation.

The Cracker Jack cards came out of their boxes boasting generous 2¼" by 3" proportions – substantially larger than a typical tobacco card. Putting the expanded dimensions to good use, the cards featured beautifully detailed, color-tint photo likenesses of the 144 individual players and employed a brilliant red background hue for the finest, eye-catching effect. Cardbacks performed two roles, with approximately one half devoted to a short player biography and the other to text advertising both the set and the product. The items were printed on thinner-than-usual card stock, which revealed a textured surface that favorably showcased the cards' brightly inked attributes.

Baseball cards and Cracker Jack – the perfect match! That is with the exception of one aspect. The Cracker Jack snack had been formulated so that each bit of coated popcorn would resist adhering to its neighbors in the box. This worked fine, in the sense that people could enjoy the confection piece-by-piece, without risk of the product clumping. Less successful, by far as it turned out, was the premise of placing a delicate trading card into close proximity with syrupy Cracker Jack, and expecting it to emerge in credible shape. Almost all of 1914's Cracker Jack cards, as a result of this lapse in judgment on the part of its maker, display stains and darkening associated with sweet-tasting "goo," as well as dents, dings and creases incurred while the piece bounced around

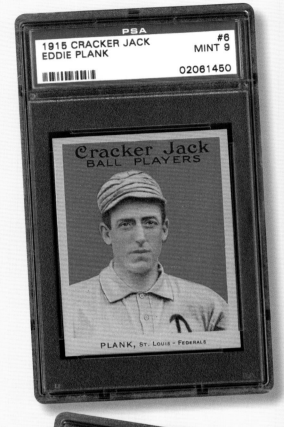

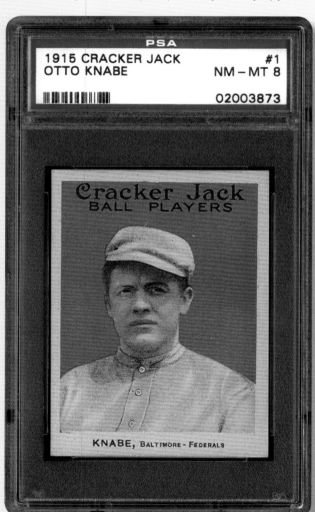

"raw" and unprotected within the container. The hobby loves its 1914 Cracker Jacks, but enthusiasts are generally required to compromise exacting condition standards in the effort to collect them.

It's gratifying to a commodity's buyers of any era when a manufacturer listens to their concerns and subsequently addresses them. Cracker Jack improved its product in its subsequent 1915 issue, in highly meaningful ways. Most importantly, a buyer could have his Cracker Jack and his high-grade cards, too! In 1915, a customer found a card inside when he purchased a box of Cracker Jack … and it was stained, just like the 1914s had been. But now, the company offered the option to obtain the whole set pristine and unsullied throughout, by mail in exchange for coupons. (A specially made album to house the cards was also furnished upon request and for additional coupons.) A collector's dream, these early "factory sets" – likely the first of their kind seen in the industry – held a full span of the series' cards that were not only unblemished, but which had been spared the rigors of packing, too.

For 1915, Cracker Jack expanded its offering to a grand total of 176 subjects. The issue (designated E145-2 in *The American Card Catalog*) was identical in appearance and theme to its 1914 counterpart. In other words, it kept intact all of the facets that had made its predecessor so appealing, and it shed all of the earlier version's liabilities. Cracker Jack is a phenomenal set, particularly in the second 1915 incarnation that allowed fans to view their favorite American, National and Federal League heroes in glorious, uninterrupted splendor!

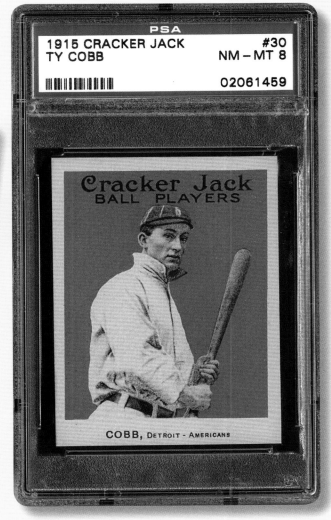

Composition

The 1915 Cracker Jack set of 176 cards constitute a gallery that many enthusiasts of the Dead Ball Era regard as fundamentally unimprovable. The expected Hall of Famers (Ty Cobb, Honus Wagner, Tris Speaker, Walter Johnson and others of that caliber) are present, as well as Miller Huggins, Max Carey, Branch Rickey, Zach Wheat and more. Unlike the foregoing stars who were among 1914's collection of 144 pieces, Edd Roush and Clark Griffith are found only in Cracker Jack's 1915 edition.

Three players are featured who would, just a few years later, make history as highly visible members of Chicago's 1919 "Black Sox" squad. Most prominent among this trio (which also included Chick Gandil and Ed Cicotte) is the card of "Shoeless Joe" Jackson. The latter piece is easily one of the most vigorously sought after and proudly held relics in the modern collecting hobby.

The majority of Cracker Jack's 1915 cards reused the enticing illustrations that had originally graced those players' 1914 entries. The most conspicuous exception is the depiction of Christy Mathewson. Shown for 1914 in a pitching pose on a horizontally oriented cardfront, *Matty's* 1915 card reverts to a dignified portrait likeness. Needless to say, both Mathewson portrayals are highly prized on the basis of their own, respective levels of grandeur.

Key Features and Rarities

Collectors of today are certainly thankful; there are no actual rarities in 1915 Cracker Jack. (It should be kept in mind that the manufacturer's willingness to dispense complete factory sets ensured some degree of evenness in production numbers.)

The predictable effects of demand scarcity and condition scarcity apply, however, and this is fully understandable given the impressive nature of the Cracker Jack cards, and their elevated properties of aesthetic allure when seen in the highest grades.

As mentioned, the 1915 issue's final group of cards – those numbered from 145 through 176, inclusive – have no direct counterparts in prior year's abbreviated production. For this reason, they're in somewhat stronger demand than many of the first group, as all of the collectors who seek to obtain a Cracker Jack card of each player and who are willing to settle for a suitable example from either year are compelled to compete with conventional set-builders for those final 32 pieces.

Bottom Line

Just like the snack they accompanied, 1915's Cracker Jack cards left consumers hungry for more. Regrettably, the onset of World War I, perhaps combined with a shift in Cracker Jack's marketing strategies, brought a close to the company's two-year-old baseball card venture. While they lasted, the productions revealed a cardmaker's art at its finest, and the second, most-refined of Cracker Jack's vaunted pair – the 1915 edition – has been revered ever since as a classic release holding undisputed "all-time" status.

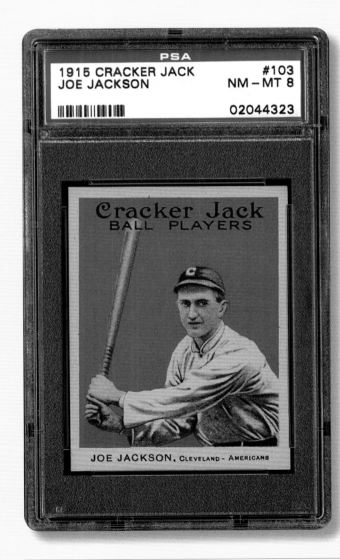

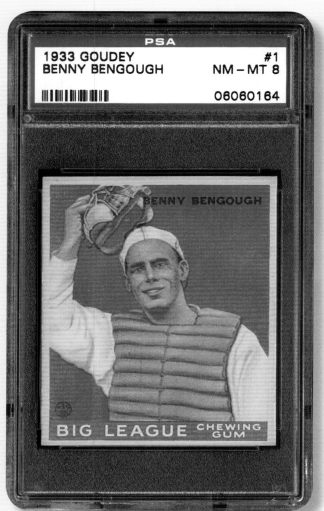

Background

Those who didn't actually live through it have difficulty imagining the mood in America during the post-Depression era. The time of the flappers gave way to a period of bread lines. What must have been a giddy feeling of 1920s prosperity, transformed reluctantly into an atmosphere of worry and desperation. The populace, accustomed to immediate gratification accompanied by the prospect of more in the offing, was now more receptive to small doses of pleasure, and sought distraction, however fleeting, from the overriding concerns of the day.

Whether by coincidence or not, the early 1930s posed the ideal environment for a positive change in the established configuration of gum and candy trading cards. Gum cards of the 1920s generally emulated their tobacco counterparts in size and format. Discreet and unimposing, those items (known in the industry as the "E"-card genre) afforded a limited opportunity for creativity in design; thus, collectors were comfortable with, but rarely dazzled by, the offerings that accompanied the confections of the day.

Into this sedate and demonstrably precedent-driven marketing environment, Goudey Gum Company of Boston launched its revolutionary "Big League Gum." For the first time, a packaged product (supposedly having undergone significant improvements in its own right) was threatened with being overshadowed by the gimmick with which it was distributed. Goudey's 1933 baseball cards enjoyed a highly auspicious debut and for reasons that immediately become apparent to anyone viewing the items, initiated a Golden Age for collectibles of their kind.

The new gum cards' most immediately recognizable and eye-catching feature is their size. Enlarged to 2⅜" by 2⅞" (much bigger than their predecessors' considerably narrower dimensions) Goudeys come well-equipped to display the magnificently colorful, artistic illustrations of ballplayers that quickly set a modern standard in terms of eye-appeal. The cards' physical enlargement also enabled the presentation of much more information on the backs. Previously, size constraints allowed just one or two lines of descriptive text, a limitation reinforced by the necessity of leaving room for the requisite advertising.

Goudey's 1933 cards were printed on thicker cardboard stock, too. Where tobacco and candy cards of the past, with their thin cardstock canvases, carried a delicate feel, the gum cards introduced an intriguing mode of substance; the cards were somehow sturdier, with more heft, than those that had come before. A pack for a penny was now an investment in a viable and not-inconsequential bundle containing a high-quality picture card and a serious slab of chewing gum, both neatly packaged within an attention-grabbing wrapper. This was a great deal ... especially in the throes of tough economic times.

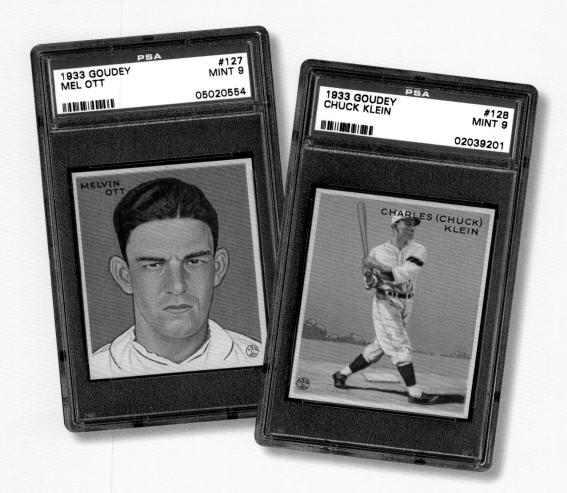

Composition

The 1933 issue, strictly speaking, accounted for 239 cards. (A 240th entry – #106, produced in 1934 in response to consumer outcries – is another story altogether!) Most prominent among the series' content is an abundance of Hall of Famers, with multiple depictions of key personnel. It must have been a no-brainer for those Goudey employees charged with selecting athletes for inclusion to go heavy on Babe Ruth. Sure enough, there are four different Ruth portrayals, and one of those (#144) was double-printed and therefore, found in packs at twice the rate of lesser figures. There are three cards of Joe Cronin (#s 63, 109 and 189) and two of Jimmy Foxx (#s 29 and 154), as well as two each of Hornsby, Hubbell and other luminaries.

Redundancy isn't always a bad thing. It should be pointed out that Goudey quite sincerely sought to "give the customers what they want." The result of this intent was not only numerous star cards, but *different* ones of the most desired figures. (In one pack, for example, a buyer might find a no-nonsense portrait of Mel Ott, and in another, there could be a view of Ott's fearsome batting posture.) In those years before the widespread distribution of color photographs, these highly visual morsels were certainly received with great enthusiasm!

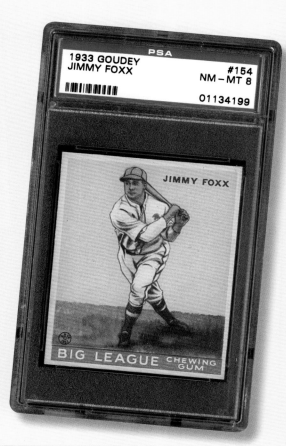

Key Features and Rarities

The 1933 Goudey cards were printed on ten different press sheets containing 24 cards apiece, and the subjects found on the first two of those sheets (the "Low Numbers") are a bit scarcer than the issue's other entries. In practice (again, excepting the anomaly posed by #106 Lajoie), realities governing differences in the popularity levels among individual players brought about a previously unheard of circumstance – *demand* scarcity – that had nothing to do with production numbers. Collectors naturally hungered for Babe Ruth and Lou Gehrig portrayals; they were, and obviously still are, much more likely to pursue those depictions than ones featuring such athletes as George Uhle and Ed Brandt.

As an aside, it should be noted that 1933 Goudey included a number of minor leaguers too. We wonder how much success a New York youngster, seeking to obtain a Goudey card of Bill Dickey or Tony Lazzeri, would have had with only the likes of the New Orleans Pelicans' Eddie Moore and Dan Howley (the Toronto Maple Leafs' manager) in his for-trade portfolio.

Bottom Line

Sure, cards had been packaged with candy in the past. But, with its fabulous combination of larger size, creatively rendered and dramatically colorful images, and unbelievably powerful player selection, 1933 Goudey is almost indisputably acknowledged as the first meaningful gum card release. To many, on an emotional level, they're the first baseball cards, period.

Ironically, Goudey's subsequent products failed to fully capitalize on the groundwork laid by the spectacular and (apparently) inimitable 1933s. The concept's expression suffered abbreviation in 1934, and became distracted in 1935. The company's string of innovations had ceased altogether by the time the onset of World War II rendered such concerns frivolous. Nevertheless, the legacy of the 1933s remains intact, instantly recognizable to the viewer of almost any subsequent production.

Background

After single-handedly reinventing and invigorating the gum card market in 1933, the Goudey Gum Company was on track for a satisfying encore performance the following year. Its clientele's expectations were high and the Boston-based confectioner delivered the goods.

The 1934 edition of Goudey's "Big League Chewing Gum" reflected the best choice its maker could possibly have selected in terms of basic premise, namely, it kept all of its glowing and trend-setting 1933 innovations intact. Such top-quality pieces as the 1933 Goudey cards must have required much more expense to produce than the smaller, less-impressive collectibles that had come before – and which were doubtless mentioned at some point by those in charge of Goudey's finances – but the company still held true to the vision established by its spectacular 1933 effort. The 1934s retained their predecessors' large size, sturdy construction, painted images and blazing color, and one can easily imagine that a buyer's excitement at first sight of the new 1934 cards was mixed with relief that the items were, once again, superb in character.

In 1934, Goudey managed to satisfy the truly difficult goal faced by every manufacturer of products that require annual revision – improving upon a concept without diluting its essence – in fine style. Goudey didn't subject its cardfronts to a drastic redesign, but it improved them. Where solid colors had been employed as many of the 1933s' backgrounds, 1934s added discreet line-drawing graphics of ballplaying figures in action. And, where 1933s offered straightforward company name blocks in the caption areas of most entries, 1934s took pains to showcase one of the game's most prominent heroes.

The bottom one-fifth areas of 1934 Goudey's cardfront player depictions, in the majority of the series' subjects, are devoted to a blue strip holding a small likeness of Yankees immortal Lou Gehrig, along with the legend *"Lou Gehrig says …"* Statements ostensibly authored by Lou appeared on the backs of the cards and

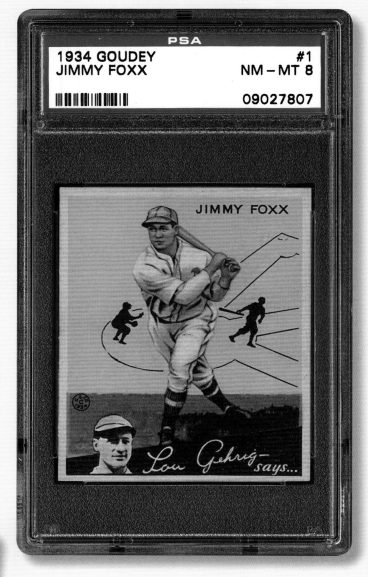

constituted the entirety of the items' descriptive texts. This was a gimmick that highlighted an explicit endorsement of the cards by one of the game's finest! To achieve balance between rival leagues, Chicago Cubs slugger Chuck Klein performed the same role, with his photo presented in a red strip at the lower edge, on most of the set's high-numbered cards. Interestingly, both men's appearances, as noted on each cardback, were arranged by Christy Walsh, the time's famously relentless promoter who is widely acknowledged as the first "sports agent."

Composition

The 1934 Goudey release is complete at 96 cards. Perhaps more were planned for later issue, but the series' roster of just eight dozen subjects reveals a thoroughness in player selection that should have inspired thrills in even the most demanding fan.

The lowest numbers in the 1934 Goudey set are packed full of superstars and future Cooperstown honorees. The flagship entry – the #1 card – pictures charismatic slugger Jimmie Foxx; he and Mickey Cochrane, Dizzy Dean, Leo Durocher and Chuck Klein are all found within the issue's first ten numbers! Following in rapid order are Paul Waner, Frank Frisch, Carl Hubbell, Lefty Grove and others. Lesser stars take over midway through the set's lineup, but the rookie card of Hank Greenberg (#62) and a high-numbered keepsake of KiKi Cuyler (#90) merit special mention.

Unlike its 1933 series, Goudey's 1934 issue avoided multiple portrayals of the same player. Only Lou Gehrig (#s 37 and 61) is afforded more than one card. The majority of enthusiasts, if questioned, would indicate he deserved the distinction and, in any case, both of Gehrig's cards display attributes of beauty that place the pieces among the most attractive and cherished of all 1930s gum cards.

Omissions? The most glaring shortcoming in 1934 Goudey would seem to be the absence of Babe Ruth, who was, at the time, toiling in his last year with Gehrig's Yankees. The set's noteworthy lack of a Ruth card is a mysterious circumstance. Perhaps, 1934 was seen as Gehrig's turn to shine, and Walsh didn't want the *Iron Horse* to share the spotlight with another larger-than-life client. Since the Babe was featured in Goudey's 1934 Premium issue (known today as R309-1, and consisting of just four subjects presented in an eye-catching 5½" by 8¹³⁄₁₆" format), it's possible that this large piece was regarded as Ruth's 1934 Goudey card. Regardless, the treatment given to the majority of the sport's most important contemporary figures is sufficiently special that even the *Bambino* is barely missed.

Key Features and Rarities

The 1934 Goudey set's "High Number" series (including #s 73-96, and, to a lesser extent, #s 49-72) are much tougher than the foregoing entries. Owing to the concentration of stars among the lower numbers, however, this situation might not have caused too much consternation during the time of 1934 Goudey's original distribution. (The same can't be said for modern collectors, many of whom encounter monumental frustration in attempting to assemble the "Highs!") The set was produced on four 24-card press sheets; on one of these, the famous 1933 Goudey #106 Napoleon Lajoie – complete with its 1933-style reverse – shares space with 23 "*Lou Gehrig says…*" and "*Chuck Klein says…*" cards for 1934.

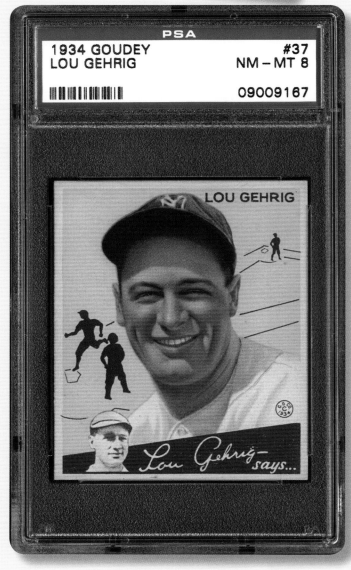

Bottom Line

The 1934 release seemed to herald more great things for Goudey's future, with the abridged nature of the 96-card set acting as the only possible cause for alarm to those who noticed it. Indisputably a treasured issue that merits "all-time" accolades, 1934 Goudey receives the highest marks for its artwork, content and overall substance … it would be quite a few years before the hobby saw another production that could have been described even remotely as its equal!

1941 Play Ball Baseball

Background

During the first administration of U.S. President Franklin Delano Roosevelt, the Goudey Gum Company of Boston completely remodeled the nation's baseball cards. Larger, bearing fuller illustrations and a relative wealth of player information, those 1930s classics had been enthusiastically received by the gum-buying, card-collecting public.

The industry's fortunes shifted somewhat quickly though, and by the time of FDR's third term in office, the direction established by Goudey was in the hands of a new caretaker.

Gum, Incorporated, of Philadelphia, maker of some of the period's finest non-sports, entertainment-themed card sets under the leadership of chewing gum entrepreneur Warren Bowman, had become the reigning baseball card manufacturer by 1941. Gum, Inc.'s "Play Ball" brand effectively seized the market in 1939 from a staggering Goudey, and handled it adroitly from the start.

Bowman's approach was safe, predictable and successful. Rather than re-invent the wheel, he presided over a maturation of the theme initiated by Goudey. For 1939's Play Ball release, a 2½" by 3⅛" approximation of the size pioneered by Goudey was retained, with large images and in-depth descriptions of the athletes' careers also present as noteworthy features. However, the similarities to earlier products ended there, as the Play Ball brand was clearly given the latitude to develop its own identity. And, as would be demonstrated, the new leading name in baseball cards was prepared to grow and evolve in the quest to hold its customers' interest.

The first Play Ball cards may have been seen as rather austere when they emerged in 1939. Each collectible's obverse side revealed a black and white, photographic image of the subject player. That's it. No elaborate logos or slogans, no dancing graphics or radiant colors – not even a caption! The effect was such that the buyer was encouraged to turn over the card and read about the ballplayer's accomplishments. (Perhaps, in the cases of lesser figures like Vito Samulis or Tom Sunkel, the turnover was mandatory if the holder wanted to know who the player *was*!) Whatever the precise motive leading to their design, the 1939s were enjoyed in their time – either because or in spite of their lack of visual histrionics – and the production provided an array of superb images to commemorate the 162 players who had been selected for inclusion.

For 1940, Play Ball stuck with the previous year's cardback style and modified the fronts in just one respect; name captions, along with unassuming borders capped by tiny bat, glove and ball graphics were added to its still all black and white frontal motif. The set was expanded to 240 players (including some tougher "High Numbers," distinguished by numerous retired Hall of Famers plus a conversation-inspiring depiction of "Shoeless Joe" Jackson) and Gum, Inc. had another winner.

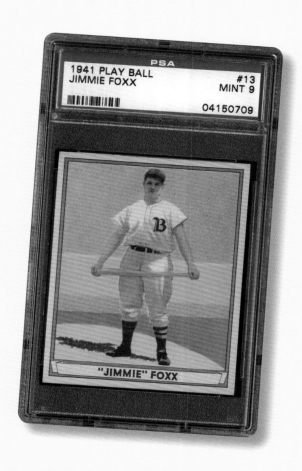

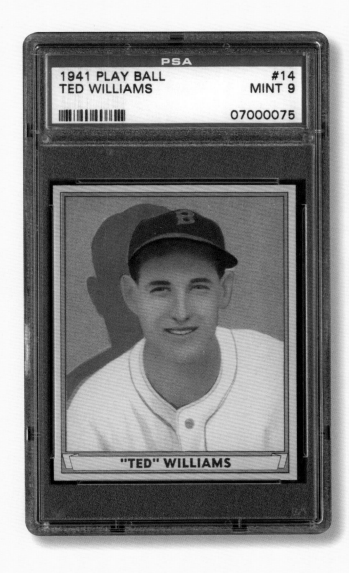

Who knows where Play Ball's discreet, thoughtful progression of style would have led, given a number of years in succession to enable blossoming to its fullest. Regrettably, the exigencies of global conflict dictated limitations, and the hobby was only allowed to experience the brand in one more stage.

The 1941 Play Ball cards showcased the most dramatic new facet seen in the brand to that point. Yes, for 1941, *color* was added to the cards' fronts. It would be a joy to recapture some of the expressions on the faces of those first Play Ball buyers in that season! Those people must have been transfixed, as the pastel colors bestowed upon the new cards' obverse sides are unbelievably graceful and elegant complements to their respective players' likenesses.

The players' poses were now accented by appropriate, flattering hues, and their backgrounds were lent glamorous touches of aesthetically-pleasing single shades or lushly artistic and geometrically derived "Deco-style" treatments. With its lovely, polychromatic new look, the third Play Ball issue easily joined the ranks of the future's "all-time" contenders!

Composition

Although just 72 cards in length, 1941 Play Ball provides a surprisingly satisfying record of a great time in the game. Ted Williams, Joe DiMaggio, Hank Greenberg and Jimmie Foxx headlined a roster that also boasted the likes of Mel Ott, Carl Hubbell, Bill Dickey, Chuck Klein and Lefty Gomez. Most of the issue's entries were granted to the day's established, regular players, but one eventual Hall of Famer, Brooklyn's "Pee Wee" Reese, was shown in his debut-year, rookie card appearance. And as an aspect that must have been a bit of an attention-grabber among fans at the time, the three ballplaying DiMaggio brothers – Joe, Dom, and Vince … all active Major Leaguers during the 1941 campaign – made their only simultaneous showing in the same trading card production.

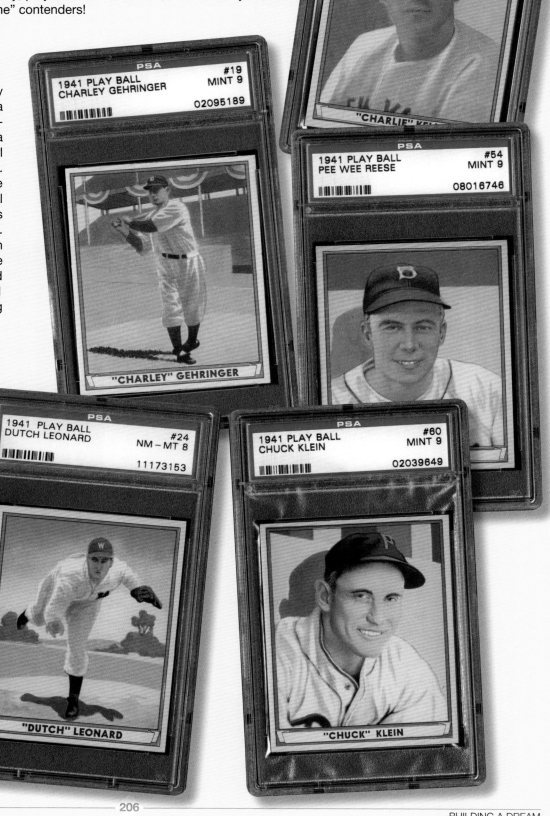

Key Features and Rarities

No rarities or significant variations distract enthusiasts from the straightforward enjoyment of 1941 Play Ball's stellar content. The release was printed on six 12-card sheets; the latter two of these holding #s 49 through 72, inclusive, yielded high number cards that are slightly scarcer than their lower-number counterparts, but not prohibitively so. Aside from an understandable and obvious preoccupation toward obtaining the set's marvelous depictions of DiMaggio, Williams and their Cooperstown-enshrined contemporaries, hobbyists are free to focus on completing a set that's wholly reasonable in number while reveling in its short-but-sweet character!

Bottom Line

Although it couldn't have been forecast with certainty as the collectibles rolled off Gum, Inc.'s presses, the 1941 Play Ball series led the gum card industry into a time of forced hiatus. As they say, sometimes things happen for a reason, and maybe that was the case here. If military people set out on their overseas travels with baseball cards on their minds, 1941 Play Ball's well-selected group of color-tinted star cards must have made for servicemen's fond memories. The last major prewar issue marked an appealing conclusion to one generation's hobby, and doubtless ensured that cards would return to the scene after the crisis passed.

1948-49 Leaf Baseball

Background

By 1948, *Rosie the Riveter* was back in her kitchen, and Major League rosters had returned to the talent-filled glory of the prewar years. Naturally, baseball cards returned, and again were embraced by America's culture. The first new product was a matter-of-fact effort by Bowman, which offered a straightforward array of rather small, completely unembellished black and white photo cards. The second, right on the heels of that no-frills product, was the comparatively flamboyant 1948-49 issue created by Chicago's Leaf Gum Company.

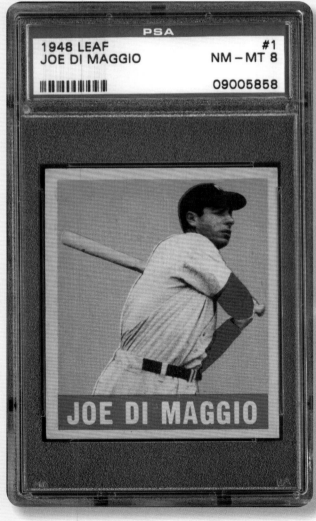

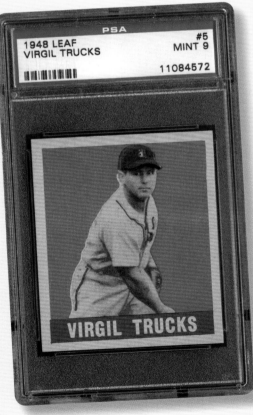

Leaf's card designs reflected gaiety, almost palpably illustrating relief at the war's passing and subsequent fading into memory. The set's bright colors, laid out in dramatic background swaths and vibrant caption blocks, nearly overwhelmed the photographic likenesses of the subjects, and the cards' dimensions (2$\frac{3}{8}$" by 2$\frac{7}{8}$") were reminiscent of their Goudey and Play Ball predecessors. The Leaf cards emerged as un-abashed attention-grabbers, and their introduction was met with delight on the part of anxious collectors.

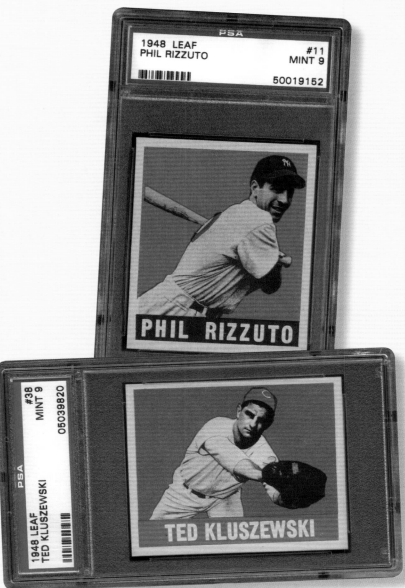

Not unexpectedly, Leaf's issue benefited from a fantastic group of newly anointed star players who, since the gum card market had gone seven years without a serious baseball-themed product, were ripe for portrayal. This staggering lineup of debut collectibles included Stan Musial, Satchel Paige, Phil Rizzuto, Warren Spahn, Ted Kluszewski, Jackie Robinson, Hal Newhouser, George Kell, Enos Slaughter and Larry Doby. Lesser rookies were also present, as well as a number of worthy holdovers from prior seasons, including Joe DiMaggio, Ted Williams, Bob Feller, Bobby Doerr and Luke Appling. Finally, deference to past greatness was shown in Leaf's card #3, which was essentially a memorial piece for Babe Ruth, and #70, an evocative tribute to Honus Wagner.

Composition

The Leaf production consisted of 96 cards, which again displayed a remarkably high proportion of important figures among their content. The release was advantageously front-loaded with key athletes (such as the #1 card, picturing Joe DiMaggio, followed by #3 Ruth, #4 Musial and so on). Buyers would see these first and become addicted to building the set! As would be discovered, 1948-49 Leaf proposed a relatively short series of numbers, so completing the entire group shouldn't be too terribly difficult … right?

Key Features and Rarities

Although only 96 entries were produced for the 1948-49 Leaf set, its cards actual numbers spanned between 1 and *168*. Explanations for this discrepancy reveal – depending upon one's point of view – the effort on the part of the manufacturer to infuse a bit of extra entertainment, or the conduct of deliberate trickery.

The Leaf baseball production was the first major issue of its type to indulge in skip-numbering, wherein the cards' consecutively numbered entries when fully assembled and complete failed to yield a correspondingly complete run of card numbers. Collectors of the day doubtless purchased many extra packs, determined to find card numbers 2, 6, 7, 9, 12 … and 67 others that were *never made*!

A benign interpretation of this circumstance allows that Leaf might have planned to issue the missing numbers later as its release expanded upon demand. In fairness, this may indeed have been the case, but just as probable is the notion that clever marketing (simply defined as, "promoting additional sales by any means necessary") yielded a shocking breach of faith between the maker and its consumers.

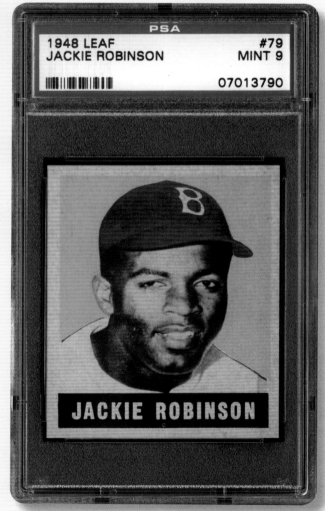

Furthermore, 48 of the cards distributed fall into a category that would become better-known in later years by a single, dreaded term – the "Short Print." Short Printing or SPs, in the most fundamental sense, means that for whatever reason, certain cards exist in smaller quantities than other ones in the same set. Often, SPs result when some designs appear more often than others on a press sheet, or when certain pieces are withdrawn, revised or replaced. In Leaf's case, however, given natural skepticism of its motives in view of the skip-numbering affair, it could probably be conceded that the company's manipulation of its clientele was taking place with the SPs too.

The 1948-49 Leaf set, for the reason just described, is filled with truly difficult cards. Its SPs are so challenging, in fact, that genuinely perplexing anomalies result: where else would Johnny Wyrostek's card be much harder to find (and "worth" more) than Phil Rizzuto's rookie, or why else would a collector pass on a Honus Wagner piece in order to seize an opportunity to acquire a more valuable collectible, like Eddie Joost? It's a frustrating predicament for an enthusiast, when a full one-half of a top quality set is demonstrably *rare*.

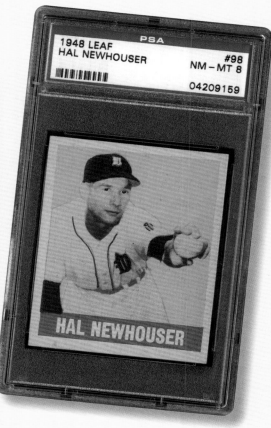

Add to this a heavy dose of condition scarcity – as Leaf cards are printed on coarse card-stock that quickly reveals wear – and demand scarcity affecting its many superstars, and the result is a series that represents a bonafide mark of distinction for the hobbyist who completes it successfully.

Not to be left out in the error realm, either, 1948-49 Leaf accounts for a very tough variation – #102 Hermansk, where haphazard printing infrequently resulted in that player's surname losing its concluding vowel – as well as the interesting but more often seen Full Sleeve (standard) and Short Sleeve (error) versions of Cliff Aberson's card, #136.

Bottom Line

Leaf's 1948-49 release had run its course by the end of the latter year, but it left consumers with tantalizing hints about what they could expect in the future. Cards of satisfying size, with colorful portrayals and star-packed player selection were on the horizon once again. Fans of the time who recalled the early Goudey cards (and the last Play Balls) certainly took heart at Leaf's creativity, built-in collecting obstacles notwithstanding, and certainly, while moving along quickly from the concerns of the past few years, reveled in the prospect of more new cards to come.

Background

While standing essentially alone in the 1951 baseball card marketplace, Bowman flourished during that year's campaign to dominate the candy counter.

Although a few lesser and regional trading card productions, like Berk Ross, Bread for Energy bread labels and Wheaties box-panel collectibles, as well as some strange game cards from an upstart manufacturer (not to be taken seriously) the colorful offerings from Bowman Gum served as the prevailing brand for anyone interested in Major League Baseball-themed gum cards. An archetype, the Bowman product conformed in size to its accompanying wad of chewy confection. Its cards' lovely artwork was embellished only by efficient name captions; the cards' backs exercised brevity in detail. In every respect of the standard of the time, Bowman cards delivered satisfactory levels of familiarity and comfort.

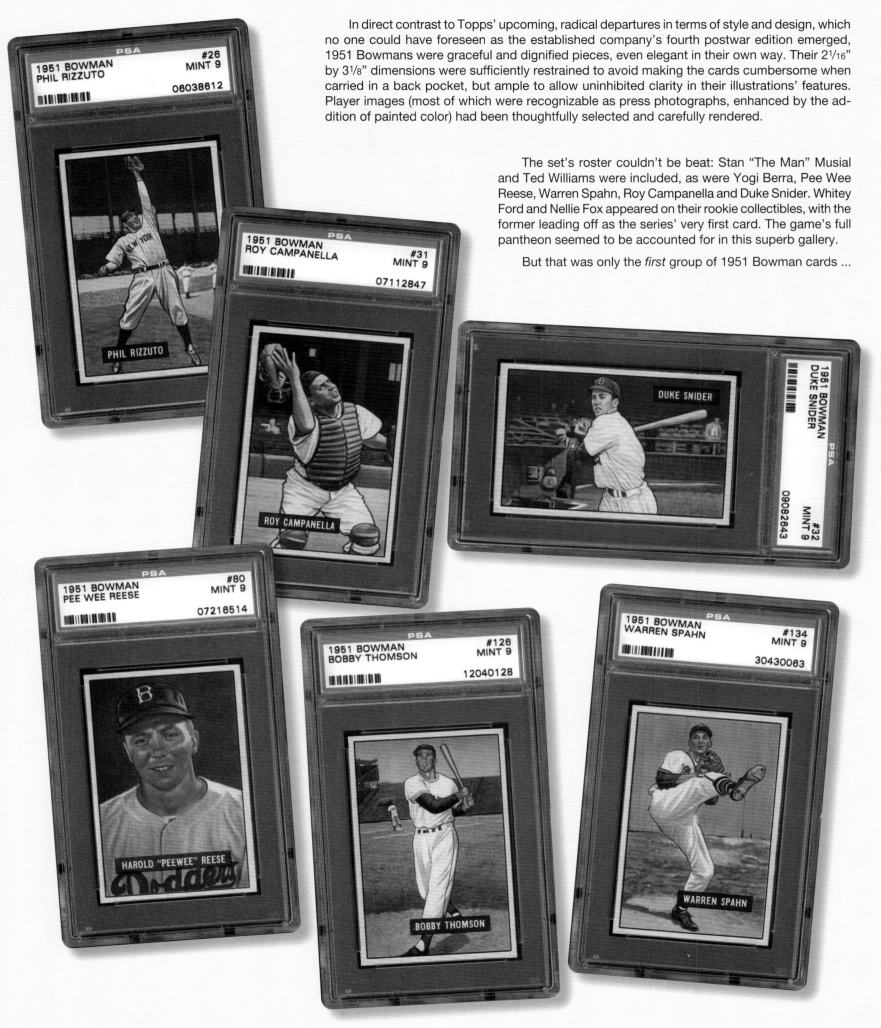

In direct contrast to Topps' upcoming, radical departures in terms of style and design, which no one could have foreseen as the established company's fourth postwar edition emerged, 1951 Bowmans were graceful and dignified pieces, even elegant in their own way. Their 2¹⁄₁₆" by 3¹⁄₈" dimensions were sufficiently restrained to avoid making the cards cumbersome when carried in a back pocket, but ample to allow uninhibited clarity in their illustrations' features. Player images (most of which were recognizable as press photographs, enhanced by the addition of painted color) had been thoughtfully selected and carefully rendered.

The set's roster couldn't be beat: Stan "The Man" Musial and Ted Williams were included, as were Yogi Berra, Pee Wee Reese, Warren Spahn, Roy Campanella and Duke Snider. Whitey Ford and Nellie Fox appeared on their rookie collectibles, with the former leading off as the series' very first card. The game's full pantheon seemed to be accounted for in this superb gallery.

But that was only the *first* group of 1951 Bowman cards ...

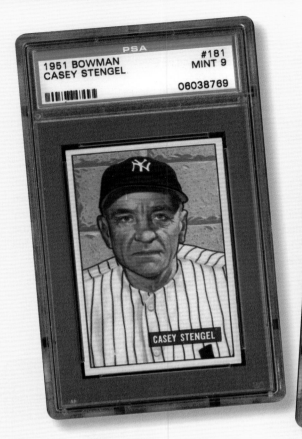

Composition

Although comprehensive and impressive when judged on its initial 252 cards, the 1951 Bowman series became absolutely breathtaking when – late in the issue's production run – it expanded to a grand and final total of 324 entries. Those last 72 pieces (the "High Numbers") elevated the production at once from the satisfying level to the hobby's "all-time" stratosphere.

The final segment of 1951 Bowman holds a worthy group of stars, minor stars and managers, but two depictions, in particular, have ensured its revered status: the rookie cards of young New York stars Mickey Mantle and Willie Mays.

Mantle and Mays were up-and-coming ballplayers who had begun to captivate the game's major market, and Bowman, the savvy, veteran producer of gum cards, eventually had recognized this fact just in time. Mantle's horizontally-oriented, over-the-shoulder batting pose became an immediate sensation among collectors, and the portrayal of his Giants counterpart, Mays, followed close behind. Today, more than 50 years after they first turned up in packs during the Fall of 1951, these are two of the most beloved, in-demand mementos in the card-collecting hobby.

Key Features and Rarities

The high-number series (#s 253-324, inclusive) is naturally a bit scarce, but Mantle and Mays are in such high demand that actual production numbers become meaningless. They're the indisputable "keys" to the set. The 1951 Bowman release contains plenty of future Cooperstown enshrinees, acknowledged stars, and popular players, and with the aforementioned caveats noted, they all enjoy general availability in roughly equal measure.

Bottom Line

Its big pair of rookies alone would seem to make 1951 Bowman a keeper, but to view the issue from the perspective of just two cards unfairly ignores its significance. The production defined a period, soon to culminate, that was well-served by a single, mainstay release. The very next year, the 1951 Bowman set's maker would encounter and try to cope with a market determined to shift toward more complex, inherently exciting products. Proven favorites, such as the nicely done (and sometimes, it seems, under-appreciated) 1951 Bowman gallery, would be left to receive their deserved glory in the future as classic objects of nostalgia.

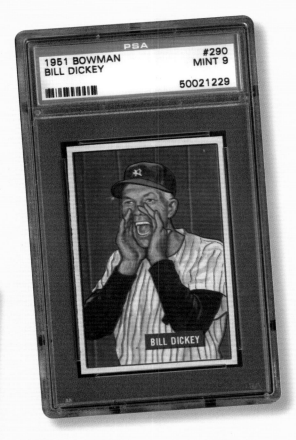

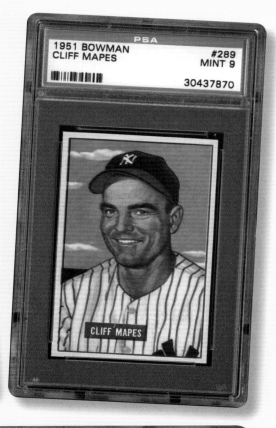

1952 Topps Baseball

Background

"Giant Size!" That was The Topps Company's succinct description – prominently printed on packs and boxes – of its new baseball trading cards for 1952, but the slogan held vastly more meaning than anyone could have recognized at the time.

America's collectors were accustomed to baseball cards that were rather small in their physical proportions. The tobacco issues of the 1910s (relatively tiny) had given way to Goudey Gum's somewhat larger standard by the 1930s. Just before and after World War II, manufacturers settled first on cards approximating Goudey's 2³/₈" by 2⁷/₈" dimensions, then down-sized even further. The time's dominant card-maker, Bowman Gum, produced collectibles measuring 2¹/₁₆" by 2½" between 1948 and 1950, and granted just a bit more surface area (2¹/₁₆" x 3¹/₈") to the cards in its 1951 and 1952 efforts.

Topps wasn't at all bashful about its motives, with respect to the company's decision to release a lavishly designed and extremely comprehensive gallery to compete with Bowman's market-leading 1952 effort. Although the Brooklyn-based manufacturer had only been making baseball cards in a meaningful fashion for a year – its 1951 products included elongated die-cuts and roster-challenged game cards – the company formulated an all-out blitz for the 1952 campaign.

The effect on the dime store candy counter's established order, where a complacent Bowman held the advantage by a wide margin, was dramatic and immediate. Topps' "Giant Size" 2⅝" by 3¾" cards were an instant hit among consumers. Not only were the single cards almost outlandishly big, allowing plenty of room for expansion of baseball cards' most popular features, they were well conceived and attractive. Their huge illustrations and starry-bordered caption areas made Bowman's discreetly small artworks pale in comparison, and the backs? No contest. Lengthy player bios and detailed statistics were immediately adjudged preferable to the now terse-seeming Bowman writeups.

As Topps, impressed by its own handiwork, began to recognize that its idea was being validated nationwide by floods of pennies and nickels from young consumers, additional series of cards were composed and released. The same buyers who had been pleased at first by the cards' creative features were now also dazzled by the number of players included in the production. Clearly, the upstart manufacturer had done its homework before mounting its challenge in the baseball card industry!

The 1952 Topps issue adroitly symbolized America's new, postwar prosperity. And as things turned out, the "Giant Size" cards would develop into a milestone holding monumental gravity for the future of trading cards in general. At the time of the cards' first appearance, they were viewed in a much simpler light. Their premium size, flashy designs and generously dimensioned images brought about the sale of a great quantity of Topps product, and won legions of new participants for the collecting hobby. A win-win for all concerned!

Composition

By the time the season ended and Topps wrapped up production of its 1952 set's final components (and probably, at that point, retired to the company's offices to begin plotting its 1953s), the blockbuster release harbored a total of 407 cards – the largest number of players ever seen in a modern card issue. It seemed that every segment of 1952s – there were six distinct "Series" groups in all – held its own objects of fascination.

As yet another indicator of thoughtful preparation in view of its target market's preferences, the various series of 1952 Topps played their cards in an insightful manner. New York customers, forming the nucleus of the time's confectionery market, found local heroes Phil Rizzuto, Duke Snider, Gil Hodges, Monte Irvin and other Yankees, Dodgers and Giants in the very first series. Certainly, gestures were made toward each team's clientele in every series (Spahn, Sauer, Kluszewski, Roberts and stars of similar caliber also represented their respective teams in Series 1, for example) but a decided New York emphasis acted as a predictable and successful theme throughout 1952 Topps' considerable span: Mize in Series 2, Martin in Series 3, Berra in Series 4, Mays in Series 5, and so forth.

For anyone who failed to spot the trend in Series 1 through 5, the New York bias was made crystal clear with the appearance of the 1952 Topps set's final push. Series 6 emerged like a Who's Who of metropolitan-area stardom, beginning with card #311, the first Topps card of the Yankees' youthful phenom, Mickey Mantle. Mantle's card was followed in succession by depictions of the Dodgers' Jackie Robinson (#312), the 1951 Giants' "Shot Heard 'Round the World" home run hitter Bobby Thomson (#313), Roy Campanella (#314) and Leo Durocher (#315). It looked like the finale at a show of fireworks! After the incredible quintet that led off the segment, such players as Pee Wee Reese, Eddie Mathews and Bill Dickey, and a respectable group of rookies highlighted by Gil McDougald, Joe Black and Hoyt Wilhelm, kept the chase interesting, and encouraged the purchase of baseball card packs well into the months of September and October.

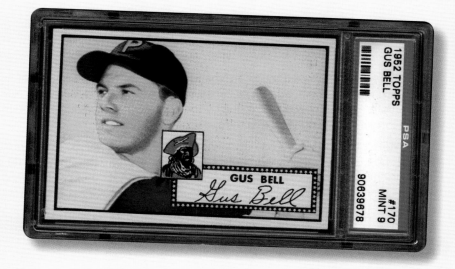

It's hard to identify any faults at all in a production that's exciting on so many levels, but fairness dictates mention of a couple of omissions. Ted Williams and Whitey Ford were away, serving their country at the time of issue, and were left out for that reason. But another key superstar, Cardinals' great Stan Musial, was under contract to Bowman and couldn't appear in a competitor's product. The 1952 season was the first time in a generation that two national manufacturers went head-to-head in marketing like-themed cards of Major League Baseball players, and Musial wouldn't be the last player for whose licensing rights Topps and Bowman were destined to compete.

Key Features and Rarities

In such an expansive gallery as the one formed by 1952 Topps, it's not surprising that key and difficult entries abound.

For starters, an *entire series* in 1952 Topps – the big-name-filled Series 6 containing card #s 311 Mickey Mantle through 407 Eddie Mathews – is considered rare. The final segment of Topps' inaugural release was only minimally distributed, as retailers, who had yet to become familiar with the allure of all those late-season Topps stars, held to the logical assumption that buying patterns of the past would once again dictate a seasonal falling-off in card sales. So orders were reduced or cancelled altogether. And it's probable that Topps anticipated this and kept Series 6 production numbers low to begin with. Hobby lore provides all sorts of additional conjectures to account for the scarcity of 1952 Topps "High Numbers." They were sold primarily in Canada, they were dropped off a ship sailing out of New York Harbor and so on – but the fact that these subjects are in perpetually short supply, for whatever reason, is indisputable.

The 1952 Topps set also unintentionally laid the groundwork for a pair of concepts that were just beginning to be understood as the set was being sold. The first condition scarcity, was felt whenever a collector tried to find the issue's first card (#1, picturing Andy Pafko) in respectable shape. It wasn't long before that card, and, to a lesser extent, its series-concluding counterpart, #80 Herman Wehmeier, was acknowledged as the customary victim of rubber-banding, and truly nice copies became quite difficult to obtain.

The second notion, demand scarcity, was thrust to a whole new level by 1952 Topps' star content, and by the uncertain distribution of its "High Numbers." Topps' cards for 1953 had barely

reached the stores' shelves, and fans were already looking for Mickey Mantle's rookie card from the preceding year. Naturally, there were (and are) precious few to be had. Mantle's card, which was actually double-printed on its press sheet and therefore twice as available, in theory, as most of the "Highs," became one of the first gum cards that collectors were willing to pay *cash* for. The Mantle Rookie, spearheaded a trend to bring about a reduction in the casual trading of the past, and an increase in the focused acquisition mode of the future.

Finally, there are just enough variations, errors and oddities in 1952 Topps to keep things interesting on those fronts, too. Each card in Series 1 (#s 1-80) can be found in Black Back and Red Back configurations; two of those (#s 48 and 49, pitchers Joe Page and Johnny Sain, respectively) are the subjects of error versions wherein each man's card has the other's printed back. And for those who love the impossibly trivial differences, the card of Frank Campos (#307) comes with and without an unusual, overprinted star on the reverse. The former is very seldom encountered.

Certainly, Topps showed the hobby how it's done, when it comes to infusing tremendous variety, innovation and intrigue into a nominally finite set of collectibles!

Bottom Line

In so many ways, 1952 Topps ushered in a new era of card collecting, and acted as the flagship release for several generations going forward. The series gave collectors what they wanted; its manufacturer took note, recognized the preferences of its clientele, and modified future offerings accordingly. The "Giant Size" cards were probably the first such collectibles whose main function wasn't simply to stiffen a pack or act as a come-on for the real product – the gum. No, these items were intended to be sought out and purchased on the strengths of their own merits. Like so many issues of the future, which were patterned in varying degree after the 1952 Topps' model, they succeeded admirably.

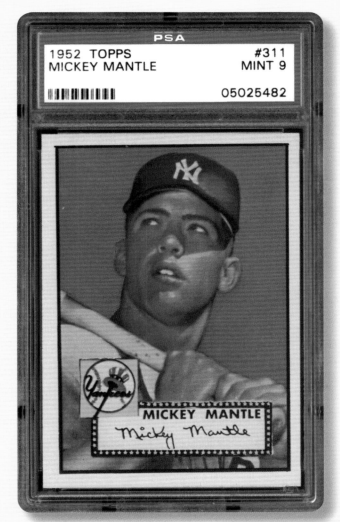

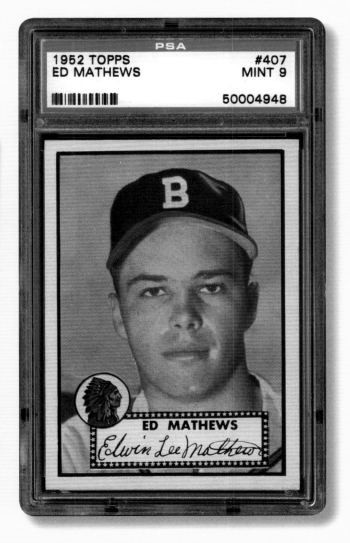

Background

For 1953, Bowman Gum answered Topps' "Giant Size" challenge with clear and crisp pictures from life – the first of their kind seen on cards! The company's new, up-sized color release, featuring exquisite, photographic images, has been widely heralded for generations as standing among the most beautiful modern-era set of baseball cards ever made.

Lofty accolades indeed, for the product of a manufacturer who'd so recently faced a rude awakening in its merchandising strategies. The company had been content for five years to create and distribute cards that, while attractive and visually engaging, were still, well … *small*. Topps' inaugural effort in 1952 proved evidently, size *does* matter. To its credit, Bowman wasted no time pondering the situation, and fired back hard in the very next season.

Bowman's 1953 cards measured 2½" by 3¾", slightly narrower than Topps 1952 collectibles but for all practical purposes like-sized. The backs presented layouts that were doubtless inspired by Topps' prior-year model (with content to match), and they bore little resemblance to their Bowman antecedents. The cards' reverse sides, however, were merely an afterthought to the awestruck consumer: the first-time buyer of 1953 Bowman Color cards, one imagines, would have been hopelessly transfixed by their *fronts*.

No captions, no team logo devices, no manufacturer's legends – just fabulous pictures! An observer could easily become immersed in the sight of a favorite player, as the set allowed full expression of each athlete's facial details and uniform features. In some of the highest-quality photographs ever presented on baseball cards of any kind, before or since, 1953 Bowman brought the viewer "up close" to Mickey Mantle's graceful follow-through, Stan Musial's relaxed humor, and Allie Reynolds' resolute gaze. The renderings seem to have been selected with their subjects' personality traits in mind – as these aspects were effectively transmitted and brought to the forefront without benefit of embellishing descriptions – and they were executed with every bit of the depth and clarity enabled by the technology of the day.

Priceless images abound among Bowman's 1953 Color cards. Pee Wee Reese's leaping in action portrayal is an all-time favorite among hobbyists. Hank Bauer, Yogi Berra, and Mickey Mantle, in one of the first multi-player shots to grace a cardfront, appear together, all smiles, on card #44, in acknowledgement of the clientele's presumptive New York leanings, Billy Martin and Phil Rizzuto share the set's other card of this type (#93). Classic single-player depictions are plentiful in the release, but those of Whitey Ford, Gil Hodges, Warren Spahn and Roy Campanella are also popular on the basis of their aesthetic merits as well as the respective prowess of their subjects.

Interestingly, Bowman also put out a 1953 Black & White counterpart to its marvelous color effort. Although less than half as many ballplayers were included in the company's less flamboyant version, the Black & White series did cover a different group of athletes, and it afforded an intriguing comparison in terms of style.

Bowman clearly did its homework and came prepared to meet its competition in 1953. The company's Color issue gave the hobby yet another high point to be enjoyed in its own right, and several of its features would inevitably serve as models for the refinement of future products.

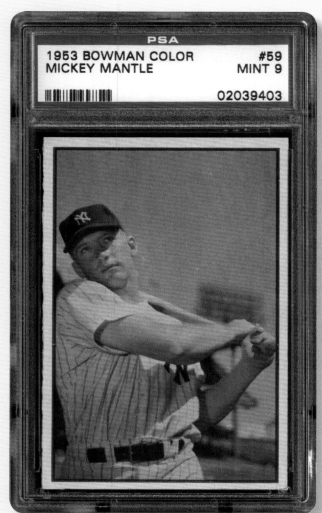

Composition

The 1953 Bowman Color issue held 160 cards, and the separate Black & White series accounted for 64 more. Although sometimes lauded more for its design than its content simply because of its extraordinary appeal in that realm, the issue delivered plenty of star power: Mantle (on his own card #59, as well as the aforementioned #44), Campy, Ed Mathews, Yogi Berra and Duke Snider are just a few of its big names. (Black & White's highlights included Casey Stengel, Bob Lemon, Hoyt Wilhelm and Johnny Mize.) Incidentally, the 1953 Color card of Stan Musial, arguably one of his most prized ever, would be his last regular-card appearance until 1959. And the series' conspicuous omissions were few. Ted Williams was still away fighting for his country in Korea as a Marine pilot, while Jackie Robinson and Willie Mays were under contract to Bowman's new nemesis, Topps.

Key Features and Rarities

Collectors of 1953 Bowman's Color or Black & White versions don't have to worry about obscure print variations or troublesome rarities, but the Color issue's "High Numbers" (113-160) are somewhat more challenging than the preceding run of 112 cards. So although Berra, Ford and Gil Hodges are found in the release's scarcer group, great solace can be taken from the realization that Mantle, Musial, Reese, Campanella and the two multi's are harbored in the set's easier component!

PSA · 1953 BOWMAN COLOR · #114
BOB FELLER · MINT 9 · 11376673

PSA · 1953 BOWMAN COLOR · #117
DUKE SNIDER · MINT 9 · 30828059

PSA · 1953 BOWMAN COLOR · #118
BILLY MARTIN · MINT 9 · 90419984

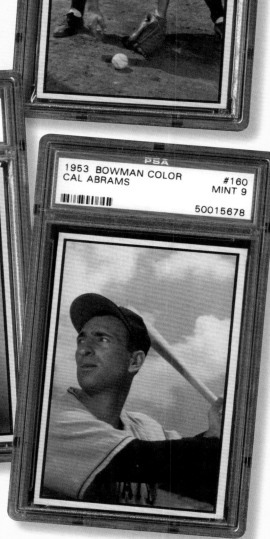

PSA · 1953 BOWMAN COLOR · #153
WHITEY FORD · MINT 9 · 50001127

PSA · 1953 BOWMAN COLOR · #160
CAL ABRAMS · MINT 9 · 50015678

PSA · 1953 BOWMAN COLOR · #121
YOGI BERRA · MINT 9 · 07112199

Bottom Line

Bowman's 1953 response to Topps, in the form of the older company's Color gallery, remains unmatched in the esteem of many enthusiasts. Upon the Bowman product's release, the series quickly earned an enduring nickname – "Pure Cards" – that would eventually come to be applied to later-issue productions, from any manufacturer, that adhered to 1953 Bowman Color's simplicity in design. A foundation piece of the 1950s-era hobby, 1953 Bowman Color is one of its period's defining gum card efforts and one of its most cherished, nostalgia-inspiring mementoes.

1953 Topps Baseball

Background

Topps' 1953 release emulated the prior year's successful "Giant Size" experiment. For its sophomore-season effort, the company concocted a largely portrait-filled issue, with favorably enticing but still-restrained aesthetic qualities suggesting the maturity of the genre … not bad for what was only its maker's second year of involvement in a demanding market!

The 1953 series is distinguished by detailed player portraits on most of its entries – the artistically rendered but still true-to-life illustrations effectively allowed card buyers to "get acquainted" with their heroes, and to recognize their faces. Stylistic enhancements on the cardfronts were limited to single bottom-corner caption areas. There, a viewer would find the featured athlete's name and position, and an in-color version of his team's current cartoon or symbol logo enabled immediate identification of his alliance. The caption areas' background fields were red for American Leaguers, black for National League subjects.

Cardbacks exhibited a busy layout, but it was a creative and effective one. Descriptive text, the preceding year's and career-to-date statistics and personal information had by 1953 become routine elements of the cards' reverse side, and these were retained. Instead of decorating the cards' fronts as in other years, a facsimile autograph was now placed atop a player's biography on the back; the scripting was inked in deep red, to match the theme staged by the backs' other elements. Topps also launched a "Dugout Quiz" trivia question feature to engage readers' interest, that consumed more than one-fourth of the back's available surface. In one form or another, the "Quiz" format would be re-employed in many subsequent seasons' Topps products.

Finally, huge numerals stating a card's number (and situated within a baseball graphic) appeared at the upper left corner of each collectible's reverse side. With that bold sequencing device, not to mention the color and logo-coded fronts, Topps cards must have been a breeze to place in order, in any fashion desired by a young fan during the summer of 1953!

Composition

Jackie Robinson's card stood as the #1 depiction in Topps' 274-piece, 1953 release. Although as initially conceived, 280 cards were foreseen, six numbers – probably casualties of last-minute pullouts owing to contract disputes with rival Bowman – were never made or distributed.

A more-than-adequate representation of the 1953 campaign's star power was included, and this time, unlike in 1952, Mickey Mantle (#82) was front-and-center in the group's low-numbered series. Customers had to wait for Willie Mays, however, as the Giants' popular center fielder (card #244) didn't surface until the issue's final segment. Among the release's other important players were Satchell Paige (on what would turn out to be his only career-contemporary Topps card), Yogi Berra, Whitey Ford, Ed Mathews, Roy Campanella, Bob Feller, Phil Rizzuto, Pee Wee Reese and Warren Spahn. Marine pilot Ted Williams was still half-a-world away from participation in baseball-themed activities and, in order to find a few key stars like Duke Snider, Stan Musial and Gil Hodges … well … buyers were left to turn to Bowman for those.

Each player was treated very respectfully by the generally unknown artists who were commissioned to adapt portraiture for use in the 1953 Topps set, and this is a pervasive value that is observable while viewing the issue's gallery. These painters seem to have been given just a bit more latitude in stylizing the release's later-numbered entries. Although a number of cards (like Mays') deliver full-length poses, and several – as a delightful exercise of artistic license in showcasing one's employer – reveal fanciful Topps advertising signs on the outfield walls behind the pictured athletes.

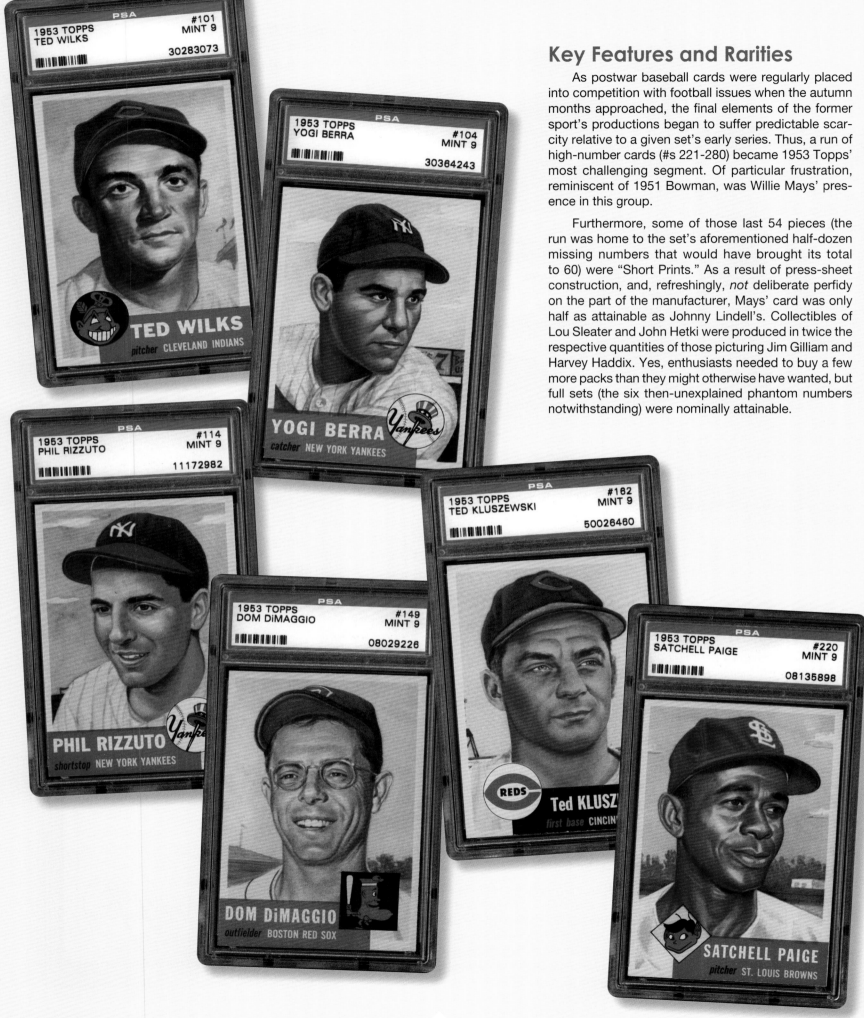

Key Features and Rarities

As postwar baseball cards were regularly placed into competition with football issues when the autumn months approached, the final elements of the former sport's productions began to suffer predictable scarcity relative to a given set's early series. Thus, a run of high-number cards (#s 221-280) became 1953 Topps' most challenging segment. Of particular frustration, reminiscent of 1951 Bowman, was Willie Mays' presence in this group.

Furthermore, some of those last 54 pieces (the run was home to the set's aforementioned half-dozen missing numbers that would have brought its total to 60) were "Short Prints." As a result of press-sheet construction, and, refreshingly, *not* deliberate perfidy on the part of the manufacturer, Mays' card was only half as attainable as Johnny Lindell's. Collectibles of Lou Sleater and John Hetki were produced in twice the respective quantities of those picturing Jim Gilliam and Harvey Haddix. Yes, enthusiasts needed to buy a few more packs than they might otherwise have wanted, but full sets (the six then-unexplained phantom numbers notwithstanding) were nominally attainable.

1953 TOPPS #244
WILLIE MAYS
NM – MT 8
07005500

WILLIE MAYS
outfielder NEW YORK GIANTS

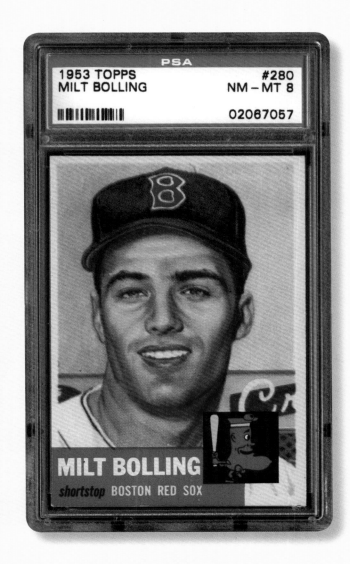

1953 TOPPS #280
MILT BOLLING
NM – MT 8
02067057

MILT BOLLING
shortstop BOSTON RED SOX

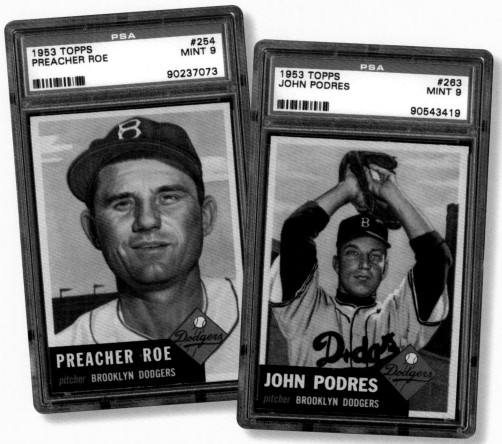

1953 TOPPS #254
PREACHER ROE
MINT 9
90237073

PREACHER ROE
pitcher BROOKLYN DODGERS

1953 TOPPS #263
JOHN PODRES
MINT 9
90543419

JOHN PODRES
pitcher BROOKLYN DODGERS

Oddly, once more a function of press sheet considerations and probably barely noticed as the 1953s hit the shelves, a few lower-series cards were also technically SPs. The weight of the first group's large volume sold must have obscured the relative difficulty of #s 61 Early Wynn and 81 Joe Black (plus three others) among "Low Number" consumers.

Nothing "rare" or especially problematic affects those who wish to construct 1953 Topps. There are a few understandable SP or "High Number" hurdles to face when piecing together the array, but to presage a trend that would last for many years, acquisition of the series' Mantle and Mays cards tends to stand as most fans' top priority.

Bottom Line

A highly encouraging symbol of continuity, Topps' second baseball release seemed to point to a company philosophy that would compel it to conscientiously build upon prior year card sets and still give collectors something new to anticipate with each release. The 1953 Topps issue, an extremely worthy group of collectibles, easily holds its own among other "all-time" classics from its era.

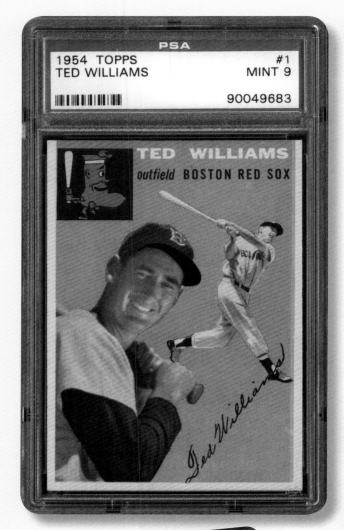

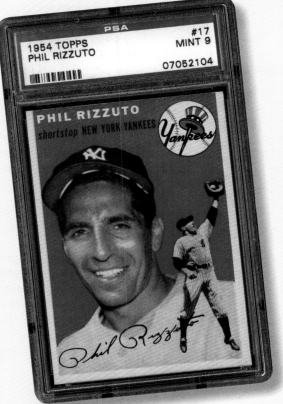

Background

A developing phenomenon, that would come to be seen as the Topps juggernaut, gathered momentum in 1954. That company, not Bowman, was now in a position to dictate baseball cards' preferred dimensions, and its 2⅝" by 3¾" size had effectively become the market's undisputed standard. Still, there was plenty of opportunity for innovation in design with respect to the features that would adorn the cards' big surfaces in a new year, and Topps took full advantage with the creation of its 1954s.

The 1952 issue had been a trendsetter, and 1953 demonstrated a solid theme, executed with restraint and dignity. But all the stops were pulled in 1954, as the new models were characterized by (for lack of a better word) "activity."

All kinds of visual elements vied for the customer's attention on the front of a 1954 Topps baseball card. A central, color image shared space with a smaller one that showed the same player in a game-action posture. A huge team logo proclaimed the subject's franchise affiliation in no uncertain terms, and each player's facsimile autograph, along with a standard caption showing name, position and (again) team, showcased his identity. A brightly-hued background color, which, unusually extended all the way to the card's top edge, set off the entire arrangement, making each 1954 Topps cardfront look like a collage-piece tribute to the featured athlete.

The horizontally-oriented backs were just as busy, with personal information, descriptive text, statistics and cartoon sequences all filling their respective allowed spaces. The aesthetically appealing cardbacks also revealed full-bleed color, with the deep-green accenting of the design's bottom-half left attractively uncontained.

In short, there was nothing tentative about 1954 Topps' manner of presentation. The cards were easily the most eye-catching collectibles of their kind produced to date, and the fervency with which the market responded to their design left little doubt about the success of the concept.

Composition

Numbering just 250 cards, the 1954 Topps release offered a technically limited but still very potent range of subjects. A satisfying array of big stars, including Berra, Ford, Hodges, Mays, Robinson, Snider, Spahn and Williams, populated its ranks, as well as a small but truly amazing group of rookie players: Ernie Banks, Al Kaline and, most significantly, Hank Aaron.

Although clearly still grappling with contractual licensing rights issues that precluded the appearance of some key players (most notably, Mickey Mantle), Topps wasn't fretting about their absence. Instead, the company capitalized on the grandest marquee name that *was* featured. Ted Williams – just back from military service and once again settling into his starring Major League role – was granted the illustrious position as the issue's #1 depiction. His card, blessed with all of the series' typical style attributes and set apart by a vibrant orange-colored background, assumed its position as the production's flagship entry. But that wasn't enough – Williams also appeared on the *final* card in the set. There, his yellow-themed, second portrayal displayed different pictures of Ted, and the back of his card #250, which is one of the most popular cards in the modern hobby, carried a full narrative in cartoon form.

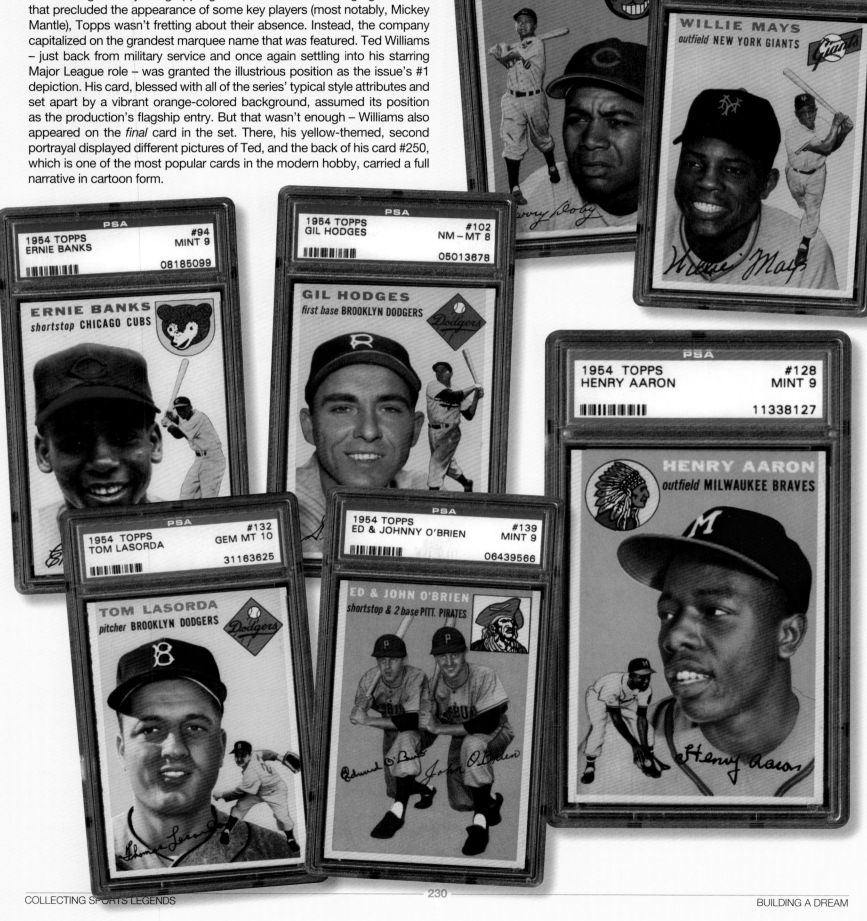

In the realm of design, the 1954 Topps cards demonstrate a quirk only a true enthusiast would notice. If one sorts a stack of the 1954 cards with all of the players facing up, the backs are jumbled if the group is examined from the back. Conversely, if the cards are put in order by number (resulting in a neatly ordered, consecutive group when viewed from the reverse), half of the obverse fronts will be upside-down when the sorted pile is looked at from *that* perspective. This odd circumstance is a result of the factory press-sheet layout, on which cards were placed top-to-top before cutting (those contiguous tops yielding the aforementioned color border at the northward edges) and the backs were similarly aligned to accommodate the borderless green effect on those sides. This pattern wouldn't be employed again for many years, and in any event brought about little or no consternation among hobbyists.

Key Features and Rarities

The awesome 1954 Topps rookie crop, highlighted by Aaron, Kaline, Banks and Tom Lasorda, stands as a focus of interest among present-day Hall of Fame collectors and speculative card-buyers. One segment of the issue (#s 51-75) is seen as mildly difficult, but there are no profoundly elusive numbers in the release. As is the case when attempting to construct many of the vintage card sets, attaining satisfactory condition poses more of a challenge than the simple location of all of its numbers.

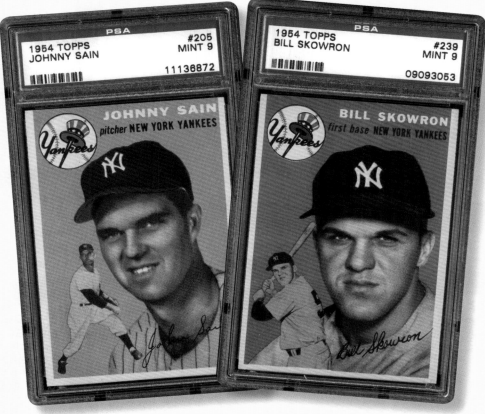

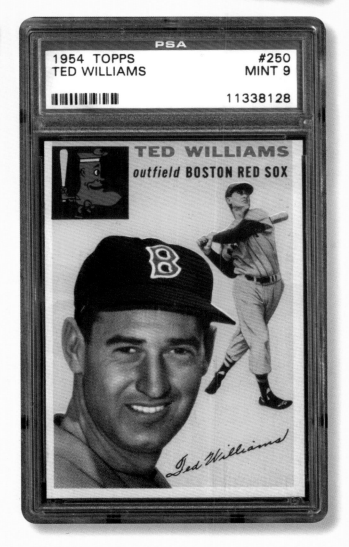

Bottom Line

As if any doubt remained at this point, in just the third year of its baseball card activity, Topps was making its intentions clear as the undisputed superior card company of the hobby during that period. The 1954 Topps productions' dual images, and player autographs, and the association of color and graphics featured on single cards were, nothing less than spectacular for their time. In another campaign that witnessed Topps and Bowman going head to head, Topps emerged as the maker of the year's "all-time" classic effort.

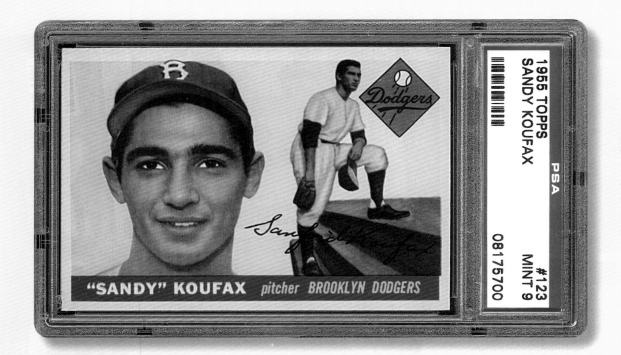

And what about Mickey Mantle, Bob Feller, and Whitey Ford? Those players, and other conspicuous absentees, were tied up in "that contract thing" once again, and most of them appeared in Bowman's competing product. To this day, though, enthusiasts tend to enjoy 1955 Topps to such a great extent that its lack of full comprehensiveness is seldom mentioned.

Key Features and Rarities

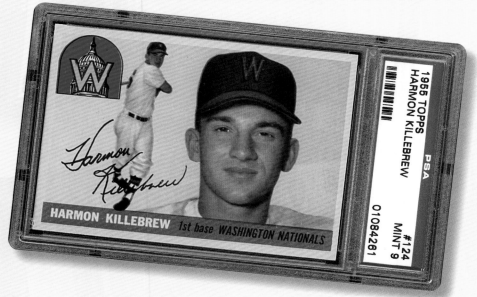

Once more, the "High Numbers," presumably hitting the market just as the season's new football cards were released, are more scarce than the issue's lower-numbered subjects. In 1955, the "Highs" included #s 161 to 210, and #s 151-160 were a bit tougher, too. So Mays, Berra and Snider are more challenging to locate, but Williams, Robinson and Aaron can readily be found … not a bad trade-off in comparison to the imbalances in other years.

Among the rookies, only Clemente is meaningfully impacted by the "High Number" stigma, although the first card of Harry Agganis (#152), picturing the young Red Sox standout who passed away suddenly in June of 1955, just prior to achieving true stardom, is typically a bit harder to obtain.

The 1955 Topps set contains no bonafide rarities – just a number of pieces that are condition sensitive – and is more of a pleasure than a chore to assemble today.

Bottom Line

With its 1955 effort, Topps demonstrated that visually inspiring cards were here to stay! After a successful run of dazzlers – the "Giant Size" 1952s, the portrait gallery 1953s, and the kinetic 1954s – the company seemed to be on a winning track, and history would affirm that this was indeed the case. The 1955 Topps set's position on an "all-time" list is assured, not by any type of groundbreaking change or attention-grabbing gimmick, but by its worthy stewardship of a concept that had proven its appeal to the card-buying public. It's a classy and attractive, much-cherished issue, and an absolute favorite among baseball nostalgists!

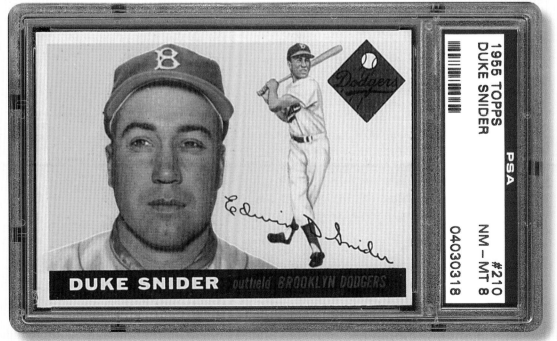

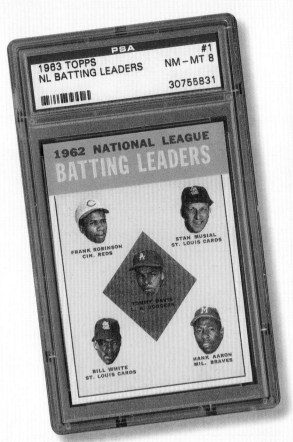

Background

By the time Topps' 1963 production hit the shelves, almost a full generation of collectors had moved along from the year of the company's boldly pace-setting 1952 issue. During the intervening span of more than a decade, plenty of developments in card sets composition had been observed; numerous innovations had been attempted, and many survived from year to year. The resultant "snowballing" of features yielded a fresh and modern production, which displayed such visual complexity and crowded content that the cards likely wouldn't have been fully understood, let alone appreciated, ten years prior. Gum card evolution had been a gradual process, though, and buyers in 1963 were more than ready for the kaleidoscope of delights in the new Topps set.

Each of the 1963 Topps player cards was highlighted by a bright and glossy, large photograph of the athlete as the primary focal point of the card. A much smaller, black and white image, centered within a circular area slightly smaller than a half-dollar at a bottom edge corner, revealed a different pose; the secondary photo, plus caption information, occupied a full-bleed band of color that formed the piece's lower margin. The cards' backs, printed in black with yellow-orange backgrounds, carried neatly arranged layouts with personal info, biographical highlights (some in text form, plus one as a cartoon), and in most cases, statistical records covering the player's entire career.

Composition

The set consists of 576 cards, which combine to cover an amazing gamut of information and a packed roster of baseball's personnel. A quick look at the range of the 1963 Topps special elements shows that the set is relatively dizzying in its scope and causes the viewer to reflect upon the fact that almost none of these features were present in standard Topps or Bowman productions from just ten years earlier. The ideas caught on upon introduction and had become, essentially, mandatory elements of card sets' construction.

Here's an overview of the 1963 Topps themes along with the year the first item of each type was introduced by the company. Remember, all of these are presented *in addition* to the issue's regular player cards:

League Leaders – First employed in 1961, the Leaders (in such categories as RBI, Batting Average, and Wins) are honored on the 1963 Topps ten opening numbers.

Managers – (1950) Managers had been shown off and on in baseball card sets since the 19th Century, and the current skippers were all present in the 1963 Topps set. An interesting design feature of the managers' cards was the replacement of the standard second picture with their team logo instead – a great touch when sorting the cards into team order!

World Series Cards – (1959) Card #s 142-148 deliver a pictorial recap of the Giants' defeat at the hands of the Yankees.

Multi-Player Cards – This idea debuted in modern times in 1954, when Pittsburgh's O'Brien Brothers shared card #139. This concept was allowed plenty of freedom in 1963, with some marvelously creative and inspired combinations affording Topps the opportunity to add some extra star cards to its production. Stan Musial and Willie Mays formed the "Pride of N.L." (#138), and four Pirates, including Clemente, constituted #18's "Buc Blasters." "Friendly Foes" Hodges and Snider appeared together on #68, Mickey Mantle and two teammates were the "Bombers' Best" (#173), and the "Dodgers' Big Three" card (#412) showed Koufax, Drysdale and Podres. It would be difficult to contend that such items didn't contribute loads of personality to a card set! Topps was finished with the multi-players by the time it concluded Series 5. Presumably, space in the lineup was needed to accommodate the concentration of rookie cards in the higher card numbers.

Rookie Cards – Each of these entries presented *four* rookie players. First-year players were taking on increased prominence in each new Topps release. Special note of a ballplayer's debut appearance began in 1960 with the company's All-Star Rookie (Trophy) cards; these awards continued in 1963 on certain athletes' individual cards. But many more young players were captured in the small circles of the 1963s' four-in-one rookie cards. Foremost among these is Pete Rose (on "High Number" card #537), whose tiny portrayal remains one of the most vigorously pursued collectibles of its era. Other up-and-comers treated in this fashion by Topps include Willie Stargell, Rusty Staub, Tony Oliva and Gaylord Perry (shown on what was actually a second-year card, as the future Hall of Famer was apparently demoted from his full-card status in 1962). By 1964, the manufacturer drew back on this approach. Rookie cards the next year would feature just two players apiece, but the four-player style allowed dozens of first-year appearances in 1963 … and Pete Rose is the undisputed king of this category.

Team Cards – (1956) With the cropped, color-background photos of each squad, these cards remained as popular as ever among enthusiasts.

Checklists – (1956) It had become customary by this time to give consumers a means of record-keeping as they built their sets. The checklists also allowed Topps a bit of self-promotion: the last few numbers on each series' checklist gave a sneak preview by revealing several players who wouldn't be available until the *next* series went on sale! The checklists were also fertile ground for hunters of oddities, as most of the cards displayed obscure variations in their color arrangement, punctuation or copyright line.

Key Features and Rarities

Late-season production and distribution drop-offs led to *two* levels of scarcity in the 1963 Topps set. Its "Semi Highs" (#s 447-522) and its "Highs" (#s 523-576) were both hard to find, with the former actually a bit more difficult than the true "Highs." The coveted Rose rookie is situated among the highest-numbered group, along with Stargell, Clemente, Duke Snider and Nelson Fox. The "Semi Highs" are notable for the presence of Lou Brock, Willie McCovey and Orlando Cepeda, as well as Harmon Killebrew and Tom Tresh – both of whom are regarded as especially elusive "Short Prints" within their already challenging numerical group.

Elevated levels of condition scarcity are attached to the 1963 Topps cards, too. Each card has two sensitive corners where solid color extends all the way to the tips, and these are prone to readily expose the slightest bit of wear. Truly uncirculated-looking 1963 Topps cards are particularly tough to obtain on the basis of this (admittedly attractive) quirk in the issue's design.

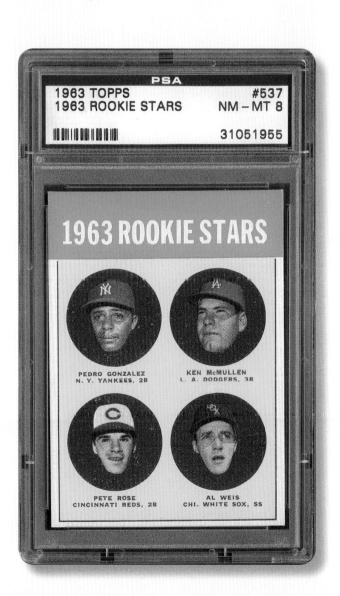

Bottom Line

The 1963 Topps release set the tone for a different decade and a different generation. The collecting public had matured since 1952, in terms of expectations, and buyers were ready to be dazzled, rather than merely satisfied, by each new season's group of cards. As an eye-catching release packed full of interesting sub-topics and multi-themed specialty pieces, the 1963 Topps set acted as yet another instance in which the premier card manufacturer's offering was perfectly suited for its time.

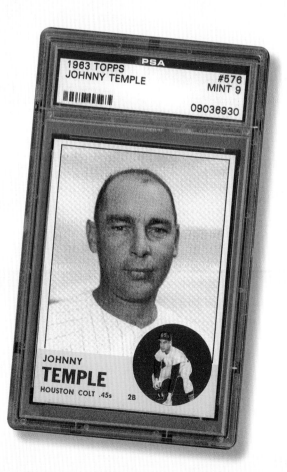

Background

With a different look for yet another new generation, 1975 Topps baseball cards came out of the gate well-equipped to impress their clientele. The first packs opened that year must have momentarily taken aback the initial consumers: a handful of 1975 Topps cards showcased a mind-boggling rainbow of colors, plenty of stars, loads of attention-grabbing features, and those splendid two-tone borders ... in other words, all of the ingredients necessary to bring about another banner year for the Brooklyn-based confectioner.

Topps had been a serious player in the trading card realm for 23 years at this point, and had completely dominated the field for two decades. The company learned its lessons well during that span, and astutely retained the most widely appreciated features in its cards from year to year. Its 1975s displayed a range of design elements that could be traced in their origins all the way back through its 1952s, its 1955s and its 1963s. The 1952 cards exhibited facsimile autographs on their cardfronts, and so did 1975s. Entertaining cartoons appeared on the backs of mid-1950s Topps cards, and here they were once more in yet another production. The early 1960s had been noteworthy for the continued development and perpetuation of full-career statistical listings, multi-player collectibles, and specialty cards honoring award winners, individual records and World Series contests – not to mention the now customary 2½" by 3½" card size. Every one of these components, and more, was evident in the bright, full-bleed bordered 1975s.

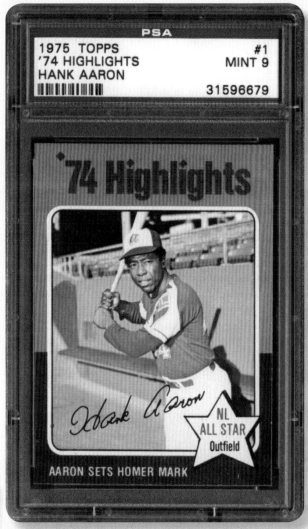

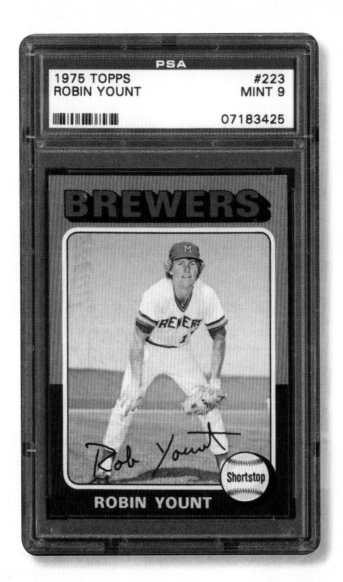

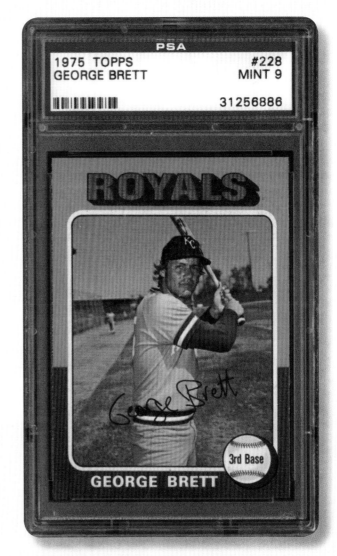

There was one big difference in 1975, though, that would have astonished a buyer who hadn't looked at cards since, say, 1963. It was immediately clear that the concept of cards in compartmentalized series no longer applied. Beginning the year before, in 1974, Topps emblazoned an enticing slogan – "All 660 Cards in One Series!," or words to that effect – on each box and wrapper. Collectors of 1975s quickly realized that they wouldn't have to wait for subsequent boxes later in the season to acquire Hank Aaron, for instance, all of the cards were available *now*. (Incidentally, Aaron is one example of Topps' marketing savvy in constructing its 1975 set: the slugger was featured on card #1, a 1974 Highlights commemorative, as well as the final entry, #660 – Hank's regular card.)

The downside? It took a *lot* of individual-pack purchases to round up 660 different cards. No doubt, the hobby's mathematicians could quote some depressing odds with respect to finding the last few cards needed for a set in this fashion. But Topps benefited from the ability to mount just one extended production run and to simply handle re-orders all year long from a stocked warehouse. In this way, presumably, the company gained a steady stream of revenue from buyers of packs all year long.

Composition

The 1975 Topps set's 660-card length was a stable and orderly size for the time. Its innovations included appealing Team cards (equipped with Checklist backs that applied to each respective squad's members) and 1951-1974 MVP cards, along with Record Breakers and Highlights. All three of the latter types afforded Topps the transparent opportunity to cram more superstar pictures into the release, but the depictions were enjoyable, nonetheless. The MVPs, utilizing cardfront designs borrowed from past Topps issues, gave collectors two big names on each card. In this way, 1975 Topps enthusiasts were treated to multiple new collectibles of recently retired legends like Mickey Mantle and Willie Mays.

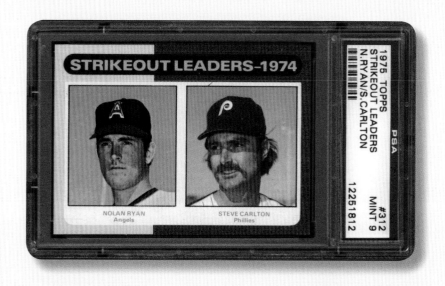

Starting in 1973 Topps had elected to cluster a majority of the set's first-year players into one segment of the issue. For 1975, numbers 614 through 624, inclusive, were devoted to Rookies, grouped by position and showing four players per card. Talented youngsters like Gary Carter, Keith Hernandez, Jim Rice and Fred Lynn debuted to the public on these Rookie entries.

Given all the planning and organization that must have gone into partitioning the Rookies, it's ironic that the two most sought-after single cards in 1975 Topps somehow eluded the agreed-upon formula. Future Cooperstown enshrinees George Brett (#228) and Robin Yount (#223) have their own cards, right in the mix – mid-set – with the game's veterans.

Key Features and Rarities

To produce its 1975 series, Topps had to merely lay out five different, 132-card press sheets of customary size and cut them into 660 cards. That process yielded the full contents of the year's set, and all cards were printed in equal quantities. No "High Numbers," no "Short Prints," no anomalies of any kind. The company had engineered its methods to achieve maximum efficiency, and the outcome was straightforward and predictable – and in some ways, pleasing. Although enthusiasts often refer in nostalgic tones to the "old days" of tracking and chasing new series of baseball cards as they surfaced in unexpected places, many found 1975 Topps' "One Series" distribution to be quite satisfactory.

As the nation's fans were building their 1975 Topps sets, few knew that the card manufacturer was simultaneously indulging in a bit of odd behavior. After the many years of tinkering and refinement that had brought about the streamlined and wholly acceptable 1975 Topps baseball product, the company opted to test another scenario. A few, limited areas of the country were chosen as venues to receive 1975 Topps "Mini" cards, which replicated the "regular" cards, detail for detail, right down to the style of their packs' wrappers. The only difference: "Mini" collectibles measured 2¼" by 3⅛" … just a little larger than a 1951 *Bowman* card! Whether Topps succumbed to its own spell of nostalgia at this point, or was just investigating the prospect of holding down the cost of raw materials in its purchases of cardboard, will likely never be known. But the "Minis" became a legitimate and recognized, stand-alone production, and 1975 Topps cards in the relatively scarce, smaller size are widely and happily pursued in today's hobby.

Bottom Line

Topps' contribution to the trading card industry in 1975 stood as yet another period-defining (and visually gratifying) release. Its colors, its features and its length all lent themselves well to a group of youngsters – at this point just two years away from the *Star Wars* phenomenon – for whom activity and vibrancy were essential qualities. The period's collectors thrived on 1975 Topps cards, which, as mentioned, were the newest in a lineage that had successfully evolved from patterns formed through traceable ancestral roots. But – witness the 1975 "Minis" – the manufacturer was still experimenting …

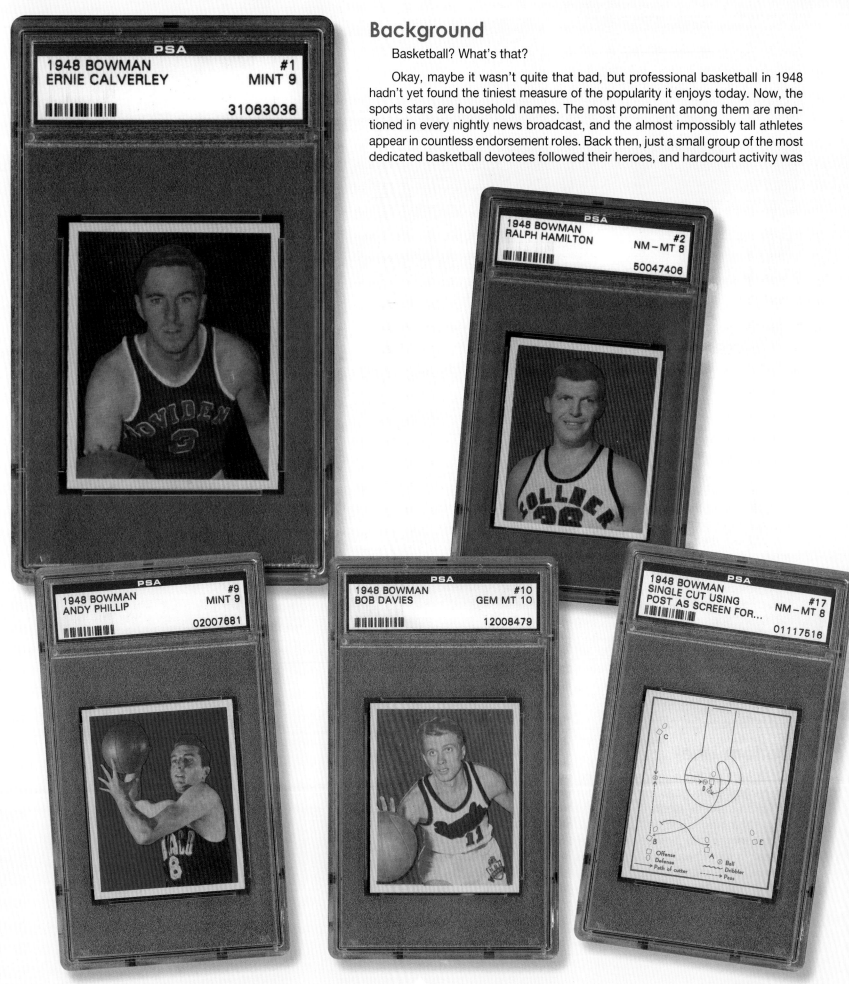

Background

Basketball? What's that?

Okay, maybe it wasn't quite that bad, but professional basketball in 1948 hadn't yet found the tiniest measure of the popularity it enjoys today. Now, the sports stars are household names. The most prominent among them are mentioned in every nightly news broadcast, and the almost impossibly tall athletes appear in countless endorsement roles. Back then, just a small group of the most dedicated basketball devotees followed their heroes, and hardcourt activity was

much less publicized than baseball, boxing, or even football. Fans at the time might have been simply unaware of the on-court exploits of Buddy Jeanette, Jim Pollard, or Joe Fulks, and they almost certainly didn't know the Providence Steamrollers' or the Baltimore Bullets' positions in the league's standings.

So it is with a measure of admiration that the hobby views Bowman Gum's inaugural and only venture into the production of basketball-themed trading cards. Utilizing the exact design format seen in its 1949 Baseball release, Bowman deployed its 72-card basketball set in 1948. The 2$\frac{1}{16}$" by 2½" cards, which primarily feature black and white, tinted photographs of individual players (each with a red or blue background) provided an initial glimpse of the young sports stars of the day. The reverse side of each card revealed black and red printed personal information, a short biography, and an offer for one of several Bowman novelty items (available upon redemption of card-pack wrappers).

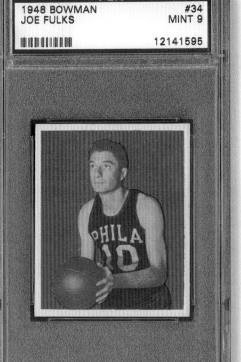

Scattered among the player cards in the 1948 Bowman lineup were a dozen Play Diagram cards conceived to introduce a few of the sport's nuances to the collecting populace. These were quite creative and informative in their own way, and it is a bit surprising that the idea wasn't used more often in other disciplines. (Only Philadelphia Gum's similar, mid-1960s football pieces, which were embellished by the presence of some big-name head coaches, come to mind by way of comparison.)

Bowman Basketball emerged as a quality product that was seeking to create its own special niche, and most collectors of today would agree that the set had all the tools necessary to achieve success.

Composition

The 1948 Bowman set of 72 cards was printed on two, 36-card press sheets; its six-dozen entries (which included 60 player cards) were adequate to cover the subject matter. Since the release was the first basketball set ever, all of its athletes were shown, by definition, on their rookie cards. Stellar luminaries (and eventual enshrinees in the Naismith Basketball Hall of Fame in Springfield, Massachusetts) included Andy Philip, Bob Davies, Red Holzman, Arnie Risen and a few others. The true attention-grabber of the series was the portrayal of Minneapolis Lakers forward George Mikan on card number 69.

Mikan was a big man whose towering 6'10" height is credited with revolutionizing the way in which the game was played. His influence was seen as overpowering, and his card is akin to those of Babe Ruth, Gordie Howe, and equivalent monumental figures in other sports. Mikan's card-back biography carries the note, "*… rated by experts as the greatest basketball player in history*." He was surrounded in 1948 Bowman by other figures who were noteworthy in their own right, but the inclusion of Mikan cemented the issue's lasting all-time significance.

Key Features and Rarities

The cards featured on the issue's pair of press sheets were not distributed simultaneously; the second group – the "High Numbers" (#s 37-72, inclusive) – were in circulation for a shorter period of time and are scarcer than the "Lows." George Mikan's card, naturally, was found in the product's more challenging component.

Although each standard card, as mentioned, employed a solid red or blue background to accent its player's photograph, a small number of grey background cards from the issue's second group have been documented. It is speculated that these unusual-looking rarities are print variations that were never intended for sale; whether any of these odd pieces ever made it into standard gum packs remains questionable.

For the would-be set builder in today's hobby marketplace, the 1948 Bowman basketball set includes a straightforward roster of 72 subjects, 36 of which are somewhat difficult, and one of *those* is the most sought-after basketball card on the planet!

Bottom Line

Bowman made a sincere attempt to cover new territory in addressing basketball, but its decision makers must have quickly concluded that the payoff was insufficient. A retailer's display, at the dawn of the prosperous 1950s, must have been a sight to behold with its Leaf and Bowman baseball cards, Leaf's boxing and football cards, a variety of enticing non-sports products, and even Topps' peculiar and self-developing Magic Photos. New and still-unfamiliar basketball cards must have been overcome by competing options that were gaudier, more exciting, and more habitual. Although perhaps a product that was ahead of its time, Bowman's basketball cards have earned plenty of retrospective appreciation … very likely from a group of collectors whose grandfathers chose something else at the candy counter in 1948!

Background

In 1957, with its baseball, football and non-sports card sets like Zorro, Planes and Hits Stars already in place and selling well, Topps entered the hardcourt realm, too. Evidently determined to cement its position as the undisputed market heavyweight in card production, basketball appeared to be a good fit for the aggressive manufacturer.

The company had seen Bowman take its lumps a few years earlier after following the same logic. Bowman's 1948 Basketball set had been a credible release, certainly, but it had demonstrated through lackluster sales that the existing client base for its theme was painfully thin.

Topps elected to defy precedent, perhaps figuring the popularity of its other products would help inspire interest in basketball, too. The company assembled an 80-card release, consisting of standard-sized, 2½" by 3½" depictions, and filled its roster with the time's best-known stars.

One can only speculate about the fact that Topps' 1957 experiment with basketball cards ended after just a single production. The cards were certainly nice enough, arguably equal in quality and creativity to the contemporary baseball and football issues, but it is indisputable that they weren't widely collected. (As anyone who's broken down an undisturbed gathering of cards from the period can attest, the basketball cards are inevitably under-represented, if at all.) In 1957, Topps was fated to repeat the same mistake Bowman made in 1948. While it was a detriment to the Brooklyn-based company, it has been a boon for the hobby!

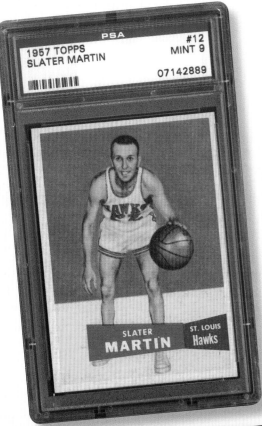

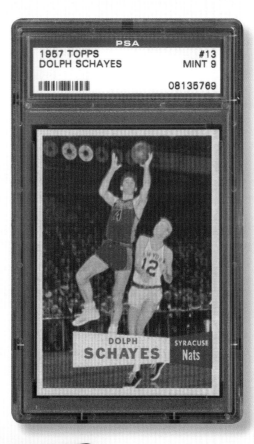

Composition

The 1957 Topps set consisted of 80 cards, and few would disagree that this number was adequate to encompass the subject matter at hand. Full-length poses, action shots and portraits were featured; some of the player's photographs were left uncropped, with generally dim and vaguely resolved backgrounds showing game day crowds, and others revealed simply the athlete, with a bright, single-color backdrop added for visual emphasis. A two-part caption banner stated the player and team names in individual compartments.

The back of each card carried personal details, a paragraph of text and a small statistical chart. A card number appeared on the item's upper-left corner inside a backboard-style graphic. In an especially creative feature that acknowledged the sport's preoccupation with player height, a diagram at the right side of each cardback, similar in concept to a youth's growth chart, pinpointed the subject athlete's stature by means of a generic ballplayer figure placed against a graduated measuring scale.

The cards were printed in top-to-top fashion on press sheets, making half of the backs upside-down relative to the fronts when sorted by number.

It had been almost ten years since Bowman's basketball venture came and went, and, once again, an entirely new group of players in their first-time portrayals were seen in 1957 Topps. This fresh generation featured such future Hall of Famers as Bob Cousy, Bill Sharman, Paul Arizin, Dolph Schayes, Bob Pettit, Jack Twyman, Tom Heinsohn and others – all of whose cards are naturally much sought-after in today's hobby. Other 1957 Topps rookies included Maurice Stokes, whose career would end tragically in 1958 and, significantly, Celtics legend Bill Russell.

Key Features and Rarities

Through circumstances brought about by press-sheet layout, about forty percent of the cards in 1957 Topps basketball are "Short Prints," and were produced in smaller quantities than the remaining depictions. In a glass is half-full or half-empty sort of way, some hobby sources don't cite "Short Prints," instead referring to the more plentiful cards as "Double Prints." Semantics aside, at least 30 cards are demonstrably scarcer than the other 50.

The issue's tougher cards include those of Bill Russell, Cliff Hagan and Andy Phillip, but Russell's entry (card #77) is seen as 1957 Topps' standout "trophy piece." A figure who dominated the sport during his time and beyond, the acquisition of a top-quality Russell example is the most adamantly stated goal of many basketball specialists.

Topps adopted the 2½" by 3½" size for cards in 1957 after several years of the 2⅝" by 3¾" "Giant Size" proportions pioneered by its 1952 baseball series. It is possible that updated factory equipment commissioned in 1957 to accommodate the smaller card size also resulted in a few quality control lapses, especially as expressed in an excessive number of cards that displayed substandard centering, grainy photos or surface "snow." The company's 1957-era baseball, football and non-sports series are notorious for imprecision in these aspects, but the basketball release seems particularly challenging. High-grade 1957 Topps Basketball cards that display nicely aligned centering and smooth, unimpeded images stand as the true rarities of the series, as many hobbyists can attest!

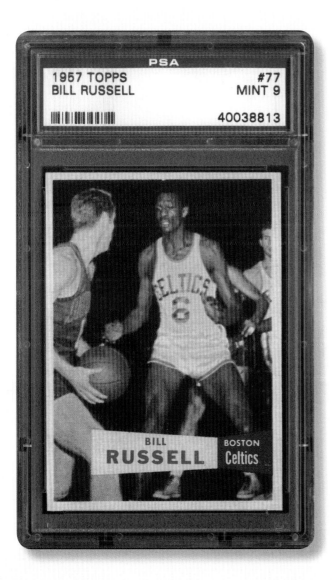

Bottom Line

Although 1957 Topps Basketball was another one-year shot at the sport on the part of card makers, the series is important when viewed in retrospect. In a practical sense, the set established a beachhead for Topps in the category, and brief as its distribution was, it undoubtedly helped pave the way for the company's revived pursuit of the sport in 1968.

Basketball has enjoyed a sketchy relationship with cards, their makers and their buyers. A review of the theme's gum card continuum from the 1940s through the 1990s will illustrate the specialty's ups and downs. A study along those lines will also declare 1957 Topps' significance as a collector favorite for a half century, and a solid "all-time"-level in card production.

1961 Fleer Basketball

Background

Up until this point, there had been one basketball gum card set per generation. In the manner of its Bowman and Topps predecessors of the 1940s and 1950s, respectively, the Frank H. Fleer Company enjoyed a golden opportunity and a clear field to produce superstar and rookie collectibles.

Fleer entered a dormant market in the early 1960s; the last prior hardcourt-themed series was released by Topps four years earlier in 1957. The Philadelphia-based company's approach was a conservative one, featuring standard-sized, 2½" by 3½" cards whose obverse provided straightforward identification of each player and his team along with his image. Cardbacks presented personal info, short biographies and statistical summaries. Each card number was set apart at the right margin inside a stylish, blue band on the reverse.

An immediate impression of the 1961 Fleer Basketball is that the series is much brighter in character than the other companies' foregoing efforts. In spite of the 1961's use of black and white photography in its player portrayals, liberal doses of color in caption blocks and team logos – which together consumed nearly one-third of each cardfront's surface – ensured a general air of vibrancy in the assembled gallery.

Of greatest interest to modern collectors, though, is this captivating, single-year issue's *content*.

Composition

The complete set consists of 66 cards and is in itself a reflection of Fleer's caution in committing to the basketball's uncertain potential in terms of the gum card market. The 66-card format lent itself perfectly to print production considerations allowing two full sets to be laid out on a 132-card factory press sheet.

In performing a task made easier by the proposed 1961 set's limited scope, Fleer could claim a high rate of success in selecting the game's truly significant players for inclusion. The set has its share of Arlen Bockhorns and Dave Gambees, but it boasts a decided preponderance of the likes of Wilt Chamberlain, Jerry West and Oscar Robertson.

Fleer certainly recognized the emergence of certain key ballplayers, and their presence in the sport was probably a huge motivator in the set's conception. Among others, Wilt, West and the *Big O* saw their rookies collectibles come forth on the

1961 Fleer set. Further, those giants of the game (and 19 others of equivalent or only slightly lower stature) appeared on two depictions apiece. Each man's lower-numbered entry was his primary card (and is, today, revered foremost as his true rookie piece), while the second served as an In Action portrayal that emphasized his prowess. The former type cast the subject athlete in a close-up pose, and the latter, as its name implies, revealed an on-court scene.

So the 1961 set was deliberately composed in a manner that would show-case the league's very best. And why not? In addition to the trio already mentioned, the set held two cards each of Bob Cousy, Tommy Heinsohn, Len Wilkins, Elgin Baylor, Clyde Lovelette, Bob Pettit, Dolph Schayes and Jack Twyman … with a number of these stars featured on debut-year collectibles. Sam Jones, Walt Bellamy, K.C. Jones, Tom Gola and Hal Green are a few more icons who were pictured. The set's roster was unbelievably formidable, especially within the context of a relatively "short," 66-card production.

Not to be overlooked was the Celtics' Bill Russell, another extraordinary gentleman of the game who also appeared on two cards (#s 38 and 62). Although not a rookie in the 1961 release, Russell's undeniable mystique contributed an element of importance to the production that can't be ovetstated. A towering presence at the time of the set's release – and long after – the sight of Russell's card in this release must have inspired immense gratification in the hearts of 1961 Fleer's first consumers.

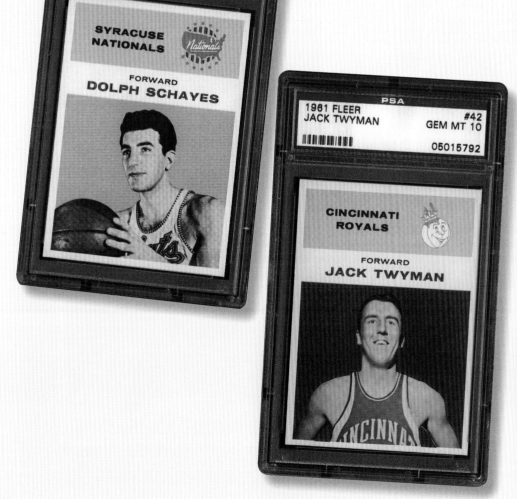

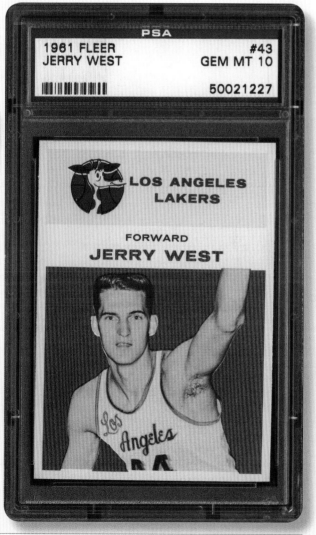

Key Features and Rarities

One big advantage to an even card count that breaks down nicely on a press sheet is, in a word, collation. The cards rolled down the production line in precisely equal quantities, and the odds of any given card winding up in a pack, or box, were evenly distributed. Thus, there were no rarities, "Short Prints," "High Numbers," or variations to confound enthusiasts. All of the series' era-defining rookies, such as Chamberlain, West and Robertson, and standout veterans (Russell, Cousy), existed in the very same proportions during the period of the set's active distribution. Only the modern hobby's tendency to create "demand scarcity" makes it seem at times that the cards of Chamberlain, Russell, West, et al are somehow especially elusive.

It's only fair to note too, that Fleer's basketball cards are a bit scarcer in general than most other nationally distributed card productions of the same period. Basketball cards were still seen in 1961 as "experimental" in nature. Today's collectors who have assembled a *nicely centered* set of 1961 Fleer cards are to be applauded for the completion of a challenging task. Fleer's quality control inspectors – to make this point delicately – tended to be lax in their adherence to the prescribed parameters of cutting alignment for the cards.

Bottom Line

After a couple of other companies' earlier basketball gum card ventures, both of which certainly contributed mightily to the formation of a hobby specialty, Fleer's 1961 issue came closer to the mark of what consumers expected from a product that related to the young sport. Fleer's basketball cards deliver plenty of satisfaction on the basis of their star-studded lineup, their winning design, and their no-nonsense composition and collation. With no apparent, built-in liabilities in sight upon analyzing the issue, one can only conclude that, at the time, the trading card market, or the basketball cards' manufacturer, were just not ready for a long-term commitment to the concept. Nevertheless, 1961 Fleer, as the single basketball release that served an entire generation of the sport's card-collecting fans, became a prized and "all-time"-level, one-year wonder.

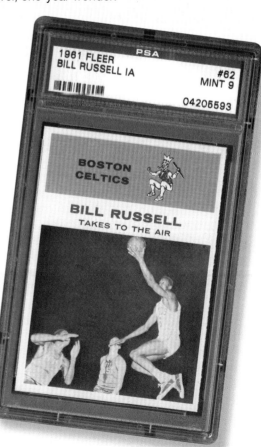

Background

Talk about the right product at the right time!

By the mid-1980s, excitement on the hardcourt generated by the rivalry between Magic Johnson and Larry Bird, helped to make professional basketball into an important force in popular culture. The sport's fan base had grown exponentially since the days of Cousy, Wilt and the *Big O*, and the NBA was selling franchises, player jerseys and tickets at a faster clip than ever before.

Even so, the game's trading card situation was in shambles. The preceding decade was characterized by uncertainty among collectors about which company would possess a given year's NBA licensing rights for cards, or what sort of collectibles would actually emerge. There had been huge cards and tiny cards (including, in diminutive scale, the important first cards of Bird and Johnson), gaudy cards and lackluster cards. In 1985, the only licensed cards were distributed in, of all things, little clear-plastic bags, not packs. Furthermore, who had even heard of a "card store" ten years prior? Yet, a determined enthusiast was forced to seek out and visit a so-designated establishment, simply to indulge the urge to buy a few cards. The system, at that stage, just wasn't working.

Fleer took the basketball-card collecting specialty back to the basics, and that approach, touted on the wrappers, boxes and cards as the "Premier Issue," was an instant success. The company took eye-catching, red-white-and-blue-bordered photo cards, gave them a straightforward design, and packaged them in good old-fashioned wax packs – with gum! Packs were available at most of the nation's big variety stores and drug store chains. In this fashion, the cards came "back to the masses," and it once again became routine to toss a couple of packs into a cart when shopping for other goods. The new Fleer cards were also available in card stores. But a special trip to one of those establishments was not a prerequisite for sampling or constructing this marvelous new set.

Composition

The manner of distribution for the 1986 Fleer release was a definite asset, but so was its content. A standard 11-card by 12-card press sheet was laid out to yield 132 collectibles, 131 of the NBA's best players, plus a Checklist card. Not only that, every pack held a "Photo Sticker" insert – yet another opportunity for buyers to acquire a superstar!

Unlike many card issues of the past, Fleer offered no teaser advertisements promising future marvels in subsequent series; all of the big guns were fired in this one staggering salvo. Bird and Magic – *at last*, it seemed – had worthy cardboard portrayals of their own. Most of their greatest contemporaries were also listed on the neatly alphabetized Checklist including, Kareem Abdul-Jabbar, Julius Erving, Moses Malone, Isiah Thomas and others. Best of all, there were the *rookies*.

Until the 1986 Fleer set came along, there had been a void in the realm of standard-issue NBA trading cards, many of the "Premier Issue's" subjects found acceptance as the first-year collectibles of their type. Highlighted by #57 depicting Michael Jordan – a card that soon became an important phenomenon in its own right – the gallery of rookies was filled with future Hall of Famers like Charles Barkley, Clyde Drexler, Patrick Ewing, Karl Malone, Hakeem Olajuwon and Dominique Wilkins.

Key Features and Rarities

One source of the 1986 Fleer set's incredible appeal is that it contains no rarities. The playing field was made level for all, in the sense that everyone faced an equal and auspicious opportunity to find the series' stars. (Remember, all cards and stickers were produced in exactly the same quantities.) Collectors quickly discovered that the purchase of a full, 36-pack box of Fleer Basketball yielded two complete sets of cards, plus duplicates. The cards' distribution and user-friendly collation, however, gave rise to an entirely different motivation. This additional incentive was the notion of the *condition rarity*. Enthusiasts sought to obtain the most well-centered copies of their favorite players, as well as examples whose delicate borders showed no trace of handling. The competition for "high-end" 1986 Fleer cards, particularly those of Jordan, escalated through the end of the decade and beyond, and drove the price of unopened packs and boxes into the stratosphere. Star cards, such as the Dominique Wilkens rookie, and commons, like #76 Johnny Moore, became hot commodities as a result of the focus on condition. As more and more 1986 Fleer cards were graded, it became clear that certain cards were clearly tougher than others.

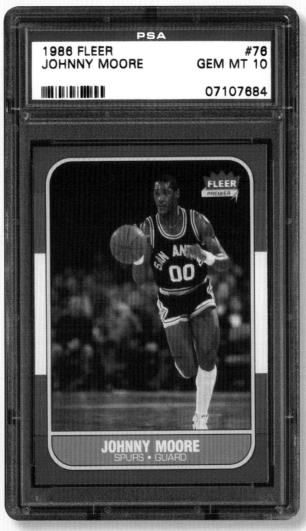

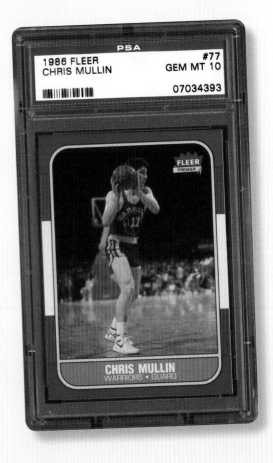

Bottom Line

Naturally, collectors have always preferred to own the nicest example that could be found of a given card. But 1986 Fleer cards – as again, precisely the right product, at the right time – lent themselves nicely to a period just around the corner as the cards were released when condition would be formally quantified. Never before had hobbyists put together hoards of specific rookie players, consisting of cards that display perfect border alignment, razor-sharp edges, and pinpoint corners. It wouldn't be long before third-party services would assess and encapsulate the cards, price guides would be revolutionized, and the once-fanciful prospect of "investment" in top-quality gum cards would be taken far more seriously. Fleer did "just right" in the execution of its 1986 Basketball cards – a factor that, by itself, would mandate its inclusion in an "all-time" listing. The series' role in shaping a growing collectibles industry's future makes it incalculably special and significant.

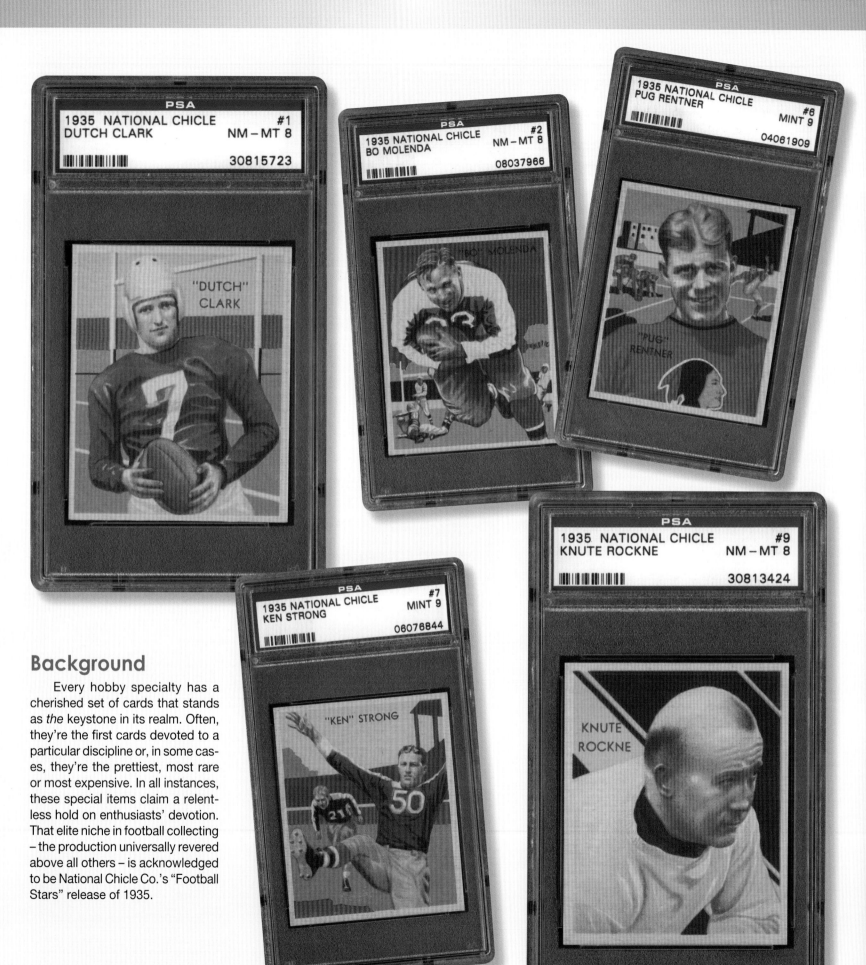

Background

Every hobby specialty has a cherished set of cards that stands as *the* keystone in its realm. Often, they're the first cards devoted to a particular discipline or, in some cases, they're the prettiest, most rare or most expensive. In all instances, these special items claim a relentless hold on enthusiasts' devotion. That elite niche in football collecting – the production universally revered above all others – is acknowledged to be National Chicle Co.'s "Football Stars" release of 1935.

National Chicle of Cambridge, Massachusetts – well-known as the makers of baseball's aesthetically comparable "Diamond Stars" – elected to take a chance with a new league (and relatively new sport) as it conceived and released the first two dozen entries in this phenomenally attractive, Art Deco-inspired series of collectibles. Although the college game was familiar to many at the time, gridiron activity at the professional level had been around for barely a decade.

Several professional "leagues" had been formed, modified and subsequently disbanded during the early 1920s, but a stable organization that satisfied the need for unity was created with the formation of the National Football League in 1922. A number of franchise owners in the now-crystallized NFL, including George Halas, Tim Mara and Curly Lambeau, ultimately became inducted into the Pro Football Hall of Fame in Canton, Ohio, as did such legendary players as Jim Thorpe and Harold "Red" Grange. By 1935, National Chicle, which had also experimented with untested subject matter in its "Sky Birds" and "Tom Mix" card sets, felt the time was right for its inaugural 24-piece treatment of football.

The initial release was deftly seeded with the era's big-name talent. The presence of period luminaries like Dutch Clark, Ken Strong and Cliff Battles was expected to draw attention, and buyers, to the colorful product. The cards also drew upon the considerable fame of Notre Dame's Knute Rockne – the acclaimed head coach who had passed away in 1931 – and featured his image on its #9 entry.

"Football Stars," which quickly became known, less generically, as "National Chicle Football," followed the classic baseball model pioneered two years prior by Goudey, and which was continued in its own "Diamond Stars." The cards' artistically rendered player likenesses were beautifully enhanced by Deco-style patterns on their uncluttered obverse sides; the back of each standard-sized 2⅜" by 2⅞" piece carried a descriptive paragraph and a couple of lines devoted to the player's position, college, age and related data. Just above the cardback's copyright information, a provocative inscription, "One of 240 football players with playing tips," announced an ambitious total number of depictions that could be anticipated by collectors.

National Chicle expanded soon after its initial release, growing by a dozen subjects to a total of 36 cards. This second group was made immediately noteworthy by the inclusion of the Chicago Bears' star fullback, Bronko Nagurski, on card #34.

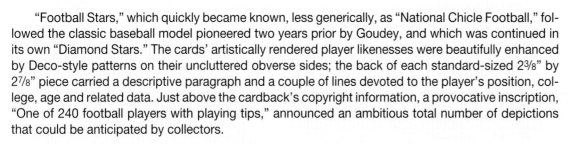

Collectors who awaited further expansion of the release after that point were destined to face disappointment. Perhaps the NFL wasn't yet ready to generate enough momentum to propel its own series of gum cards. Or, since National Chicle was facing financial peril at the time (largely due to its expensive artwork and production costs), it's possible that the company didn't hold sufficient faith in the fledgling market to justify prolonging the Football Stars venture. The rough-and-tumble pastime was gradually increasing its hold on the population's imagination, but after National Chicle Football, more than a decade would pass before another card company was willing to tackle further development of the game's collectibles.

Composition

Just 36 cards … but what a roster! The highest-profile elements of a different and newly refined athletic discipline were gathered in one of the most visually appealing and stunning spectacles afforded by the one-and-only National Chicle Football.

Each National Chicle Football card has become, quite legitimately, a stand-alone, origin-piece treasure in a hobby category that now boasts hundreds of football-themed card sets, with dozens more arising every season. The 1935 issue's depictions of Turk Edwards, Shipwreck Kelly, Beattie Feathers and their contemporaries are coveted by hobbyists to a degree that dwarfs the magnitude of the impact made by those cards at the time of their brief availability in packs of gum.

The cards of period superstars Rockne and Nagurski hold additional, specific significance. Rockne's is one of the very few items from the era that pays suitable homage to the immortal figure. Nagurski appears on what is widely seen as the most valuable and desirable football card of all. Particularly in view of its short-lived period of distribution, National Chicle Football's ongoing degrees of recognition and importance are essentially incomparable.

Key Features and Rarities

The National Chicle Football issue's "High Numbers" – #s 25-36, inclusive – are at least twice as scarce as their lower-numbered predecessors. And, this tougher group harbors the hobby's "Holy Grail" in the form of the Bronko Nagurski portrayal.

But all National Chicle Football cards can be seen as "rare," and certainly so in the highest grades. The items are demonstrably "condition sensitive" with cardstock that's prone to reveal toning from age, and corners that readily concede wear. The set's opening and concluding subjects (#s 1 Clark and 36 Bernie Masterson, respectively) fell victim to rubber-banding and exposure to light in higher proportions than other numbers, and their surviving population totals suffer accordingly. Finally, focus problems and centering mishaps affecting many National Chicle cards constitute yet another aspect that contributes to a persistent lack of top-grade pieces. National Chicle Football cards in their pack-fresh state are wondrously captivating collectibles. And very few of them have been observed in modern times.

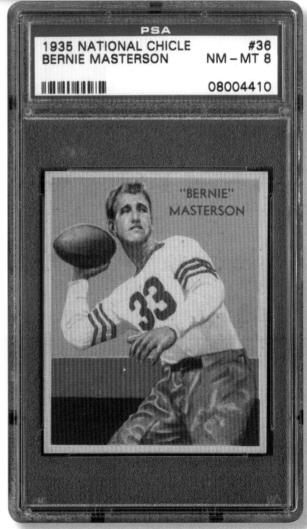

Bottom Line

National Chicle Football broke ground in unexplored card-market territory, and in hobbyists' estimation, vacated its claim much too readily. The 36-card set holds relics that showcase vintage football in a manner that historically-minded present-day fans can appreciate in a way that no other football cards can match. The Chicles comprise a short set numbers-wise, but the cards have earned character and value assessments that are certain to remain unequaled. An absolutely pivotal release!

Background

Sports cards have always been seasonally-oriented commodities. This concept was especially fundamental many years ago, when a product needed to be made available for sale at just the right time to capitalize on its moment of greatest appeal and relevance. It was necessary for a set to include the athletes who had captured the public's attention (or who were likely to do so soon), and it needed enough "style" to be considered exciting and timely. Failing these requirements, a production could expect to be overcome by competing offerings in the perennially competitive sports card market.

Those imperatives, while always true, didn't seem terribly compelling during late 1951 and early 1952. Bowman Gum of Philadelphia essentially controlled the nation's sports card activity. The company was a satisfying steward of the trade, producing quality sets of baseball and football cards year after year, but its efforts projected an air of complacency. Its cards were routinely sized (2¹/₁₆" by 3¹/₈") and adhered to an identical format. Bowman's 1951 football release, while visually engaging and sufficiently thoughtful in construction, was merely a gridiron counterpart of its 1951 baseball effort. The same scenario was poised to recur, yet again, the next year, as Bowman prepared its "new," but actually just slightly modified baseball and football card sets for 1952.

Baseball card collectors in particular can relate to what happened next. The familiar Bowmans from 1952 were met head-on by spectacular "Giant Size" baseball cards from the Topps Company of Brooklyn. Bowman's accountants must have asked, "What in the world is going on?" midway through the 1952 baseball season, as sales lagged behind expectations. Something had to be done, and fast.

Another football card set was already on the drawing board at Bowman. One more routine 144-piece set, same card size, same color paintings, and so on. All of the images were in place, and the cards' text was written ... still, there had to be a way to salvage a year's bottom line. But how?

Well, if Topps' successful innovation had been a matter of size, Bowman would try that, too. The company simply took its fully pre-pared prospective 1952 football release and *physically enlarged all of the cards*.

Although still smarting from the spanking it had received from Topps in the baseball arena, Bowman was justifiably proud of its own "Large" 1952 football cards. The big cards measured 2½" by 3¾" (the size would be retained in its subsequent baseball issues) and beauti-fully showcased their correspondingly up-sized player images.

Several card series of the 1950s and 1960s illuminated the "glitches" that could be encountered in laying out large-sized card designs on the standard-sized press sheets then in use, and the 1952 Bowman Large set represents the ultimate example of this dilemma. Consequently, the release is heavily populated by "short prints" – cards made in smaller quantities than others – that are particularly scarce. A number of the most sought-after portrayals in the set are "SPs," including the cards of Gifford, Conerly, Marchetti, Van Buren, Kyle Rote, and George Connor. A present-day collector's 1952 Large want list will inevitably take shape in a manner reflective of the SPs' patterns: all of the set's "Divide by 9" and "Divide by 9 plus 1" entries (for instance, #s 9, 18, 27, 36 and #s 10, 19, 28, 37, respectively) are unfailingly difficult to obtain, especially in high grade. Yet another, exceedingly tough "SP" card – the last card in the set, #144 Jim Lansford – was reputedly destroyed in large numbers during the series' production, and it has become one of the hobby's most highly prized football cards of the modern era.

For good measure, Bowman also released the other, smaller-sized version of the 1952 football cards, but its "Large" attempt to address its market stands out for several reasons as the distinctively "all-time" caliber variety.

First, as Topps' baseball cards revealed earlier, the bigger size made the subjects' depictions "come alive." The impressive appearance of the cards, with those bright, wonderfully detailed paintings must have been irresistible. Second, a revised look tends to invigorate a consumer base, and Bowman Large was well received by the collecting public. A final consideration that accounts for the issue's longevity as a collector favorite wouldn't become apparent until the advent of the "modern" collecting industry.

Composition

Bowman's Large 1952 football cards, totaling 144 in number, followed a proven design formula, their namesake size upgrade notwithstanding. Unembellished artwork (with a pennant-shaped caption block as the only aesthetic imposition) dominated the front of each card. The backs carried horizontally aligned text and basic player details. Veteran superstars like Sammy Baugh, Elroy Hirsch, Bob Waterfield and Otto Graham had their professional affiliations noted on their cards' fronts; newly arrived figures – notably USC's Frank Gifford in his debut year – were identified by college on their entries' obverse sides and by pro team on the backs.

Rookies and superstars are abundant in the 1952 Bowman Large set. Such notable first-timers as Art Donovan, head coach George Halas, Gino Marchetti, Hugh McElhenny and Andy Robustelli shared space on the set's roster with the likes of Tom Landry, Norm Van Brocklin, Y.A. Tittle, Steve Van Buren and Charley Conerly.

Large-sized cards in what was still a small-card world left Bowman Large collectibles highly susceptible to wear caused by handling. The resulting "condition scarcity" of the series' top grade cards, combined with the many manufacturing scarcities brought about by the various SPs, yield a recipe for difficulty to all who want to build a set. No pain, no gain … the issue's merits easily outweigh whatever frustration is brought about by its challenges!

Bottom Line

The 1952 Bowman Large production is arguably *the* classic release of the 1950s, and it was beyond doubt a Bowman triumph. By any measure a noteworthy and pace-setting series, the issue demonstrated an admirable capacity for rapid adaptation on the part of an established company. The means it chose to do so remains a nostalgic wonder as well as a delightful collecting adventure.

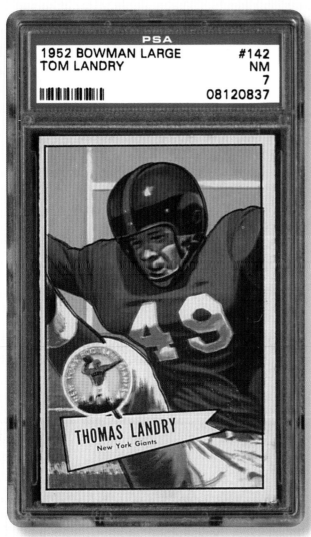

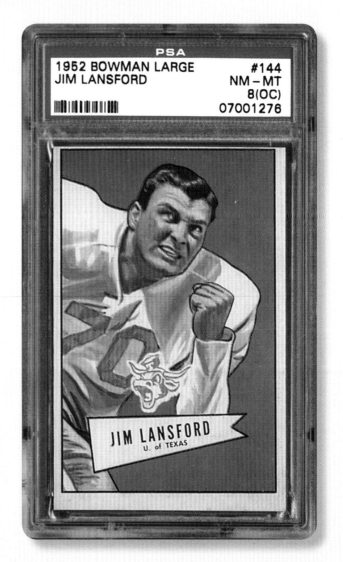

1955 Topps All-American Football

Background

One fact was clear going into the 1955 season, Bowman Gum was king of the football card market. The Philadelphia-based manufacturer had solidified its hold on the attention of gridiron enthusiasts through a well-conceived, black and white photo production in 1948, and followed that milestone with increasingly alluring full-color releases in each succeeding year from 1950 through 1954. It was presumed by all observers that Bowman's 1955 offering would be comparable in style and quality – and degree of success – to its immediate predecessors.

The Topps Company, meanwhile, was seeking to perpetuate the aggressive posture it had demonstrated through the first half of the decade. Its determined pursuit of candy counter market share had yielded considerable reward with the baseball theme, and the company was responsible during this period for dozens of non-sports productions covering a mind-boggling variety of topics. Not yet known was the fact that this same, proactive stance on the part of Topps toward its gum card business would result in a takeover of Bowman by the end of 1955.

It must have been frustrating for Topps during the early 1950s, as the company no doubt sensed there was a real market for football cards, but felt powerless to engage it. Bowman held an iron grip on the NFL's contract rights – and what was Topps to do? Its attempts to enter the category had been limited to a gimmicky series of tiny, part-cloth collectibles in 1950 and an equally problematic, scratch-off effort in 1951. Both of those issues featured then-current collegiate players, and the company's retrospective assessment of that very limited talent pool apparently led to a boardroom revelation as the 1955 season dawned.

"How about college players from the *past*? We'll find *loads* of big-name players if we look into the college game's history!" Having articulated a concept in this imaginary and possibly oversimplified fashion, Topps proceeded to create one of the most attractive and generally appealing card sets that's ever been associated with the football collecting specialty.

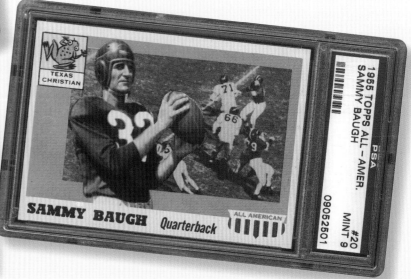

Heisman Trophy winners and Hall of Famers – some of whom had played their last down several decades ago as well as some who had recently retired – shone from the ranks of the 1955 Topps series' lineup. The set, christened "All-American," brought great college coaches to the modern public's attention, gave quite a few powerhouse college programs a moment in the sun, and showcased numerous legends who had never before appeared on a football card.

A noticeable aspect to the gallery was found in the fact that none of the players' professional teams were mentioned in any way; to avoid contractual conflicts, the athletes' illustrations, captions and referenced highlights noted only their one-time college affiliations. (This feature, far from acting as a negative, actually came to be seen as an element of "purity," and as rather charming.)

Composition

The 1955 Topps All-American set contains 100 cards. Its spectacular player selection confirms that this relatively short span of numbers is a suitable one, and it was probably just right for a year-ending sports season that wasn't as lengthy as baseball's. Into this group of 100 subjects, Topps stuffed what is arguably more "greatness," card for card, than any other production seen to date.

The college-only framework opened plenty of avenues, turning a vast group of stars into "fair game" for inclusion. Olympian Jim Thorpe, 1920s superstars "Red" Grange, "Turk" Edwards, "Fats" Henry and Beattie Feathers; stand-out Heisman winners who never reached the pros such as Jay Berwanger (the first Heisman Trophy recipient) and Nile Kinnick; plus greatest-ever coaches Knute Rockne and Amos Alonzo Stagg, are all represented in the special 1955 Topps array. Players who until a couple of years prior could be found in Bowman's annual regular issues included Otto Graham, Sammy Baugh, Sid Luckman, Leo Nomellini and Alex Wojciechiwicz.

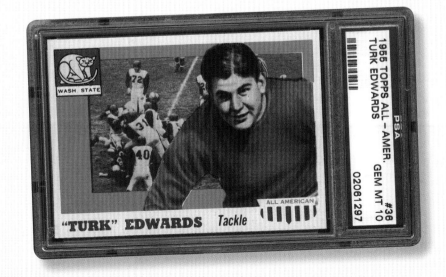

Key Features and Rarities

Topps' 100-card set was printed on press sheets that held 110 designs. Under this formula, clearly some cards would be produced in lesser quantities than others. "All-American" is home to more than 25 "Short Prints" ("SPs") who are tougher to obtain than their set-mates. Among these particularly difficult entries are Tom Harmon, Ace Parker, Mel Hein, Berwanger, Nomellini, and all of the numbers from 93 through 100 (including #97 Don Hutson and #100 Henry). The most hungered-for "SP" of all is #68, which features an especially popular depiction of all four of the players who comprised Notre Dame's 1924 backfield combo: The Four Horsemen.

All of the series' entries received "star treatment" in aesthetic terms. The prevailing-standard card dimensions of 2⅝" by 3⅝" were employed – none of that oddball small stuff, which Topps had tried before – and attractive border hues were used to complement each player's color-enhanced photographic image. A black and white "action" photo was placed as a tasteful backdrop to each man's likeness, and a picturesque rendering of his respective alma mater's symbol occupied one corner of every card's obverse. (A red-and-white "All American" logo, at another corner, afforded balance in design.) The cards' backs, printed in black against a two-tone blue color scheme, revealed collegiate career highlights in a paragraph of text, and a cartoon/trivia item also was featured.

There are tempting pieces for variation collectors in this set, too. The cards of Gaynell Tinsley (#14) and future U.S. Supreme Court Justice "Whizzer" White (#21) can be found with or without the back of the other man's card. A.A. Stagg's collectible is also known with an error in place. In all of these cases, the proper, "corrected" version is much more widely available.

Although no true "rarities" exist within the All-American's composition, the unremitting effects of "demand scarcity" (brought on by the issue's star power), "short printing," and general condition-sensitivity ensure that the gathering of "only" a hundred different cards isn't quite as easy as one might assume!

Bottom Line

Here's a wonderful product, which must have emerged out of the blue. 1955 Topps All-Americans form a timeless, enduring effort showcasing football history in its most exciting and favorable light. The following year would see Topps take over where Bowman would leave off, as the growing confectioner became the new leader in football card production. Though its maker quickly and pragmatically abandoned their concept, these "All-Americans" were left behind as a marvelous and indisputably "all-time" level, one-year effort.

1957 Topps Football

Background

By 1957, the Topps Company was quite well established as the market leader in the field of baseball cards, even though they had taken a tentative approach to football cards prior to that season. Perhaps energized by the success of its 1957 Baseball release, which was newly standard-sized with 2½" by 3½" cards and which promenaded a superb, real-photo theme, the company decided on a much more serious commitment to football than it had demonstrated in the past.

A quirky felt-backed issue, a group of odd "scratch-off" collectibles, and the colorful "All-Americans" highlighted Topps' gridiron heritage to this point; all of these featured only college players. Dabbling in the NFL realm for the first time in 1956 (after rival manufacturer Bowman was no longer a factor), the result was essentially a much-abridged version of 1956 Baseball. 1956 Topps Football provided a short, 120-card roster that accommodated Team Cards as well as depictions of established stars.

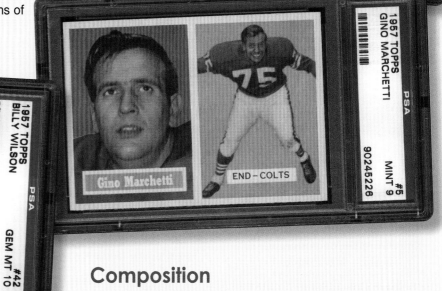

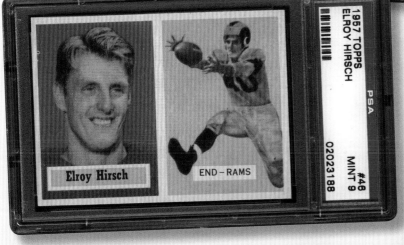

Composition

The 1957 Topps Football issue consists of 154 cards. A set that's relatively short and quite efficient in its construction, 1957s are memorable in style; each player is featured on the obverse in a portrait likeness placed side-by-side with an "action" scene. The cards are horizontal in orientation, with the athletes' names, teams and positions identified on the fronts, and biographical and statistical information – plus cartoons, which were becoming a Topps hallmark – decorating the backs.

The 1957 issue, in addition to solving the various shortcomings that resulted from its maker's prior indecision with respect to the sport, inaugurated a pattern of football-card continuity that would serve Topps nicely for the next several decades. At last, the company was prepared to be thoughtful and methodical with respect to a pastime that was becoming increasingly important to America's sports fans.

Each 1957 entry seems to have been carefully selected, an aspect that jives satisfactorily with its brevity. Virtually all of the day's significant stars are present, including such legends as Frank Gifford, Y.A. Tittle, George Blanda and Bobby Layne. Additionally, whoever made the final call in terms of content took care to recognize the NFL's future superstars. The set's formidable rookie triumvirate, Bart Starr, Johnny Unitas and Paul Hornung, is among the most powerful group of debut collectibles in any sport, and other first-year Hall of Famer appearances include cards of Ray Berry, "Night Train" Lane and Tommy McDonald.

Key Features and Rarities

The 1957s, possibly because a bit of tentativeness remained among Topps' decision makers, were released in two series: the first group of 88 cards was followed by a smaller, 66-card run of "High Numbers." The latter bunch is slightly more difficult to obtain, and naturally, it contains the "Big Three" within the release's rookie crop. Furthermore, although 1957 Topps' "Highs" as a category are not excessively tough to find, certain numbers in that run were short printed and are correspondingly elusive.

The "regular" cards, the stars and the rookies form the general-interest portion of 1957 Topps' story, but there are also two sub-plots that have captivated enthusiasts for 50 years. In a very real sense, 1957 Topps Football solidified the importance of two specialty elements, the "Error Card" and the "Checklist."

The former is occasionally observed on card #58, which features the Rams' Willard Sherman. In a very few instances, the team name (which *should* occupy the caption block at the card's right side) was left unprinted. Sherman is left soaring in a midair "action" portrayal on these rare "Error" pieces, and the cards look strangely incomplete. Although misprints were nothing new to trading cards, "Sherman – No Team" has steadily gained popularity as a scarce and quantifiable variation piece of which, significantly, a much more plentiful "Corrected" version was produced.

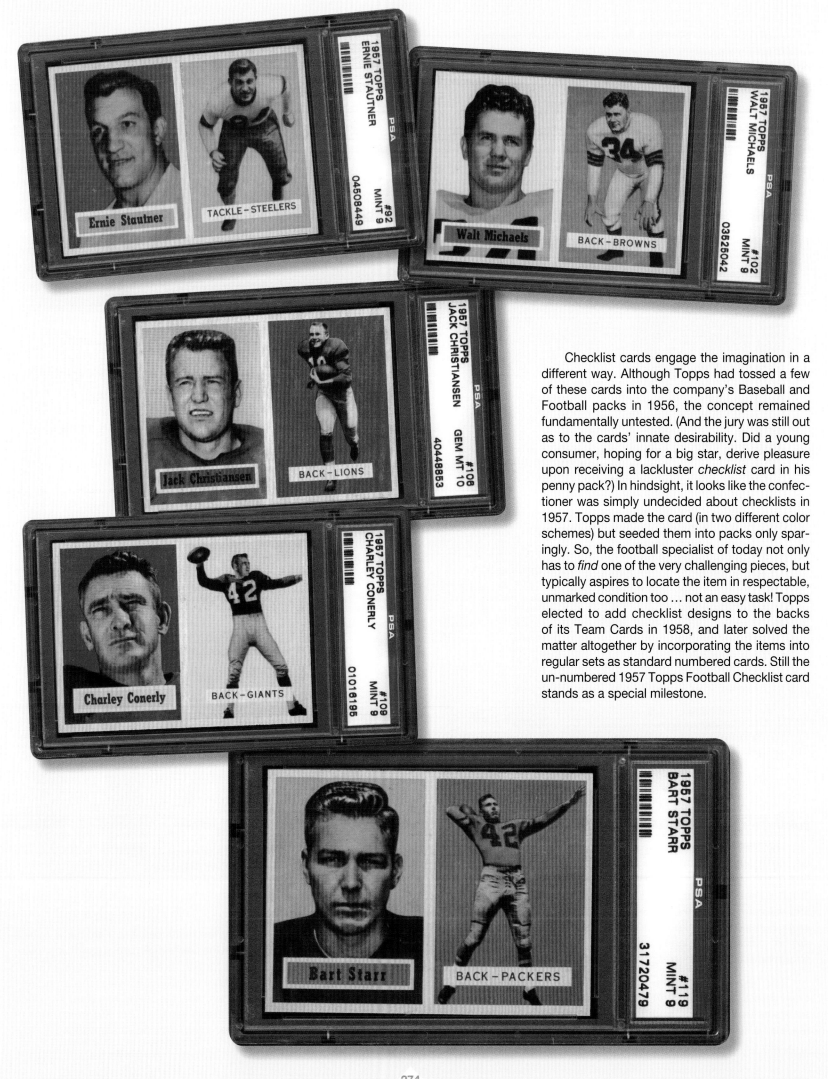

Checklist cards engage the imagination in a different way. Although Topps had tossed a few of these cards into the company's Baseball and Football packs in 1956, the concept remained fundamentally untested. (And the jury was still out as to the cards' innate desirability. Did a young consumer, hoping for a big star, derive pleasure upon receiving a lackluster *checklist* card in his penny pack?) In hindsight, it looks like the confectioner was simply undecided about checklists in 1957. Topps made the card (in two different color schemes) but seeded them into packs only sparingly. So, the football specialist of today not only has to *find* one of the very challenging pieces, but typically aspires to locate the item in respectable, unmarked condition too … not an easy task! Topps elected to add checklist designs to the backs of its Team Cards in 1958, and later solved the matter altogether by incorporating the items into regular sets as standard numbered cards. Still the un-numbered 1957 Topps Football Checklist card stands as a special milestone.

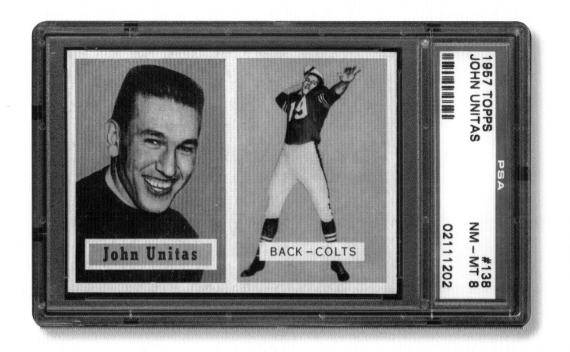

Bottom Line

Topps' 1957 Football production marked an observable turning point. The company was finished with large-sized cards, college players and novelty themes that tended to trivialize a sport which was beginning to rival the World Series as a source of autumn-season enthusiasm. Its 154 cards were ideally conceived and attractive, and its player content was appropriately robust. With the emergence of its 1957 Football production (and with the influence of its competitor, Bowman, now two years removed into the past) one thing became clear: Topps was determined to take charge in a new realm.

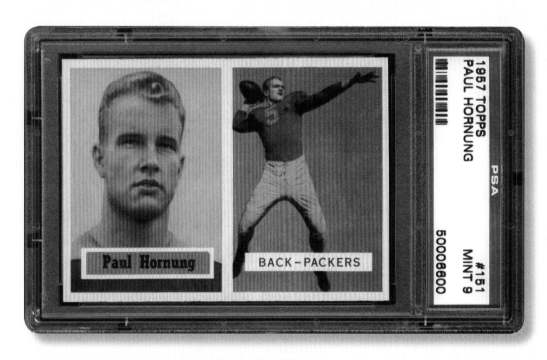

1965 Topps "Tall Boys" Football

Background

"Hey, who the heck are *these* guys?" Exclamations like that were routine in the early autumn of 1965, as collectors experienced the Topps Company's new "Tall Boys" football cards for the first time.

Topps had offered American Football League cards once before in the preceding season, but AFL subjects still took a bit of getting used to. Rival manufacturer Philadelphia Gum held the competing National Football League's licensing rights, and collectors were forced to turn to them in order to obtain collectibles of their favorites. Unitas, Starr, Tittle, Jim Brown and all of their contemporaries were found only in Philadelphia Gum's standard-sized packs, while Topps' premium-proportioned release featured some of its own luminaries like Jack Kemp, George Blanda and Len Dawson, along with more than its share of such under-the-radar athletes as Walt Suggs, Dalva Allen and Cosmo Iacovazzi.

The disparity in public recognition levels between the players in the time's two rival leagues undoubtedly prompted Topps to become daring in "expanding" its AFL release for 1965. Conventional "cards" of the day had only two surfaces with which to work – a front and a back. This aspect left a finite, restrictive window for experimentation, so the designers at Topps proceeded to simply elongate both of the available canvases. The formula had been successful in dramatic fashion once before with the "Giant Size" baseball cards of 1952 which had, after all, helped launch Topps to the pinnacle of the card-market heap – and it was felt that bigger pictures and bigger features would help the cause once again.

So, maybe Topps didn't have football's biggest names, but did produce the sport's *biggest cards*. Width was kept "standard" at 2½", but the items' top-to-bottom spans grew substantially from the usual 3½" to a generous 4¹¹/₁₆".

The extra space was almost entirely consumed by larger photos on the front of the cards. Large team-name headings at the depictions' top edges and smaller name/position notations at the bottom complemented the cards' easy-to-see images. A bright, cropped-in background hue was consistent among members of each team represented in the series, making color-coded sorting a simple matter.

The cards' backs were divided into two panels, both of which were printed in black ink with salmon-toned accents. The left side held the card number, player information and a descriptive paragraph, and the right half featured a cartoon based on a highlight from the athlete's career.

Larger cards meant, naturally, larger packs, and when they appeared on retailers' shelves in 1965, they must have presented an eye-catching display on the basis of size and visual spectacle alone. The "Tall Boys" packages, each equipped with big cards, a slab of gum and a "Magic Rub-Off" insert, appeared more than ready to confront Philadelphia Gum's NFL "regulars."

Composition

The 1965 "Tall Boys" account for 176 cards. With the exception of two checklists, these were all designated to portray individual players. The athletes were alphabetically sequenced in team groups, and then alphabetically by name within those team segments. A mixture of full-length poses and portraits adorned the cards' fronts.

The unconventional size led to improvisation in the laying out of factory press sheets: more than half of the set is "Short Printed," and those "SP" subjects are noticeably less plentiful than other entries. Interestingly, some collectors have observed that many "SPs" appear to feature a relative lack of clarity in their illustrations. Perhaps a number of the SP players were last-minute "fillers" in press sheet composition, or maybe some of these individuals were seen as less important than other selections. Regardless, an overview of the entire set does lend credence to this informal assessment.

Like any other seasonal, sports-oriented production, the 1965 Topps held several players' first-year cards. Foremost among these was card #122 of the New York Jets' young, news-making quarterback Joe Namath. Other prominent "rookies" included Willie Brown, Fred Biletnikoff and Ben Davidson.

Key Features and Rarities

The "SPs" proved to be a serious complication for set-builders in 1965, as they are to this day. All four of the issue's most important rookies are "SPs," and the placement of Joe Namath's card in this category served to make the item especially desirable and elusive.

Namath's card was released at the onset of his heyday, as the news media released almost daily accounts of the brash superstar's fur coat, his shag carpet, and his playboy escapades. The Namath piece captured its time like no other football card, and has almost single-handedly ensured that constant hobby attention is drawn to the "Tall Boys."

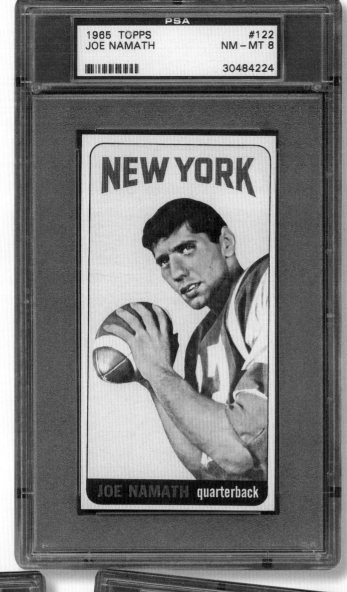

Due to their size, the cards are condition sensitive, and many otherwise "pack-fresh" examples suffer from haphazard centering. These factors complicate the construction of a high-quality 1965 Topps set, but again, Namath remains an aspiring enthusiast's greatest obstacle.

Incidentally, those short-lived and unusual "Magic Rub-Off" inserts are especially scarce and delicate. If one thinks that building a set of 1965 Topps *cards* is difficult, imagine trying to collect the inserts in high-grade!

Bottom Line

The "Tall Boys" came at an important time of soul searching for Topps. The company recognized a problem – it held less-interesting content options than by its competitor – and used creativity to address the quandary. The offshoot was a one-year experiment that led to the only football card set of its type ever made. (And the 1965 Topps set's exact specifications would be re-employed four years later in the company's second attempt to promote basketball cards.) In a way, it's unfortunate that the Namath card grabs the lion's share of 1965 Topps' headlines. The production is a worthy and appealing array in every respect, and it's easily its decade's most memorable "all-time" candidate.

1951 Parkhurst Hockey

Background

Among the many homefront disruptions brought about by war was the interruption of bubble-gum production ... the materials used to make it were more valuable to a nation elsewhere. During the World War II era in Canada, lack of gum translated into a lapse in the manufacture of that country's sports fans' beloved hockey cards. But finally, by 1951, peace and prosperity had returned sufficiently for a new and eagerly awaited hockey-themed release.

After the long enforced halt to production brought on by the Canadian war effort, Parkhurst, a leading confectioner in Toronto, reintroduced hockey cards to collectors. These hockey cards were crude in physical terms, but entrancing and highly meaningful in the emotional realm.

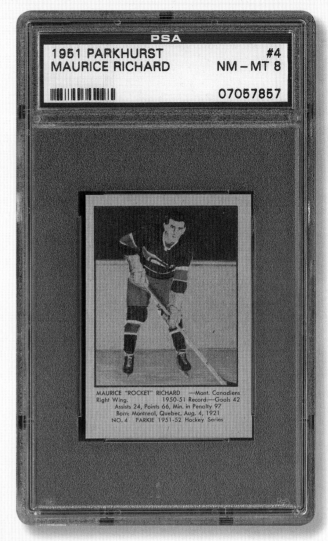

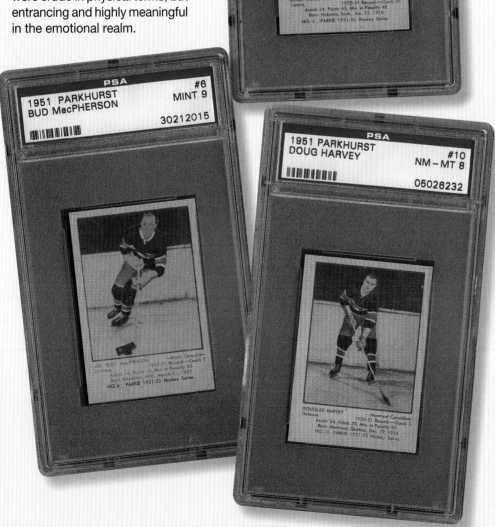

Parkhurst's inaugural 1951 effort showcased the sport's storied "Original Six" teams – Detroit Red Wings, Toronto Maple Leafs, Montreal Canadiens, Chicago Blackhawks, New York Rangers and Boston Bruins – through color-tinted individual poses of the squads' most prominent members. The likeness of each player were about the size of postage stamps, and were placed against an off-white background on a cardboard canvas measuring just 1¾" by 2½." The cards' backs were blank.

Clearly, a nation's sporting culture was ready for an apt diversion, and these new cards, which delivered a certain extra charm by their very simplicity, were met with genuine enthusiasm when they first appeared on the shelves of candy retailers.

Composition

The "minimalist" production 1951 Parkhurst contained just 105 cards – all that were necessary to relaunch a genre and provide inspiration for the future. As is the case in any collectibles undertaking that addresses a sport following a long hiatus, the series is chock-full of rookie commemoratives. Eventual Hall of Famers like Maurice Richard and Terry Sawchuk were seen for the first time on suitable keepsakes, and their cards, like the athletes themselves, were destined to achieve "national treasure" status among Canadian enthusiasts. Other esteemed players such as Alex Delvecchio, "Boom Boom" Geoffrion, Doug Harvey, Red Kelly and Ted Lindsay were also among 1951 Parkhurst's honorees.

But one man (and his one card) thoroughly endeared the project to collectors: Gordie Howe. A unique and undisputed idol-on-ice, *Mr. Hockey* was regarded as the Canadian version of America's Babe Ruth. Although Howe would toil for additional decades on the rink (most of that time spent with one team), and continue to add to his considerable list of records, he was already well-recognized at the time of 1951 Parkhurst's emergence. Howe's first "Parkie" almost immediately became a crucial acquisition in the eyes of every hockey collector, and the card has maintained its singular cachet for more than a half-century. Even after the rise to prominence of a more-recent hockey legend – Wayne Gretzky – the 1951 Parkhurst #66 Gordie Howe collectible remains diligently sought after, with its formidable mystique fully intact.

Key Features and Rarities

No rarities have been noted in the 1951 Parkhurst's content, but the series itself is challenging. As a new product in competition for customers with other confections, the hockey cards needed time to establish a following. (And the supply of product made available to collectors for the long term would have been restricted accordingly.) Though with its abundantly star-packed roster, "demand scarcity" is the quest to obtain particularly renowned players, an important factor in collecting these relics.

Interestingly, and of critical concern to enthusiasts who desire 1951 Parkhurst cards that reflect "pack-fresh" condition, an unexpected liability affects the series. Parkhurst's methods were rudimentary at the beginning of their approach to hockey card production, and several sources have reported that the company purchased a *cement mixer* to ensure random distribution of cards as they were prepped for packaging. If indeed the delicate items were tumbled by a heavy apparatus of that sort, it's not surprising that 1951 Parkhurst collectibles bearing sharp corners and crease-free surfaces are especially hard to find today!

Bottom Line

Who could imagine a National Pastime without trading cards? That was Canada's predicament prior to the arrival of the 1951 Parkhurst collectibles. These items filled a void, and they set the stage for all future hockey productions. Glorifying the items' aesthetic qualities may not be warranted in the strictest artistic sense, but immense significance of the cards was felt through other, less tangible avenues. The 1951s made the statement that hockey cards had returned, and ever since, the little blank-backed pieces have been the beneficiaries of a hobby's sincerest appreciation.

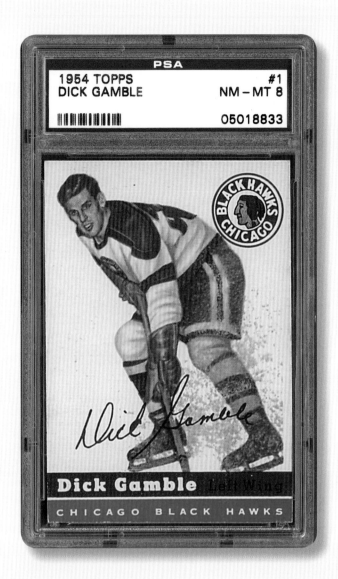

Background

Sheer drama on ice! Chilly looking white backgrounds and players in color-ful uniforms with specks of playing surface flying off the blades of their skates ... that's what Americans saw upon glancing at their first home-grown, modern-era hockey cards!

Few series of cardboard collectibles capture the "feel" of their respective sports as effectively as the artistic showpieces contained in Topps' 60-card hockey release produced for the 1954-55 season. The viewer of these items can almost feel the frigid atmosphere of the games. The individually depicted athletes' poses display a palpable quality of "action," and conspicuous details among the graph-ics include large-sized team logo devices on the cards' fronts and stick designs on the backs. A red-white-and-blue motif characterizes each card, apparently in deference to the presumptive United States orientation of their target audience. (A less subtle, regional bias is evident in the series' actual composition; Boston, Chicago, Detroit and New York squads were well-represented, while Montreal's and Toronto's were not at all.)

For three years prior to the creation of Topps' masterpiece, the Canadian national pastime was ably served in terms of hockey trading cards by that country's own Parkhurst brand. Once it decided to compete, however, Topps hit their mark on the first attempt. The 1954-55 Topps hockey cards assumed a position of prominence that begged comparison to its landmark 1952 baseball effort – and that highly complimentary parallel is still widely acknowledged today.

Composition

Topps used generous 2⅝" by 3¾" cardstock canvases for its initial rink-themed portrayals. These collectibles were the same size as the company's baseball items that had been successfully touted to youngsters upon introduction as "Giant-Sized" pieces and they blew away Parkhurst's relatively coarse-looking offerings. The cards' ample dimensions and the issue's very favorable printing standards enabled the presentation of exciting illustrations featuring Alex Delvecchio, Harry Howell, Ted Lindsay, Terry Sawchuk and many other stars, a number of whom eventually gained enshrinement at the Hockey Hall of Fame in Toronto.

Key Features and Rarities

As a rule, a classic card set can be counted upon to incorporate at least one "key" figure or a very rare, standout entry. Fortunately for collectors, the 1954-55 Topps single group of 60 subjects appears to have been well-collated and evenly distributed. As a result, no particular card has gained notoriety by virtue of being simply "harder to find" than its counterparts. "Star power" is another matter, however, and the inaugural Topps product had the ultimate: Detroit's Gordie Howe.

Although Howe's "rookie card" resided among the austere portrayals of the 1951-52 Parkhurst gallery, Topps' 1954-55 card #8 of the great player landed in the manner of a thunderbolt on a young hockey-collecting specialty. Like its set-mates, a beautiful, lavishly-hued keepsake, the card delivers a charismatic image, and it's a sight demanding to be cherished. Just as the 1952 Topps Mickey Mantle, the 1954-55 Howe is sometimes chided (almost always by a non-owner) as "not a rookie." But its role as many enthusiasts' all-time favorite card is equally secure.

Bottom Line

An apparently humble group of just five dozen cards – which, in hindsight, makes one wonder if it was conceived as a "test issue" – the 1954-55 series by itself inspired a new category of collecting. Hockey cards today are sought after with great vigor by devotees of the sport, and they are treasured with the same fervency as those hobbyists whose allegiances lie with baseball, football or basketball. Topps made a small but classy and very well done foray into a new market with its 1954-55 hockey cards. In so doing, the company set the standard for decades of future enjoyment among the fans of a growing sport.

1933 Goudey Sport Kings

Background

Here is a single, united gallery revealing the full array of a Golden Era's standouts! Far more ambitious in scope than any set of cards that restricted its attention to just a single athletic discipline, Goudey Gum Co.'s priceless "Sport Kings" release of 1933 attempted to capture the entirety of a culture's focus by featuring virtually every aspect of organized competition.

Having just recently established a viable market in colorful gum cards with its "Big League" baseball effort in 1933, Goudey thought that it could *run the table* with Sport Kings. The company assembled four dozen key figures from more than 15 sports, and placed them together in one, majestic and visually consistent release. Each of its superstar subjects received a treatment similar to the design pioneered by the 1933 Goudey Baseball's motif – a brightly rendered illustration on the obverse of a 2⅜" by 2⅞" card, with green-inked commentary text on the reverse.

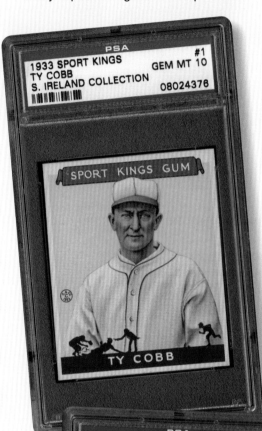

The significance of a project like Sport Kings, which showcased Hall of Fame-caliber individuals from baseball, football, golf, hockey, basketball and other arenas is difficult to overstate. The equivalent in today's world would see Brett Favre on one card and A-Rod on the next. Tiger Woods and Natalie Gulbis would be included (the former perhaps a greater certainty than the latter), along with Barry Bonds, Roger Federer, Oscar de la Hoya and, quite likely, standouts from the emerging "Extreme Sports." The licensing and contractual ramifications of such an array in today's context would be nightmarish!

But Goudey made it happen, and the result was of great benefit, not so much for the focused fan as for the generalist. Each Sport Kings entry was credible on his or her respective merits, and upon those of their distinctly different sports. With such tremendous variety, and an egalitarian approach to all of the pastimes represented, Sport Kings aptly defines its time as much as it outlines the state of athleticism during the period.

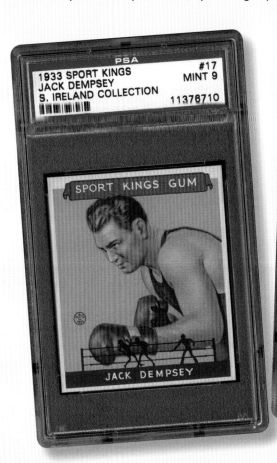

Composition

Sport Kings consists of 48 highly engaging cards that capture the fascination of the observer in a manner unrivaled before or since. A smorgasbord, wholly populated by "big guns," the issue's portrayals carry the same "Sport Kings Gum" top caption, and a black rectangle at the bottom edge holds the subject's name. A tiny silhouette, for which the lower-edge caption block forms a base, shows a touch of intriguing "action" of relevance to the sport practiced by the card's featured athlete. And the centerpiece of the item is a beautifully painted likeness of the specifically commemorated star.

The cards' back text descriptions were written to acquaint the reader with an athlete's sport, more so than to dazzle with statistics. On Billiards player Willie Hoppe's entry, for example, the eloquent paragraph begins, "Shakespeare tells us that Cleopatra played billiards during the days of Julius Caesar…" and continues in that vein before moving along to discuss Hoppe's American League Tournament success in 1928.

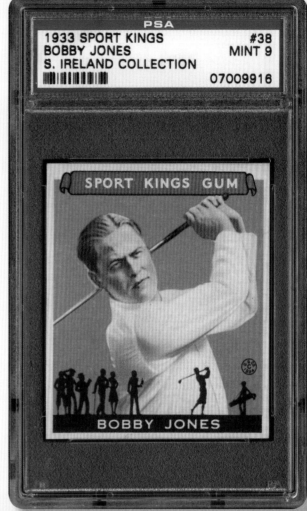

Eclectic to the greatest extent imaginable, Sport Kings nevertheless had its priorities straight in terms of worthy candidates for selection. Baseball players honored by inclusion were Ty Cobb (retired by this time but still a "King"), Babe Ruth and Carl Hubbell, and football employed Jim Thorpe, Red Grange and Knute Rockne as its highlights. Four basketball players and four hockey players – legends all – appeared, as well as golfers Bobby Jones, Walter Hagen and Gene Sarazen and such renowned pugilists as Jack Dempsey, Gene Tunney and Max Baer. By no means stopping there, stars from aviation, tennis, bicycling, dog-sled racing, and several more activities were afforded their own cards.

Two deserving female athletes made the cut, in an unusual acknowledgement of talent for the era. Swimmer Helene Madison and all-around phenom Babe Didrickson (whose specialty was cited simply as "Track") represented their gender on collectibles that remain especially popular. Another specialty favorite is the card of Hawaiian icon and quintessential surfer Duke Kahanamoku, who, like his equally accomplished set-mate Johnny Weissmuller, was placed in Sport Kings' "Swimming" category.

Key Features and Rarities

Twenty-four of the issue's cards are scarcer "High Numbers," but the "demand scarcity" attaching to high-profile stars is the defining consideration when evaluating specific Sport Kings' relative difficulty. Each sport's partisan has its particular favorites, and card collectors compete heavily with niche enthusiasts to obtain their chosen heroes. The release's biggest names – Ruth, Grange, Thorpe – are obvious "keys," but the cards of Bobby Jones, Carl Hubbell and Hockey Hall of Famer "Ace" Bailey (all of which are "High's," with numbers placed in the set's tougher segment, #s 25 through 48) are deceptively challenging acquisitions for the aspiring set builder. No print-quantity anomalies or obscure variations have been confirmed in Sport Kings' content.

Bottom Line

An amazing and incredible undertaking that would be impossible in today's fully copyrighted, trademark-focused environment, Sport Kings is an extraordinary tribute to the first half of the 20th Century. Rumors persist that one of today's modern manufacturers is contemplating a similar production – more than 70 years after the superlative and inimitable original made its debut – but the thought of such an attempt, at this stage, evokes skepticism. There's no way that any sort of "new cards," even if gifted with an equally stellar lineup drawn from another era rich in athletic talent, could deliver the same flavor, or support a comparable mystique. Sport Kings stands by itself as a wholly unique, "all-time" production.

Collecting Sports Autographs

By Rob Rosen

Au-to-graph ... noun, from the Latin *autographus*, meaning a) something written by one's own hand. b) a person's handwritten signature. The latter definition is the more pragmatic usage as it pertains to the hobby of collecting autographs, also known as philography. Autograph collecting is one of the most popular and rewarding forms of collecting and easily dates back several hundred years. This begs the question, "What drives the collector to obtain the signature of another?"

As an autograph collector of thirty years, I can only answer based on my own experiences of collecting, since what is enjoyable and rewarding to collect for one person may not be the same for another. However, I do believe there is a common thread running through all autograph collectors ... a strong passion for and respect of history.

Almost all autograph collectors, often without realizing it, are history buffs and, to some degree, collectors and curators of history. What better way to explore the history of baseball, for example, than collecting autographs of its players? Autograph collecting not only tends to help the hobbyist build a better knowledge of a particular player, but of the sport itself, potentially introducing the collector to the history of ballparks, cities, culture and ultimately to American history.

Baseball is not called our national pastime on a whim. It binds generations and connects fathers and sons in a way that can't be explained. Since the birth of baseball in the mid-1800s, there's not a single piece of American history that cannot be seen and studied through the eyes of this grand sport and autograph collecting truly preserves a piece of our past.

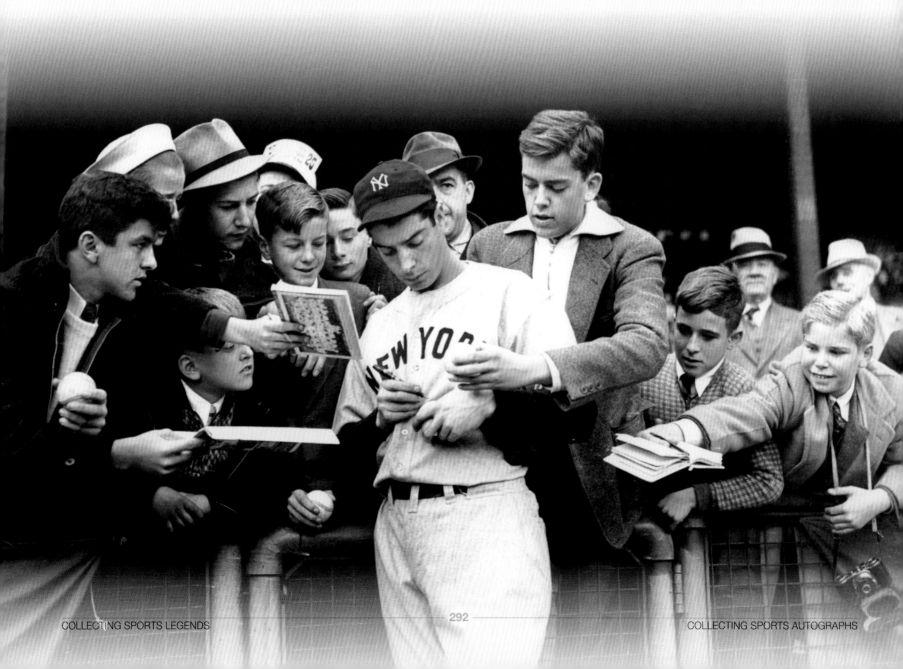

Many collectors believe a signature tells a great deal about the person who did the signing. For example, look at the large, bold signature of Babe Ruth in contrast to the smaller, lighter signature of his more demure teammate Lou Gehrig. Further, Gehrig's signature is usually found on the side panel of most baseballs, avoiding, as in life, becoming the center of attention. We admire the fluid, graceful "sweetness" of a Walter Payton signature. We respect the strength, confidence and quiet resolve of a Jackie Robinson-penned item as well as the stately and regal manner in which Joe DiMaggio leaves his signature.

A player's signature can go through many changes during the course of the player's life, often mirroring the struggles and triumphs endured by the man himself. A collector of Mickey Mantle autographs will notice the smaller, tighter and more unsure signature of a young Mantle fresh out of Commerce, Oklahoma. He doubted himself and was initially unable to handle the pressure of carrying the torch of Yankee greats that was bestowed upon him at such a young age. That signature went through a metamorphosis. It appears to have changed each year into a larger, bolder and more confident signature as both the player and the man grew into a success and an American icon.

In addition, autograph collecting can be financially rewarding. The price of autographs, particularly vintage examples, has steadily increased over the years. Some have outpaced other non-traditional investments such as fine art and antiques, as well, as many traditional investments.

There are several factors that determine the value of an autograph, including who the signature is from, the medium signed, and the condition of both the autograph and medium.

The most important factor in determining the value of the signature is the signer. The fame of the person and their place in history are the most determinative factors to be considered here. The signatures of athletes such as Babe Ruth and Muhammad

Ali will always have far greater value than Barry Bonds and Mike Tyson. All four were either homerun champions or world heavyweight boxing champions in their prime, but their impact on their respective sport and the world around them in general Is what separates the value and appeal of these particular athletes.

I mention these particular athletes to merely state a point. Comparing Babe Ruth and Muhammad Ali to any other athlete in terms of value and appeal is unfair as Ruth and Ali are the only ones in history to transcend sport. Their contribution to culture and history is of equal importance to their unparalleled feats of greatness in their respective sport. If you ask most autograph collectors to identify the most important signature in the hobby, they will tell you the answer is, without hesitation, Babe Ruth.

Another factor in determining the value of an autograph is the medium upon which it is signed. This is as subject to individual taste as is the theme of what genre of autographs to collect. In the baseball collecting arena, the most popular item to have signed by a player is the baseball itself. Regarding contemporary signatures, the type of baseball signed is important but not nearly as important as it pertains to vintage, pre-1960s signed items.

Assuming the condition of the autograph and baseball are comparable, a Jackie Robinson signature, for example, is far more valuable on an official National League Ford Frick baseball than on a commercial baseball of the same period. Taking this one step further, a Babe Ruth signature on a "Barnard" baseball is of greater value than on a "Harridge" baseball. It almost assuredly tells the collector that this was a *playing day*

signature of Ruth, signed while he was still wearing Yankee pinstripes, hitting home runs and winning championships.

Photographs are also a very popular choice of autograph collectors. The appeal of this medium is obvious since you have captured not only the player's autograph, but a moment in that player's life. Many vintage photographs are appealing without an autograph but, if one of these prized images happens to be signed, the collectible can be enhanced significantly. Further, many collectors of autographed photos prefer an image of the player in uniform as opposed to street clothes or those taken after their playing career, since the former represents the player as most fans are able to, and want to, remember him.

A handwritten letter is easily the rarest of autograph mediums, and depending on the letter's content, may provide a very special and unique insight into the player's personal life that all other mediums are unable to provide. Most collectors of handwritten letters prefer that the letter contain either content about that player's sport or something about an integral part of the player's personal life. In this medium, the content of the letter can greatly enhance the value of the autograph.

Other very popular mediums for collecting sports autographs are on sportscards, government postcards, Hall of Fame plaques or index cards. Each of these types has its own appeal. Depending on rarity, condition and eye-appeal, the item can vary in value.

Regardless of whose signature it is and what has been signed, autograph collectors care greatly about the condition of both the autograph and the medium upon which it rests. The item must have eye-appeal, a display-oriented factor that makes the item pleasant to look at and present. A smeared signature, a stained index card, a photograph with torn or frayed edges, or a badly scuffed baseball will greatly affect the eye-appeal and value of the autograph. Strength of the signature is also a very important factor and, in most instances, the determining factor in the value of an autograph. Bold, clear and legible signatures are preferred for obvious reasons over faded or light examples.

Another factor that affects eye-appeal is the legibility of the autograph itself. The reader shouldn't have to rely on guesswork to figure out who signed the item. What would be the point of having an autograph if you are unable to tell who signed it? Regarding condition, it is important to remember that the items with the most potential for an increase in value are the best of the best, both in regard to the condition of the medium and strength of the autograph. These are the items that most astute collectors look for and, therefore, command a premium in the hobby.

This brings us to the top 100 sports autographs in the hobby. The final list came to rest based on a variety of reasons, but those reasons are truly a peripheral matter. Aside from Babe Ruth perched on top, we truly hope the rest of the list causes the same stir, laughter and scintillating debate it caused us. These discussions and debates will once again allow you to smell the grass, taste the hot dogs, hear the roar of the crowd and revisit the day that the championship was yours to enjoy.

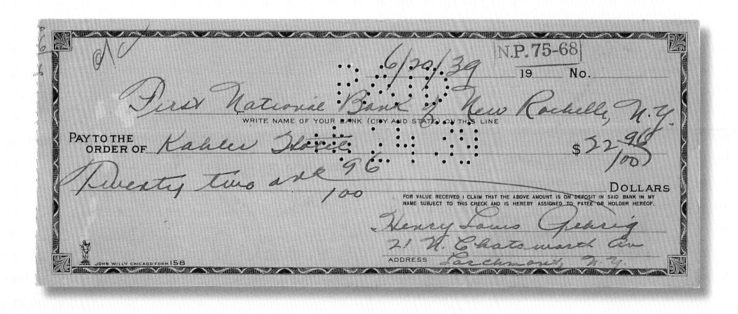

The Top 100 Autographs in the Hobby

Ranking the Top 10 Most Important Signatures

By Steve Grad

The hobby of collecting autographs has been around since Abraham Lincoln was President. In the late 19th Century, collectors used to obtain signatures of famous politicians and, as we entered the 20th Century, attention shifted to actors, war heroes and sports stars. A baseball legend by the name of Babe Ruth helped revolutionize the hobby of autograph collecting and, thanks to his immense popularity, the demand for his signature exceeded that of anyone in the world.

The hobby, as we know it today, came into its own in the 1940s and 1950s when fans began to mail requests to retired players. These were sent to primarily early Baseball Hall of Fame members. This practice continues, but the hobby has certainly evolved from "snail mail" signature requests to in-person chasers, sports memorabilia shows and private signings. Collectors are passionate by nature; it is just something in their blood. I was 10 years old when I was first introduced to the world of autographs. I remember running down the third-base line at Comiskey Park in Chicago with a scrap of paper in hand and a pounding heart. I had absolutely no idea whose autograph I was chasing, but what I do remember is that I felt an amazing rush of adrenaline.

When I finally reached my desired target, I stuck out my paper and, in less than two seconds, it was returned to me with this strange handwriting. Years later, I recognized it as Rich Dotson's signature, a former pitcher for the Sox. But, at that moment, I was hooked for life. Collecting autographs is a lot of fun. I discovered that if you start at an early age, with a little focus and determination, you can build a fairly substantial collection. Through the years, the lessons I learned as a 10-year-old have stayed with me as an adult. These lessons are about how to be a successful "chaser," the importance of how and what to collect, and the dangers of fraudulent signatures. As collectors, we must constantly improve our base of knowledge and recognize the pitfalls that exist. If you decide to collect, it is always best if you collect with purpose and stay focused on your goals.

Whatever you collect, make it the best collection you can. For example, if you build the ultimate baseball collection or construct a collection of football Hall of Famers, make sure you focus your energy on that part of your collection and excel at it. It's important to learn as much as you possibly can. To know your subject matter is to know how to better collect. Be wary of the "bad guys," otherwise known as forgers. They've been around a long time – as long as autograph collecting has been a hobby. Their job is to mimic the signatures you desire. It is not uncommon for collections to be filled with autographs that are not authentic or signed via proxy, either by a secretary or a clubhouse attendant. It happens to nearly everyone, but if you study your subject and get to know it, the less likely you will fall victim. I have been lucky enough to turn my collecting passion into a full-time job. There is nothing more gratifying, as the principal authenticator at PSA/DNA, than to be a part of the hobby I became hooked on as a 10-year old. Hopefully, you can experience the same in your collecting pursuits.

In the following chapter, we list and discuss what we consider to be the most important autographs in the collecting world, starting with our *Top 10*. From baseball to boxing, from football to golf, the top autographs from each respective sport were included in assembling this exclusive list. Each signature was selected based on a combination of factors with the ultimate two factors being popularity and historical significance.

Let the journey begin...

1

Babe Ruth

In the world of autographs, there is nothing more symbolic than this man's graceful stroke. Babe Ruth's autograph is, quite simply, the most desired in the hobby. Ruth was, perhaps, the most prolific signer of his era. Nevertheless, the zeal for items signed by the *Sultan of Swat* has not wavered in nearly 80 years, leaving demand to outweigh supply.

Fittingly, Ruth's signature was quite representative of the man – bold, flamboyant and striking. During the prime of his career, Ruth often would place quotes around "Babe" when signing his name. This practice mainly ceased during the late 1920s. In the latter stages of his life, when Ruth was being treated for cancer, he had a nurse sign some of his fan mail. Although these were non-malicious forgeries, it is still important to note.

There are also several variations of his signature. From the abbreviated "GH Ruth" often found on cancelled checks, to his popular "Babe Ruth" to his rare, full-name version "George Herman Ruth," they are all highly desirable. Any one of the Babe's signatures would sit center stage in a serious autograph collection.

Ruth died in 1948 at the age of 53.

2

Muhammad Ali/Cassius Clay

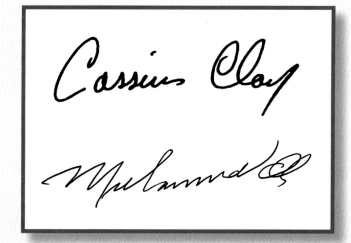

Born Cassius Clay, a man who later changed his name (Muhammad Ali) to coincide with his religious beliefs, Ali was a charismatic boxer with a penchant for causing trouble and stirring the pot wherever he went. A man who could "float like a butterfly and sting like a bee ..." was an Olympic Champion and later World Heavyweight Champion. Ali's career started in the 1960s and ended in 1981. He fought some of the most memorable bouts in boxing history, clashing with legendary champions like Sonny Liston, Archie Moore and contemporary champions like Joe Frazier, George Foreman and Ken Norton.

Hobbyists can collect two versions of Ali's signature, his original given name, Cassius Clay, and the second one, Muhammad Ali. When comparing the availability of the two signatures, the first version is very scarce compared to the second one. While Ali occasionally signed his given name for collectors in the 1980s and 1990s, his preference was to sign his full name when asked by fans. In 1984, Ali was diagnosed with Parkinson's disease, which has made it quite difficult for him to sign his name. Ali's signature can be described as anything from long, flowing and large to something that resembles a Richter Scale reading. To this day, he continues to sign his name with the demand outweighing the supply.

3

Mickey Mantle

Years after his death, Mickey Mantle's autograph is still coveted. Mantle's signature continues to be a driving force in the sports memorabilia market. For most, capturing Mickey's signature as a young player is the key. The problem is that very few remain. His signature has always been a simple and straightforward, "Mickey Mantle." While his autograph evolved throughout his professional career, it has remained very legible.

In the 1950s, his signature went through some small changes, going from a very upright and innocent looking signature to a more stylish version. In 1956, this more stylish version of his signature took hold and it became slightly more flamboyant as the years went on. During much of his playing career, Mantle rarely signed. Occasionally, he signed an autograph at the ballpark, team hotel or during spring training. He rarely signed team baseballs or fan mail. It is a daunting task to find a New York Yankee team ball signed by Mantle. Typically, this was a clubhouse attendant's job. As a result of his fame, Mantle's signature has been heavily forged. Despite being a frequent signer on the show circuit in the 1980s and 1990s and part of Upper Deck Authenticated for a short time, the demand still outweighs the supply when it comes to his signature. Take extreme caution when purchasing a Mantle signature and make sure it has been properly authenticated.

The 16-time All-Star, who played hard on and off the field, died from liver cancer in 1995 at the age of 63.

4

Michael Jordan

Michael Jordan's autograph is highly coveted and he helped change the way autographed memorabilia was marketed to the hobby. A courteous signer in college and throughout his early years in the NBA, Jordan became a marketing tool for Upper Deck in its second year of business. With exclusive signed photos, jerseys, basketballs and cards, Jordan changed the way people collected autographs.

His signature has evolved drastically through time. In college, it was simple but every letter of his autograph was penned. By the time he hit the court for the Bulls in 1984, Jordan had become very used to signing his name. By the early 1990s, Jordan had shortened his autograph and became more efficient, but it was tougher to read. Even though MJ's signature is readily available, it is still a cornerstone of many autograph collections.

Lou Gehrig's signature remains one of the most desirable in all of sports. While he had plenty of time to sign his name as a member of the New York Yankees, Gehrig autographs remain quite scarce. As a rookie in 1923 and into his second and third seasons, Gehrig's autograph was very basic and childlike. As his popularity grew, Gehrig learned the art of signing his name. Not one to turn down many requests for signatures, Gehrig typically scrawled his name on a number of items during his playing days, especially album pages, which are the most frequently seen.

5

Lou Gehrig

Gehrig's autograph was typically penned so every letter was legible but, if hurried, he would occasionally sign an abbreviated version dropping the "ou" and just signing "L. Gehrig." After his retirement from baseball in 1939, Gehrig signed very few items, with most of his correspondence and requests for his autograph handled by his wife Eleanor. His career and life was cut short by Amyotrophic Lateral Sclerosis (ALS). Gehrig died in 1941, two years after retiring from baseball. Most of the Gehrig material that survives has been penned on team-signed baseballs. As was the custom with the Yankees and anywhere Babe Ruth played, the *Sultan of Swat* graced the sweet spot of baseball. Gehrig typically signed on a panel adjacent to Ruth's autograph. Single-signed examples of Gehrig's signature are rarely seen and are typically penned on the side panel of the ball, as if Gehrig was still awaiting the great Ruth to place his name on the sweet spot. While many fans and collectors realize the significance of having Gehrig's signature a part of their collection, what they fail to realize is how truly rare his signature is. When it came to social behavior, Gehrig was the antithesis of Ruth. Since Gehrig was a private man, he signed infrequently compared to his boisterous teammate.

6

Jackie Robinson

Jackie Robinson's number (42) is officially retired by every major league ballpark and his legendary status continues to grow to this day. Throughout his career, Robinson was very cordial and a good signer for fans and collectors. During several periods of his life, Robinson would occasionally employ a secretary or clubhouse attendant to sign his mail, but was known to respond to a great number of requests for his signature.

His signature developed throughout time and evolved from a slowly signed signature with very little authority to a fast flowing signature with authority. This transformation began prior to his professional career and continued up until his death. Thanks to the sale of his cancelled checks and correspondence, signed Robinson material is not rare, but it is valuable. Single-signed baseballs, especially examples signed on the sweet spot, are quite scarce, with Robinson electing to sign most on the side panel.

Robinson died in 1972 at the age of 53.

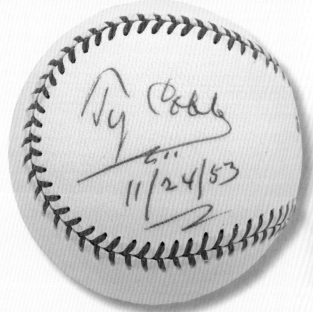

7

Ty Cobb

Ty Cobb, who was tenacious on the field, signed frequently off the field. Most of the material known of Cobb is from his post-playing days. Signatures from Cobb's playing days exist in decent numbers, but are certainly tougher to find than ones penned after his retirement from the game. One of the most prolific letter writers in baseball history, Cobb would often pen long letters of correspondence to family, friends and fans alike. In addition, his signature took many shapes and forms during his life.

Early in his career, Cobb would sign his full name, "Tyrus R. Cobb," however, most of his correspondence and signatures from his playing and post-playing career were signed "Ty Cobb." He would typically date items and add a small personalization if asked. Cobb also retained his surliness later in life. When the same collector would repeatedly write Cobb, asking for signatures, he would typically write back, telling the recipient that he would no longer sign for them. A good in-person signer for fans and collectors, Cobb signatures are not in short supply. In addition to baseballs, photographs, 3x5s, GPCs and cut signatures, Cobb signed a great deal of his personal checks, which have made their way into the marketplace during the last 25 years.

Cobb died in 1961 at the age of 74.

8

Tiger Woods

As an amateur, Tiger Woods was an accommodating signer. While at Stanford, Woods signed for fans and signed all of his fan mail. Few people watched him play and even fewer asked for his autograph. The more recognition he gained, the more desirable his autograph became. Woods' signature has evolved through the years into the eloquent signature it is today. As a teen, Woods' signature featured a stand alone upper case "T" followed by the rest of his first name. His last name, an impeccable, "Woods" with every letter readable, including the double "oo"s. As demand for his signature increased, Woods retained the stand alone "T" but instead of spelling out the rest of his first and last name, the rest of his first name would flow into his "W" where he ends with a small case "d". As Woods reached elite status, Upper Deck signed the star, offering everything from autographed flags to photos. The lone exception has been golf balls. While Woods has signed them in the past, he stopped the practice when he went pro in August, 1996. A few recent examples have surfaced since then, but they are a rare find.

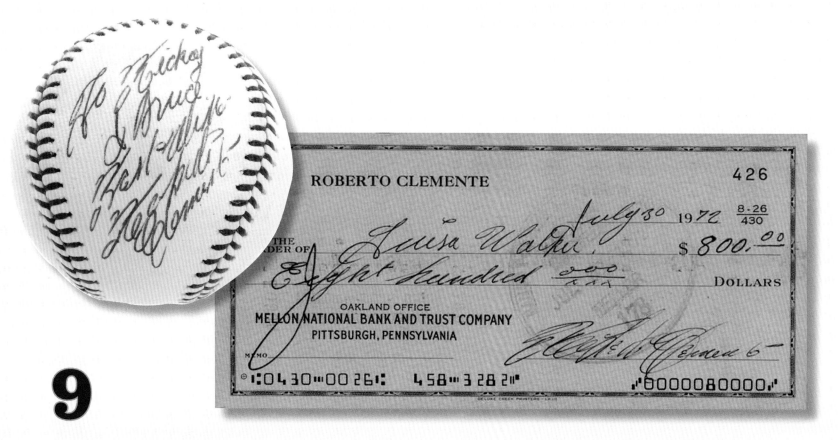

9

Roberto Clemente

Roberto Clemente, who perished in a plane crash in 1972 while en route to Nicaragua, possessed one of the most desirable signatures in baseball. Obviously, his autograph is scarce for the above-mentioned reason but it is also tough as a result of something else.

During the final five or six seasons of his career (1967-1972), Clemente's assistant and valet (Phil Dorsey) signed a large amount of his fan mail. What is found in the marketplace today is Dorsey's signature, though once thought to be Clemente's. Discerning the difference between the two signatures can be quite difficult. In the 1950s, Clemente featured a long flowing signature on one plane, "Roberto Clemente." By 1960, Clemente started to stack his signature with his first name above his last. Clemente's signature is most commonly found on team baseballs, scorecards and 3x5s. Single-signed baseballs are found, but at a hefty price. His personal checks, most originating from the 1970s, can be found but, they too, come at a premium price.

10

Sandy Koufax

Pride is always something that has been synonymous with Sandy Koufax throughout his career and life. His signature reflects that. From his early years as a Dodger to the present day, Koufax's signature is handsome and legible. Though his signature has become less precise from what it was in the 1960s and 1970s, it is still a gorgeous creation.

Throughout his career and during his post-baseball life, Koufax was very obliging to autograph seekers via the mail and in person. But now, thanks to some very smart marketing, Koufax's signature has become a hot commodity. Koufax's signature is now very limited and he signs autographs only once a year, all done during a private signing. Koufax single-signed baseballs command a serious price in the marketplace and are in great demand.

Baseball Autographs

Hank Aaron

Owning a Hank Aaron autograph is a cornerstone to any Hall of Fame autograph collection. Until recently, finding one was relatively easy. A ready and willing signer for most of his career, Aaron became a regular on the show circuit in the 1980s, before curtailing his appearances in the mid- to late-1990s. Currently, Aaron makes only a few appearances per year. Thus, the demand for his signature has skyrocketed.

While playing with the Braves, Aaron had a very small and compact signature. He would typically sign "Hank Aaron" and, occasionally, "Henry Aaron." By 1960, he stuck with "Hank Aaron." In recent years, Aaron's signature has become much larger and less legible. In addition, Aaron rarely adds anything to his signature. In the past, he would occasionally add his home run total (755) or his uniform number (44). There are no known examples featuring the year of his Hall of Fame induction (1983), since Aaron refuses to sign that inscription.

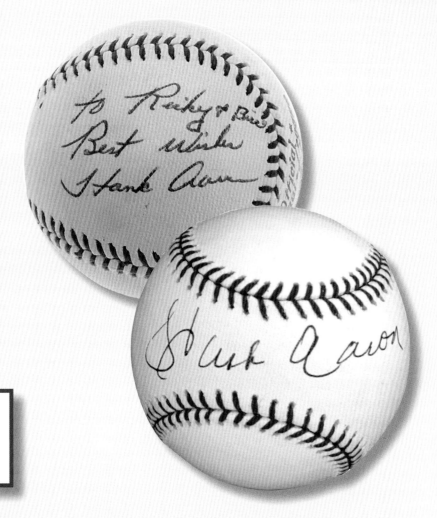

Cap Anson

Cap Anson passed away in 1922 before collecting autographs became a hobby, making his signature extremely rare. After his retirement from baseball in 1897, Anson took on a number of jobs, including Chicago City Clerk and, later as a vaudeville performer. What remains of Anson today is mostly relegated to signed letters and documents. Finding Anson's signature on a team baseball from his playing days is not likely to happen and there are few single-signed examples known.

His signature was a very simple "Adrian C. Anson." Several documents have surfaced where he signed "Capt." and those are from his vaudeville years in the early 1900s. Be extremely cautious when approaching Anson material. Items signed during his days working for the City of Chicago were mostly secretarial in nature and finding cut signatures are difficult. His autograph is one of the scarcest of all 19th Century players.

Anson died in 1922 at the age of 69.

Johnny Bench

A long-time guest at autograph shows, Johnny Bench is no stranger to collectors. His signature has remained virtually the same since his rookie year in 1967, a very simple "Johnny Bench." With a small and powerful slant to the right, Bench's signature flows from his hand gracefully. His signature can be found on any number of baseball-related items, but finding a vintage signature of Bench is more of a challenge. While he signed his fair share of autographs during his early years in baseball, not many have survived, especially tough to find are single-signed baseballs.

Yogi Berra

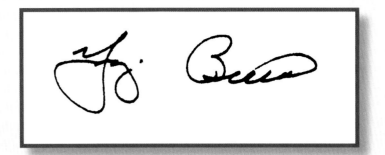

Yogi Berra's autograph is abundant. His signature is a flawless "Yogi Berra." While playing with the Yankees in the 1940s, he signed "Larry Berra" before switching to "Yogi." Well after his playing days, Berra created his own company, LTD Enterprises, Inc., which provides signed memorabilia direct to the hobby. The LTD stands for Larry, Tim and Dale. Tim and Dale, who help run the operation, are Yogi's two sons. Berra's signature is an undeniable treasure, a symbol of Yankee greatness.

Barry Bonds

Starting at Arizona State in the 1980s, to his current day, mass-produced signature, this all-time home run leader's signature has taken on many shapes and forms. The true vintage signature of Barry Bonds and the most desirable example is from the 1984-1987 period, when he was a college senior to his rookie year with the Pirates. His signature, during this time, was a very distinguished and legible "Barry L. Bonds."

As his popularity grew, so did the demand for his signature. By 1988, Bonds' signature was a far cry from what it was just a season before. Throughout the years, his signature has gone from showcasing every letter, to being almost unreadable, then back to an every letter version, though much more pronounced and neater than his signature from the mid-1980s. Bonds has actively marketed his signature to fans, dealers and collectors through his own company. His autograph can be found on virtually any kind of baseball memorabilia.

George Brett

George Brett, known for his toughness on the field, was tough off the field as well. Early on, as a rookie in 1975, Brett was an accommodating signer, penning his full letter name, "George Brett." Through the years, Brett cut down on his signature and shortened his first name to either a simple "G" or a sloppier version of his first name with a few, barely legible letters. An in-person Brett signature was quite difficult during the 1980s, typically signing "G Brett." Finding Brett's autograph in the modern world of autograph shows and signings isn't much of a challenge. However, obtaining a Brett signature from his early days is a must for collectors and poses a real challenge.

Roy Campanella

A gracious signer throughout his career, Roy Campanella signatures are not in short supply, but remain a hot commodity in the collecting world. A frequent signer in person and via the mail, his signature was slightly angled to the right and was signed with authority. During his career, Campanella would occasionally employ a proxy, with a clubhouse attendant or a secretary handling some of his signing duties. An expert eye is needed to differentiate between the two signatures. Signed photographs, 3x5s and GPCs are the most commonly seen with single-signed baseballs being a rarity.

Thanks to the aid of a machine developed in the mid-1980s, Campanella was able to continue signing his name, well after an auto accident left him paralyzed for life in 1958. Campanella's right arm was strapped into a harness and a machine helped guide him. The end result was a fairly legible, but choppy and large signature. A key component of the Brooklyn Dodgers of the 1950s, Campanella is regarded in many baseball circles as one of the finest catchers in the history of baseball.

In 1993, Campanella died of a heart attack at the age of 71.

Alexander Cartwright

Alexander Cartwright is considered by many to be the inventor of the game of baseball. His New York Knickerbockers, playing in their inaugural game in 1846, lost 23-1 to the New York Nine. By 1849, he was in Hawaii starting a new professional league that would later be used as a model for the American and National Leagues. A 1938 inductee into the Baseball Hall Fame, Cartwright died in 1892.

His signature is in short supply. Having died in 1892, Cartwright signed very few, if any, autographs. Most of the material signed by Cartwright is in the form of checks, documents or handwritten letters. His authentic signature is stunning. It's very ornate and large, which Cartwright signed two different ways. The first style, one that is rarely seen, was "Alexander Cartwright" and the second and more common was "Alex J. Cartwright." His signature is one of the most important in the Hall of Fame and one of the scarcest on the list.

Henry Chadwick

The *Father of Baseball* was partially responsible for turning baseball from a club sport into one of the most popular American games in sports history. A journalist, statistician and historian, Henry Chadwick helped promote the game like no one else had. He edited the first baseball guide on public sale, as well as annual guides on the sport. In a time when his opinion mattered more than anyone else's, Chadwick helped sculpt the public's perception of the game. Born in 1824, Chadwick died in 1908 and was elected to the Baseball Hall of Fame in 1938.

His signature remains scarce and is rarely seen in authentic form. Hoards of documents and papers purported to have been signed by Chadwick have surfaced in recent years, but many have now been dismissed and should be treated with caution. Signed photographs, baseballs, and documents are virtually non-existent. His signature, when seen in its authentic form, is typically printed with every letter visible and is often accompanied by a small inscription or salutation. In his later years, Chadwick's signature became more erratic and sloppy.

Chadwick's signature is one of the most important in the hobby.

Roger Clemens

The Rocket's autograph has made some amazing transformations through the years. As a rookie and into his second year, Roger Clemens didn't really have a true autograph. He was more or less just printing his name. Most of his signature was printed with very few connected letters. By 1986, he started to develop more of a true autograph and that style stayed with him through the years. His autograph can be big or small and it greatly depends on what medium he is putting his signature on. Today, Clemens' autograph is very simple, with his first name and last name running quite close together.

Of course, finding early Clemens material can be a challenge. Most commonly seen are 3x5s or gum cards that were autographed by Clemens during his early years. A must have for any Cy Young and MVP collector, finding the ideal Clemens signature shouldn't be too arduous.

Eddie Collins

Who is Eddie Collins? Playing alongside players like Ty Cobb and Joe Jackson, Collins could hold his own. A career .333 hitter, Collins finished his career with 3,315 hits and four Championship crowns.

An original inductee into the Baseball Hall of Fame, Collins' signature continues to garner attention and is a key piece to anyone's HOF collection. Collins' signature was very stylish, specifically as he started to get older and wiser. The older Collins became, the more authority his signature exuded. Most commonly, Collins would sign "Eddie" Collins. The quotation marks added by Collins indicated he was signing "Eddie" as a short for Edward. His signature, one of beauty, is attainable, but at a price. What is available today are signed contracts from the 1940s when Collins was the general manager of the Red Sox.

Signed photographs do not surface often and black and white HOF plaque cards can command five figures. Even more scarce are single-signed baseballs; only a few examples exist in the hobby. Signed 3x5s and GPCs are more common and many of these were signed by Collins via mail until his death in 1951.

Dizzy Dean

During his playing days, Dizzy Dean would sign his name many different ways. The most typically seen is "Dizzy Dean." At times, especially early in his career, Dean signed his initials or even his first name "Jerry" before signing the rest of his name. For most of his career, Dean signed predominantly two ways. They were very similar, but around 1938, Dean started running his first and last name together. He would continue to sign in this manner for the rest of his life.

There are several things to keep in mind when looking for Dean's signature. Most of the correspondence Dean replied to in the late 1940s and early 1950s was secretarial signed. His wife would occasionally sign mail requests for him sent in care of The Baseball Hall of Fame or to his home.

His signature is coveted on single-signed baseballs. When Dean graced a ball with his autograph, he would typically sign on the side panel. Sweet spot signed baseballs are rarely found. During the 1930s, while playing with his brother Paul, they both signed baseballs, occasionally on the sweet spot. While some would argue that Dean isn't worthy of HOF consideration, there is no question that his wit and humor make him one of baseball's most memorable players.

Dean died in 1974 at the age of 64.

Joe DiMaggio

In 1951, Joe DiMaggio retired from baseball and became known to generations of Americans as Marilyn Monroe's husband and *Mr. Coffee*. The former outfielder can be credited with changing and revolutionizing how his autograph was sold and marketed. A smart businessman, who kept the first dollar he earned, DiMaggio was a staple on the autograph circuit for much of the 1980s and 1990s. Through it all, his autograph hardly changed in appearance from the 1940s until his death in 1999. Fans and collectors were always treated to a beautiful signature of DiMaggio, who signed his name legibly on every item he signed.

His autograph went through developing stages early in his life, when he was still wrestling with exactly how to sign his name. While his signature went through some changes in the 1940s, it remained almost the same throughout his life. As the years progressed, especially after the 1970s, DiMaggio's long and looping "g"s in his last name became smaller but, overall, his autograph remained a work of art. Vintage material of DiMaggio is not as scarce as some contemporaries of his period. DiMaggio was constantly besieged by fans to sign autographs and was typically gracious, signing his name to baseballs and autograph books.

As was a common practice with major league players, DiMaggio employed the services of clubhouse attendants to sign team baseballs from time to time and, for a short period during the late 1970s and 1980s, his sister would sign his fan mail.

A legendary Yankee and member of the Baseball Hall of Fame, DiMaggio's autograph is an important part of any collection.

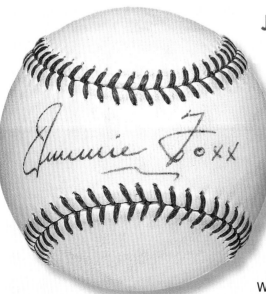

Jimmie Foxx

While Jimmie Foxx wasn't a prolific signer during his playing career, he certainly was after his playing days were over (1945). During that time, and especially during his early years (pre-1930), Foxx toyed with his signature, signing many variations of his name, including "Jim Foxx", "Jimmie Foxx" and "Jimy Foxx." His signature not only changed in content, it changed in style. The "J" in his first name went through a metamorphosis, looking dramatically different over the years.

About 1930, just as his career was starting to blossom, Foxx's signature stayed relatively consistent and is very similar to how he signed up until his death in 1967. Most of the authentic Foxx material seen on the market is from the 1950s and 1960s.

The marketplace is not saturated with Foxx autographs, but they are relatively easy to find on 3x5s and album pages. Collectors should be cautious with vintage signed letters, photos and postcards. His brother and a clubhouse attendant would regularly sign his name on these items during the mid-1930s. Foxx's autograph remains in high demand because he was a Triple Crown Winner and a member of the 500 Home Run Club.

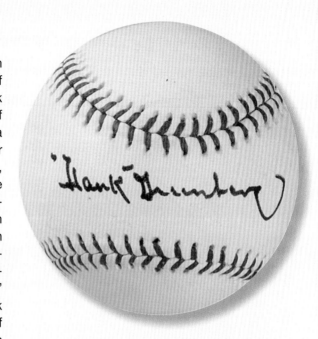

Josh Gibson

This powerful Negro Leaguer's autograph is almost a thing of legend. While some examples exist, they rarely surface. When they do, they command staggering prices. His autograph is worth more than almost anyone he played against in the 1930s and 1940s. Josh Gibson's signature is elusive and the reason was simple – Negro League players were very rarely asked for their signature. When they were, they were not placed on premium items. Most players signed scraps of paper and scorecards, with many items lost or discarded over time.

The former catcher's scrawl was just that, very childlike, slow and deliberate, Gibson struggled to sign his name. The examples that survive today feature Gibson signing in three different styles, including "Joshua Gibson," "Josh Gibson" and "J. Gibson." All are quite legible and feature every letter of his name. Recently, several Gibson autographs have reached a bidding frenzy in auction, including the only signed image of him known to exist. That piece, which was double-signed (back and front) by Gibson, garnered more than $80,000 in auction.

Signed baseballs are few and far between, especially baseballs signed during his days with the Pittsburgh Crawfords or Homestead Grays. Through the years, several balls signed by Gibson and his former teammate Satchel Paige have surfaced. Those were reportedly signed during the war years in the mid-1940s, while on tour, to raise money for the war effort.

Gibson died in 1947 at the age of 35.

Hank Greenberg

One of the American League's top performers of the 1930s and 1940s, Hank Greenberg was the class of the Tigers and he possessed a great signature. A willing signer throughout much of his career, Greenberg always took pride in signing his name. Every letter of his name can be seen in his striking autograph, which graces a number of baseball-related memorabilia. His signature reads a simple "Hank" Greenberg and typically took up an enormous amount of real estate when placed on a baseball, photo, 3x5 card or government issued penny postcard. Vintage signed pieces from Greenberg's playing days are still rather abundant in the hobby.

Also available for collectors are signed letters and contracts from his days as a general manager. A willing signer via the mail, Greenberg signed his fair share of 3x5s and photographs with most signatures from the Baseball Hall of Fame member strong and placed perfectly on every item. Single-signed baseballs are in short supply. While baseballs signed during the 1970s can be found with other players scribbled on other panels, finding Greenberg's scrawl on a single-signed Bobby Brown ball can be a challenge.

Greenberg, due to his death in 1986, could only have signed one kind of American League Bobby Brown ball. This ball features a black Haiti stamp below the Rawlings logo, giving Greenberg a short time to sign them but making it certainly possible. The balls were manufactured from 1984 to 1990, giving the popular slugger about a two year window. Typically, when signing a single-signed baseball, Greenberg used a black Sharpie or Flair marker to sign his name.

Rogers Hornsby

While Rogers Hornsby's life could certainly be described as turbulent, his autograph was strikingly beautiful. From the earliest examples that exist up until his death in 1963, his autograph remained graceful. His playing-era signature is characterized by a long paraph that would flow under his autograph when he was finished signing an item, a trademark he kept throughout his life.

a

A fairly accommodating signer during his lifetime, Hornsby's signature can be found adorning baseballs, photos, 3x5s, GPCs and autograph pages. He was around baseball almost his entire life, so he had plenty of time to sign for fans and collectors in person and through the mail. Only during one period of his life (in the 1950s) did Hornsby supply fans with ghost signatures. Typically, fans received a reply from Hornsby, only to have it penned by a girlfriend.

His autograph is highly sought after on single-signed baseballs as those are considered quite rare. A member of baseball's *All Century Team*, Hornsby is one of the leading second baseman of all time.

Joe Jackson

Finding a real signature of Joe Jackson is monumentally difficult. His signature appears on a number of stock certificates kept in his family and willed to his sister, who sold them in the early 1990s. Most are double-signed and rarely surface. These have been buried in private collections over time.

After his playing days, Jackson faded from public life and most collectors had no idea on how to find him. He resurfaced in the 1940s and mail was then sent to him to sign, although most was signed by his wife, Katie.

Jackson's illiteracy was public knowledge and his signature was childlike. He wrote his name with Katie's help. The end result was choppy and barely legible, which explains why he did it so infrequently.

Jackson died in 1951 at the age of 63.

Reggie Jackson

Unlike *Shoeless Joe*, finding this Jackson signature is not problematic. It's readily available as Reggie Jackson is a frequent guest on the show circuit. His signature is typically accompanied by his jersey number "44" placed in the large bottom loop of the "J" in Jackson. On the other hand, finding an authentic Jackson signature from his playing days can be more of a quest. For most of his career, he employed the services of a clubhouse attendant to sign team baseballs and, during his later days in the major leagues, he would employ a secretary to sign his mail.

While Jackson did occasionally sign in-person, his "in person" signature tended to be quite illegible. There is very little single-signed material of Jackson that pre-dates the 1980s. Finding a single-signed ball from early in his career would be a daunting task. His autograph can typically be found on baseballs, photographs, bats and jerseys. In many cases, it's difficult to find authentic examples of his autograph on baseball cards with many of those secretarial-signed throughout the years.

Today, Jackson remains a Yankee favorite and one of the greatest home run hitters of all time.

Derek Jeter

As the 11th team captain in Yankee history, Derek Jeter immediately recognized the value of his signature and, not long after his rookie campaign, he signed on with New York-based Steiner Sports, who marketed Jeter's autograph to the masses. His popular signature is compact and to the point. His autograph has certainly evolved from his high school and minor league scrawl to his major league signature. Finding Jeter's autograph shouldn't be an issue with baseballs, photos and jerseys readily available in the marketplace. Early signatures of Jeter, signed before he hit the major leagues, are in short supply and should be considered rare by modern standards.

Walter Johnson

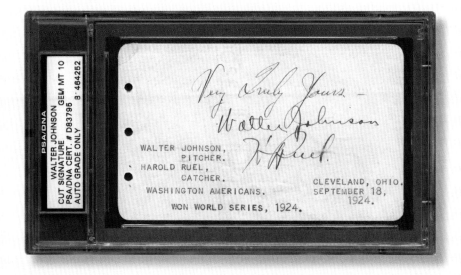

A gracious signer in person and through the mail, the most abundant source of Walter Johnson's signatures are from cancelled checks sent to collectors by his wife after his death and sold via his estate in the 1980s and 1990s. Johnson's signature was typically very neat and almost always legible. When signing the sweet spot of a baseball, his signature would take up the entire space, making for a beautiful keepsake. Johnson passed away before mailing requests to players' homes was commonplace, making his autograph tough.

Johnson died at the age of 59 in 1946.

Larry Lajoie

Little is known of Larry (Napoleon) Lajoie's signing habits while a player and manager. His autograph is almost non-existent with the few examples remaining on team baseballs and several handwritten letters. Most of the material that remains today was signed after his retirement when corresponding with fellow retirees.

Never one to slight a collector, Lajoie featured a methodical, legible signature "Larry Lajoie" and occasionally would sign his full name "Napolean Lajoie." As an added bonus, Lajoie dated virtually all of his correspondence under his signature. A gracious signer in the mail and in person, most of what remains in the marketplace are signed 3x5s and GPCs. Occasionally, a signed photograph or postcard will turn up. From time to time, a single-signed baseball will find its way into the hobby, but they are the rarest of all items signed by Lajoie. A small number of handwritten letters have been discovered, which always exhibit his beautiful penmanship.

Lajoie died in 1959 at the age of 84.

Roger Maris

This Yankee legend's autograph has been the target of forgers since he died in 1985 and finding a nice Roger Maris autograph requires some patience. Single-signed Roger Maris baseballs are a commodity and he signed very few before his death. For every 1,000 Mickey Mantle signed baseballs, there is probably one Roger Maris signed baseball.

A better-than-average signer throughout his life, especially during his post-baseball career, he remains one of the most desired Yankee autographs. His autograph was a simple "Roger Maris" and is very similar in size and shape throughout his career. As an interesting note, the young outfielder would sign his given last name "Maras" early on. Very few of these examples remain and most are from the early- to mid-1950s. Photographs, 3x5s, a select number of bats and single-signed baseballs can be found in the marketplace.

Beware of baseballs signed by Maris bearing a black "Haiti" stamp under the Rawlings logo on official American League baseballs with Bobby Brown as the commissioner. Maris had a limited window to sign these baseballs. Moreover, be cautious of baseballs that have been purportedly signed by Maris on Official American League Bobby Brown baseballs with no Haiti stamp. This indicates the ball was made in the 1990s, long after Maris' death in 1985. Also, more disturbing, are Maris signed balls on reprint World Series baseballs from the late 1970s. The originals always featured a black "HAITI" stamp on the sweet spot.

One of the most desired modern era autographs, Maris' signature is in a class by itself, outdistancing even that of his former teammate Mickey Mantle.

Connie Mack

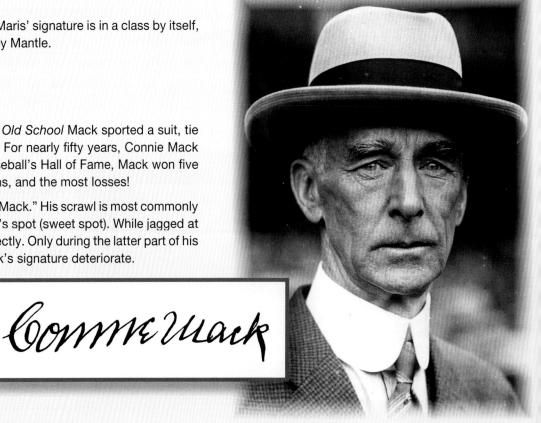

One of the greatest managers in baseball history, *Old School* Mack sported a suit, tie and fedora, rather than a traditional baseball uniform. For nearly fifty years, Connie Mack managed the Philadelphia Athletics. A member of baseball's Hall of Fame, Mack won five World Series titles. He left the game with the most wins, and the most losses!

His signature is rarely anything other than "Connie Mack." His scrawl is most commonly seen on team baseballs where he signed the manager's spot (sweet spot). While jagged at times, Mack's signature was flowing and scripted perfectly. Only during the latter part of his life, especially right before his death in 1956, did Mack's signature deteriorate.

His signature is widely available and can be found on most mediums relating to baseball. He was a productive signer during his managing career and rarely used a "ghost" or secretary to sign his mail.

Greg Maddux

This masterful pitcher's autograph, or scrawl in Greg Maddux's case, reads like a seismograph. He abbreviates his first name with a large "G" followed by a large "M" for his last name, followed by a few jagged lines. With all the Maddux autographs signed through the years, few are legible. Going as far back as 1986 (his rookie year), Maddux signed items very sloppily, a trend that has continued to this day. Don't let that discourage you. Maddux is in an elite club of pitchers, a certain Hall of Famer, and his name is mentioned in the same breath as Walter Johnson and Sandy Koufax.

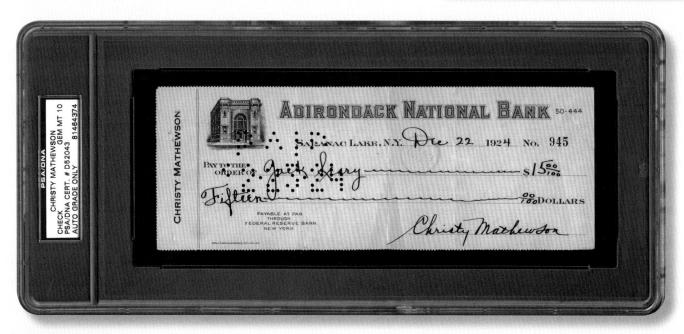

Christy Mathewson

This Hall of Famer's signature scrawl is a rare and valuable autograph. During Christy Mathewson's playing time with the Giants and later with the Reds, signing autographs was not a common practice. The practice of fans asking players for autographs didn't start in earnest until the 1920s, as the popularity of Babe Ruth helped change the game.

A handful of Mathewson checks from the 1920s have made their way into the hobby, mostly thanks to his wife who used to honor fan requests by sending his cancelled checks through the mail. They are coveted and bring a premium in the marketplace.

Rarely is a Mathewson signed-single baseball discovered. In 1922, the Giants held a fundraiser at the Polo Grounds for Mathewson, who was battling tuberculosis. Fans met the WWI vet and received an autographed ball in exchange for a small donation. Today, those balls sell upwards of $150,000. His elegant, long flowing signature is a rare gem few collectors possess.

Mathewson died in 1925 at the age of 45.

Willie Mays

A frequent guest on the show circuit in the 1980s and 1990s, Willie Mays' signature has increased in value through the years. As he ages, his signature has evolved from the 1950s to his modern signature, which is very small and condensed.

Collectors in pursuit of a Mays' signature shouldn't have much of a problem, they are affordable. Vintage autographs of Mays, while not in short supply, bring a premium when sold and finding single-signed baseballs and photos that Mays signed, early in his career, can be difficult.

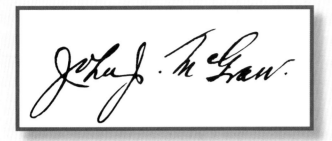

John J. McGraw

John McGraw, a pioneer in the sport of baseball, was one of the most successful skippers the sport has ever known. Mainly associated with the New York Giants, McGraw compiled 2,763 wins and his team won 10 National League Pennants and three World Series Championships.

McGraw's signature, elegant and flowing, was scripted "John J. McGraw." On team-signed baseballs or multi-signed baseballs, his signature dominated a large portion of the sweet spot. A few examples are known where McGraw abbreviated his first name with a simple "J." Typically, this is seen on a multi-signed baseball where he didn't have room to write out his full signature.

His autograph became popular after his death at 60 in 1934. What remains of his signature are scattered throughout the hobby. Commonly seen are check cuts originating from his family. In the 1940s and 1950s, autograph seekers wrote to his wife for memorabilia signed by her late husband. They would typically receive a signature cut from the "signee" portion of the check. Those signatures of McGraw make up most of what remains in the hobby. Signed photographs, baseballs and letters are scarce, as are full- signed checks by McGraw. Only a few are in existence in their full and unaltered state.

Mark McGwire

Few players have dominated baseball in a way that Mark McGwire did. As a rookie with the Oakland A's in 1987, he hit an amazing 49 home runs. In 1998, he was the first player since Roger Maris in 1961, to hit 61 or more home runs in a season, finishing with 70. This record wasn't broken until 2004 when Barry Bonds slugged 73.

Despite his off-the-field woes, McGwire maintains his popularity in Oakland and St. Louis and his autograph remains quite coveted. The McGwire signature most desired is his early signature from his days spent with the 1984 US Olympic Baseball team, and items signed before the 1987 season. McGwire's signature was tall and upright and was always signed quickly.

As his popularity grew in the late 1980s, the demand for his signature increased and McGwire became a frequent guest at card shows. In the 1990s, his autograph morphed and became hastily signed with very few legible letters and just a "MCG" visible. He also disappeared from the show scene. During the late 1990s, especially during his chase of the home run record, McGwire's autograph hit new heights in terms of demand. He can be found on nearly any piece of signed baseball memorabilia.

One of the most significant and important players of the late 20th Century, Mark McGwire and his legend live on.

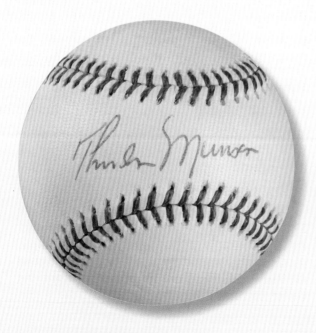

Thurman Munson

As a born leader who possessed unrivaled work ethic, Thurman Munson was a future Hall of Famer in the making. A star catcher in the 1970s, Munson was a clutch hitter, batting .373 overall in three straight World Series. Sadly, Munson's love of flying was his weakness. In 1979, at the age of 32, he perished as his own plane crashed.

Munson remains high on the list of desired autographs for collectors. As a player, Munson could be quite difficult to approach and was known to say "no" more than "yes" when asked to sign. Therefore, his autograph is in short supply. The most desirable Munson signatures date to his early years in the league (1971-72) where he signed every letter of his name, "Thurman Munson." As the years passed, Munson shortened his signature. He's most commonly found on team-signed balls, 3x5s and programs. Rarely is Munson's signature found on single-signed balls or bats. Both bring a premium in the open market.

Stan Musial

An icon in St. Louis, where he spent his entire career, Stan Musial has been a very accommodating signer throughout his life. From his early years in the majors up until modern time, Musial has signed his name the only way he knows how, "Stan Musial." His autograph always featured an every-letter signature. Through time, it has transformed and shrunk considerably in size and shape, but remained much like it did in the 1940s.

Finding a gorgeous Musial signature on any medium related to baseball shouldn't be a challenge with plenty of signed memorabilia available in the marketplace. In fact, Musial created his own sports memorabilia company during the hobby boom called Stan the Man, Inc., which provides signed Musial memorabilia direct to the hobby.

Mel Ott

Mel Ott's catch-phrase "keep it classy," was reflected in his signing habits. While Ott was one of the top stars in the game, he was also one of the best signers. His name was short, but that didn't keep it from making a beautiful autograph. Simply penned "Mel Ott" for the majority of his career, his autograph was very legible. During the late 1920s, he signed his full name "Melvin Ott" from time to time, mostly on team-signed baseballs. Also during the 1940s, a clubhouse attendant occasionally signed team baseballs for him. Ott's autograph can be found on a variety of items, including 3x5s, GPCs and album pages, which are the most common.

Finding a single-signed baseball can be a challenge and Ott is definitely the most difficult of all the *500 Home Run Club* members. He died in 1959 at the age of 49. During his time with the Giants and after his playing career, he was rarely asked to be a single signer on a baseball. The few single-signed examples that do exist are typically found signed (and sometimes inscribed) on the side panel of the ball.

Satchel Paige

Satchel Paige was a gracious signer for autograph collectors. Most of the Paige autographs in existence are from the late 1960s and 1970s when fans wrote to Paige requesting his signature. Paige died in 1982, around the time that many former Negro League players starting cashing in on their fame by appearing at sports memorabilia conventions.

The most commonly seen signature style of Paige was "Satchel Paige." At times, he would sign his name "Satchell Paige" adding an extra lower case "l." His autograph, which was usually signed with every letter, is in high demand on baseballs and photographs. Typically, Paige would inscribe baseballs on a side panel using a simple inscription, "To (name) from (Paige would also add an extra "m" in "from") Satchel Paige." In the early 1980s, his wife or daughter would sign his correspondence from time to time.

Cal Ripken, Jr.

During Cal Ripken, Jr.'s entire career, his availability and fan-pleasing attitude made him a delightful in-person signer. Brought up in a baseball family and reared by his father Cal Sr., he learned the value of signing his name neatly and perfectly every time he penned it. His early signature was scripted simply "Cal Ripken Jr." Every letter was present and that continued throughout his career with some minor changes. For the most part, it remained stylish and graceful.

The stories of Ripken's signing are legendary. During the years of the famous streak, specifically 1997 and 1998, fans would line up along the railing at ballparks and Ripken would graciously sign his name. While his signature is easily found on virtually any kind of baseball-related memorabilia, his autograph is vital to any collection.

Pete Rose

There is a plethora of Pete Rose autographs. Here's one case where supply outweighs demand. His autograph hasn't changed much through the years, especially since the 1980s. He signs a simple, clean "Pete Rose." It's big and remains on one easy-to-read plane. More elusive is Rose's vintage signature, especially from his rookie campaign of 1963. Most collectors covet Rose's early signature and those from his days spent with the Reds in the 1970s, a period when Rose excelled at the plate.

While Rose has come clean and admitted that he bet on baseball and the Cincinnati Reds, whom he managed at the time, the damage is already done. One of the living members of baseball's *All Century Team*, Rose continues to cash in on his name, signing autographs for more than 175 days a year at a Las Vegas casino.

Nolan Ryan

Nolan Ryan's autograph could be compared to his best pitch, a fastball. It was typically signed quickly by Ryan who was an accommodating signer during his entire career and afterwards. His autograph stayed relatively the same throughout. As a rookie in 1966 with the Mets, Ryan's autograph was small but legible. By the time he reached the Angels in the 1970s, his autograph was large, full of life and character.

His signature, signed simply "Nolan Ryan," featured an uppercase "N" and "R" each followed by the rest of his letters in his name. An occasional signer at memorabilia shows, Ryan now takes more time when signing his name and makes it even more attractive, adding inscriptions such as his Hall of Fame induction year or his all-time strikeout mark. For several years, Ryan has been signing large quantities of autographs for charity. *The Nolan Ryan Foundation* provides signed memorabilia to the public and the proceeds are used to provide resources for education and community development.

George Sisler

George Sisler's career spanned 16 years and included some of the most incredible single-season batting marks in the history of the sport. An original inductee into the Baseball Hall of Fame in 1939, Sisler owned American League pitching. From 1917 to 1922, a six-year span, Sisler averaged a .374 mark at the plate, topping the coveted and now-impossible .400 mark twice! His 257 hits in 1920 stood until Ichiro Suzuki broke it in 2004, taking eight more games to do so. Originally a pitcher like Babe Ruth, Sisler was too valuable to play once every four days and found his mark as a hitter.

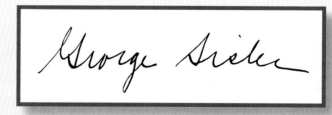

His autograph is fairly easy to find. Sisler lived until 1973, well into the autograph-collecting craze of the era, which started in the 1950s. While his autograph changed in shape and size throughout the years, it remained a gorgeous script throughout his life. An every-letter signature from Sisler adorned each item he signed. Typically found signed by Sisler are 3x5s, GPCs, HOF plaque cards and photographs. Baseballs are scarce, but not impossible to locate. He rarely dedicated anything and obtaining a pure signature of Sisler is quite easy. While he's one of the greatest hitters in major league history, his autograph remains somewhat overlooked.

Tris Speaker

Autographs of Tris Speaker, signed during his career, are few and far between.

Most of the Speaker "playing day" material originates from the 1920s with very few examples seen from the teens. While his autograph evolved through the years, it remained virtually unchanged in structure, reading a clear "Tris Speaker." A coach in the 1950s and a willing mail-signer throughout his life, Speaker was a relatively easy signature to obtain.

Much of the material that has survived in the hobby is featured on 3x5s, GPCs and photographs. Presenting more of a challenge to collectors is finding a single-signed Speaker baseball. While Speaker was never shy about signing his name in person, he typically gravitated to the side panel of a baseball.

Speaker died in 1958 at the age of 70.

Ted Williams

On July 5, 2002, Ted Williams passed away, but his memory lives on. His autograph was highly marketed in the 1980s and part of the 1990s while Williams was a fixture on the sports memorabilia show circuit. His signature remained relatively consistent from the 1960s, until 1994, when Williams had the first of his two strokes. Following his first stroke, Williams was unable to successfully execute a signature on a baseball, only signing flats and bats. Because of the curve of the baseball, Williams could no longer successfully sign his name on a sphere.

Ted Williams' signature was always unmistakable, large and graceful. There wasn't a time in his life that Williams didn't feature a large, every-letter signature. From his early days with the Boston Red Sox through his retirement and post-baseball career, he featured one of the most attractive autographs. During periods in his life, specifically in the 1940s and 1950s, a clubhouse attendant would sign his name on team baseballs. In addition, most of his mail correspondence sent to him during the season was outsourced to a proxy signer. In the 1950s, the Boston Red Sox clubhouse man, Johnny Orlando, was famous for signing Ted Williams' name.

Williams' autograph can be found on any number of baseball-related memorabilia, including bats, photographs, baseballs, jerseys, 3x5s and cards. A word to the wise about Ted Williams; in the 1990s, forgers took advantage of the general public and started to forge Williams' signature in huge quantities. It is said that there are more fake Ted Williams' signatures than real ones. Williams, who signed memorabilia as part of Upper Deck Authenticated for a short time, also signed memorabilia for a family-owned business. That company, which was run by his son at the time, was originally called Green Diamond Sports, Inc. and then became known as Ted Williams Family Enterprises later on. There were rumors within the hobby that a percentage of those autographs may have, in fact, been signed by his son and not by Ted Williams himself. When buying a Ted Williams autograph, make sure proper authentication accompanies the piece.

Harry Wright

A baseball innovator, Harry Wright is largely responsible for the development of major league baseball. Known to baseball historians and fans as the "Father of Baseball," Wright was the first 19th Century baseball manager, leading some of the top teams of the era. From 1871 to 1893, his teams won six championships and, as a player in 1868, he teamed with his brother George to form baseball's "famous nine." Wright died in 1895, just shy of his 61st birthday.

For a serious challenge, try locating Harry Wright's signature. It's rare in any form. His signature was elegant, written in the Spencerian style of the 19th Century. Handwritten letters and clipped signatures remain from the Baseball Hall of Fame member. Finding a signed baseball or piece of baseball memorabilia, other than what is mentioned, is not likely. Thanks to the sale of items in his estate, scorecards that he filled out from his managerial career have made their way into the marketplace. On these scorecards, Wright would fill out the entire lineup and sign his abbreviated name "H. Wright" in the scorer area.

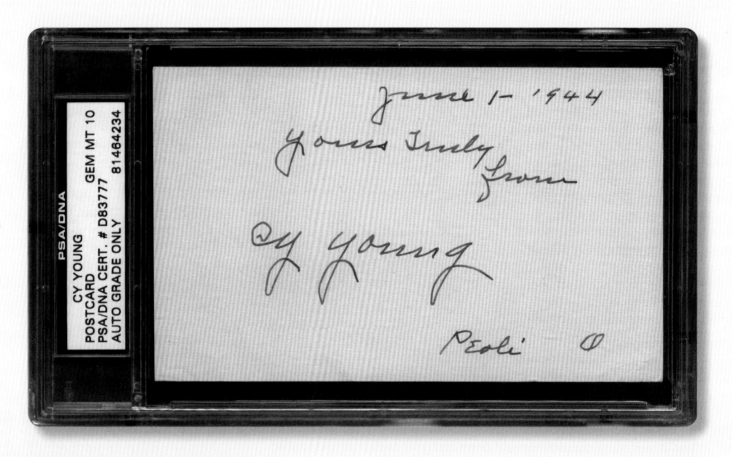

Cy Young

This great pitcher's autograph is a key component to any Hall of Fame collection. A prolific signer and letter writer during his post career, Cy Young was a great signer via the mail and in person, signing autographs right up until his death in 1955. His autograph is not in abundance, but finding a signature on a 3x5 or government postcard is not a challenge. He would typically sign items very simply "Cy Young."

At times, his autograph would include a date or inscription and he was also known to add the town name where he lived, Peoli, Ohio. Material signed by Young during his playing days is virtually non-existent. Single-signed baseballs are very difficult to acquire, but they do exist and are sold in the marketplace on occasion. Nevertheless, they are hard to find signed on the sweet spot with most of them penned on the side panel. Signed photographs also are in short supply and quite desirable.

Basketball Autographs

Kareem Abdul - Jabbar/Lew Alcindor

For the autograph collector, this particular athlete poses an interesting dilemma. What to collect? For the pure collector, finding a Lew Alcindor autograph is a challenge. He only signed this way during his collegiate playing career and up until 1971, when he officially changed his name. Finding a single-signed basketball bearing an Alcindor signature is a near impossible task, with most of the Alcindor material to be found on programs, 3x5s and basketball cards.

His current name, "Kareem Abdul-Jabbar," is typically seen signed just "Abdul-Jabbar" or a standalone "Kareem." Rarely does he combine the two. This autograph can be found on basketballs, jerseys, photos and cards. He typically signs his name with very large letters, making for a nice presentation piece.

Larry Bird

Players who played against him, teammates who played with him and fans that encountered him, realized one thing about Larry Bird – he was ornery. A competitive player, who played every game like it was his last, Bird was ferocious on and off the court. A tough in-person autograph by any standard, fans were lucky if Bird scrawled a "B" for his autograph. Thanks to some very limited signings, finding a genuine signature of Bird is realistic.

During his years at Indiana State University in the late 1970s, Bird's signature was at its best. It was almost innocent looking, lacking real authority. It's the signature most coveted by collectors and it is in short supply. His current signature has been heavily distributed and, thanks to his appearance as a Dream Team member in the 1992 Olympics, he signed a great deal of memorabilia related to that team, including basketballs, photos with Magic Johnson and Michael Jordan and single-signed jerseys.

Kobe Bryant

Kobe Bryant's autograph has taken several different turns and twists during his young career. Before hitting the NBA hardcourt, his signature was a sloppy but readable "Kobe Bryant." Perhaps some of the nicest Kobe Bryant signatures are from his days in high school in suburban Philadelphia. A big attraction to basketball fans, Kobe would pack high school arenas and fans would typically have him sign programs and scraps of paper. His early signature was very legible and it is one of the most collectible of his signature styles.

During his rookie season in 1996, Bryant still featured a full-name signature adding his jersey number (8) to his first and last name. But he quickly dropped his last name when signing a year or two later to "Kobe 8." His signature has remained relatively consistent until 2006 when Bryant switched his jersey number to 24.

Bryant's current autograph simply features his initials "KB."

Wilt Chamberlain

As a signer, Wilt Chamberlain typically obliged fans, especially during the height of his career in the 1960s, and he loved the attention. Chamberlain rarely traveled with an entourage, which is now typical of many modern players. His autograph was a bold and striking, "Wilt Chamberlain." Typically, he stacked his first name on top of his last name, possibly to avoid running out of room on the item he signed.

Through the 1960s and 1970s, Chamberlain's signature quickly deteriorated, with most of the letters in his name becoming illegible. By the 1980s, and especially into the 1990s, Chamberlain became a guest at memorabilia shows, wherein most fans and collectors were left with a beautiful autograph.

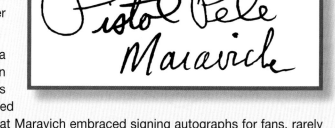

Throughout his career, a "ghost signer" was employed by Chamberlain to occasionally sign random team items and some fan mail, though Chamberlain also found time to sign fan requests during his playing years and during his retirement. His autograph can be relatively easy to locate, with his vintage playing career signature the tougher variety to find.

Chamberlain passed away in 1999 at the age of 63.

Magic Johnson

A great signer throughout his career and post career, Magic Johnson is rarely seen in public without a smile. His autograph, while more condensed than it was as a rookie in 1980, is very legible. On rare occasions, he will add his first name "Earvin" before the nickname "Magic."

During his time in college at Michigan State, Johnson featured a beautiful signature, one where you could make out every letter of his name. It would also feature his nickname sandwiched in between his first and last name. This style remained constant during his early NBA days as well but, as his fame and the demand for his signature grew, his autograph became illegible and condensed. His autograph is easily obtainable on nearly any piece of basketball memorabilia imaginable. Along with Michael Jordan and Larry Bird, Johnson is one of the most recognizable players in basketball history.

Pete Maravich

While warming up to play a pickup basketball game in 1988, Pete Maravich collapsed and died of a heart attack. He was only 40 years old. It was less than a year after becoming the youngest player ever to be inducted into the Basketball Hall of Fame.

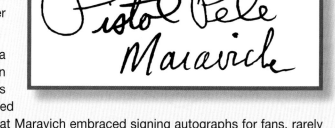

His signature is highly desired and finding the perfect one can be a challenge. As a player, Maravich was known to be a very difficult signer and would regularly turn down autograph requests via the mail and in person. That explains why Maravich autographs are so tough. Most of the autographed material available is from the mid-1980s, signed after he retired and after becoming a Christian. It was during this time (1982-1988) that Maravich embraced signing autographs for fans, rarely turning down a request.

The price of his autograph continues to escalate. Single-signed basketballs, photos and trading cards sell for a premium. Signed checks, which were made available via Maravich's estate, are easily located but still carry a steep premium. His signature also varied through the years. Maravich had many different styles including his full name, his nickname, "Pistol Pete," and he would occasionally sign his full name with his nickname or without it. Following his religious conversion, Maravich also added a bible verse after his signature.

Named to the 50 greatest NBA players in history in 1996, Maravich is one of the paramount players in league history and his signature is one of the most elusive basketball autographs.

Shaquille O'Neal

To say Shaquille O'Neal has refined his signature through the years would be an understatement. His autograph has gone through a metamorphosis. His years in college at LSU produced a beautiful, legible signature "Shaquille O'Neal" followed by his jersey number. Upon entering the NBA in 1992, O'Neal's signature became less legible and more quickly drawn. Currently, his signature appears very similar to his mid-1990s signature. It includes a large "S" that quickly leads into what is left of his last name and a jersey number after the signature.

As one of the league's top centers and most charismatic players in NBA history, O'Neal's signature rates near the likes of Wilt Chamberlain and Kareem Abdul-Jabbar in terms of demand.

Oscar Robertson

An accommodating signer throughout his life, Oscar Robertson has several different variations of his signature. As a college student at the University of Cincinnati, Robertson signed his full name and kept that practice for the majority of his career. Occasionally, he would shorten his signature and offer fans a very easy alternative, "Big O." Utilizing his nickname, Robertson would typically adorn items with that signature. His autograph is readily available in the marketplace, but shouldn't be overlooked. He is regarded as one of the 10 best players in NBA history.

Bill Russell

During his playing years and post-career, Bill Russell was a very private man and remains that way to this day. He would rather shake someone's hand than sign an autograph. For years, Russell was notorious for not signing autographs at all. Until very recently, he started to sign his name for a fee, doing several in-person shows, but most of the signings are done in private. In addition, his signature is very legible.

Vintage material, signed during his playing days, is extremely rare and signed photographs from the 1960s are virtually non-existent. The few signatures that have surfaced from Russell's playing career, have been on programs with a handful of team-signed basketballs. Finding his modern-era signature is a different story and virtually any form of basketball memorabilia has been signed by Russell at one time or another.

Jerry West

The pinnacle moment for most athletes is having their jersey raised to the rafters and retired. Take that one gigantic leap further and you have Jerry West's peak. His league honored him by using his dribbling silhouette as the NBA logo, imprinting his image in the minds of basketball fans everywhere.

A guest from time to time at sports memorabilia shows, West is still associated with the NBA and has been a visible face of the league since his rookie season in 1960. His autograph is readily available, but has clearly deteriorated over the years. His early signature is full and neat. Through the years, as demand has increased, West's signature has become less and less legible. His autograph, in vintage form, is highly desirable and rarely seen. The advent of collecting basketball autographs wasn't a phenomenon until the 1970s, long after West's rookie campaign of 1960.

Boxing Autographs

Bob Fitzsimmons

One of the most powerful punchers in boxing history, Bob Fitzsimmons was one of the greatest bare-knuckled fighters of the 19th and early 20th Century. His professional career started in 1883 and continued through 1914. By the time he was finished, Fitzsimmons was a world champion in three different weight classes, including Middleweight, Light-Heavyweight and Heavyweight. His career included some legendary fights, including ones with James Jefferies, Jim Corbett and Jack Johnson. According to boxing historians, his 1914 fight with Bob Sweeney was the first ever captured on film. Fitzsimmons died in 1917 of pneumonia at the age of 54.

Due to his early death, very few Fitzsimmons signatures are known. Since he died before autograph collecting was an organized hobby like it is today, few people ever obtained his autograph. What remains are several contracts for his fights and a smattering of correspondence that are typed and signed or completely handwritten by Fitzsimmons. His signature was large and flowing. He typically signed his full name, "Robert Fitzsimmons," and would occasionally shorten his first name to "Robt."

Joe Frazier

"Smokin'" Joe Frazier was Muhammad Ali's biggest nemesis in the 1970s and considered by many to be one of the greatest heavyweight champions of in history. His three fights with Ali is one of the greatest trilogies in the history of the sport. Frazier's non-stop pursuit of opponents, especially Ali, made for great viewing for millions of boxing fans. Although he fought as a professional only 37 times, his record is impressive: 32 wins, four losses and one draw.

A gracious signer throughout much of his life, Frazier's signature has remained relatively the same since the 1960s. It appears as a large "J" with the "oe" of his first name in the loop of his "J" followed by his last name. When asked, Frazier will add "Smokin'" to his signature. His autograph can be found on a number of boxing related ephemera. Being the constant gentleman and entertainer, Frazier enjoys having fans stop by his South Philadelphia gym for visits

Evander Holyfield

Known to boxing fans as the *Real Deal*, Evander Holyfield was exactly that during the 1980s and 1990s as one of the most recognizable names in the world of sports. A former Olympian, Holyfield was a champion multiple times in both the Cruiserweight and Heavyweight divisions. His epic battles with Riddick Bowe and Mike Tyson are both legendary. His second fight with Mike Tyson in 1997 is one of the most memorable matches of all time. In this bout, Tyson bit Holyfield twice, the second time severing the top of his ear. Tyson was disqualified, the fight ended and a riot erupted. Holyfield continues to fight in 2008, searching for a heavyweight title shot.

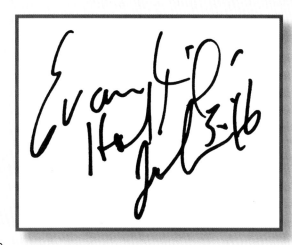

While a Holyfield autograph was relatively easy to obtain during the early part of his career, he changed his signing habits and style of his autograph as his popularity grew. Holyfield's early career signature contained every letter and typically featured a bible verse (Phil 4:13). As his autograph continued to evolve, Evander dumped his first name and would just sign his last name with his bible verse. That change came in the early 1990s and his autograph has remained the same to this day.

One of the most influential boxers of the 20th Century, Holyfield's place in boxing history is secure. Through years of perseverance and with a no-quit attitude, Holyfield has become one of the greatest boxers in the sport's history.

Jack Johnson

Locating Jack Johnson's signature isn't an impossible task, but it can be difficult to find on a premium item. A typical Jack Johnson autograph was signed on one plane, with the beginning of his last name overlapping the end of his first name. Johnson, arguably the first dominant heavyweight champion in boxing history, would typically add a small salutation, the date or the inscription "Former Champion."

Very little autographed material has survived from his career and most of the autographs of Johnson that exist date to his post fighting days. Johnson lived until 1946, passing away at the age of 68. Finding signed gloves or trunks are a virtual impossibility as most of the items signed by Johnson are photos and cuts.

Sugar Ray Leonard

For a time, the face of boxing was Sugar Ray Leonard. During the late 1970s and 1980s, Leonard commanded the ring with lighting jabs and unfettered energy.

He was one of the most decorated amateur boxers in the sport's history. When Ali was on his way out in the early 1980s, Leonard revived the sport. In the 1980s, Leonard's "superfights" featured him against boxing's best contenders.

Throughout his career, Ray Leonard has been fairly accessible and a terrific signer. A typical Leonard signature features his full name, "Sugar Ray Leonard" adorned with a small smiley face after his autograph. His autograph, one continuous name, is easily identifiable. It is easily found on photos, gloves, trunks and most other boxing items.

Sonny Liston

Sonny Liston, one of boxing's most powerful punchers, was also one of the Heavyweight division's most troubled fighters. After doing time in prison in the 1950s for serving as a "bonecrusher" for the mob, Liston embarked upon a controversial career. During his 18-year career in the ring, Liston fought some of the greatest heavyweights, losing only four times in 54 fights.

His most memorable fights were against Floyd Patterson, who he floored twice in the first round and Muhammad Ali, who beat Liston twice. The photo from the second fight (in which Liston was knocked out by what was called a "phantom punch" because it appeared Ali never made contact with Liston) was featured on the cover of *Sports Illustrated* and is one of the most famous pictures in sports history. The image captures Ali looking down on Liston sprawled out on the canvas. His death, at 37 in 1971, was ruled a drug overdose, but many have speculated that Liston was murdered.

Growing up with little education, Liston wasn't the most able of signers throughout his life. His autograph remains in short supply to this day as it was apparent that Liston struggled to sign his name. Nevertheless, signed pieces of paper, album pages and several photographs have surfaced. It's unlikely that Liston ever signed his name to a pair of boxing gloves since none have surfaced in the marketplace. Photographs bearing the signature of Joe Louis and Liston have been discovered, with a handful making their way to auction over the years.

Joe Louis

The *Brown Bomber's* signature is highly desired and for good reason. He's one of the best fighters in the history of the sport and a true American hero. Vintage-signed Joe Louis material can be located, but authenticating it can be tricky. During the height of his career, in the 1940s, many of his signature requests via the mail were signed by a secretary. Typically seen are secretarial-signed photos and government penny postcards, which would usually bear an inscription and date.

As an in-person signer, Louis was ready and willing to sign when asked. His autograph was a very simple "Joe Louis." Often times, his signature featured a large oversized "J" that would connect to his last name. He kept this style throughout much of his life with his signature becoming less legible during his late-in-life years. Louis died in 1981 at the age of 66 and the demand for his signature continues to escalate.

Rocky Marciano

Finding a real Rocky Marciano autograph can be a daunting task, but it's not impossible. During and after his career, Marciano would employ a secretary to sign his name and, many times, would send back a rubber-stamped signature. In person, Marciano was a willing signer and the end result was a striking full-name signature. His personal checks are available and many are signed with his full last name "Marchegiano." Rarely seen are signed boxing gloves with only a handful coming up for sale. Photographs, 3x5s, typed letters and handwritten letters are the most commonly seen mediums with his autograph. In 1969, Marciano died in a plane crash at the age of 46.

John L. Sullivan

While he was a generous signer for fans, John L. Sullivan's autograph remains in short supply. He featured a long, flowing signature that was typically inscribed to recipients. A small number of photographs, documents, handwritten letters and cut signatures find their way into the marketplace from time to time. Collectors are attracted to his signature in part because of the legend of his bare knuckle brawls and the fact that he was a true 19th Century champion. He died in 1918 at the age of 59.

Mike Tyson

What could have been? That's the question raised when talking about Mike Tyson. Tyson's missed opportunities are well known. Nevertheless, for a short time in the 1980s, he captivated fans like no one has before or since.

From 1985 to 1990, Tyson simply owned the sport. Tyson was not only one of the most powerful punches the sport had ever seen, he also was an incredible defender. He typically knocked out his opponents in one or two rounds. During the 1980s, he charged through the Heavyweight division with ease. On February 11, 1990, his career came to an abrupt halt. Fighting in Tokyo, coming in as a 42-1 favorite, Tyson was knocked to the canvas for the first time in his career by Buster Douglas and the rest is history. Tyson fought

for another 15 years, but was never able to match the intensity he previously brought to the ring.

His autograph, like the fighter, is intense. Heavily slanted to the right, it resembles Pikes Peak, with his name scribbled at a frantic pace. As a young boxer in 1984, his autograph was much more laid back, written out slowly by Tyson, but as his career skyrocketed and the demand for his signature increased, his autograph changed. His early autograph is rarely found, especially anything from the mid-1980s. Nevertheless, several contracts have surfaced. An accommodating and friendly in-person signer, Tyson rarely turns down an in-person autograph requests. That being said, Tyson was known to use a secretary or assistant to sign his mail.

Football Autographs

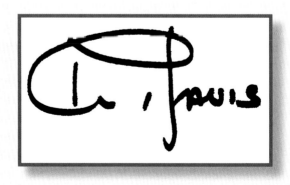

Al Davis-Owner-Oakland Raiders

When Al Davis makes an appearance, fans and collectors clamor like paparazzi spotting a superstar. Unfortunately, Davis' deteriorating health prohibits him from signing much today. Since the 1980s, Davis has been a notoriously difficult autograph to obtain. A former coach, commissioner and now owner of the Raiders, Davis is a football legend. His signature, a simple "Al Davis," is in very short supply. Goal Line Art cards, signed in black Sharpie marker, are collector favorites. Most football Hall of Fame collectors have struggled to obtain his signature, since so little is in the marketplace.

John Elway

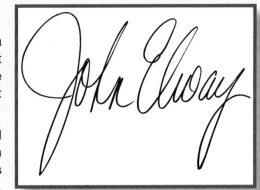

A generous and gracious signer throughout his career, John Elway adopted, at an early age, a very simple autograph style. His signature has remained the same to this day, "John Elway 7." At times, his jersey number was excluded from his signature. His autograph has remained virtually the same since the late 1980s, with a large oversized "J" being the focal point of the signature. The rest of his autograph flows together with his first name virtually attached to his last name.

Finding an Elway signature shouldn't be much of a problem with photos, jerseys, helmets and footballs readily available in the marketplace. Considered more scarce is his vintage signature from 1983, when Elway was a minor leaguer in the New York Yankee farm system. Elway signatures from this period are the scarcest versions and the few examples that have surfaced feature a long, flowing signature, showing every letter of his name.

Brett Favre

Brett Favre's autograph has remained virtually the same since coming into the league in 1991. A very simple "Brett Favre" followed by his jersey number (4) is the norm. As a tradition for football players, most included their number after their signature. As a young player with the Packers, it took a few years before Favre became a fan favorite. After leading the Packers to the Super Bowl in 1996, his popularity soared and the demand for his signature increased. Favre regularly took part in private signings with Wisconsin-area dealers and his signature is one of the most coveted in the NFL. His autograph is easily identifiable and fairly easy to locate on any type of football related memorabilia.

Nile Kinnick

A gentleman, scholar and gifted athlete, Nile Kinnick is considered one of the best college football players ever. The talented halfback excelled in the 1939 season. That year, he led the Iowa Hawkeyes to a 6-1-1 mark. But more amazing are the records he set that still stand today. Kinnick was involved in 107 of the 130 points that Iowa scored that season and played 402 of a possible 420 minutes.

That season, Kinnick set 14 school records, six of which still stand. He was honored with virtually every major award in the country including the Walter Camp Award, Maxwell Award, Associated Press Male Athlete of the Year (beating out Joe DiMaggio and Joe Louis); Big Ten MVP and he was a consensus first team All-American. In 1939, he also won the Heisman Trophy.

Spurning professional football overtures, he returned to school but left after a year to join the naval reserves. His life was cut short in 1943 during a routine training flight off the coast of Venezuela. He died at 24, his body was never recovered.

His autograph, considered one of the scarcest in the autograph hobby, is quite desirable. So scarce are Kinnick signatures, that less than 20 are known to exist. A Kinnick signature symbolizes authority and is quite bold. Occasionally, a 3x5 or small photograph will surface. His correspondence rarely finds its way into the marketplace. The last holographic letter was offered to the public in 2004. Signatures of Kinnick range in price from $3,500 to $5,000. During Kinnick's life, autograph collecting was in its infancy and few collectors requested them, making Kinnick signatures virtually impossible to find.

Vince Lombardi

When one speaks about great football coaches and motivators, Vince Lombardi is at the top of the list. The driving force of the Green Bay Packers from 1959 to 1967, Lombardi and the Packers helped redefine winning. During his nine-year run in Green Bay, the Packers captured five NFL Championships, mainly due to Lombardi's grueling training regimen and demand for excellence.

His signature was long and flowing. His autograph is commonly seen on team-signed footballs from the 1960s, team correspondence from his days in Green Bay and occasionally on a signed photograph. It's questionable whether Lombardi signed his mail. There are numerous ghost-signed materials, stamped or printed signatures originating from fan requests.

While certainly not the most valuable football HOF signature, the master tactician's autograph is extraordinarily popular.

Joe Montana

Joe Montana's signature has certainly evolved over time, and, during the late 1980s, Montana settled into his modern signature which is best described as "J Mont." His oversized "J" flows into what resembles an "oe" followed by his last name which is an oversized "M" followed by a loop for the rest of his autograph. As a standout at Notre Dame, his signature was legible and quite clean. By the time Montana played a few years in the NFL, his autograph started to develop a rushed feel and eventually became what it looks like today.

While finding Montana's signature on any kind of football-related piece of memorabilia is relatively easy, a piece of Montana memorabilia should have a place in everyone's collection.

Dan Marino

Dan Marino's autograph has varied throughout the years, from revealing every letter to a hastily-signed rookie-era autograph to his modern-era autograph of "D Marino 13." During his rookie year and several years thereafter, Marino was a very untidy signer, rushing through his autograph. As typical with football players, Marino usually added his jersey number (13) after penning his signature.

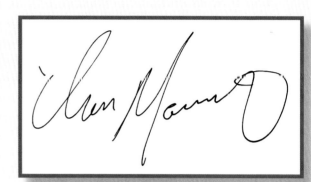

Always accessible to fans during his career, Marino was a gracious signer in person, regularly playing in golf tournaments and appearing at sporting goods shows during the off-season. Throughout the years, his signature has become more refined and quite aesthetically pleasing. A frequent signer at autograph shows, Marino autographs are easy to obtain and can be found on virtually any item pertaining to his football career.

Joe Namath

An occasional guest on the sports memorabilia show circuit, Joe Namath still draws a crowd. His autograph is highly desired and Namath is well aware of his popularity, years after his playing days. His signature is always large and fluid and signed in a legible fashion. His current signature doesn't vary much from the one used during his playing days. It is always signed neatly and strategically placed on an item. At times, Namath adds a salutation, including "Go Jets," his nickname "Willie" or his jersey number (12).

One of the greatest competitors in football history, Joe Namath will always be remembered as a clutch player, delivering on the biggest promise of his career.

Walter Payton

Walter Payton's signature would occasionally feature his number (34) or his nickname "Sweetness." After his playing career ended in the mid-1980s, Payton started to market his signature to the masses. His company sold items including helmets, footballs, cards, photos and jerseys signed by the former Bears star. Payton was a gracious signer for adoring fans, sometimes scrawling a graceful full signature and, occasionally, shortening his signature so he could sign for everyone.

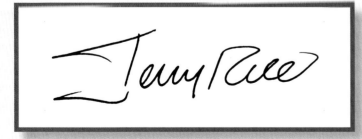

Payton died from a rare liver disease and subsequent cancer in 1999 at the age of 45. The only item signed by Payton that is truly scarce is a signature from his college days at Jackson State University. Experts have only seen a handful in the marketplace.

Jerry Rice

During the late 1980s, a friendly and accommodating Jerry Rice signed often for his fans. He penned a simple "Jerry Rice #80" most of the time. During Rice's early years, he would typically stack his signature with "Jerry" above "Rice." Later, Rice stretched his signature across an entire item and added his jersey number.

As the years have passed, Rice's signature has become more rushed and illegible but he remains a frequent signer, even after his retirement from the game. Even though his signature remains readily available, thanks to signings and sports memorabilia shows, no collection is complete without a signature of the greatest wide receiver in NFL history.

Knute Rockne

His autograph is as legendary as the man himself. Highly desired in any form, Knute Rockne's signature is extremely rare. Rockne was an obliging signer in person but, at the time, collecting was not popular. Most commonly seen are signed letters on Notre Dame letterhead, written while he was the head coach for the Irish. His signature can be found in two forms, "KK Rockne" and "Knute Rockne." Some of the more unique signed items of Rockne are the 1928 All American Certificates, which are signed not only by Rockne but by Tad Jones and Glenn "Pop" Warner.

Difficult, though not impossible to find, are signed and personalized photos and cut signatures. Rockne's iconic status makes his autograph one of the most important of any college athlete or coach. Rockne died in 1931 at the age of 43.

Barry Sanders

Barry Sanders' autograph, as a college player and during his early years in the NFL, was nothing short of magnificent. During his first season and a half with the Lions, Sanders' autograph was very legible and commonly accompanied by a brief bible verse. As the years passed and as his popularity grew, his autograph became much more rushed. Occasionally, Sanders would add his jersey number below his signature, which was often stacked with his first name on top of his last name.

Sanders' place in NFL history is solid. He's a Hall of Famer and ranks right at the top of almost every rushing category. He left the NFL as one of the greatest running backs in history and is worthy of being mentioned in the same breath as Jim Brown, Walter Payton and Emmitt Smith.

Bruce Smith

There are two Bruce Smiths. The first Bruce Smith, the 1980s and 1990s football player, is most commonly remembered as the former Buffalo Bills defensive lineman, a standout at his position and one of the best players in recent NFL history.

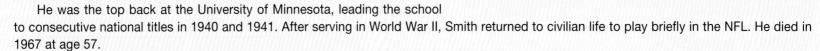

Most people would find it difficult to name the **other** famous Bruce Smith. He also was a football player, but played college ball in the 1940s. In 1941, this Bruce Smith was awarded with the Heisman Trophy award.

He was the top back at the University of Minnesota, leading the school to consecutive national titles in 1940 and 1941. After serving in World War II, Smith returned to civilian life to play briefly in the NFL. He died in 1967 at age 57.

His autograph is rare in any form. Considering his life span, Smiths' signature should be more abundant. For reasons unknown, it's not. What survives of Smith are his college signatures from the 1940s and several examples from his time in the NFL. Little, if anything, signed past 1950 has surfaced. During a period (1950s) when autograph collecting became a serious endeavor, very few hobbyists sent requests to Bruce Smith, asking for his signature.

Smith's autograph is legible, beautiful and flowing. The former Golden Golpher scripted a very simple "Bruce Smith." Of the handful of examples that exist, cuts and team-signed sheets are the most common. Several photos have surfaced in recent years, with most of the keepsakes from his estate offered at auction. Of Heisman Trophy winners, his signature is the second most elusive behind that of Nile Kinnick.

Emmitt Smith

During his career, Emmitt Smith was a very reluctant signer, especially during the Cowboys' heyday of the mid-1990s. Trying to get Smith to sign in-person was a tall task. During his early years in the league, Smith was one of the first players to market his signature, doing so via a sports memorabilia and card store that he co-owned with his father. His father was a regular on the show circuit in the mid-to-late 1990s and most of the product he sold was signed by his son.

Since his retirement, Smith has become a semi-regular guest on the autograph show circuit and finding his signature on any type of football memorabilia is a relatively easy task. His signature features a large oversized "E," the dominating component of his autograph. A series of up and down lines finish his first name followed by a large "S" and some flashy looping. Smith typically finishes his signature with "22," his jersey number.

Jim Thorpe

For years, finding a valid Jim Thorpe signature was a challenge. But, as a result of several major auction house finds, a number of signed Thorpe autographs have made their way into the marketplace. Signatures from Thorpe's athletic days are very scarce, with most of the available material dating to the 1940s and 1950s.

A frequent guest on the banquet circuit in the 1940s, Thorpe signed numerous programs, papers, and ticket stubs. Most signatures from this period are crowded and rushed. Though 8x10s are not readily available, photos from his football playing days and premium items such as signed letters and correspondence from the 1920s can be located from time to time. As of the time of this writing, a signed Thorpe contract has not surfaced. Most commonly seen are signed books by Thorpe entitled *Fabulous Redman*.

He passed away in 1953 at the age of 64.

Golf Autographs

Walter Hagen

Walter Hagen is credited for making golf the sport it is today. He was golf's first millionaire and a major figure in the game in the first half of the 20th Century. His 11 Majors rank him third behind Tiger Woods and Jack Nicklaus. He totaled 45 PGA wins in his career, including winning the PGA Championship five times. A key figure in the development of golf, Hagen is a member of the World Golf Hall of Fame.

While Hagan had plenty of time to sign his name, his autograph is in short supply. His signature was very legible and he would often add the inscription "Golfingly" and a small paraph under his signature. Typically seen are signed album pages and the fly page from his book, *The Walter Hagen Story*, which is usually personalized, inscribed and dated by the golf legend. In short supply are signed golf balls, with only several to have surfaced through the years.

Hagen died in 1969 at the age of 76.

Ben Hogan

In the world of professional golf, very few could strike a ball in the manner like Ben Hogan could. Hogan's consistency, along with his studious approach to golf, made him one of the greatest competitors in the sport's history. Hogan started as a professional in 1931, but it wasn't until 1953 when he had a breakout season, winning three Majors, that his career took off. In his career, he won The Masters twice, the U.S. Open four times and the British Open once. He retired in 1971 after 64 PGA Tour wins. He died in 1997 at the age of 84.

A gentleman on and off the course, Hogan was a relatively easy autograph to acquire. A gracious signer via the mail and in person, Hogan accommodated autograph requests much of his life. His signature was always very fluid and legible, penned in every-letter fashion. His signature can still be found on photos, 3x5s, letters, and, in rare cases, signed golf balls and Masters Tournament pin flags.

Bobby Jones

Early autographs of Bobby Jones, from the 1920s, are hard to come by. During that time, Jones' signature was at its best. A willing signer in person and via the mail (rare in the 1920s and 1930s), Jones penned a beautiful signature that included his middle initial "T" and "Jr."

It was quite common for Jones to add a date or an inscription to his autograph. Beginning in the 1930s and continuing throughout the rest of his life, Jones would sometimes sign "Bob Jones" instead of the full version "Robert T. Jones, Jr."

During his lifetime, Jones would often respond to autograph requests and corresponded with many people, making his signature available in the marketplace. Perhaps the rarest of signed Jones items are golf balls. Since the surface of a golf ball is very slick, it doesn't take well to ink. There have only been a handful of signed Jones golf balls that have surfaced. Also, as Jones' health waned in his later years, he would occasionally employ a secretary to handle some of his correspondence, but still tried to sign most of the photos and 3x5s that were sent to him. His efforts resulted in shaky signatures that are very hard to read. In 1948, he was diagnosed with syringomyelia, a rare disorder that affects the spinal cord. He died in Atlanta in 1971 at the age of 69.

Jack Nicklaus

Jack Nicklaus was the Tiger Woods of the 1960s and 1970s. A gifted amateur athlete, Nicklaus was one of the top golfers in the country, finishing his career with 73 PGA Tour wins. In 1962, Nicklaus became the youngest golfer to win the U.S. Open. His intense rivalry with Arnold Palmer transformed golf into an exciting spectator sport.

Nicklaus, always a gracious signer, has a very strong collector base. Throughout his pro career, Nicklaus has typically met the demand posed by collectors, signing at tournaments and via the mail. Periodically, Nicklaus turned to using an autopen machine to sign his name.

His autograph is an impeccable "Jack Nicklaus." As a young pro, his signature was large and flamboyant. Through the years, his signature has become condensed, but is still legible. Highly desired by collectors are single-signed Masters pin flags and golf balls. Nicklaus has become reluctant to sign premium items in recent times. On occasion, you can spot an authentic example on the Internet.

Arnold Palmer

Arnold Palmer was golf's first major superstar of the television era. Now retired, Palmer won four major championships including The Masters four times in eight years (1958, 1960, 1962 and 1964). A prolific and willing signer during much of his career, Palmer remains a polite and courteous signer.

Collecting autographs from golf stars has changed considerably in the past decade. Today, thousands of signature hawks swarm events hoping to be one of the lucky few actually granted an autograph.

Palmer's autograph hasn't changed much since the late 1950s. It is very simple and easy to read. Palmer's autograph is readily available on a number of items, mainly 8x10 photos. Unfortunately, Palmer has resorted to using an autopen machine from time to time, which signs his name for him when receiving autograph requests in the mail.

Hockey Autographs

Wayne Gretzky

Playing in what is the most fan-friendly sport of the major sports, Wayne Gretzky was its goodwill ambassador, a title he has kept in his retirement. A willing signer for fans and collectors his entire life, Gretzky has rarely disappointed anyone seeking out his autograph. His early signature from the 1980s was very slow, choppy and almost childlike. By the late 1980s, Gretzky had found his groove and developed a very quick and easy-to-read signature. Gretzky's autograph remained the same for the rest of his career. Gretzky will typically add his jersey number (99) when signing his name.

Gordie Howe

While Gordie Howe's signature is not elusive, it is one of the most desirable in sports. While he goes by *Gordie*, his autograph usually features his full name of "Gordon." Finding vintage material signed by Howe can be a challenge. As hockey struggled to gain popularity in the 1940s and 1950s, very few people collected hockey autographs in comparison to baseball autographs. Few examples have surfaced from this time period.

During his retirement, Howe has been quite accommodating to fans and collectors who request his signature in person or via the mail. While he keeps his personal appearances to a minimum, Howe manages to make a few autograph show appearances a year. His autograph can easily be found on jerseys, hockey pucks and photos, thanks in part to his own website, www.mrhockey.com, which offers Howe signed items to the public.

Bobby Hull

Bobby Hull's autograph is a thing of beauty. When signing his name, Hull typically stacked his autograph, signing "Bobby" then "Hull" underneath. Most examples of his signature feature this signature trademark. Hull's signature is typically signed with every letter visible, occasionally accompanied by his jersey number (9) and his nickname, "The Golden Jet." A gracious signer (as are most hockey players) Hull's autograph is readily available, but is of major importance.

His stature in hockey lore is cemented forever. He retired in 1980 as the second leading goal scorer and his resume includes almost every possible award and trophy given by the league.

Mario Lemieux

Mario Lemieux's autograph has certainly evolved through time. As a rookie and for the first few years of his career, Lemieux's signature was legible, featuring a large "M" followed by a lower case "a" and a series of bumps and lines. It was during this time that Lemieux was an accommodating signer via the mail and in person.

As his popularity grew through the years, Lemieux instructed someone else to sign his mail due to the overwhelming volume of requests. In addition, his in-person signing habits drastically changed with more and more collectors left out in the cold when pursuing his signature. His last name, similar to his first, featured a large "L" followed by a lower case "e" and a series of bumps and lines. His current autograph, the same one he has featured since the late 1980s, resembles a "ML" followed by his jersey number (66).

Mark Messier

A fierce competitor who wore his emotions on his sleeve, Mark Messier is the only player in the NHL to captain two different Stanley Cup Trophy-winning teams. The former center, who retired from the NHL in 2004, is second in all-time scoring. Messier played on six Stanley Cup winners and retired with a house full of hockey hardware.

His ferocious nature also applied to his life off the ice. Obtaining his autograph in-person could be quite a task. Very few autographs from his early years in the NHL exist. While he did sign autographs in-person, not many hobbyists collected signatures from hockey players, explaining the relative scarcity of his early career signature.

His signature featured two identical and very large "M"s each followed by the rest of his name. As the years passed, his autograph became less and less legible. Most commonly seen are signed jerseys, photos, pucks and hockey sticks. Like most modern athletes, Messier has an exclusive deal with a memorabilia company to sell his signature, making his autograph readily available in the marketplace.

Bobby Orr

Bobby Orr's signature has a striking lean to the left. It is not stylish, outlandish or over the top; it is simply elegant. Penned with every letter of his name, "Bobby Orr," his signature exhibits an elegant flow that compliments any piece he graces.

During his playing career, Orr was an outstanding signer via the mail and in person. During his post retirement, Orr has been more reclusive and makes very few appearances on the show circuit. His autograph isn't rare, but it can be difficult to find on premium items such as jerseys or hockey sticks.

Miscellaneous Autographs

Billy Jean King

The owner of 12 Grand Slam singles titles, Billy Jean King is widely considered to be one of the greatest tennis players of all time. In 1973, she defeated Bobby Riggs, a former number one ranked player in men's tennis, in the televised "Battle of the Sexes." The game's most dominant player, of either men or women, King was at the top of her game during the 1960s and 1970s, retiring for good in 1983.

Her signature is very legible and exhibits her full name, "Billy Jean King." A gracious signer throughout her playing career and thereafter, King has been receptive to fans and collectors, signing in person and via the mail. Her legacy is forever cemented in the history of tennis and she's considered a trailblazer in a sport where men once dominated.

Pelé

The world's greatest soccer player, Pelé was a hero in his native Brazil, crowned as the *The King of Football*. In America, they call it soccer; the rest of the world simply knows it as football, and Pelé is revered as the most famous of its players. The all-time top scorer in the history of Brazil's national team, Pele has been retired since 1977 and has served as an ambassador for the game.

His signature can be found in two different styles. The very easy-to-write "Pelé" is the most commonly seen and is in greater supply, thanks to Pelé signing his name to soccer balls, photos and jerseys for memorabilia companies. His full name signature is the more desirable version and is signed "Edison Pelé." Taking his first name and nickname, he combines the two together to form a beautiful signature. His autograph, the most important in the world of soccer, is in short supply in vintage form but can easily be found in its modern incarnation.

Babe Didrickson-Zaharias

Babe Didrickson's autograph is in short supply and it commands a premium when offered for sale at auction or privately. Given her nickname after legendary Baseball HOFer Babe Ruth, Babe Didrickson-Zaharias was a gracious signer and had a stunning autograph. She signed her name three different ways. The first is the nicest and the longest, "Babe Didrickson Zaharias." She also shortened that full name by signing her first name followed by an initial for her middle name "D" and her last name. At times, she would just sign "Babe Zaharias." Those signatures were often penned in person.

Babe's autograph is elegant and flowing as she typically would inscribe an item to its bearer. One of golf's greatest competitors, her signature remains one of the most important in sports autograph collecting.

Legendary Lumber
A Look at Collecting Game-Used Bats

By Joe Orlando

Hitting ... it's considered the single most difficult task in sports. If you fail seven out of 10 times at the plate, you are considered a star. From opposite-field line drives that graze the chalk to titanic home runs that soar into the far reaches of the stadium, fans are drawn to those who are masters with the bat. For Picasso, it was his paintbrush. For Shakespeare, it was his pen. For the Gladiator, it was his sword. For the Hitter, it is his bat. The bat is his weapon, the ultimate tool of the trade.

For the most part, fans do not come to the ballpark to watch a mound magician like Greg Maddux spot his changeup; they go to watch the hitters swing the bat. While some fans may dream about throwing a fastball by a powerful slugger or snapping a curveball to make a hitter look ridiculous, most fans dream about being at the plate with the game on the line.

Players come and players go, but a few batsmen become legends along the way. It is this select group of men who possessed the ability to change a game with one swing and the skill to instill fear into opposing pitchers. At some point in their careers, these hitters were the ones who little leaguers emulated across the nation. For collectors of game-used bats, these players and their bats represent the top of the legendary lumber list.

Collecting game-used equipment has always been an intriguing endeavor. Unlike most collectibles, including the types listed in this book such as trading cards and autographs, pieces of game-used equipment are tied directly to the player and to the accomplishments that made that athlete famous. That is what makes things like jerseys, gloves or bats so different from other collectibles. They are not merely symbolic; they are a direct and tangible piece of sports history. They are also, in the vast majority of cases, extraordinarily scarce.

This list was compiled considering a number of factors. These factors include, but were not limited to, offensive accomplishment, player popularity and, to a lesser extent, scarcity. For example, there are only a handful of Monte Irvin bats known; however, his offensive accomplishments do not justify his inclusion on this list. In contrast, Rafael Palmeiro is one of only four players in history to reach 3,000 hits and 500 home runs, but his bats are plentiful and his popularity is marginal compared to other stars of the era.

Here are, in my opinion, the 40 most desirable game-used bats in the hobby. Each bat pictured in this section is an ideal example, featuring many of the specific player characteristics discussed within the text.

1
Babe Ruth
(1914-1935)

A game-used bat from this legend is one of the most prized collectibles in the hobby. Imagine holding the lumber that once belonged to the *Sultan of Swat*. Babe Ruth was known to use a monstrous piece of wood, ranging from the mid-30s to the upper-40s in terms of ounces. Can you imagine using a bat that's 36 inches and 42 ounces?

Earlier in his career, Ruth used bats at the heavy end of the range. As he grew older and his body started to show signs of dramatic deterioration, the bats became lighter but were still a force to be reckoned with. Ruth also used a balanced bat with a thicker handle earlier in his career but eventually went to a thinner-handled, top-heavy piece of wood. During his entire career, Ruth often hit with the centerbrand facing down, resulting in ball marks predominantly showing up on the left barrel. This is documented in many vintage photographs.

During a very brief period of his career, Ruth carved notches into his bat, around the centerbrand, to keep track of every home run he hit. It sounds like the stuff of legend but it's true. In fact, five such bats are known to exist with one on permanent display in the Hall of Fame (28 notches) and one in the Louisville Slugger Museum (21 notches). The other three are privately owned, with one exhibiting eight notches and the other two showing 11 respectively.

Ruth was elected to the Hall of Fame in 1936.

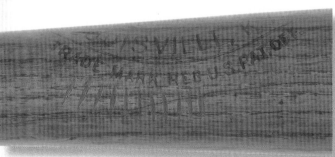

2
Ty Cobb (1905-1928)

This is one of the toughest bats on the list, and these weapons were used by a man whose career batting average may never be approached. Can you imagine anyone hitting .366 for a career? I can't fathom most players hitting .366 for a season or two. Ty Cobb was not the most likable player in baseball history, but he was a fierce competitor. His bats are very difficult to obtain and much scarcer than Ruth examples.

Well-used Cobb bats are usually seen with tobacco juice stains and spike marks along the barrel. Cobb used his spikes in more ways than one and opposing infielders weren't too happy when he was running the bases. Luckily, his bats had no feelings. Cobb was also known for using two unique taping methods along the handle. One method left space between the taped portions of wood while the other, more common method was spiral in nature without any gaps. The spiral method appears to be the one more commonly used by Cobb as evidenced by many vintage photographs.

Cobb was elected to the Hall of Fame in 1936.

3
Ted Williams (1939-1960)

Teddy Ballgame wanted to be known as the greatest hitter who ever lived, and you will get no argument from me on that count.

As for his bats, they are among the most desirable bats in the hobby. Ted Williams was one of the first players to use a lighter bat (for more control and bat speed). Williams, like his idol Babe Ruth, often hit with the centerbrand facing down resulting in ball marks along the left barrel. He also used pine tar or a combination of olive oil and rosin to improve his grip from time to time. Some well-used gamers exhibit heavy applications of each substance. Williams would often clean the handle of his bats with alcohol to prevent heavy buildup of either grip enhancer.

In addition, Williams would occasionally score the handle for grip and the knobs of his bats are also quite interesting. Starting in the 1950s, the bat boy for the Boston Red Sox used to hand paint the number "9" with a line underneath it on the knobs of Ted's gamers and then, towards the end of his career, his number would be noted with black marker. If a bat doesn't have this distinguishing mark there's no need to worry, but it is a unique feature on some of his gamers.

According to Williams, he used Hillerich & Bradsby bats exclusively even though he did order a few Adirondacks along the way. Finally, it cost as much as $5,000 or more to have Williams sign game-used bats during the 1990s. The high price for Teddy's autograph makes signed gamers a prized treasure.

Williams was elected to the Hall of Fame in 1966.

4
Jackie Robinson (1947-1956)

Jackie Robinson is a true American icon who helped change the game of baseball forever. Robinson will always be remembered for breaking down the color barrier in 1947 after spending time in baseball's Negro Leagues, but many people forget that he was also an outstanding hitter.

Robinson's bats are, arguably, the most valuable pieces of wood from his era. The only bats that rival Robinson examples, in terms of current market value, are those that once belonged to Mickey Mantle. Extremely high-end examples have fetched well in excess of $100,000, a price point reserved for an elite group of lumber. As a hitter, Robinson preferred H&B bats according to factory records and he used a fairly hefty piece of lumber. Most of his bats are in the 34-36 ounce range.

Robinson was elected to the Hall of Fame in 1962.

5
Lou Gehrig (1923-1939)

For the first 10 years of his career, the *Iron Horse* was overshadowed by Babe Ruth. To some degree, Lou Gehrig's own offensive prowess was overshadowed by his 2,130 consecutive game streak. Until a guy named Cal Ripken, Jr. came along, Gehrig held the record. What some people forget is that he was a devastating offensive machine.

Gehrig game-used bats are one of the true rarities in the hobby. Less than 20 examples are known to exist, a number that may shrink if they keep cutting old bats into pieces for modern trading cards. Some Gehrig gamers have been found with a unique taping method along the handle, with spacing in between ringlets of tape. Not all Gehrig gamers have this taping method. In fact, most Gehrig bats do not.

In addition, due to his declining strength, Gehrig's bats were gradually made lighter so a weakened Lou could handle the weight. With so few authentic examples in existence, combined with his legendary status, Gehrig bats are extremely desirable.

Gehrig was elected to the Hall of Fame in 1939.

6

Mickey Mantle (1951-1968)

He is quite simply the most beloved player in baseball history and a man who possessed unrivaled raw power during the 1950s and 1960s.

Mickey Mantle's power is quite evident on his well-used bats. I have handled many bats through the years but, of all the bats I've seen, the Mantle gamers exhibit the most deeply embedded ball and stitch marks. Seeing these marks in person can really help the collector appreciate the power that Mantle possessed. It truly is a sight to see. Like Mays and Aaron, Mantle seemed to alternate with his use between Adirondack and H&B bats. According to most experts and photo studies, Mantle seemed to use Adirondacks for a fair amount of time in the late-1950s and early 1960s, but primarily he used H&B's throughout his great career.

Mantle would also alter his use of pine tar. Mantle seemed to use very little tar, if at all, during the 1950s but then, sometime in the early 1960s, he started to show a pattern of pine tar use. Many authentic gamers have "caked" tar about 8-12 inches up from the knob in a concentrated area. This is certainly not true of all Mantle gamers but the pattern does exist. In addition, like Williams, autographed Mantle gamers are especially coveted.

Another interesting aspect to Mantle gamers is the fact that most authentic examples don't show his number (7) on the knob. Other players were fanatical about this, but not Mantle. Some have a number 7 and some don't. Either way, there's no need for concern. Last but not least, because Mantle was a switch hitter, most of the use should be located on the right barrel since there are far more right-handed pitchers in the league than lefties.

Mantle was elected to the Hall of Fame in 1974.

7

Joe DiMaggio (1936-1951)

The Yankee Clipper is considered by many to be one of the greatest all-around players in baseball history, but it was his work with the bat that made him famous.

Joe DiMaggio bats are highly desired by collectors, with early examples fetching a premium. The one aspect of DiMaggio bats that may confuse some collectors is the great disparity between the value of his bats. A bat used during his 1941 56-game hitting streak sold for $345,596 in 2004, one of the highest prices ever paid for a game-used bat. I have seen DiMaggio bats sell for as much as $75,000-$100,000, and I have seen others sell for under $40,000.

Most DiMaggio bats exhibit ball marks on the left barrel as he was known to hit, predominantly, with the centerbrand facing upward. It is important to note that his bats do not often exhibit the types of unique characteristics mentioned in this section such as a particular style of handle preparation.

While game-used items from his days with the San Francisco Seals are rare and desirable, in my opinion, the Yankee bats are more important. That is where DiMaggio did his damage as a major leaguer and where he became a legend. At one time, DiMaggio bats were considered to be among the scarcest in the hobby. While a few more have been found during the last five years, the demand still outweighs the supply.

DiMaggio was elected to the Hall of Fame in 1955.

8

Shoeless Joe Jackson (1908-1920)

Of all the bats on this prestigious list, this is the toughest. For collectors, owning a piece of lumber from *Shoeless Joe* is merely wishful thinking. As of the writing of this book, only two documented examples are known from his playing days and only one of those examples is a vault-marked, signature model H&B. Both of these bats sold for $577,610 and $206,529 respectively, proving the intense demand for his bats.

Joe Jackson, known for using very heavy and thick-handled bats, was someone who often hit with the centerbrand facing down. This approach was copied by Babe Ruth, an avid fan of Jackson, and some of the best hitters in the game today use the same approach. Jackson was also known for naming his bats and the most famous bat of all was his *Black Betsy*, a name that would eventually be used for a particular style of bat years later.

After his 1920 ban from baseball, Jackson was relegated to barnstorming tours, and you will see bats from this time period offered on occasion. These bats, while valuable in their own right, do not command near the price that an example from his MLB career would. These bats represent the missing link in almost every major collection in the hobby.

9

Honus Wagner (1897-1917)

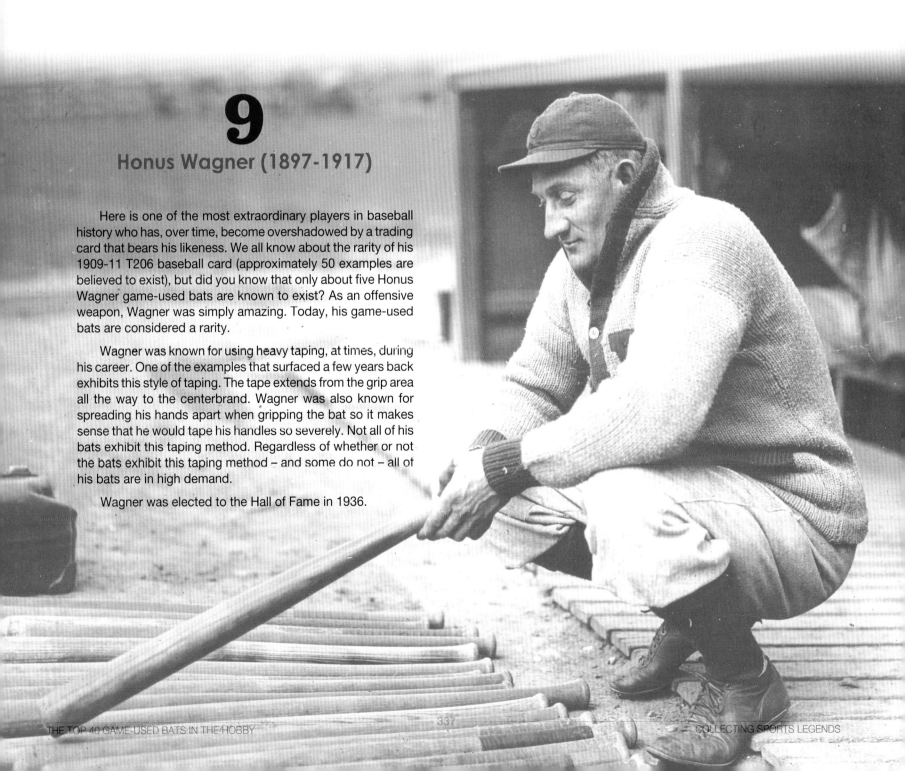

Here is one of the most extraordinary players in baseball history who has, over time, become overshadowed by a trading card that bears his likeness. We all know about the rarity of his 1909-11 T206 baseball card (approximately 50 examples are believed to exist), but did you know that only about five Honus Wagner game-used bats are known to exist? As an offensive weapon, Wagner was simply amazing. Today, his game-used bats are considered a rarity.

Wagner was known for using heavy taping, at times, during his career. One of the examples that surfaced a few years back exhibits this style of taping. The tape extends from the grip area all the way to the centerbrand. Wagner was also known for spreading his hands apart when gripping the bat so it makes sense that he would tape his handles so severely. Not all of his bats exhibit this taping method. Regardless of whether or not the bats exhibit this taping method – and some do not – all of his bats are in high demand.

Wagner was elected to the Hall of Fame in 1936.

10
Jimmie Foxx (1925-1945)

The Beast, though a very kind and personable man, was an intimidating figure at the plate. His freakish strength terrified opposing pitchers and his glare paralyzed them. Lefty Gomez once said of Jimmie Foxx, "He wasn't scouted, he was trapped." After Gomez shook off every sign the catcher gave him and refusing to throw a pitch, a meeting was called on the mound. The pitcher whispered to his backstop, "If we stay out here long enough, maybe he'll (Foxx) just go away." According to spectators, no one, not even Babe Ruth, had as much raw power as Foxx did.

When it comes to his bats, Foxx examples are very difficult to find. Foxx often used ash bats, but he also used hickory bats. The hickory bats have a darker appearance and they really give you that vintage feel. With the exception of Mel Ott bats, Foxx bats are the most challenging for the *500 Home Run Club* collector. Like most players, early examples from Foxx's days with the Philadelphia Athletics, sell for a premium.

Foxx was elected to the Hall of Fame in 1951.

11
Mel Ott
(1926-1947)

Of all the fashionable bat-collecting themes, perhaps no other is as popular as *The 500 Home Run Club*. Many of the biggest names in the game are part of that exclusive club, from Ruth to Mantle to Bonds. There are some very difficult bats needed to complete the set but, of all the bats on the list, none is more arduous to find than those wielded by this man.

Surrounded by the big bruisers of the club, Mel Ott was not the prototypical power hitter. In fact, at about 5'9", 170 pounds, Ott might very well be the smallest member of the group. Generating power with an extraordinarily high leg kick, Ott was able to power 511 baseballs over the wall in his career, taking advantage of a short porch in right at his home field, The Polo Grounds in New York.

Unlike many of the bats on this list, Ott's do not possess identifiable characteristics such as a unique taping method, pine tar application or handwritten notations. This is due, in part, to the era that Ott played in. Players did not place their numbers on the knobs of their bats and rarely used pine tar or handle tape. Ott is a fixture on this list since his bats usually represent the final hole to fill for a collector of super sluggers.

Ott was elected to the Hall of Fame in 1951.

12

Rogers Hornsby (1915-1937)

This man is considered by many to be the greatest right-handed hitter in baseball history, compiling a .358 career batting average. Rogers Hornsby, unlike many of the names on this list, does not fit neatly into some of the major collecting themes such as *The 500 Home Run Club* or *The 3,000 Hit Club* (he narrowly missed with 2,930 career hits) but his significance cannot be overlooked.

When it comes to Hornsby bats, the most notable aspect is the style of his knobs. Hornsby-style knobs, as they are referred to today, appear to be a compromise between the traditional protruding knobs seen on most bats and the flare knob (which is really no knob at all) seen on some gamers. This would allow for a hitter to comfortably place his bottom hand around the base of the bat. In addition, Hornsby would occasionally employ a taping pattern along the handle. Some examples found today show evidence of the tape residue left by Hornsby's application.

Hornsby was elected to the Hall of Fame in 1942.

13

Willie Mays (1951-1973)

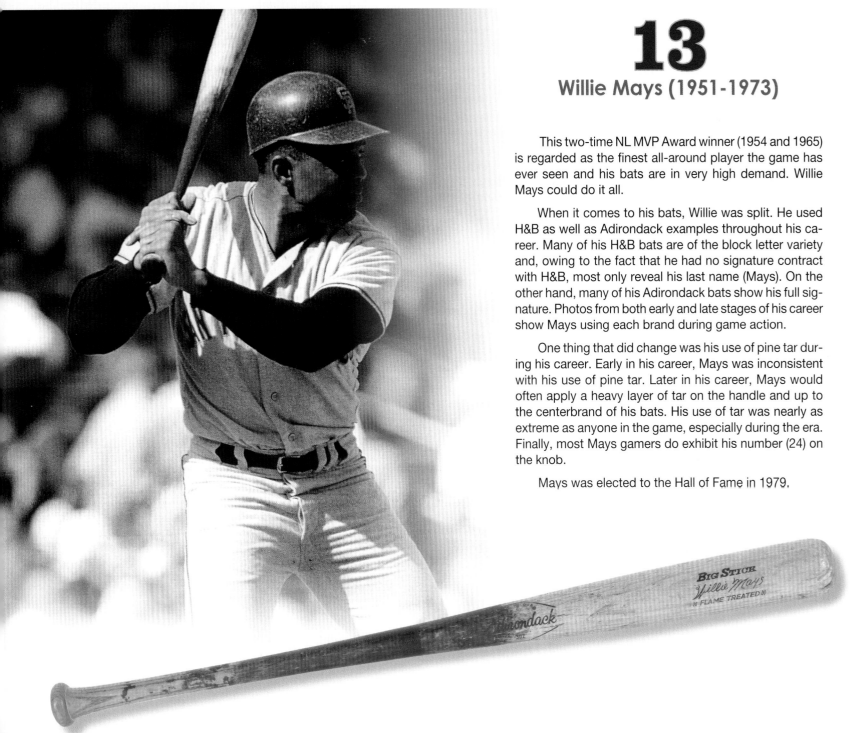

This two-time NL MVP Award winner (1954 and 1965) is regarded as the finest all-around player the game has ever seen and his bats are in very high demand. Willie Mays could do it all.

When it comes to his bats, Willie was split. He used H&B as well as Adirondack examples throughout his career. Many of his H&B bats are of the block letter variety and, owing to the fact that he had no signature contract with H&B, most only reveal his last name (Mays). On the other hand, many of his Adirondack bats show his full signature. Photos from both early and late stages of his career show Mays using each brand during game action.

One thing that did change was his use of pine tar during his career. Early in his career, Mays was inconsistent with his use of pine tar. Later in his career, Mays would often apply a heavy layer of tar on the handle and up to the centerbrand of his bats. His use of tar was nearly as extreme as anyone in the game, especially during the era. Finally, most Mays gamers do exhibit his number (24) on the knob.

Mays was elected to the Hall of Fame in 1979.

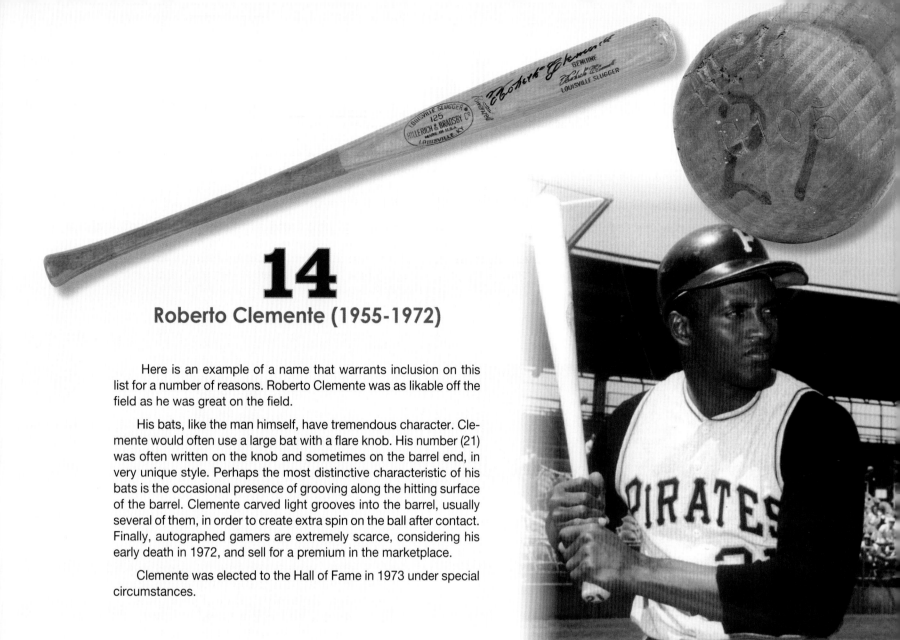

14
Roberto Clemente (1955-1972)

Here is an example of a name that warrants inclusion on this list for a number of reasons. Roberto Clemente was as likable off the field as he was great on the field.

His bats, like the man himself, have tremendous character. Clemente would often use a large bat with a flare knob. His number (21) was often written on the knob and sometimes on the barrel end, in very unique style. Perhaps the most distinctive characteristic of his bats is the occasional presence of grooving along the hitting surface of the barrel. Clemente carved light grooves into the barrel, usually several of them, in order to create extra spin on the ball after contact. Finally, autographed gamers are extremely scarce, considering his early death in 1972, and sell for a premium in the marketplace.

Clemente was elected to the Hall of Fame in 1973 under special circumstances.

15
Hank Aaron (1954-1976)

We all know that *The Hammer* was the all-time home run leader with 755 long drives until Barry Bonds came along, but what most fans and collectors don't know is that Hank Aaron also excelled in virtually every facet of the game.

During his career, Aaron was known for using both H&B and Adirondack bats. His final year came in 1976 when he used the popular Bicentennial H&B bats. Early in his career, Aaron was not known for using heavy pine tar but that changed in the early 1970s. Some of his 1970s examples are found with very heavy tar. Most Aaron gamers do feature his number (44) on the knob and sometimes on the barrel end as well.

Due to his assault on Ruth's home run record in the early 1970s, many Aaron bats were either taken from the locker room or given away during the time period. This is the main reason why you see many early 1970s examples with little or no use. People knew Aaron was going to break the record so his bats became a hot commodity.

One of the most challenging bats to find on this list would be a game-used Aaron bat from the 1950s. Only a handful of them have been offered publicly during the past 10 years or so. Another interesting aspect to his gamers is that there are documented Aaron home run bats in the hobby. Only a few regular season examples and one All-Star Aaron home run bat (1972) have been made available for sale. These are great pieces to own, but make sure you have rock-solid documentation to accompany the bat.

Aaron was elected to the Hall of Fame in 1982.

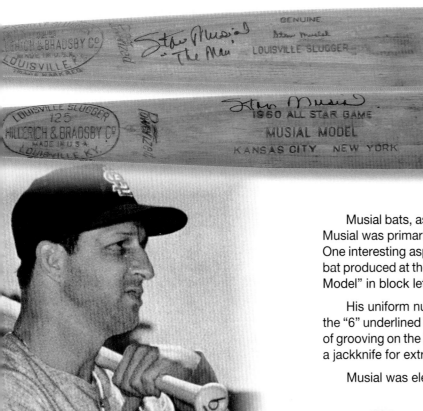

16
Stan Musial (1941-1963)

How would you define consistency in a hitter? Would 1,815 base hits on the road and 1,815 at home for a total of 3,630 career hits and a .331 batting average suffice? If Ted Williams is the greatest pure hitter who ever lived, then *Stan The Man* is certainly a close second.

Musial bats, as you might expect, are a very hot commodity in the game-used bat market. Musial was primarily an H&B user, although he did order a few Adirondacks during his career. One interesting aspect about Musial bats is the fact that Musial actually had a signature model bat produced at the beginning of his career but, for the most part, his bats were labeled "Musial Model" in block letters.

His uniform number (6) was often noted on the knobs of his gamers in black marker with the "6" underlined at times. Perhaps, the most unique Musial bat characteristic is the existence of grooving on the handles. Musial was known to occasionally score or groove the handles with a jackknife for extra grip, a practice that has been documented in several books.

Musial was elected to the Hall of Fame in 1969.

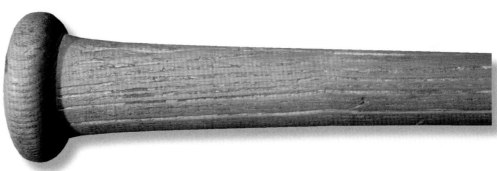

17
Yogi Berra (1946-1965)

With three MVPs under his belt (1951, 1954 and 1955), a slew of memorable quotes and a vault filled with championships, Yogi Berra is clearly a *Top 40* selection. Mantle may have been the marquee star for the New York Yankees, but Berra was the team leader.

When it comes to his bats, there are some interesting aspects to note. Some of Berra's bats were purposely turned in such a manner that the hitting surface (sweet spot) appeared on the backside of the barrel, an oddity among professional bats. Remember this is only true for some and not all of his gamers, but it is a unique characteristic of Berra gamers. Berra started ordering "turned" bats later in his career.

As seen in vintage photographs, Berra did note his uniform number (8) on his bats with some regularity when the practice became commonplace in the league. Berra bats from the 1950s and earlier are valued higher than bats from his last few years in the 1960s. Berra won all three of his MVPs during the 1950s, making gamers from that decade very popular.

Berra was elected to the Hall of Fame in 1972.

THE TOP 40 GAME-USED BATS IN THE HOBBY

18

Pete Rose (1963-1986)

Forget about the gambling and the ban from baseball, collectors seem to love this guy. As the all-time leader in hits, Pete Rose is an automatic choice for collectors.

Rose used a variety of bats throughout his career including many orders of H&B bats and some Adirondack specimens. Later in his career, Rose used Mizuno bats the vast majority of the time. Mizuno would eventually print bats with the number "4192" on the barrel (the number needed to break Cobb's record for career hits – though Cobb's hit total has now been reduced to 4,189) as a motivator for Rose. Once he surpassed Cobb, the acronym "ATHL" (All Time Hit Leader) replaced the "4192" on the barrel. Both versions are very collectable and eye-appealing. Most of these bats were made with a black finish but some were also made using the natural blonde color.

Early Rose bats sell for a major premium but they are very difficult to obtain. Rose bats from the 1980s are much easier to acquire in comparison to bats from earlier decades. Like Aaron before him, everyone knew Rose was approaching a major record so his bats became hot commodities. With 4,256 hits under his belt, a mark that almost seems unreachable, it's easy to see why Rose bats make this exclusive list. A player would need to bang out 200 hits per year for 20 straight seasons and then add another 256 just to reach Rose. Good luck!

19

Barry Bonds (1986-2007)

Whether you like him or not, Barry Bonds is going to go down in history as one of the most devastating offensive machines and best all-around players ever, not to mention the fact that he is baseball's single-season and all-time home run king.

During the first half of his career, his bat of choice was Louisville Slugger but, since the late 1990s, Bonds has used the maple wood SAM bats almost exclusively. Bonds was fairly consistent about his bat usage characteristics. On earlier gamers, usually Louisville Sluggers, Bonds often placed a coating of pine tar, sometimes light and sometimes heavy, on the upper handle. Grip marks, near the base of the handle, are also common. After transitioning to SAM bats, Bonds applied a very unique taping pattern to the handles of his bats for grip. He has used both a criss-cross method and solid spiral taping pattern during his career.

Since about 1997 or so, Bonds has provided and sold his bats directly to the hobby with his own hologram and authentication system. You might have to pay a premium but, in my opinion, it is worth it if you select a well-used piece of lumber. While early bats from his career are harder to find, many collectors prefer the visual appeal of the SAM bats that Bonds has made famous during his extraordinary offensive run.

20
Roy Campanella (1948-1957)

This Brooklyn Dodger favorite has always been popular with bat collectors. Despite a short career in the majors, Roy Campanella was awarded three NL MVP Awards (1951, 1953 and 1955) for his great work at and behind the plate.

Campanella bats are among the scarcest of the era. Very few have been offered publicly in the last 10 years. His bat of choice was H&B although he did not have a signature contract with the bat company. This resulted in his bats only containing "Campanella" in block letters along the barrel. Due to his accident and scarcity of his gamers in general, autographed examples are almost impossible to find. Campanella was an avid user of pine tar but was also inconsistent in placing his uniform number (39) on the knob.

Campanella was elected to the Hall of Fame in 1969.

21
Duke Snider (1947-1964)

Here's another member of that great Brooklyn Dodger team of the 1950s. During that time period, one of the great debates in baseball involved Duke Snider. Who was the best centerfielder of the 1950s? The only real choices were between three New York players: Mickey, Willie or *The Duke*. They were all well-rounded players who could do it all on the field.

When it comes to Snider bats, there is one player characteristic that is unique to Snider. As seen in many vintage photos, Snider would often apply a criss-cross taping method along the handle to enhance his grip. It is unlike any taping method I have seen on any bat from any era. This not only gives Snider bats great character, but it also provides excellent evidence about use. Very few bats today have the original tape intact but some can be found with remnants of tape residue along the handle. Snider would also tend to place his number (4) on the knob from the mid-to-latter part of his career.

Snider was elected to the Hall of Fame in 1980.

22
Ernie Banks (1953-1971)

Mr. Cub is certainly a fan favorite, and not just among Chicago Cub fans. His affable personality and deceptive power ensured his popularity. With 512 career homers, Ernie Banks is part of the exclusive *500 Home Run Club* and his back-to-back NL MVP's in 1958/1959 solidify him as an all-time great. Along with Michael Jordan and Walter Payton, Banks is one of the few true Chicago-area sports legends.

When it comes to Banks bats, there are a couple of keys to note. First, as with most players of his era, 1950s examples are much more difficult to locate than examples from later in his career. Second, you can often find "Yosh" marks near the centerbrand of his bats. These are small notations, usually found on the right side of the centerbrand, made by the Chicago's equipment manager Yosh Kawano during the 1960s/1970s era. Finally, Banks would often place a small "14" (his uniform number) on the knob in black marker.

Banks was elected to the Hall of Fame in 1977.

23
Mike Schmidt (1972-1989)

All I have to say is that Mike Schmidt was the greatest 3rd baseman to ever play the game. Brooks Robinson may have been a better defensive player (but not by that much), Eddie Mathews may be a match for Schmidt in the slugging department and George Brett may have been a better hitter for average, but no other third baseman in baseball history can compete with Schmidt as an all-around player.

When it comes to his bats, Schmidt had a few interesting habits. First of all, Schmidt generally preferred Adirondack to H&B bats, but used both during the course of his career, and he often noted his uniform number (20) on the knob. One of the most interesting bats you may find is a Schmidt H&B gamer with red tape around the mid-point of the bat. Schmidt did this to make the bat appear like an Adirondack on television (Adirondacks are known for having a colored ring around the mid-point of the bat). Schmidt most likely did this as a result of a contract with Adirondack. He didn't do this to all his H&Bs, but you can find some examples with this interesting mark.

In addition, Schmidt, during the tail end of his career, would mark his bats when he connected for a homer. Usually the mark is placed near the centerbrand with either the number of the career homer or the number needed to reach the magical 500 home run mark, a countdown notation. It was usually done in some type of marker and many of the home run bats have a circle or dot near the home run number. These bats sell for a significant premium and not many exist.

Schmidt was elected to the Hall of Fame in 1995.

24
Hank Greenberg
(1930-1947)

This man was one of the best sluggers in the history of the game. Unfortunately, his career was limited due to military duty. Despite losing nearly four years to the service, Hank Greenberg posted some amazing numbers with his potent bat, played with dignity and became a Jewish-American role model to many.

Greenberg game-used bats can definitely exhibit character, as he would often score the handle of his gamers. In addition, he was an avid pine tar user during an era when few batsmen used the substance to enhance their grip. He would apply a thick layer of tar near the base of the handle, about six to eight inches from the knob up. Keep in mind that he did not score all of his bats, nor did he apply large amounts of tar on all of his gamers. The existence of either pattern merely provides additional evidence of Greenberg's use.

Greenberg was elected to the Hall of Fame in 1956.

25
Tris Speaker (1907-1928)

The Grey Eagle was one of the most overshadowed players of his generation. Playing against headline makers such as, Ty Cobb and Honus Wagner certainly didn't help in this regard as they would often steal the headlines. Tris Speaker was a defensive innovator, playing extremely shallow in the outfield so he could take away base hits and bloopers from the opposition. Regardless, on both the offensive and defensive end, Speaker was among baseball's elite.

Speaker bats are certainly desirable as an elite hitter and member of *The 3,000 Hit Club,* but they are also very tough to find. Some Speaker bats exhibit evidence of tape along the handle, much like Ty Cobb gamers. However, finding the tape still intact has been a futile endeavor for high-end bat collectors as none are known to exist in that condition.

Speaker was elected to the Hall of Fame in 1937.

26
Frank Robinson (1956-1976)

If I had to pick the most underrated player in baseball history, it might just be this man. A lot like Speaker, Frank Robinson was a victim of a talent-rich era. With Hank Aaron, Roberto Clemente, Mickey Mantle, Willie Mays and a host of other outstanding outfielders in the league, Robinson was often overshadowed during the 1950s and 1960s.

When it comes to his bats, there are a few characteristics to observe. Robinson, for a time, would mark the end of his knobs in a unique fashion by noting both his uniform number and the approximate weight of the bat (in ounces) in black marker. You will also notice cleat marks and shoe polish along the barrel of many of his gamers as Robinson would often bang his cleats at the plate. Finally, pre-1968 gamers are significantly rarer than those made after 1968.

Robinson was elected to the Hall of Fame in 1982.

27
Harmon Killebrew (1954-1975)

Along with Mickey Mantle, this 500 Home Run Club member epitomized brute power and was considered one of the most feared right-handed sluggers of the 1960s.

There are a few keys to look for when it comes to Harmon Killebrew gamers. First, Killebrew was an avid user of pine tar for most of his career. He would often apply a thick layer of tar along the handle, extending towards the centerbrand, to enhance his grip. The only exception to this characteristic would be bats found from his rookie-era (1954-1957).

In addition, Killebrew was very consistent about noting his uniform number (3) on the knob. In some cases, he would note his uniform number and an additional digit, for the ounces, alongside – usually a small "1" or "2" to the immediate right. Both number notations were applied with either black paint, sometimes seen early in his career, or marker.

Killebrew was elected to the Hall of Fame in 1984.

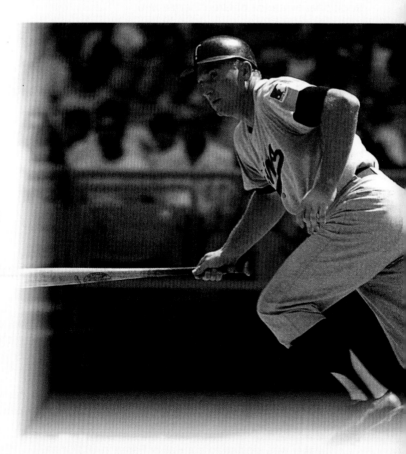

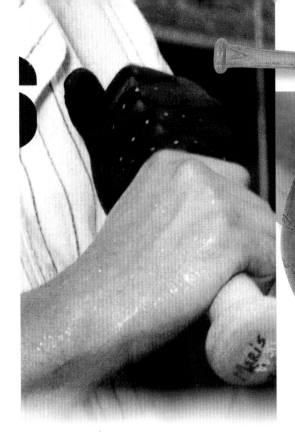

28
Roger Maris (1957-1968)

For a time, this man combined with Mickey Mantle for the most fearsome 1-2 punch in the American League. Roger Maris, who often played in the shadow of his ultra-popular teammate, won back-to-back AL MVP Awards in 1960 and 1961. Of course, the summer of 1961 was a magical one for Maris as he out-homered Mantle in an epic battle, ultimately reaching 61 home runs and surpassing *The Babe's* single season mark.

When it comes to his bats, there are a couple of characteristics to note. There are actually four different styles of knob notations seen on Maris gamers. "Roger" or "Maris" notations on the knob can often be seen in vintage photographs. It is believed that these notations were actually made by Maris himself and they have a very distinct look.

You can also find Maris gamers with an "RM" or an underlined "9" on the knob on occasion. Maris was a user of pine tar and the placement of the tar is usually seen on the upper handle area in a concentrated six-inch area. With the exception of rookie-era gamers, it is clear that Yankee-era bats are valued higher than bats used during his St. Louis Cardinal days.

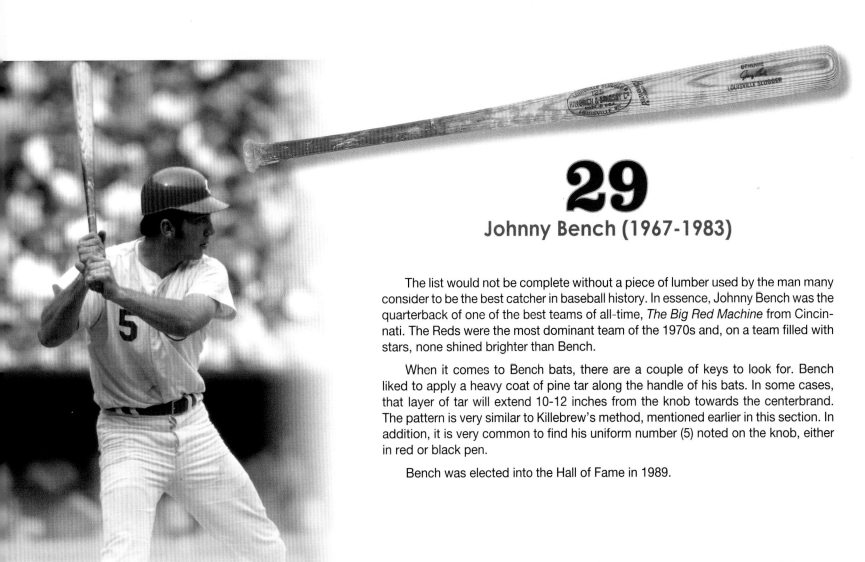

29
Johnny Bench (1967-1983)

The list would not be complete without a piece of lumber used by the man many consider to be the best catcher in baseball history. In essence, Johnny Bench was the quarterback of one of the best teams of all-time, *The Big Red Machine* from Cincinnati. The Reds were the most dominant team of the 1970s and, on a team filled with stars, none shined brighter than Bench.

When it comes to Bench bats, there are a couple of keys to look for. Bench liked to apply a heavy coat of pine tar along the handle of his bats. In some cases, that layer of tar will extend 10-12 inches from the knob towards the centerbrand. The pattern is very similar to Killebrew's method, mentioned earlier in this section. In addition, it is very common to find his uniform number (5) noted on the knob, either in red or black pen.

Bench was elected into the Hall of Fame in 1989.

30
George Brett (1973-1993)

When it comes to the pure visual appeal of collecting game-used bats, this man's lumber is near the top of the class. Not only was this 1980 AL MVP a great hitter with 3,154 career hits, 317 home runs and a career batting average of .305, George Brett also helped make his own bats famous with a most memorable moment called *The Pine Tar Incident*.

The unforgettable incident, which took place at Yankee Stadium in 1983, was a result of a disputed rule by Yankee manager Billy Martin. After Brett homered off Rich Gossage in the 9th inning to give Kansas City a one-run lead, Martin emerged from the dugout. He pointed to Brett's bat and told the umpire that the pine tar exceeded the 17-inch limit allowed by the rulebook. Brett was ruled out after the measuring took place. Brett then charged the umpire in a tirade and the rest is history. After further review, AL President Lee MacPhail allowed the home run to stand and the game was eventually resumed at a later date.

Here comes the obvious. The characteristic most desired on well-used Brett bats is … heavy pine tar. Some of his gamers look like they have been dipped repeatedly in the substance and these examples exhibit great character. Keep in mind that early Brett gamers from the 1970s do not feature this heavy tar application.

In addition, Brett would note the knob of his gamers in unique fashion at times. The traditional "5" can be seen alone on some gamers while "GB" with a "5" directly underneath can be seen on others in black marker. Finally, concentrated ball marks on the right barrel are another Brett characteristic to look for.

Brett was elected to the Hall of Fame in 1999.

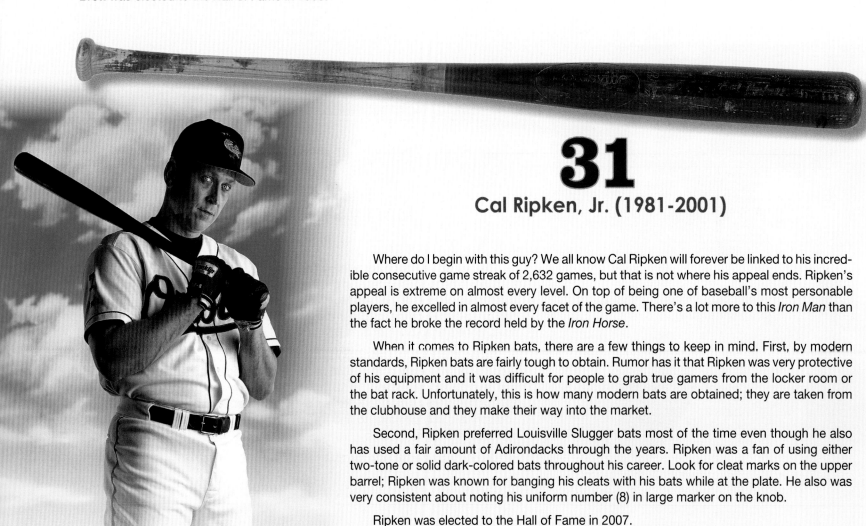

31
Cal Ripken, Jr. (1981-2001)

Where do I begin with this guy? We all know Cal Ripken will forever be linked to his incredible consecutive game streak of 2,632 games, but that is not where his appeal ends. Ripken's appeal is extreme on almost every level. On top of being one of baseball's most personable players, he excelled in almost every facet of the game. There's a lot more to this *Iron Man* than the fact he broke the record held by the *Iron Horse*.

When it comes to Ripken bats, there are a few things to keep in mind. First, by modern standards, Ripken bats are fairly tough to obtain. Rumor has it that Ripken was very protective of his equipment and it was difficult for people to grab true gamers from the locker room or the bat rack. Unfortunately, this is how many modern bats are obtained; they are taken from the clubhouse and they make their way into the market.

Second, Ripken preferred Louisville Slugger bats most of the time even though he also has used a fair amount of Adirondacks through the years. Ripken was a fan of using either two-tone or solid dark-colored bats throughout his career. Look for cleat marks on the upper barrel; Ripken was known for banging his cleats with his bats while at the plate. He also was very consistent about noting his uniform number (8) in large marker on the knob.

Ripken was elected to the Hall of Fame in 2007.

32
Reggie Jackson (1967-1987)

When you buy a seat at the ballpark, you want to be entertained. No one during his era was a better entertainer than Reggie Jackson. Everyone was aware of Reggie when he strolled to the plate, whether you loved him or hated him. He received booming cheers from his fans and thunderous jeers from those who rooted against him. Whether he struck out and fell to his knees or crushed a titanic home run and watched it soar into the stands, everyone was entertained.

When it comes to his bats, the demand can vary depending on the era of the bat. Reggie moved around a bit during his career as he played for the A's (twice), Orioles, Yankees and Angels. Bats used during his Yankee days and first stop with the A's sell for a premium. In addition, Reggie used H&B bats during the early stages of his career but gradually transitioned into Adirondacks for the remainder. Reggie was also fairly consistent about placing his number on the knob. As a member of the A's in the 1970s, his uniform number (9) would often be underlined in black marker.

Jackson was elected to the Hall of Fame in 1993.

33
Mickey Cochrane
(1925-1937)

This man was one of the fiercest competitors and extraordinary catchers in baseball history. As a key figure on both the Philadelphia Athletics and Detroit Tigers, Mickey Cochrane's leadership and potent bat helped both teams to several World Series appearances. Unfortunately, his playing career came to an end after being plunked in the head by a Bump Hadley pitch.

At the plate, Cochrane was an outstanding hitter. He finished his career with a .320 batting average, a career that saw Cochrane hit .300 or better nine times. His career-best was .357 in 1930, a season where he also scored 110 runs. As part of the powerhouse A's, his job was to get on base ahead of run producers Jimmie Foxx and Al Simmons and he did that often. Prior to his career-ending injury, this player/manager was still going strong with a .306 average for the season.

Cochrane game-used bats are extremely difficult to locate. In fact, there are less than 10 known examples in the hobby. When it comes to specific player characteristics, Cochrane was not known for unique handle preparation or the like. Finding them at all is the key for any collector of legendary lumber.

Cochrane was elected to the Hall of Fame in 1947.

34
Eddie Murray (1977-1997)

There is no question this man is one of the most underrated players in baseball history. It was not due to his lack of skill, but possibly due to his lack of flash and lackluster relationship with the media. Eddie Murray, a switch hitter, was quite simply one of the most dependable and consistent players of his generation.

At the end of his career, Murray became one of three players to reach the 3,000 hit and 500 home run milestones along with Hank Aaron and Willie Mays. He has since been joined by Rafael Palmeiro to bring the number to four, but Murray is certainly in rare company. He finished with a .287 batting average, 3,255 hits, 504 home runs and 1,917 RBI. Murray won three consecutive Gold Gloves (1982-1984), was the AL Rookie of the Year in 1977, and an eight-time All-Star.

Eddie Murray gamers can certainly have their share of character. The knobs on Murray gamers will usually feature his uniform number (33) and that number would occasionally be highlighted with a color marker on top of the black ink. In addition, Murray would often employ a very unique handle taping pattern to the handle for grip. Murray would place several very small, thick ringlets of tape along the handle with slight gaps in between. This pattern is very unique to Murray and while he did not use this method all the time, the existence of the pattern provides a fingerprint of his use. Finally, large amounts of cleat marks are often found along the barrel of well-used Murray gamers.

Murray was elected to the Hall of Fame in 2003.

35
Carl Yastrzemski (1961-1983)

Carl Yastrzemski had one of the most difficult jobs in Boston Red Sox history. He had to replace the legendary Ted Williams in left field. Even though no one could replace *Teddy Ballgame*, *Yaz* came as close as anyone could've hoped.

When it comes to specific bat characteristics, there are two key elements to look for. *Yaz* would often place his uniform number (8) on the knob in large black marker. You may also find the word "Game" written on the knob of his bats, referring to the bat that was reserved for game action and not batting practice.

Furthermore, he occasionally applied a very distinct taping method along the handle. The tape was spiral in nature but with gaps between the continuous stretch of tape, extending towards the centerbrand. Occasionally, he would place pine tar on the upper handle for grip. Early examples, dating to the 1960s, have been far more difficult to locate than examples from the 1970s and 1980s.

Yastrzemski was elected to the Hall of Fame in 1989.

36
Tony Gwynn (1982-2001)

This man was one of the most consistent hitters and personable players in baseball history. In many ways, this consummate student of the game was a throwback player, which includes the fact that he played with the same team (San Diego Padres) his entire career in an era dominated by free agency and trades.

Tony Gwynn game-used bats are easier to obtain than most sticks on this exclusive list. In fact, Gwynn provided game-used equipment to the hobby via his own company during the last few years of his career. His bat of choice was certainly Louisville Slugger, but he did use other brands along the way. Bats from the latter part of his career are often characterized by unique handle treatment in the form of thick tape near the base of the handle or other forms of grip enhancers. He also was fairly consistent about placing his number (19) on the knob. In some cases, you may also see the weight of the bat noted (in ounces) in small numbers.

Gwynn was elected to the Hall of Fame in 2007.

37
Hack Wilson (1923-1934)

With one of the most unique body types in baseball history, this man used his compact frame to generate tremendous power. Imagine a man who stood 5'6" but weighed 200 pounds, a man that had the neck of a heavyweight boxer but wore size six shoes. That was Hack Wilson, a man whose first name said it all.

While his career was brief, Wilson's impact was significant. From 1926-1930, Wilson went on an absolute tear at the plate. He won four home run titles during that span, including a season where he led the Chicago Cubs to the World Series (1929) after blasting 39 homers and driving in 159 runs. His best season came in 1930, one of the most outstanding offensive seasons in baseball history. Wilson hit .356 with 56 home runs and established a single season MLB record of 191 RBI, which still stands today.

When it comes to Wilson game-used bats, they are not only very unique in design but are very scarce. Using an ultra-thin handle for the era, Wilson was able to generate great bat speed. The handle extends upward from a small but protruding knob, unlike a flare handle and more dramatic than a Hornsby-style knob. Due to the unique character of his bats and of Wilson himself, his bats found a home on the *Top 40* list.

Wilson was elected to the Hall of Fame in 1979.

38
Lou Brock (1961-1979)

This man went from relative obscurity as a member of the Chicago Cubs to a future Hall of Famer as a member of the St. Louis Cardinals almost overnight. Brock was one of the first players in history to show that you could change the outcome of the game on the bases. While Brock was, perhaps, best known for his speed and ability to steal bases, he also was an outstanding hitter, especially in the World Series.

When you consider all of his accomplishments, including entry into *The 3,000 Hit Club,* it is no wonder Brock bats are in such high demand. Well-used gamers are often characterized by either a heavy application of pine tar or tape along the handle to enhance Brock's grip. Brock was also fairly consistent about the noting of his number on the knob (20) in black marker.

Brock was elected to the Hall of Fame in 1985.

39
Eddie Mathews (1952-1968)

This nine-time All-Star was part of the most prolific slugging duo of all-time, along with teammate Hank Aaron. As teammates, they slugged more homers than Mantle and Maris, more than Mays and McCovey, even more than Gehrig and Ruth.

When it comes to his bats, there are a few keys to observe. Eddie Mathews was someone who often noted his uniform number (41) on the knob in black marker. In addition, some of his gamers exhibit a spiral taping pattern along the handle, but the vast majority of his gamers do not feature such a characteristic. Heavy cleat marks along the barrel are another fingerprint of Mathews, who did use both Adirondack and H&B bats regularly.

Mathews was elected to the Hall of Fame in 1978.

40

Mike Piazza (1992-2007)

When it is all over for Mike Piazza, while not known for possessing exceptional defensive skill, he will go down as the greatest hitting catcher who ever lived. He hit for average, power and drove in plenty of runs. His uncanny knack for hitting the ball the other way with authority made him one of the most dangerous hitters in the majors during the 1990s and 2000s, as he routinely powered home runs to right field.

Another facet of his game that fans enjoy is his intensity. Great intensity is basically inherent when you are talking about a catcher, but Piazza takes it to another level. He has taken a beating behind the plate, but Piazza is resilient. That's what makes this 1993 NL Rookie of the Year's numbers so amazing. He is the all-time leader in home runs by a catcher (with 423 total); breaking the MLB record formerly held by Carlton Fisk and has a career average of .308. In 1997, Piazza had his best season. He hit .362 with 40 homers and 124 RBI, finishing second in the MVP voting.

Piazza's bat of choice has been Mizuno through the years, but has been known to occasionally use Adirondacks in recent years. He also used Worth bats and Louisville Slugger bats at times during the early stages in his career. His primary uniform number (31) can often be found on both ends of his Mizuno gamers in black marker.

Autographed gamers are extremely difficult to find because Piazza has not been a frequent signer during his career. Many of his well-used bats have a light coating of pine tar on the upper handle area, but not all bats exhibit this characteristic. Fine hitting catchers are extremely rare, and Piazza is the best of the group as he rounds out the *Top 40*.

Collecting Sports Tickets

By Joe Orlando

During the past few years, collectors have become increasingly exposed to and interested in sports tickets. The problem has been and continues to be a real lack of available information about them. How scarce are they? What are they worth? What collecting themes are popular? The questions are numerous, but there's no doubt that tickets are gaining in popularity.

The appeal of tickets is simple. They are relatively scarce and, in most cases, incredibly rare in comparison to trading cards. Trading cards were and still are mass produced each year. The number of sport tickets made for events such as the World Series or a Super Bowl is miniscule in comparison to the number of trading cards produced annually. Furthermore, sport tickets must be saved and preserved, which happens infrequently.

This leaves collectors with a tough chore in completing some of their ticket collections. Much like the appeal of vintage trading cards, it is amazing how some of the tickets survived. The journey some of these fragile, paper relics had to endure is a story in and of itself.

For example, completing a collection of single-signed baseballs from all the members of *The 500 Home Run Club* is challenging because there are a few scarce and valuable autographs needed to complete the run, such as Jimmie Foxx and Mel Ott. In comparison, completing a collection of tickets from the game each player hit their 500th home run is many times more difficult. Collecting the single-signed ball set is mere child's play when compared to collecting tickets.

Sometimes, difficulty can discourage hobbyists from starting a collection. While some tickets may be scarce, there are plenty of the great ticket runs and individual tickets available to collect. Even with Super Bowl tickets, the most popular ticket collecting theme of all, the presence of certain rarities within the set does not discourage people from collecting them. The rarities within the set may be hard to come by but, with a little patience and the financial wherewithal to afford them, they are feasible to acquire. As in the autograph, game-used bat and trading card world, there are *Holy Grails* in the world of ticket collecting. These elusive tickets are, at best, rare and, at worst, unknown. Nevertheless, the idea that a major rarity could surface at any time is an exciting prospect for the collector.

What you have to keep in mind as a collector is that tickets, unlike trading cards, were never intended to be collectibles. They were intended to be a consumable, something actually used to gain entry into an event. That was the sole purpose of a ticket, nothing more and noth-

ing less. As a result, most tickets were discarded after the game, tossed in the trash alongside hot dog wrappers, empty peanut bags and beer cups. Most tickets ended up buried in the trash. Perhaps some fans simply forgot to keep their tickets as they stumbled aimlessly towards the exits. (I place emphasis on stumbling aimlessly after consuming large quantities of some unnamed beverage. I am sure you get the picture.)

Tickets that were saved almost always exhibit severe condition problems. Whether they were shoved into someone's back pocket, folded inside a program or mildly sautéed in a variety of condiments, most tickets had to endure obstacles just to return from an event in one piece. Keep in mind, full tickets

are even more elusive since most used tickets were torn at the gate before entering the event. Today, some venues like the MLB All-Star Game offer scanning instead, giving tickets a chance to make it into the hobby in full form. This, in turn, gives hobbyists a chance to add a pristine example to their collection. There are rare cases where tickets go unused but, since most desirable tickets are related to significant events, the amount of these tickets still in circulation is almost nil.

In addition, tickets are directly related to the event itself. In fact, they are an actual part of the event. Tickets are a tangible piece of sports history. When you hold a ticket in your hand, it's fun to imagine what it was like to actually be at that particular game or event. With the help of video footage and classic sports programs, fans can relive great moments of the past on television. What was it like to be at the game when Willie Mays made his miraculous catch in the 1954 World Series? Can you imagine the electricity of the crowd when Nolan Ryan struck out Roberto Alomar for the final out of his 7th No-Hitter?

Still, I think you'll agree, there is no substitute to being present at the event and watching it unfold. With ticket in hand, I remember being at Game One of the 1988 World Series. My brother and I were sitting near the right field foul pole, only a few rows up from the field. We watched Dennis Eckersley stroll confidently from the bullpen toward the mound to secure the victory for the seemingly invincible Oakland A's. The crowd became very quiet as the Hall of Fame closer recorded two quick outs.

Suddenly, the crowd began to chant, rooting for the improbable Dodger comeback. Mike Davis drew a walk and then Kirk Gibson limped to the plate. Gibson looked overmatched before he even took a swing and, when he did swing, it looked awkward and painful at best. One hanging slider later … boom … the ball took flight towards the right field stands and kept drifting until it landed in the frenzied crowd. When it did, the deafening cheers nearly burst our eardrums.

I was rooting for the A's that night and everyone around me knew it. My brother and I were dressed from head to toe in green and gold. We were certain the A's were going to win, especially after *The Eck* emerged for the save. On the way out of the stadium, I was taunted mercilessly by the Dodger faithful. To be present at one of the greatest moments in the history of the game is still indescribable. The sounds, the scene and the excitement of the moment were priceless. It was worth all the taunting I received because if you love the sport itself, the purity of the game, it takes precedence over the one loss for your team. As great as it was to watch on television, I guarantee you it was better in person.

As a collectible, tickets are not just for the hardcore ticket collector. Tickets, like some other pieces of memorabilia, make great complimentary pieces to an existing collection. If you collect Hank Aaron baseball cards, why not add a ticket from the game Aaron hit his 715th home run to pass Babe Ruth on the all-time list in 1974? If you collect memorabilia relating to Wilt Chamberlain,

wouldn't it be terrific to hunt down a ticket from his amazing 100-point game? If you are a big New York Yankees fan and collector, how amazing would it be to own at least one World Series ticket from every championship season? You can come up with so many ways that one ticket or group of tickets can compliment an existing collection.

Another fascinating aspect to ticket collecting is the diversity in design. Some tickets are plain in appearance and others exhibit fine artwork or eye-catching holograms. While their visual appeal may vary, few question their significance. These collectibles are not manufactured items created to commemorate an event; they give the public access to the event. This increases their desirability and adds to their charm.

The Top 15 Sports Tickets in the Hobby

Now that the appeal of collecting tickets has been covered, it is time to select the best of the best. The following list was compiled by looking at a variety of factors including, event significance, team or player popularity, visual appeal and scarcity. While scarcity is important, there are tickets much tougher to find than the ones listed here. There also are many tickets more valuable than the ones on this exclusive list. I wanted the list to be representative and diverse while still maintaining its integrity.

Like other sections of this book, I fully expect the debates to begin. With so many outstanding tickets to collect, it was nearly impossible to limit this list to just 15 slots. For example, if the list was constructed on pure popularity, I would simply fill each slot with a different Super Bowl ticket. It's the same challenge that presented itself in constructing the individual trading card list. I could simply list every single Sandy Koufax, Mickey Mantle and Willie Mays card, but that would be too easy and not nearly as interesting.

In the following pages, I have constructed a list of some of the most intriguing tickets in the hobby, covering a variety of sports. Each ticket is linked to an unforgettable moment in history. These are the type of events that sports fans yearn to be a part of and wish they could have a front row seat to. Even if we couldn't be present at these great events, owning any of these tickets is a superb addition to a serious collection. These tickets evoke memories and stir feelings inside anyone who appreciates the competitive spirit of sports.

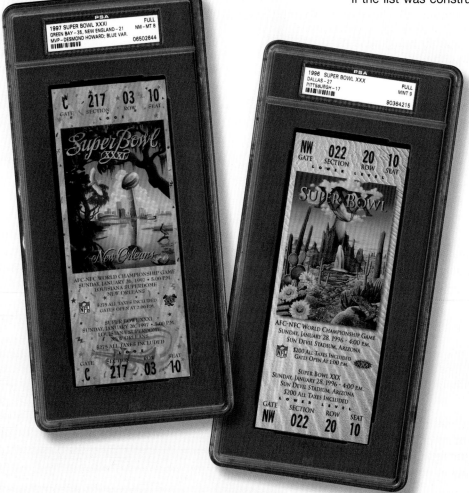

The Top 15 Sports Tickets in the Hobby

1932 World Series, Game 3

Wrigley Field
Chicago, IL
October 1, 1932

The 1932 World Series pitted the New York Yankees against the Chicago Cubs. The Series, which opened in New York, was marked by a high level of animosity between the two teams from before the first pitch was thrown. By the end of Game 2, with the Yanks having yet to taste a victory, the tension was palpable.

In Game 3 at Wrigley Field, Babe Ruth stepped into the batter's box with one out in the fifth inning to the deafening catcalls of Chicago fans and players alike. Ruth took a called strike on the first pitch from Charlie Root. Two balls and another strike later, the Cubs fans were mercilessly taunting Ruth. *The Sultan of Swat* responded by allegedly pointing to the bleachers in Wrigley's center-field. Root wound up and released a pitch that Ruth then smacked into the exact place to where he had pointed. Forever known as Ruth's "Called Shot," this home run would also prove to be Ruth's last in World Series play, sparking the Yankees on to a 7-5 victory in Game 3, and ultimately the World Champion-ship. Whether Ruth actually pointed is arguable but, regardless, the moment was impressive as Ruth answered the abusive fans and the relentless Chicago bench by silenc-ing them with one mighty swing.

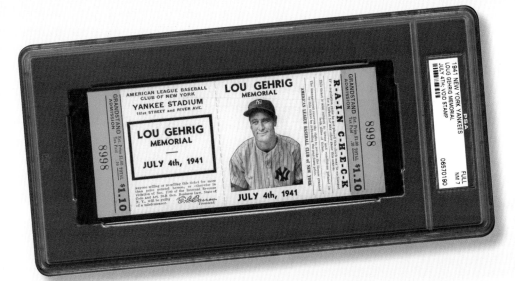

1941 Lou Gehrig Memorial Day
Yankee Stadium
Bronx, NY, July 4, 1941

Lou Gehrig's humility, accomplishments and premature death took his status as a legendary athlete and transcended it to that of an authentic American hero. Having played in 2,130 consecutive games, Gehrig's playing days ended in May of 1939. Doctors at the Mayo Clinic diagnosed him with a rare degenerative disease called Amyotrophic Lateral Sclerosis. With Gehrig's playing days over, New York sportswriter Paul Gallico suggested the Yankees have a recognition day to pay tribute to Gehrig.

On July 4, 1939, a memorial was held at Yankee Stadium where Gehrig's number "4" was retired. In his Yankee uniform, Gehrig stood alongside his teammates and fought back tears as he told 62,000 fans he was "… the luckiest man on the face of the earth." At the close of Gehrig's emotional speech, Babe Ruth put his arm around his former teammate and spoke to him the first words they had shared since 1934. On June 2, 1941, Lou Gehrig succumbed to ALS at the age of 37. Two months later, on July 4, 1941, the New York Yankees honored Gehrig's memory by issuing a ticket that bore the image of *The Iron Horse*.

1951 National League Championship Series, Game 3
Polo Grounds
New York, NY, October 3, 1951

The 1951 National League Championship Series was one of the most exciting in baseball history. The Brooklyn Dodgers and the New York Giants fought it out down to the wire, finishing the regular season in a dead heat. As a result, it was necessary to play a three-game playoff series. The Giants won the first game of the series that took place at Brooklyn's Ebbets Field. The second game, played on the Giants home turf of the Polo Grounds, saw the Giants shutout in a 10-0 Dodger victory. The final and deciding game also was played at the Polo Grounds. At the end of seven innings of play, the game was tied at a 1-1. In the eighth inning, Brooklyn scored three times and looked like they were handily cruising to victory. In the bottom of the ninth inning, the Giants scored a run, and with two men on base and one out, third baseman Bobby Thomson came to the plate. Thompson smacked a Ralph Branca pitch deep into the left field stands giving the Giants the National League pennant for the first time in 14 years. Thompson's homer, dubbed "The Shot Heard 'Round the World," is one of the most famous in baseball history. That moment, documented for eternity on film, has been watched over and over by sports fans of all ages. You can still hear the exuberant cries of Giants play-by-play announcer Russ Hodges who repeatedly screamed, "The Giants win the pennant! The Giants win the pennant!"

THE TOP 15 SPORTS TICKETS IN THE HOBBY

1956 World Series, Game 5
Yankee Stadium
Bronx, NY, October 8, 1956

The New York Yankees took on the defending World Champion Brooklyn Dodgers in the 1956 World Series. A rematch of the 1955 World Series, the Yankees would go on to wrangle away the crown in seven games marking their 17th World Series title. The highlight of the 1956 Series came in Game 5 when Don Larsen threw a perfect game. The unlikely hero was coming off his best season, going 11-5 with a 3.26 ERA. In Game 2, Larsen was less than spectacular. In fact, it was a terrible outing for Larsen as he walked four Dodgers and allowed four runs in only 1⅔ innings. The Yankees lost 13-8 and fell behind 2-0 in the Series. When Game 5 approached, Larsen wasn't sure if he would get the nod but, when he arrived at the stadium, he was penciled in on the mound. Twenty-seven outs later, the 64,000-plus in attendance went wild as history was made. A jubilant Yogi Berra jumped into Larsen's arms after the right hander struck out Dale Mitchell as the Yankees won 2-0. Larsen finished his 14-year career with a record of 81-91 and an ERA of 3.78, making this day the clear highlight in a relatively mediocre career. Named the Most Valuable Player of the 1956 Series, Larsen's feat stands as the only no-hitter in the history of Major League post-season play.

1960 World Series, Game 7
Forbes Field
Pittsburgh, PA, October 5, 1960

The 1960 World Series saw the Pittsburgh Pirates challenge the New York Yankees for baseball's top honor. The Series is remembered most for Bill Mazeroski's Game 7, ninth-inning, walk-off home run over the towering wall in leftfield that drove the crowd into a frenzy. After a five-run 8th inning comeback by the Pirates, Mazeroski's blast won the game 10-9 in the ninth. The Pirates won the Series four games to three, giving them their third World Championship and their first in 35 years. It also avenged their 1927 destruction at the hands of *Murderer's Row* – the 1927 Yankees. Mazeroski became the first player to hit a walk-off home run to win a World Series. Thirty-three years later, Joe Carter would become the only other player to end the World Series with a home run, doing so for the Toronto Blue Jays in the 1993 Series. Even though Mazeroski's home run dominated the headlines, Game 7 is the only game in World Series history that saw no strikeouts recorded by either side. This game was also historic because Bobby Richardson was named Series MVP, the only time a player from the defeated team captured that honor. The game also marked the legendary Casey Stengel's last World Series appearance.

1968 AFL-NFL Championship Game
Orange Bowl
Miami, FL, January 14, 1968

The second AFL-NFL Championship Game, later to be known as the Super Bowl, was a match-up between the Green Bay Packers and the Oakland Raiders. Kicker Don Chandler hit on four field goals and defensive back Herb Adderly turned in a 60-yard interception for a touchdown as the NFL Champion Packers defeated the AFL Champion Raiders by the score of 33-14. Green Bay quarterback Bart Starr was tapped as the game's MVP. Starr hit on 13 of the 24 passes he threw for 202 yards and one touchdown. In the week preceding this game, rumors swirled throughout the sports world that the Pack's legendary head coach, Vince Lombardi, might retire after the game. The rumors proved to be true as Lombardi did call it quits. As the final gun sounded, Coach Lombardi was hoisted on to the shoulders and carried off the field by his victorious team, providing one of the more memorable images in professional football history.

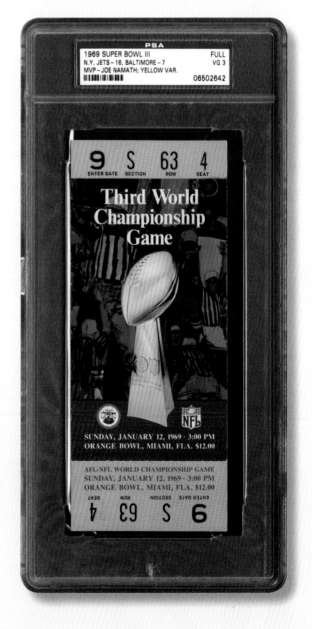

1969 Super Bowl III
Orange Bowl
Miami, FL, January 12, 1969

The third AFL-NFL Championship Game, which pitted the underdog AFL Champion New York Jets against the highly favored NFL Champion Baltimore Colts, was the first to be officially tagged as the Super Bowl. This battle for professional football's world title has gone down in the books as one of the greatest upsets in sports history. It is also credited as being the game that helped the American Football League earn respect. While it had been three years since the AFL forced the NFL into a merger agreement, the AFL was limping along precariously. The new league gained little respect and its future was questionable. The AFC was handed defeats in the first two Championship Games, and many thought a Colts victory would be the league's final blow. That was not to be. Three days before the game, the Jets brash, young and controversial quarterback, Joe Willie Namath, told a gathering at the Miami Touchdown Club that his team would win. In fact, he guaranteed it. Namath's bold guarantee was splashed on the front of every paper's sports page, raising the ire of their opponents who laughed off the audacity of this long-haired kid who wore white shoes. When the final seconds ticked away and into history, it was Namath and company who were doing the laughing. *Broadway Joe* had completed 17 of 28 passes for 206 yards and was named the game's Most Valuable Player as the Jets downed the Colts by the score of 16-7.

The Fight of the Century

Muhammad Ali vs. Joe Frazier
Madison Square Garden
New York, NY, March 8, 1971

Billed as *The Fight of the Century*, the 1971 showdown between Joe Frazier and Muhammad Ali guaranteed a then-record purse of $2.5 million dollars. Witnessed by 20,455 at Madison Square Garden, and an estimated 300 million more viewers watched the fight from all corners of the world, via closed-circuit television. The fight had huge social ramifications. Ali, the most outspoken man in all of sports, was supported by those who opposed the war in Vietnam. While Frazier, a humble man from the south, was supported by a more conservative crowd. From the opening bell, it was clear Ali was not in top form. For 15 rounds, Frazier controlled the match as he levied his devastating left hook. Ali countered with jabs and left-right combinations that his opponent seemed to take in stride. Ali had predicted a sixth-round knockout, but six rounds came and went. Five rounds later, with 49 seconds to go, Frazier dazed Ali with a hook and then landed another devastating blow. Ali was in trouble. Amazingly, Ali survived the 11th round and went the distance. Deep into the 15th round, just as Ali prepared to deliver a right uppercut, Frazier countered with a left hook that put Ali on the canvas. Getting back to his feet, the wobbling Ali again continued on but it was clear the fight was over. Frazier won by a unanimous decision. Ali and Frazier would go on to meet two more times with Ali winning by decision twice. Their trilogy stands as one of boxing's most brutal wars.

Hank Aaron's 715th Home Run
Atlanta Fulton County Stadium
Atlanta, GA
April 8, 1974

Although Hank Aaron always downplayed his chase to tie and pass Babe Ruth's home run record, he seemed to be the only person alive who did. Sports fans and the media were obsessed as they covered *Hammerin' Hank* closing in on baseball's most coveted record.

As the 1974 baseball season began, Aaron's pursuit was clearly at hand. His team, the Atlanta Braves, opened their season on the road. The Braves front office, expressing their desire to have the record broken on home turf, made the decision to have Aaron removed from the lineup until they returned to Atlanta. That decision sent MLB Commissioner Bowie Kuhn into a tizzy and he ultimately ruled Aaron had to play in at least two games of the opening series. Hank did, in fact, play two of those games and tied Ruth's record in his very first at bat against pitcher Jack Billingham. Then, back in Atlanta, on the evening of April 8, 1974, the Braves took on the Los Angeles Dodgers. In the fourth inning of that game, before a record-attendance crowd of 53,775, Aaron surpassed *The Babe*. Number 715 was an Al Downing-offering that Hank hammered into the Braves bullpen. Aaron's teammate, relief pitcher Tom House, caught the ball as the Atlanta Fulton County Stadium crowd wildly celebrated the milestone, who many believed would never be challenged.

1975 World Series, Game 6
Fenway Park
Boston, MA, October 21, 1975

The 1975 World Series between the Boston Red Sox and the Cincinnati Reds has been called one of the greatest Series games ever played. The Reds took the crown in seven games, winning on a ninth inning single by Joe Morgan.

Game 6 of that Series is, however, the one people still talk about today. The contest proved to be a 12-inning battle rife with moments that had frenzied fans on their feet. In the eighth inning, Red Sox pinch hitter Bernie Carbo slammed a game-tying home run. In the bottom of the ninth, Reds relief pitcher Will McEnaney pitched his way out of a bases loaded, no out situation. In the 11th inning, the Reds Dwight Evans made an incredible grab to rob Joe Morgan and the Reds of a go-ahead run. While this game is remembered for many exciting moments, none hit the scale like the last play of the game – Carlton Fisk's walk-off home run that came in the bottom of the 12th. Fisk's homer gave Boston a 7-6 win and sent the Series to a seventh and deciding game, which Cincinnati won to clinch the first of the *Big Red Machine's* back-to-back Championships. This game, and the Series, also served to bolster the "Curse of the Bambino" legend.

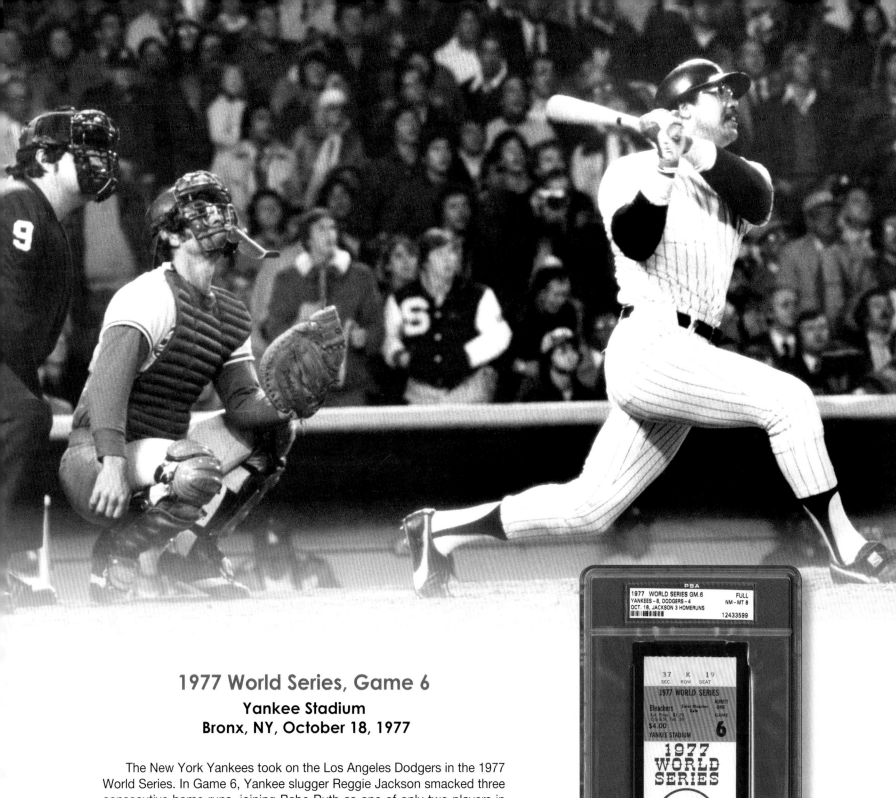

1977 World Series, Game 6

Yankee Stadium
Bronx, NY, October 18, 1977

The New York Yankees took on the Los Angeles Dodgers in the 1977 World Series. In Game 6, Yankee slugger Reggie Jackson smacked three consecutive home runs, joining Babe Ruth as one of only two players in Major League Baseball history to hit three homers in a single Series game. *Mr. October's* first blast gave the Bronx Bombers a 4-3 lead. He crushed the first pitch from Burt Hooton into the right field seats. In the fifth inning, with two outs and Willie Randolph on first, Reggie smashed the first pitch from Elias Sosa into the right field seats of *The House That Ruth Built*. Reggie completed the hat trick in the eighth inning when he put one deep into the centerfield bleachers off a Charlie Hough off-speed pitch, a classic tape measure blast. Each home run traveled further than the last. Three pitches, three home runs and the rest is history. The 56,407 fans on hand went wild as Reggie and the Yanks held on to their 8-4 lead, giving them their 21st World Championship title and their first in 15 years. Jackson, who was named the Most Valuable Player of the series, chalked up an amazing .450 Series average with a total of five home runs and eight runs batted in.

US Olympic Hockey Team vs. Russians

Olympic Ice Arena
Lake Placid, NY, February 22, 1980

Known as "The Miracle on Ice," the United States Olympic Hockey team's win over the long-dominant Soviets has been credited with lifting the nation out of a decade of gloom and reviving American patriotism. While there were actually two games that made up the entirety of "The Miracle" – it was the 4-3 win over the mighty Soviet team on February 22, 1980 that garnered as much, if not more, excitement than the 4-2 Gold Medal clincher against Finland. The U.S. team, made up of college players and amateurs like Mike Eruzione and Buzz Schneider, defeated a Russian team that dominated the Olympics since 1964. When Eruzione scored the go-ahead goal with 10 minutes remaining in the game, American TV viewers were glued to their seats. The U.S. boys held on to a one-goal lead and, as the clock wound down to the final few seconds, shouts of "USA! USA!" filled the arena as sportscaster Al Michaels delivered one of the most memorable lines in broadcasting history, "Do you believe in miracles? Yes!" The miracle was not just that the Americans beat the Soviets, but that amateur, working-class American kids beat well-seasoned Russian professionals. The team, coached by NCAA coach Herb Brooks, also included Neal Broten, Dave Christian, Mark Johnson, Ken Morrow and Mike Ramsey, all of whom went on to impressive NHL careers.

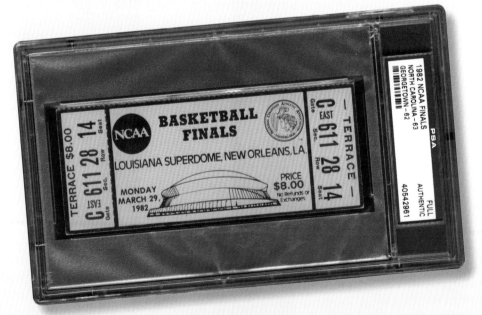

1982 NCAA Division 1 Championship Game

Louisiana Superdome
New Orleans, LA, March 29, 1982

The Georgetown Hoyas, and Patrick Ewing received the call to face the North Carolina Tar Heels and James Worthy to decide the 1982 NCAA Division 1 Championship. The teams seemed well matched and the tight score throughout the game bore out that fact. Late into the fourth quarter, the Tar Heels were down by just one point and, with only 17 seconds left in regulation play, it looked like the Hoyas would soon be celebrating. That didn't happen. It didn't happen because of one person – a 19-year old named Michael Jordan.

As those precious seconds ticked away, Jordan hit a two-pointer to put North Carolina ahead by one. But Georgetown was not finished yet. They frantically set up what they planned to be the game's final, game-winning shot. Then things fell apart for Georgetown. Jordan confused Hoya guard Fred Brown with a block and he mistakenly passed the ball to Tar Heel James Worthy, who was immediately fouled. Both free-throws were missed. Georgetown had no timeouts left and it was the Tar Heels who were celebrating their 63-62 victory in the center court of the Louisiana Superdome. For many basketball players, such a pivotal shot and follow-up defensive move in a game as important as this one would have marked the highlight of their career. For Jordan, it was just the beginning of what many consider to be the greatest career in NBA history. This single moment brought Jordan and his amazing talents into a new light.

Nolan Ryan's 5000th Strikeout
Arlington Stadium
Arlington, TX, August 22, 1989

A hard-throwing right hander whose pitches regularly soared toward the plate at a speed of 100 miles-per-hour, Nolan Ryan chalked up 27 seasons of Major League play for the New York Mets, California Angels, Houston Astros and Texas Rangers between 1966 and 1993. The Ryan Express was an eight-time MLB All-Star and his 5,714 career strikeouts rank first in Major League history. His career strikeout total is one many baseball experts feel is unreachable. To put that number in perspective, a pitcher would have to strikeout 250 batters per season (a number that is usually close to leading the league) for 20 straight years just to reach 5,000. In 1989, Ryan did just that. With the Texas Rangers, Ryan went 16-10 and led the Majors with 301 strikeouts. On August 22 of that year, in a game between the Rangers and the powerful Oakland Athletics, Ryan struck out Rickey Henderson to become the first and only pitcher to record 5,000 career strikeouts. That 5,000th "K" came in the fifth inning at 8:51 p.m. on a three-and-two fastball that Ryan delivered at 96 mph. As soon as Rickey Henderson swung and missed, the sellout crowd of 42,869 gave Ryan a standing ovation. After the game in the Oakland locker room, Henderson, who knew he forever would hold the dubious distinction of being Ryan's 5,000th strikeout victim, told the press, "If he ain't struck you out, then you ain't nobody." Ryan defied all natural laws with his longevity and none of his records provide better evidence of that than this incredible accomplishment.

Cal Ripken Breaks
Lou Gehrig's Streak
Oriole Park at Camden Yards
Baltimore, MD, September 6, 1995

In 1939, knowing he had a terminal disease that would never allow him to play again, Lou Gehrig did not appear on the New York Yankees active roster for the first time in 2,130 consecutive games. It was an amazing feat, widely considered to be untouchable. The record stood solid for 56 years, until September 6, 1995, when Baltimore Oriole Cal Ripken, Jr. surpassed that incredible streak. There was a full house on hand at Oriole Park at Camden Yards, now known as "The House That Cal Built," as Cal galloped passed *The Iron Horse*. As most sports fans know, a Major League Baseball game is not deemed to be official until it reaches the fifth inning. On that early September day, as soon as the last out was made in the fourth, Ripken left the Orioles dugout and took a victory lap around the park. Ripken would go on to play in 2,632 straight games. Ripken was an outstanding player in many respects but he had never shone brighter than on that unforgettable night, a great night for the game of baseball.

Tempting Treasures
A Look at Collecting Unopened Packs

By Joe Orlando

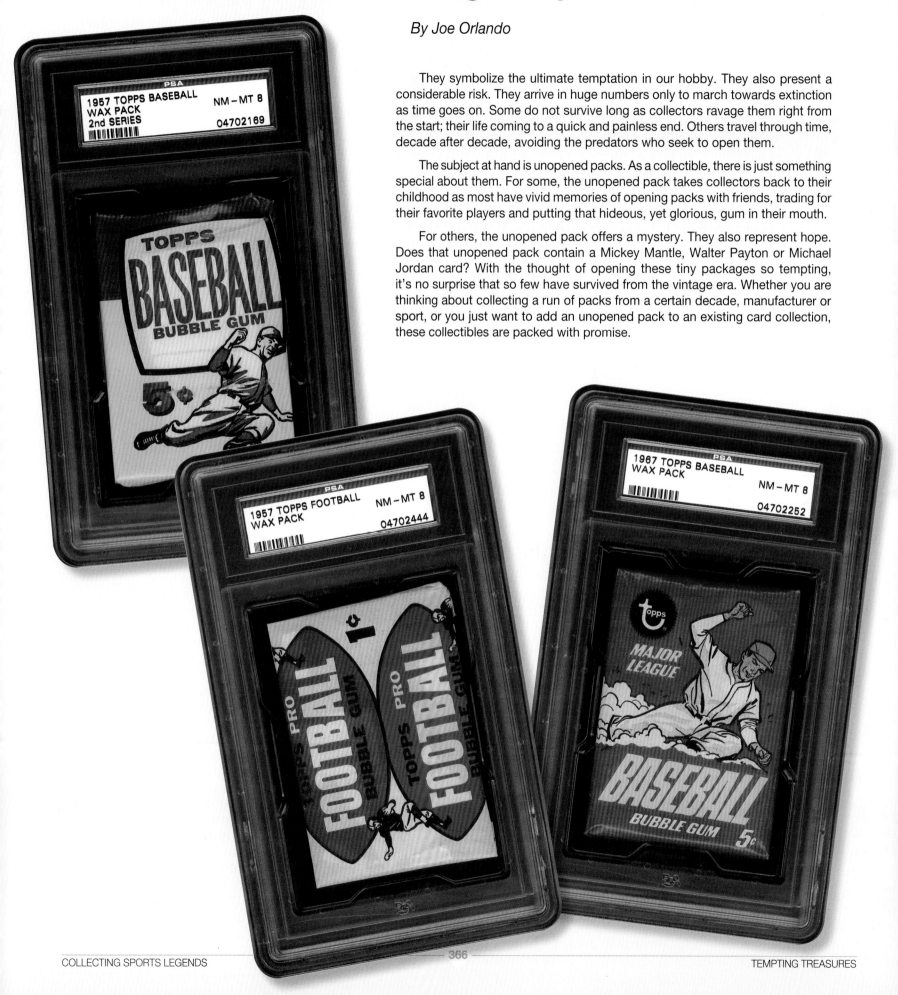

They symbolize the ultimate temptation in our hobby. They also present a considerable risk. They arrive in huge numbers only to march towards extinction as time goes on. Some do not survive long as collectors ravage them right from the start; their life coming to a quick and painless end. Others travel through time, decade after decade, avoiding the predators who seek to open them.

The subject at hand is unopened packs. As a collectible, there is just something special about them. For some, the unopened pack takes collectors back to their childhood as most have vivid memories of opening packs with friends, trading for their favorite players and putting that hideous, yet glorious, gum in their mouth.

For others, the unopened pack offers a mystery. They also represent hope. Does that unopened pack contain a Mickey Mantle, Walter Payton or Michael Jordan card? With the thought of opening these tiny packages so tempting, it's no surprise that so few have survived from the vintage era. Whether you are thinking about collecting a run of packs from a certain decade, manufacturer or sport, or you just want to add an unopened pack to an existing card collection, these collectibles are packed with promise.

In the following section, we put together a list of the top 25 unopened packs in the hobby. The list covers a wide range of packs, everything from the ultra-rare 1933 Goudey Sport Kings pack to the ultra-popular 1986 Fleer Basketball pack. Keep in mind, while some of the packs in this section are extremely scarce, we compiled the list with packs that actually exist. We did not consider unknown packs on this list even though packs of that nature may be discovered, though highly unlikely, over time.

Since packs were literally made to be opened, very small numbers of packs survived from the pre-1968 era. To further complicate matters, the advent of trading card grading had a huge impact on the survival rate of unopened packs. But do not be fooled, this is a risky proposition. Anyone with experience will tell you that the vast majority of vintage cards do not emerge from packs in great shape. This is even true of many 1970s and 1980s issues.

There is a common assumption that cards coming direct from unopened packs are destined to be in Mint condition. This could not be further from the truth as quality control was a bit erratic back in the day. Many cards are riddled with print defects, cut off-center and are stained from either wax or gum. That changed in time as the quality control improved dramatically at the manufacturer level and that sentimental gum was removed from the packaging.

Today, most cards that are removed directly from current packs would grade in PSA NM-MT 8 or better condition, but there are no guarantees. One condition obstacle, such as colored borders, or a manufacturing flaw, such as the presence of surface wrinkles, can give a collector something to think about before they take the chance of opening a pack. It is a matter of weighing the pros and cons.

Despite repeated warnings, many hobbyists cannot resist the temptation of opening those packs because there is always a chance that a pristine gem awaits. During the 1970s and the hobby explosion of the 1980s, more and more hobbyists became aware of the value in preserving unopened packs, boxes and cases. That said, the grading boom in the 1990s changed all of that. Hoards of unopened product that had been collecting dust in storage for years was being opened at a record pace, leaving fewer and fewer packs untouched.

In the end and with all of the above considered, the experience of opening the pack is priceless. This is why collectors have been left with so little when it comes to the more desirable issues, both vintage and modern, in the hobby. In the following section, we break down the appeal of each pack and provide insight as to why it made our elite list.

The Top 25 Unopened Packs in the Hobby

By Steve Hart

1
1952 Topps Baseball

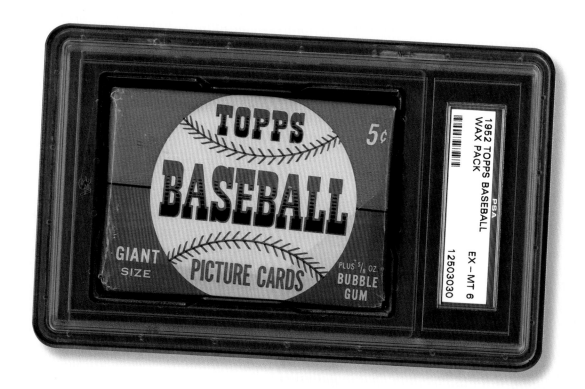

Considered to be the "grand daddy" of unopened packs, there have been a few small finds through the years that have made this highly desirable pack available. The most notable of these finds was the discovery of several dozen first-series unopened packs on the West Coast and a semi-high/high number wax box (24-count) that surfaced in Canada. Almost every pack that has turned up is from the first series, where the elusive high-grade Andy Pafko #1 card may reside. Documented packs from other series of this issue are extremely rare. During the West Coast Find, groups of eight, nickel packs (re-wrapped in clear cellophane from Topps) were unearthed. These eight-pack lots have, for the most part, been broken into single packs for distribution in the hobby; however, some eight-pack groups still exist with the original wrapping.

2
1933 Goudey Sport Kings

As far as prewar packs go, there may be others that are considered to be more desirable; however, this is one of the only prewar packs that has been documented as authentic (note: A few One-Cent OPC hockey packs from the 1930s are also known to exist). Furthermore, we also excluded tobacco-issued packs since it is extremely difficult to tell if the card inside the tobacco pack is a sportscard. This 1933 Goudey Sport Kings pack may include some of the most desirable cards in the hobby such as those of Babe Ruth, Ty Cobb, Red Grange and Bobby Jones. These packs are extremely difficult to find and rarely surface in public auctions. When these packs do come up for sale, they are usually of the One-Cent variety, which includes one card and one piece of gum.

3

1951 Bowman Baseball

This issue contains some of the most important, and only recognized, rookie cards in the hobby. This includes those of Mickey Mantle, Willie Mays and Whitey Ford, the very first card in the set. For unopened pack collectors, this rarity remains on almost everyone's wish list. Unfortunately, these packs seldom become available. Their rarity stems from the fact that there have been no major finds of 1951 Bowman packs. It is also very difficult, if not impossible, to look through the wrapper to see a card number, which is the only way to determine the series of the cards. Therefore, a 1951 Bowman pack from the high number series is one of the holy grails of unopened packs.

4

1953 Topps Baseball

While this set was light on rookie offerings, it presented a generous supply of the most legendary players ever to be enshrined in Cooperstown's hallowed halls. In addition, since these cards have such fragile, colored borders along the bottom, in both black or red, high-end examples are hard to come by. A pack that has always been in high demand, it is nearly impossible to locate. As of a few years ago, this pack was virtually non-existent. That changed with a Canadian find that produced a 1952 Topps box and a 24-count box of this extremely desirable issue. To the surprise of many hobbyists, this pack is far more difficult to find than its 1952 counterpart.

5

1986 Fleer Basketball

When it comes to modern packs, this is *THE* pack to own! Even though it is available for collectors in decent quantities, supply never keeps up with demand. Once upon a time, demand for this lightly-issued set was so low that it was often used for door-prizes or giveaways. That changed in the late 1980s when the popularity of basketball cards started to grow and savvy collectors realized how little of this issue was around. The set is filled with Hall of Fame rookie cards. In fact, it contains the most popular rookie card in the hobby – Michael Jordan. Moreover, this set was manufactured in a small print run by modern standards and has tough, colored borders that frame each card.

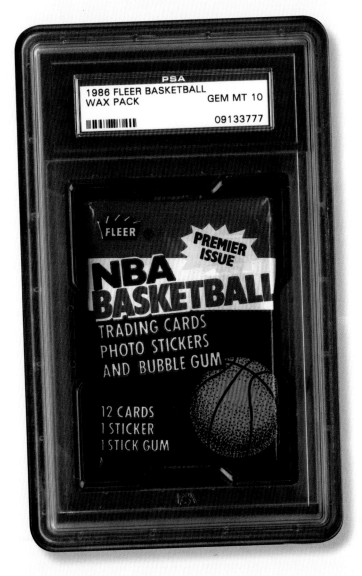

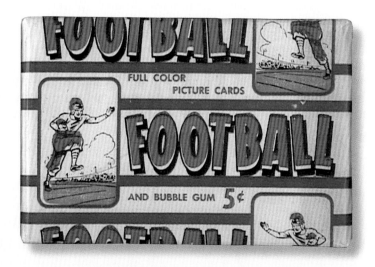

6

1953 Bowman Football

Like most Bowman football packs of the era, this 1953 offering is not simply coveted but, perhaps, the most desired of all packs produced during the 1950s. One of the toughest Bowman packs to find, its colorful wrapper offers great aesthetic appeal and the set is one of the most popular in the hobby. While the 1954 and 1955 Bowman football packs are readily available, the 1953 packs were produced in more limited quantities. Only a handful of authentic 1953 Bowman packs have surfaced during the last several years. Also, unlike the 1954 and 1955 Bowman packs, there have been no known significant finds of this issue to increase the supply to collectors.

7

1957 Topps Series 2 Football

When it comes to football cards, this pack is from the series/ issue that offered three of the most important NFL rookie cards of all time – the cards featuring Bart Starr, Johnny Unitas and Paul Hornung. All three cards are considered to be all-time classics by collectors of gridiron greats. An extremely popular set with collectors, this pack is to football collectors what the 1951 Bowman baseball pack is to hardball collectors. While these packs are by all means rare, they are not impossible to find for those who are diligent hunters. Since the set is considered one of the most important in all of sportscard collecting, demand for these packs has remained strong through the years.

8

1955 All-American Football

This Topps issue is one of the most popular of all football sets, booming with eye-appeal and filled with legendary names. Unfortunately for hobbyists, very few unopened packs exist. There have been some cello packs that surfaced in the past, but most of them have been opened. This 100-card set is loaded with stars and Hall of Famers including those of Otto Graham, Sammy Baugh, Jim Thorpe and Sid Luckman. It also contains a card capturing the legendary Four Horsemen of Notre Dame, one of the most desirable football cards in the hobby. Since the huge cello packs usually contain between 20 and 22 cards, it was very tempting to open them. One-Cent and Five-Cent wax packs are extremely hard to find and rarely show up on the open market.

9

1965 Topps Football

You didn't have to be Joe Namath to "guarantee" that this issue, which includes *Broadway Joe's* rookie card, would become incredibly popular with collectors. Along with Namath's highly coveted rookie card, this set also included the rookie cards of Fred Biletnikoff, Willie Brown and Ben Davidson. The colorful 176-card set is also filled with short prints and two very tough checklists that have provided serious obstacles for the high-grade collector. While this "Tall-Boy" offering is very rare and expensive, these packs do become available to collectors from time to time so keep an eye out for an opportunity.

10

1989 Upper Deck Baseball

There are some who may be surprised to see this issue listed so high on the *Top 25* list since it was produced in the millions and the key card in this set, the Ken Griffey, Jr. rookie, was manufactured in even greater numbers. But this pack is, and always will be, one of the most desired unopened packs because it single-handedly changed the way sportscards were produced and packaged. Back when card companies were issuing wax packs with 30 to 50-cent price tags, Upper Deck put out this tamper-proof, foil wrapped pack at an unprecedented $2 per pack on the retail market. This issue raised the bar for pricing and Upper Deck's model was soon followed by every major card company. With the release of this issue, a simple wax pack was no longer acceptable. Companies now needed to compete with the new world of tamper-proof wrappers.

11

1948 Bowman Basketball

If you are using this section as a guide for which packs to collect, you may want to leave this one off the list. For all intents and purposes, this pack is virtually impossible to find. They are as rare as they come. Only a few authentic packs have ever surfaced. They came in a little cardboard package that included the cards and three pieces of gum. The packs that surfaced sold in excess of $20,000 each, proving how desirable they really are. When there's a chance you could pull the most important basketball in the hobby, the George Mikan rookie, it is easy to see why. This pack is used to being at the top of virtually every collector's want list, but don't get too frustrated if you can't find one. There are many collectors in the same boat.

12

1957 Topps Basketball

Until recently, this pack was not even known to exist. A few years ago, reports that a very small find of a few dozen unopened packs became big news within the sportscard hobby. An extremely attractive pack that is desired by almost every serious collector, it is a classic issue. It includes a large number of Hall of Famers along with a plethora of desirable rookie cards such as ones featuring Bill Russell, Bill Sharman and Bob Cousy to name a few. In addition, since these cards are so condition sensitive, pack-fresh examples are always in demand. Since they exist in such miniscule numbers, these packs seldom surface. When they do, they command an extremely hefty price because of the importance of the issue.

14

1969 Topps Basketball

While this pack does come available on the open market on occasion, it remains highly desired by unopened pack collectors. When we say this pack is available on occasion, we certainly don't mean that you are likely to find them at your local card shop. If you are looking for this pack, you will have to follow the major auction houses each season, when high-end material is offered. This "Tall Boy" set contains the rookie issue of Lew Alcindor, John Havlicek, Bill Bradley and many other NBA stars, including a great #1 card of Wilt Chamberlain. A great looking, colorful pack, this one is on virtually every pack collector's list.

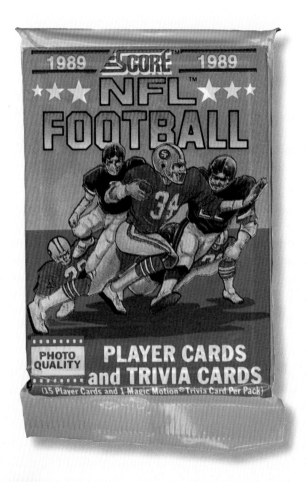

13

1961 Fleer Basketball

One of the biggest problems with the packs included in this *Top 25* list is that so many of them are either not available or are exclusively available to collectors with big checkbooks. That is not the case with this NBA issue. This pack always has been relatively affordable to collectors who want to own it. The fact that this pack does exist in reasonable numbers for a vintage issue has done little to make it any less desirable or diminish its value. There were a few sealed cases of these packs discovered back in the late 1980s and again in the early 1990s. Those finds made this pack available for those who were serious about obtaining it. While it is a rather small set at only 66 cards; it is chock full of great rookie and Hall of Fame offerings, including keys of Elgin Baylor, Wilt Chamberlain, Oscar Robertson and Jerry West.

15

1989 Score Football

This set is in great demand for much the same reason as the 1989 Upper Deck Baseball pack – rookie and Hall of Fame power! This set includes the inaugural offerings of such legends as Troy Aikman, Michael Irvin, Thurman Thomas and one of the greatest running backs of all-time, Barry Sanders. While it may be one of the most common and affordable packs on this list, the issue itself had a huge impact on the modern football card market, which should not be overlooked.

16

1954 Topps Hockey

If you are a hockey card collector and are a bit perturbed that there have been no hockey issues on the list as of yet, we apologize. The reason for this is that many hockey issues from the pre-1969 era do not even exist. If any were lucky enough to survive, they exist in such small numbers that most collectors have never even seen one much less have the opportunity to own one. When it comes to this particular set, the first Topps hockey issue and one of the most eye-appealing issues of all-time, there have been a few authentic packs known to surface. Whenever they do show up, they are scooped up fast and at top dollar. The fact that these cards are extremely condition sensitive, with fragile, colored borders, make these packs tempting to open.

17

1966 Topps Hockey

There are two words that best describe the 1966/67 Topps Hockey pack – VERY TOUGH! This is one of those packs most collectors can only dream of owning. As is the case with the majority of pre-1969 hockey issues, this pack is almost impossible to locate. The reason that this pack is labeled as "almost impossible to find" is that the set contains one of the most desirable and valuable hockey cards ever produced – Bobby Orr's rookie issue – making it hard for hobbyists to resist the temptation of opening them. The fact that the cards are surrounded by brown borders, thus extremely difficult to find in high-grade, just adds to the temptation.

18

1979 OPC Hockey

This set is very similar to the 1986 Fleer Basketball issue because it was produced in a very limited quantity. In fact, the run of this issue was even smaller than the Fleer Basketball set. Take the short run into consideration and add in the fact that this issue includes the rookie card of the NHL's premier star – Wayne Gretzky – and you can understand why it remains near the top of collector want lists. In addition, the blue-colored borders, coupled with the traditional OPC rough-cut, make these cards condition sensitive. Enough said!

19

1964 Topps Hockey

This "Tall Boy" pack is in great demand and extremely rare. During the past several years, only a few examples have surfaced via auction. When they do show up, they are often accompanied by a bidding frenzy, resulting in prices realized that can reach several thousand dollars. The set is very tough and, of all the Topps "Tall Boy" cards of the 1960s, this issue is the toughest to find due to extremely limited distribution. It is infinitely tougher to find than its basketball and football counterparts. Ask to see the wish list of any collector who is on the prowl for unopened packs and you are sure to see this issue high on the list.

20

1955 Topps Baseball

The 1955 Topps issue has always been considered one of the true favorites in the hobby. Exhibiting tremendous eye-appeal and featuring countless key cards, this set has found many collector homes over the years. Knowledgeable pack collectors are aware of a famous find of these packs, making them available for the first time in the late 1980s. That said, those same collectors also know that the packs found were all slightly damaged due to mildew. The gum bled into the wrappers that most likely aided in the mildew damage to the cards. Still, despite the fact that these cards suffer from condition problems, the packs are highly desired and command thousands of dollars. If (and believe us, that is a big *IF*) a PSA NM-MT 8 1955 Topps Baseball pack were ever to surface, it would cause a major stir in the hobby and demand an astonishing price.

21

1948 Leaf Baseball

One of the most popular sets ever manufactured, this one offers a major challenge for collectors due to its plethora of short prints. Collectors know how tough it is to find these short prints and they will pay a premium when they surface in respectable grade. In fact, the entire set is plagued by condition problems. When an unopened pack does surface, one has to hold it and wonder – could there be a PSA NM-MT 8 Satchel Paige card inside? While this is an arduous find by today's standards, a couple of boxes did surface a few decades ago, which resulted in many of the high-grade cards we see today. Unfortunately, many of the packs were opened since the set is packed with so many valuable cards.

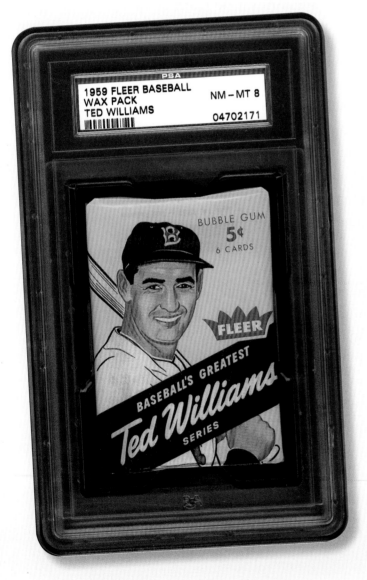

22

1959 Fleer Ted Williams Baseball

The 1959 Fleer Ted Williams Baseball issue is one of the most desired in the hobby. There have been finds of these packs over time, including full boxes and even a complete case. The discovery of those treasures has made this pack more accessible to collectors, but it is still not easy to find as many of the packs were opened over the years. A wildly popular item that contains a historical view of Ted Williams and his career, both on and off the field, this pack was issued in two variations. One pack included six cards and a piece of gum. The other, a far tougher version, came with eight cards and no gum. Both packs are visually striking, picturing the man they call *Teddy Ballgame.*

23

1963 Fleer Baseball

Serious card collectors know why this pack was so special. It did not offer gum, but rather a cookie! These packs came with five cards and one cookie, an odd companion to our prized cardboard. This is an extremely popular pack with collectors despite the fact that the great majority of the existing packs are not in the best shape (largely due to the contents of the cookie, which wreaked havoc on the wrapper). This is a very colorful pack, one that offers a chance at finding several eye-appealing stars inside. This extremely popular set is rife with Hall of Famers like Roberto Clemente, Sandy Koufax and Willie Mays. In addition, the extremely tough checklist card remains the set's most valuable card in PSA NM-MT 8 condition.

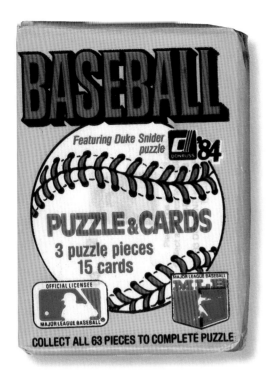

24
1984 Donruss Baseball

This modern pack comes from what most collectors and hobby experts consider to be the most popular baseball issue of the 1980s. In addition to the ever-popular Don Mattingly rookie, a card that became the talk of the hobby for quite some time and one of the first post-1980 cards to reach and surpass the $100 mark, the set offers one of the best designs of the era. In fact, it was the set that helped Donruss set itself apart from Topps and Fleer during that time period. The set's popularity helped Donruss gain momentum as their 1985-1987 issues stayed at the top of the manufacturer heap.

25
1964 Topps Football

Along with the 1960 and 1961 issues, this 1964 pack is probably the most difficult of all Topps Football offerings to find. The pack, which included the rookie cards of Daryle Lamonica, Bobby Bell, Buck Buchanan, John Hadl, a solid supply of Hall of Famers and many tough short prints, was issued in two versions. One pack came with five cards, while the second edition offered a few more with eight total cards. Even though the set is not considered extremely popular, the packs remain a challenge for the advanced collector.

Honorable Mention

1971 Topps Baseball

If we were to continue down from number 25, the next pack on the list would be from the 1971 Topps baseball issue. The years surrounding this particular issue (1970, 1972 and 1973) are readily available in the market today. This one is slightly more difficult to come by due to the popularity of these little blue packages, which are on the wish list of just about every pack collector. The condition sensitive nature of these black bordered beauties makes pack fresh examples extremely desirable and these packs very tempting to open. The set offers the advanced collector a challenge that very few pre-1971 issues can. This has resulted in a limited supply of these packs available to collectors.

Image Credits